Drive Around
Italian Lakes and Mountains
with Venice and Florence

YOUR GUIDE ... REAT DRIVES

Titles in this series include:

- Andalucía and the Costa del Sol
- Bavaria and the Austrian Tyrol
- Brittany and Normandy
- Burgundy and the Rhône Valley
- California
- Catalonia and the Spanish Pyrenees
- Dordogne and Western France
- England and Wales
- Florida
- Ireland
- Italian Lakes and Mountains with Venice and Florence
- Languedoc and Southwest France
- Loire Valley
- Provence and the Côte d'Azur
- Scotland
- Tuscany and Umbria
- Vancouver and British Columbia
  and

- Selected Bed and Breakfast in France (annual edition)

For further information about these and other Thomas Cook publications, write to Thomas Cook Publishing, PO Box 227, The Thomas Cook Business Park, 15–16 Coningsby Road, Peterborough PE3 8SB, United Kingdom.

Drive Around

Italian Lakes and Mountains

with Venice and Florence

The scenic masterpiece of northern Italy's lakes and mountains, taking in the Renaissance splendour of Venice and Florence, and the glamorous resort towns of the Italian Riviera, with suggested driving tours.

Barbara Radcliffe Rogers,
Stillman Rogers with Paul Karr

Thomas Cook
Publishing

www.thomascookpublishing.com

Published by Thomas Cook Publishing,
a division of Thomas Cook Tour Operations Limited
PO Box 227
The Thomas Cook Business Park
15–16 Coningsby Road
Peterborough PE3 8SB
United Kingdom

Telephone: +44 (0)1733 416477
Fax: +44 (0)1733 416688
E-mail: books@thomascook.com

For further information about
Thomas Cook Publishing, visit our website
www.thomascookpublishing.com

ISBN 1-841574-68-6

Text: © 2005 Thomas Cook Publishing
Maps and diagrams:
Road maps supplied and designed by Lovell Johns Ltd, OX8 8LH
Road maps generated from Collins Bartholomew Digital Database
© Collins Bartholomew Ltd, 1999
City maps prepared by RJS Associates, © Thomas Cook Publishing

Head of Thomas Cook Publishing: Chris Young
Series Editor: Charlotte Christensen
Production/DTP Editor: Steven Collins
Project Administrator: Michelle Warrington

Written and researched by: Barbara Radcliffe Rogers,
Stillman Rogers and Paul Karr

About the authors

Barbara and **Stillman Rogers** have lived and travelled in northern Italy since post-university days, when they moved to Verona. Although they have included Italy in other books, such as *Exploring Europe by Boat*, this is their first guidebook to the country. Their travels have followed their personal interests, which include mountain hikes, medieval villages, local foods, architecture and history. They return to Italy year after year because, although it may seem as though every corner of the country has been catalogued by the 'Grand Tour' writers, many surprises still await the curious traveller. The Rogers are authors of the Signpost Guide to Portugal and Travellers Milan and the Italian Lakes, and have contributed to four other Thomas Cook guides. They are also the authors of *New Hampshire off the Beaten Path*, *Adventure Guide to the Chesapeake Bay*, *Adventure Guide to Canada's Atlantic Provinces* and several other books on New England, Atlantic Canada and elsewhere in the world.

Paul Karr has authored, co-authored or edited more than two dozen guidebooks for a variety of publishers, including guides to Rome, Vienna, Montreal, Denmark, and *Vancouver and Victoria for Dummies*.

Acknowledgements

Barbara and Stillman Rogers wish to thank all the people who helped them in their travels and writing: Stephanie Jukes-Amer, Guy Geslin, Randy Stuart, Melissa Parella and Sandra Milani, who operates Bassano del Grappa tourist office, the most helpful we encountered in the whole of northern Italy. Particular thanks go to Marina Tavolato and Chiara Angella for introducing us to some of Italy's finest hotels and restaurants. Also thanks to friends who enriched our travels by sharing their own favourite Italian places: Sara Bergstresser, Juliette Rogers, Erick Castellanos and Christopher Catling, and to Liz and George Bowden for our first introduction to our Italian home.

Paul Karr gives very special thanks to Martha Coombs for research assistance and companionship.

The authors would also like to thank Deborah Parker, Edith Summerhayes, Charlotte Christensen, Karen Beaulah and Stuart McLaren for their wise guidance and editing.

Contents

About Drive Around Guides

The Anglicised spellings of Florence, Genoa, Mantua, Milan, Padua, Turin and Venice have been used throughout this Guide. However, their Italian spellings (Firenze, Genova, Mantova, Milano, Padova, Torino and Venezia) have been added whenever they are mentioned in the gazetteer tour sections. This will make it easier to recognise road signs and also make it possible to ask directions from local residents, who might not recognise the English version.

Symbol Key

- ❶ Tourist Information Centre
- ❷ Advice on arriving or departing
- ❿ Parking locations
- ❷ Advice on getting around
- ➔ Directions
- ⓫ Sights and attractions
- ❿ Accommodation
- ⓫ Eating
- ⭘ Shopping
- ⑨ Sport
- ⭘ Entertainment
- ⓦ Website

Thomas Cook's Drive Around Guides are designed to provide you with a comprehensive and flexible reference source to guide you as you tour a country or region by car. This guide divides northern Italy's lakes and mountains region into 24 touring areas – one per chapter. Major cities form chapters of their own. Each chapter provides enough attractions for at least a day's activities, usually more.

Star ratings

To make it easier for you to plan your time and decide what to see, sights and attractions are given star ratings. Three stars indicate a major attraction, worth going out of your way for. A two-star attraction is well worth seeing if you are in the area and a one-star attraction is worthy of a stop, especially for travellers with a special interest. To help you further, individual attractions within towns are graded so that travellers with limited time can quickly find the most rewarding sights.

Chapter contents

Each chapter begins by summing up the area's main attractions and characteristics, including any special travel information, such as road conditions. A ratings box highlights the area's strengths and weaknesses – some areas may be more attractive to families travelling with children, others to wine-lovers visiting vineyards and others to people interested in finding castles, churches or beaches. Each chapter is then divided into an alphabetical gazetteer, with a suggested tour. You can decide whether you just want to visit a particular sight or attraction, choosing from those described in the gazetteer, or whether you want to tour the whole area. If the latter, you can construct your own itinerary, or follow the suggested tour at the end of each chapter. In cities, these are walking tours.

The gazetteer

The gazetteer section describes all the major attractions of the area: villages, towns, historic sites, natural areas or parks, and the most interesting museums and sights in a city. Maps of the areas highlight the places described in the text. This comprehensive overview of the area helps you choose which sights to visit. One way to use the guide is simply to find individual sights that interest you, using the index, overview map or star ratings, and reading what the authors have to

Practical information

The practical information in the page margins will help you locate services you need as an independent traveller, including the tourist information centre (TIC), car parks and public transport. Here, too, are opening times and addresses of museums, churches and other attractions, as well as useful tips on parking, shopping, market days and festivals.

say about them. This will help you decide whether to visit the sight. If you do, you will find plenty of practical information, such as the street address and opening times. Alternatively, you can choose a hotel, perhaps with the help of the accommodation suggestions contained in this guide and decide what to see in its area. Use the 'northern Italy at a glance' map on pages 10–11 to tell which chapters in the book describe cities and regions closest to your chosen touring base.

Driving tours

The suggested tour is just that – a suggestion, with plenty of optional detours and ideas for making your own discoveries, under the heading 'Also worth exploring'. The routes are designed to link the attractions described in the gazetteer and to cover outstanding buildings, historic sites and scenic coastal, lakeside, mountain and rural landscapes. The total distance is given for each tour, as is the time it will take you to drive the complete route. Bear in mind that this time just covers driving; you will have to add on extra time for visiting attractions along the way. Many of the routes are circular, so you can join them at any point. Sometimes you will use one part of an itinerary as a link route to get from one area of the book to another. Other links are suggested at the beginning of each route, helping you to tie these routes together into your own custom-designed itinerary. As you follow the route descriptions, you will find names picked out in bold capital letters – this means that the place is described fully in the gazetteer. Other names picked out in bold indicate additional villages or attractions worth a brief stop along the route.

Accommodation and food

In each chapter you will find lodging and dining recommendations for individual towns and villages, or for the area as a whole. These cover a range of price brackets, concentrating on more characterful small hotels and restaurants, while also identifying the best options. In addition, you will find details in the 'Travel facts' chapter on international chain hotels, with a telephone number you can ring for information. The price indications used in this guide are in Euros and have the following meanings:

€   budget
€€   typical/average prices
€€€ de luxe

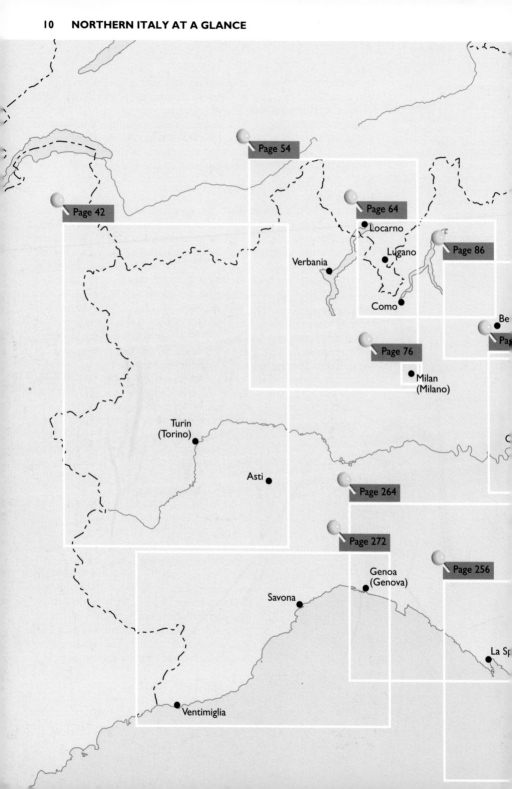

Page 54

Page 42

Page 64

Locarno

Lugano

Verbania

Page 86

Como

Be

Pa

Page 76

Milan
(Milano)

Turin
(Torino)

Asti

Page 264

Page 272

Genoa
(Genova)

Savona

Page 256

La Sp

Ventimiglia

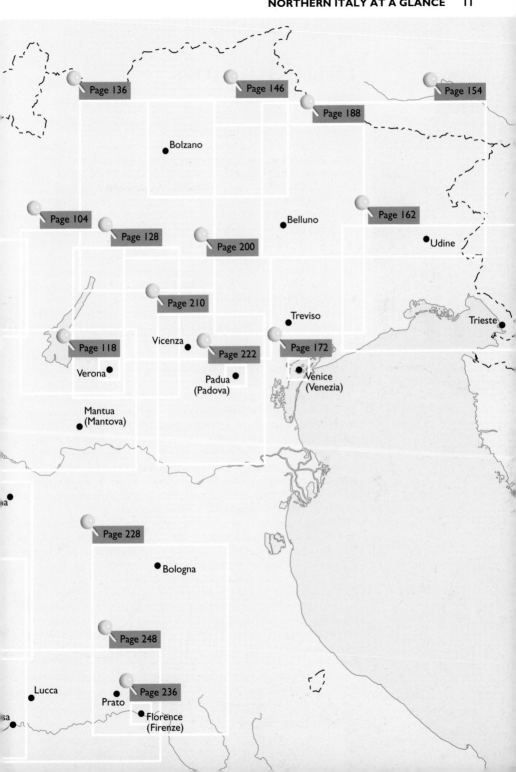

Page 136

Page 146

Page 154

Page 188

Bolzano

Page 104

Page 128

Belluno

Page 162

Page 200

Udine

Page 210

Treviso

Page 118

Vicenza

Page 222

Page 172

Verona

Padua
(Padova)

Venice
(Venezia)

Trieste

Mantua
(Mantova)

Page 228

Bologna

Page 248

Lucca

Page 236

Prato

Florence
(Firenze)

Introduction

The very name – Italy – brings a dreamy look to the eyes of those who have travelled or lived there. But a special fraternity exists among those whose time was spent in the north – for north and south are, even in the minds of many Italians, two separate Italys.

Northern Italy is a physically beautiful land. Overlooking its dark blue lakes, candy-coloured villas cluster on lush green hillsides with white mountain peaks behind them. Deep green vineyards spread along the valley floors and climb the foothills. Where the land drops to the sea, it spills into long, white beaches on the Adriatic and falls in breathtaking cliffs into the Mediterranean. In an easy day, the traveller can drive from sea level at the Venetian lagoons to mountain passes of more than 2000 metres. The Ligurian Coast south of Genoa is hardly undiscovered, especially the postcard town of Portofino artfully arranged about its harbour full of the pleasure craft of the rich and famous. But other less well known towns are equally pleasant: including the five cliff-hung villages of the Cinque Terre, which you can explore from a walking path that skirts the vertiginous headlands. Castles guard the Adige Valley from their craggy pinnacles, while a handful of towns – Castelfranco, Marositca, Soave and others – are completely encircled by defensive walls. Entire villages and city centres are filled with buildings whose ages are counted in centuries. Other sites – from baths and villas built by the Romans to medieval castles – lie in splendid and romantic ruin, leaving much to the traveller's imagination. Like a glittering gem in this setting is Venice. Images of its canals are so familiar that nearly every traveller dreams of someday standing in Piazza San Marco. But no matter how familiar its scenes, Venice continues to charm and to offer new secrets to those who stray from the usual St Mark's-to-Rialto route.

Echoing some of Venice's influence, but overlaid with their own individual histories and architecture, are the golden trio of Padua, Verona and Vicenza. These three cities are quite different in appearance – Vicenza seems a living design book of the great architect Palladio – but share a warmth and local ambience that is harder to find in Venice. They also share a wealth of the world's great Renaissance art. Villas, basilicas, cathedrals and modest parish churches here and throughout the Veneto have major works by Giotto, Tintoretto, Titian, Veronese and their contemporaries. At the southern edge of this guide's scope is Florence, birthplace of the Renaissance and perhaps the world's greatest repository of its art. Like Venice, few corners have escaped description, although even here a traveller can penetrate the veneer of tourism, but not before joining the throngs to see the unmatched treasures the city displays.

Yet northern Italy offers so much more than castles, canals, art and dramatic scenery. Hidden in its valleys and dotting its lagoons and craggy coast are stunning gardens, prehistoric carvings, Celtic and Longobard sites, medieval villages, fresco-painted buildings, towns devoted to a single variety of wine and tiny regions with their own unique cultures and even languages. The culture of this region is rich and ancient, benefiting from the many peoples who have invaded or passed through. Many of the latter were so charmed by the land that they settled there, adding their own civilisation to that they found. As you travel you will meet examples of art, architecture, traditions, even languages that reflect everyone from the barbarian hordes to the Hapsburgs and Napoleon. The Lombards and the Roman legionnaires who stayed to found the Ladin communities are good examples of those who chose to stay. A unique layer of culture even history, has also been added by the many foreign visitors – mainly writers and poets – who lived here, including Goethe, Byron, Browning, Joyce and Hemingway. So enchanting are the surroundings that everyone from Shakespeare to Cole Porter has used it for a setting, adding yet another layer to its mystique.

While it may seem that hardly a sight in Italy has escaped the catalogues of centuries of *ciceroni*, you can still discover delightful places unmentioned in guidebooks or in the memoirs of the Grand Tour's *literati*. Approach Italy with a sense of discovery. Stray awhile from its well-trod cities, into its soaring mountains, into the 'little Venices' of the Veneto, up Alpine slopes for an unfamiliar perspective on the Matterhorn, into the vineyards of the Cinque Terre and to the eastern-influenced towns of the borderlands. You'll meet an Italy few travellers know.

Below
Venice from the Grand Canal

Travel facts

Accommodation

Italy offers a full range, from some of the world's most elegant hotels to places you'd rather not stay. Fortunately, the latter are few. Lines are blurred between a small *albergo* (hotel) and a *locande* (inn) or *alloggi* (lodging house), although the latter are usually cheaper. Another alternative, *agriturismo* (agricultural tourism), brings you closer to local life by staying at farmhouses or wine estates. Many serve meals featuring the farm's products, such as their own cheeses. Since each has only a few rooms, always phone ahead or ask a TIC to call. Each region has its own listings booklet, often with pictures. Always ask the rate when reserving and ask for a fax confirmation when booking ahead. Always book ahead and get a fax confirmation for the month of August, the Easter holidays, in big cities and for your arrival night. Lodgings are inspected regularly and given stars, and although the criteria are often irrelevant to travellers, the stars do give some guidance. Two-star hotel rooms usually have private bathrooms, three-star rooms telephones and television.

Airports

Northern Italy's major international airport is Malpensa, north of Milan. Flights from within Europe arrive and depart Milan's smaller Linate airport and at airports in Bologna, Genoa, Florence, Pisa, Venice and Verona. Malpensa is about halfway between Milan and Lake Maggiore, so motorists bound for it or Lake Como can avoid encountering the city. Buses connect Milan's Centrale railway station to Malpensa every half hour €€ and Linate every 20 minutes €.

International chain hotels

Best Western:
Aus (1 800) 222 422
Ire (800) 709 101
NZ (09) 520 5418
SA (011) 339 4865
UK (0800) 393130
US (1 800) 528 1234

Comfort Inn:
Aus (008) 090 600
Can (800) 888 4747
Ire (800) 500 600
NZ (800) 8686 888
UK (0800) 444 444
US (1 800) 228 5150

Ibis:
www.ibishotel.com or contact individual hotels direct.

Labour strikes are very common in Italy and may occur suddenly as you are about to board your plane for Pisa or Milan, cancelling all flights. Alternatively, a rail strike may begin the day you leave, making it difficult to get to your departure city without a car. Try to arrange pick-up and return of cars at the airport, or to allow extra time to reach your departure point. During a rail strike, rental cars are almost impossible to get.

Above
Street car, Milan

Right
Hams and sausages, Bergamo

Children

Although Italians do not travel often with their children, they are most tolerant and quite pleasant about fussy children or crying babies. Don't expect special seats or menus for children in restaurants. It is wise to bring a folding high chair. Bring safety seats for children, too, as many car rental companies add an extra daily charge for these, if they have them. Lodgings can often supply a baby cot or rollaway bed: ask when booking. Supermarkets supply infant needs, but plan ahead for limited Italian opening times.

Climate

The northern mountains moderate what would otherwise be a hot, dry, Mediterranean climate, but summer is hot nearly everywhere. In the mountains, rain showers are common in spring, summer and autumn, and snow accumulations are high in winter. In the lakes region, sunshine averages 3–4 hours daily in the winter and more than nine in summer. In the Venetian plain, Milan, Turin and the Po Valley, summers are very hot and sunny, but winters (Dec–Feb) are surprisingly cool – colder than London – with snow, fog and rain common. In Tuscany, temperatures are hotter in the summer, more temperate in winter. Tuscany's summer heat can be unremitting in lower and coastal areas.

Currency

Currency exchange facilities are in all airports, near the arrival gates; those in Malpensa are open 24 hours. Avoid the cash changing machines; the rates are usurious. Also avoid carrying large amounts of cash, but if you do, hide it well. Safer are travellers' cheques and easier are credit or debit cards. Travellers' cheques are accepted at banks (after much paperwork), large hotels and by some larger stores in cities and major tourist areas, but are difficult to cash elsewhere. If possible, bring at least one major credit card; Visa is the most commonly accepted. Most small hotels, *agriturismo* properties and small restaurants do not accept cards. Expect trouble trying to cash Eurocheques except in large Milan banks.

Automated teller machines (*bancomat*) offer the best exchange rates, are found everywhere and never close. Check with your bank or card issuer before leaving home to learn what network you can use in Italy. Make sure that your PIN number can be used abroad. A credit card is less economical to use for cash advances than one issued by your bank that draws directly on your account, but either assures the best commercial exchange rate. Banks are usually open Mon–Fri 0830–1300 or 1330, often reopening for an hour later in the afternoon. Don't let your supply of Euros get low on a weekend, since banks, often even in

train stations and airports, will be closed. ATMs may be out of money or out of order. Try to arrive with Euros, especially on a weekend.

Customs and entry formalities

Citizens of the European Union (EU) can enter Italy for an unlimited stay with a valid passport. Citizens of Australia, Canada, New Zealand and the US, can also enter Italy with a passport (valid for at least three months from entry date); no visa is required for a stay of up to 90 days. There are no taxes or duty on articles for personal use that you take into Italy, including reasonable amounts of tobacco and alcoholic drinks.

Eating and drinking

Tip waiters about 5 per cent over the included service charge, unless a waiter has gone to extraordinary measures. Expect a modest *coperto* or cover charge at most restaurants.

Good food is so widely appreciated that dining places abound. Locals eat out frequently, so except in large cities, most restaurants offer good value at moderate prices. A *trattoria* usually has a more limited menu and lower prices than a *ristorante*. In smaller ones, there may be no menu at all, but the waiter will describe the day's offerings. An *osteria* is a wine bar that serves snacks and sometimes a few dishes, usually changing daily. When a place has a written menu, it will be posted at the door.

Fish and shellfish, except *calamari* (cuttlefish), are pricier than meat. A standard *primo* (first course) is a large serving of pasta or *risotto* (rice). A *secundo* (main course) is typically smaller, containing only the meat and perhaps a garnish. Vegetables and salads are ordered separately. Part of the fun of dining in Italy is sampling the infinite variety of pasta shapes, flavours and textures. Each town seems to have its own special kind, often a variation on the *ravioli*, filled with anything from cheese or meat to pumpkin. If breakfast is not included in the lodging price, cafés are a better value than hotel breakfasts. For plain bread rolls, ask for *panini*. Coffee with hot milk – *cappuccino* or *caffè latte* – is drunk only at breakfast in Italy. Coffee ordered at any other time

Left
Rapallo Castle

Right
Harbour, Vernazza

Electricity
Italy operates at 220 volts. UK appliances will work, but require an adaptor to the European-type plug with two round prongs. American appliances need a transformer and an adaptor.

of day will automatically be *espresso*. Traditionally, Italians eat their main meal in the middle of the day, although this is changing somewhat in cities. Meal hours are generally lunch 1200–1430 or 1500, dinner 1900–2200, later in summer resort areas and cities. In small towns, hours may be more limited. Italians usually arrive for the evening meal at about 8 p.m., so go earlier if you don't have a reservation on a busy night.

Italy is not known for 'great' wines in the way France is, but it has many very good ones. These itineraries take you through some of Italy's best known wine regions. You may recognise many of the towns described here as familiar from wine labels: Bardolino, Valpolicella, Soave. Wine areas are scattered, but most are in pockets in the north. From Piedmont try Barbaresco, Barbera d'Alba and Barolo for reds and Gavi or Roero Arneis for whites. In the Veneto the best reds are Valpolicella (fairly light) and the heartier Bardolino from the shores of Lake Garda; for whites taste Soave, Lugana and Bianco di Custoza. The best known Italian wine, Chianti, comes from Tuscany, around Florence. No matter where you are, the local *vino di tavola* is always worth a try. Ask 'prova?' for a taste.

Health

Italy is generally a healthy place to travel; drinking water is normally safe (although savvy travellers usually drink bottled varieties). No immunisations are required to enter. For minor medical problems, ask at a chemist's (*farmacia*). These take turns staying open for emergencies; normal hours are Mon–Fri 0830–1230 and 1630–1900. For more serious illness or injury, a TIC or hotel can suggest English-

speaking doctors. Bring enough prescription medications for the entire trip, with a copy of the prescription in generic form, plus aspirin, available only in chemist's.

Information

Towns of any size have tourist information centres (TICs), usually called APT or ARPT, and usually found at the main railway station or *piazza*. Except in large towns, these are normally closed in the midday period. Normal hours are Mon–Sat 0900–1300 and 1600–1800 or 1900; shorter in winter.
Some can make lodging reservations, all can suggest options. They vary greatly in helpfulness and you usually have to request brochures singly rather than being able to gather them from display racks. Some offices offer useful booklets of detailed dining, shopping, lodging and attractions listings, with current opening hours. Remember opening hours in Italy change faster than the phases of the moon!

Information online

Some websites are more useful than others and they change rapidly. These are a few of the more useful:

- *www.enit.it*   Italian state tourist office
- *www.regione.umbria.it/turismo*   Umbria tourism
- *www.beniculturali.it/index.asp*   the Ministry of Culture, with links to museums

- *www.english.firenze.net*   Florence tourism
- *www.lagodigarda.it*   Lake Garda tourism
- *www.veniceforvisitors.com*   Venice visitor information
- *www.aguestinvenice.com*   events and art in Venice
- *www.turismovenezia.it*   Venice tourism.

Insurance

Experienced travellers carry insurance covering their belongings and holiday investment as well as their bodies. Travel insurance should include provision for cancelled or delayed flights, as well as immediate evacuation home in the case of medical emergency. EU citizens are entitled to free emergency medical care in a public hospital. Showing a

Postal services

Post offices are normally open Mon–Fri 0830–1400 (often until 1930 in cities) and Sat 0830–1200. Be sure you go to the right counter for *francobolli* (stamps), or buy them in a *tabacchi* (tobacco shop). Mail delivery is unreliable.

Public holidays

The major public holidays are:
1 Jan New Year's Day
6 Jan Epiphany
Mar/Apr Easter Monday
25 Apr Liberation Day
1 May Labour Day
15 Aug Feast of the Assumption
25 Dec Christmas Day

Below
On the shore of Lake Stresa

passport might be enough but you should carry a form E111. (UK citizens can pick one up at the Post Office.) Non-EU citizens are only covered if they have travel insurance.

Italy's tourism offices

Australia *Italian Consulate, Level 26, 44 Market St, Sydney NSW 2000; tel: 02 9262 1666.*
Canada *1 Place Ville-Marie, Suite 1914 Montreal PQ H3B 2C3; tel: 514 866 7667 and 514 392 1492.*
New Zealand *Italian Embassy, 34 Grant Rd, Thorndon, Wellington; tel: 04 473 5339.*
UK *1 Princes St, London W1R 8AY; tel: 020-7408 1254, fax: 020-7493 6695 (brochure request line 0891 600280).*
USA *630 Fifth Avenue, Suite 1565, New York, NY 10111; tel: 212 245 4822, fax 212 586 9249. 500 North Michigan Avenue, Suite 2240, Chicago, IL 60611; tel: 312 644 0990, fax: 312 644 3109. 12400 Wilshire Boulevard, Suite 550, Los Angeles, CA 90025; tel: 310 820 0098, fax: 310 820 6357.*

Language

Italian is one of the easiest languages to learn. There are almost no silent letters, so once you learn the few simple pronunciation rules, you can pronounce a word when you see it. Italian has fewer words than most other Latin-based languages and synonyms are few. Those who read other Romance languages, especially Spanish, will be able to read Italian. Italians are hospitable and quite adept at speaking with their hands, so you will find understanding and being understood quite easy and often entertaining. In the Dolomites, especially in the Sud Tirol (southern Tyrol) and around Lake Garda, German is widely spoken. Always ask, for good manners' sake, if someone speaks English or another language, before launching into it. In heavily travelled areas, those who deal most with travellers speak some English. Italians are good-natured about their language and your

Senior citizens

Older people are usually treated with respect by young people, especially in smaller towns. You will sometimes find discounts, but may find that Avis is the only car hire agency that will provide cars for drivers over the age of 70. Leasing a car from Renault Eurodrive is a way of getting around this regressive policy.

Toilets

Petrol stations on the *autostrada*, museums and bus and train stations will nearly always have toilets (*Uomini* for men and *Donne* for women). Elsewhere, public toilets are a rare surprise. Most cafés don't object if you go in just to use the bathroom. Although they are less common with each passing year, be prepared in smaller and rural settings for the 'Turkish toilet' – essentially a hole in the floor flanked by two ceramic footprints.

inability to speak it, and are very pleased when you try even a smiling 'Buon Giorno'. (*See also page 282.*)

Opening times

Expect all but the largest museums, shops and offices to close during the midday period. Closing times vary from 1200–1300, reopening is most often at 1400 or 1500, but maybe even later, especially in the summer. Churches are notoriously irregular and inconsistent in their opening hours, but are usually open 0900–1300 and 1500–1900. These and smaller museums may not even be open during the hours that are clearly posted on their tightly closed doors. Don't blame your guidebook, tourist brochure or the tourist office for not having up-to-date opening hours; these may have changed last Tuesday and will change again next Friday. This is Italy, where time is often secondary to nearly everything else. Many shops are closed on Mon morning. Food stores are usually closed on Wed afternoon. Only major supermarkets near large cities and petrol stations on the *autostrada* stay open during the middle of the day. In tourist places or during the summer, shops may remain open longer. However, many businesses, even restaurants, take a holiday in August. Banks are generally open Mon–Fri 0830–1300 and 1430–1600 (later on Thur).

Packing

Pack comfortable clothing that you can layer for warmth. The Italians are a bit more formal in the evening than other Europeans, even in beach resort areas, but are not overly dressy otherwise. Even casual clothes are usually smart and stylish. Jeans are acceptable daywear nearly anywhere, but shorts are usually not allowed in churches and frowned on at evening meals. Take a raincoat or umbrella; warm clothes and waterproofs are essential for the mountains year-round. Bring suntan lotion or block for the beach and high altitudes, where the sun is stronger. Essential medications should accompany you, not be packed in checked baggage. A small daypack is handy for carrying picnic lunches, guidebooks and small items, and can double as a spare carry-on for the trip home. Travelling to Italy it can fold flat in your suitcase. If you plan to buy Venetian glassware or pottery, bring several sheets of bubble-wrap packing material for the trip home.

Safety and security

Crimes against tourists in Italy are usually from pickpockets, purse-snatchers and car thieves. Be careful, especially in cities and major tourist areas, of your personal possessions. Thieves use motorcycles to approach as close as possible to pedestrians, grab cameras or handbags and speed off into traffic. Florence has a real drug and crime problem, so take special care there. Gypsies can be a problem, especially in the Milan train stations. Some use children, who slip up unnoticed and filch a wallet with deft small fingers. Always carry money and documents in body-wallets, with only enough out for immediate needs. Lock cars and hide any sign of being a tourist, such as maps or guidebooks. Tourists' cars are a target, since they are assumed to have luggage in the boot. If a robbery does occur, report it immediately to the police, to support insurance claims. Carrying identification, such as a passport, is required by law. Although Italian drivers are usually skilful at avoiding pedestrians, they often come perilously close. Before stepping into a street, be sure you're not sharing it with a car.

Below
Arcaded street, Conegliano

Shopping

Shops close during the midday period, usually at 1300. Except in resorts, they close Sun and often Mon morning. Tourist shops may open longer hours. Local crafts include ceramics and pottery, glass (Venice), lace (be careful, most is imported), leather goods, gilded wooden boxes and trays (Florence), and hand-bound books and marbled papers (Florence and Venice). The latter may include beautifully crafted albums or items as small as a bookmark or pocket address book. In Venice, buy carnival masks from a studio where they are made. Italian fashions are very pricey, but even the most expensive shops have sales in July. Street and flea markets are good places to shop, but don't expect to see many real antiques. Be careful shipping goods home; be sure the store is reliable and used to dealing with international shipments. The success rate of Italian mail is about 50 per cent.

Sports

While active sports are less generally enjoyed by Italians, those who do cycle, climb, hike or ski are very enthusiastic. In the Dolomites, hiking trails are well-marked and generally in good repair, but Italians elsewhere are not avid walkers, so trails in other places are relatively few. One notable exception is the corniche path connecting the towns of the Cinque Terre in Liguria. Italian drivers are usually quite considerate toward cyclists (more so than they are of pedestrians) who share the roads. Tuscany and the Piedmont are favourite venues of packaged cycling tours. Skiing, especially downhill, is popular in the Dolomites, where there are world-class ski resorts. For watersports, Lake Garda is the best, especially for wind-surfing, although their sails are a common sight on northern Lake Como, as well.

Telephones

Home Country Direct

To access your own telecom service when placing a call from Italy, use the following direct dial numbers:
Australia: Optus 172 1161; Telstra 172 1061
Canada: 172 1001
Ireland: 172 0353
New Zealand: 172 1064
UK: BT 172 0044; Cable & Wireless 172 054
US: AT&T 172 1011; MCI 172 1022; Sprint 172 1877

Time

Italy is GMT plus one hour in winter and two hours ahead from the end of March to the end of September. To many Italians, especially in smaller towns, time is not particularly important, so be prepared for delays and for doors closed even when the sign on them says they should be open.

Telephone numbers are changing, so if you can't get through, check to see if a digit has been added. Printed materials – even 'official' – often lag far behind reality. Ask a TIC or hotel desk to help if you cannot reach a number. Avoid making international calls from your hotel room; the surcharges can far exceed the price of the call. Mobile phones in Italy use the GSM European standard. The easiest way to make a telephone call is to buy a card (carta telefonica) from any news stand. Some of these work only in certain phones, so it is wise to buy them in small denominations. If you find a phone that doesn't use your card, the nearest tobacconist or news stand will have the right one. You must snap the corner off a phone card before using it. To call or fax Italy from outside the country, dial the international network access code 00, then the country code 39, then the area code, including the initial 0, and then the number. To make an international call from Italy, dial the international network access code 00, then the country code (Australia = 61, Republic of Ireland = 353, New Zealand = 64, UK = 44, US and Canada = 1), followed by the local number, omitting the first digit.

Travellers with disabilities

Except in the cities, where a few more places have wheelchair access, facilities for mobility-impaired travellers are poor. In Venice they are virtually unknown. Airports are mostly wheelchair accessible and major hotels usually have a few rooms adapted, but travel can be very difficult otherwise. Most museums, theatres and public buildings are not ramped. Parking is free in special blue zones for cars with an international disabled sticker. For current information, contact **RADAR** *12 City Forum, 250 City Rd, London EC1V 8AF; tel: 020 7250 3222.*

Driver's guide

Accidents

Emergency telephone numbers

Police (*carabinieri*) tel: 112.

Ambulance (*ambulanza*) tel: 113.

ACI Breakdown Service (Italian Automobile Association, for road assistance) tel: 116.

You must stop after any accident. Summon the police, *carabinieri* (tel: 112, the EU universal emergency number) or *pronto soccorso* (tel: 113) for medical assistance. Place emergency triangles in the road to alert approaching vehicles. Exchange insurance details with other drivers and complete a European Accident Statement form, which you should obtain from your own insurers before leaving home. Remain at the scene until police arrive, stay calm and request an English-speaking interpreter to assist you in making a statement. Notify the police of any injury, however slight. One of the advantages of the popularity of mobile telephones in Italy is that accidents are reported and help summoned almost immediately.

Automobile clubs

Automobile Club d'Italia (ACI) *Via Marsala 8, 00185 Rome; tel: 064 998 234.*

Members of UK automobile clubs can extend their services to Italy, which gives them access to the Automobile Club d'Italia (ACI) *Via Marsala 8, 00185 Rome; tel: 064 998 234.* For advance assistance with motoring routes and up-to-date road information, visit *www.theaa.com* (for AA members) or *www.rac.co.uk* (for RAC members).

Autostrade

Most major limited-access motorways in Italy are *autostrade* (singular: *autostrada*) toll roads, designated by 'A' in their route number. Rare exceptions are those motorways whose route numbers are prefixed with 'E', which do not charge tolls. On most, you take a ticket as you enter the *autostrada* and pay according to the distance travelled as you exit. You can pay tolls with euros in cash or by VISA credit card.

Breakdowns

The first thing to do if you have a breakdown is to pull over, if possible; then place a warning triangle 100m behind the vehicle (or a passenger with waving arms). Then call 116 for assistance. The tow truck driver will probably not speak English but he will come equipped with a multilingual auto parts manual. You will have to pay for towing and parts. Members of automobile clubs in their own country should be able to arrange for coverage. Enquire at your local automobile club about a letter of introduction or ETI booklet. If you are not a member of an automobile club that provides this service, it is

Drinking and driving

Italy has strict limits on the level of blood alcohol a driver can have – 0.08 per cent. To exceed this is to risk stiff penalties. A driver with a high level who is involved in an accident also risks being automatically held at fault.

Essentials

All automobiles must carry a portable warning triangle to place in the road in case of breakdown or other traffic-blocking situation. This device is called a *triangolo*. A recently-passed law requires wearing a reflective safety vest if you are walking on a motorway. While you are not required to carry one, you will be breaking the law if you must walk to an emergency phone without one. These may be obtained by post from *www. advancedsafetyproducts.co.uk*. If you drive your own vehicle from the UK, you must have headlamp converters to adjust the beam to the right.

wise to take out a continental breakdown insurance policy, so that the details will be handled by a multilingual specialist.

Caravans and camper vans (trailers and RVs)

Camping and caravanning is not so popular among Italians as it is among northern Europeans, and campsites are not as plentiful. But they do exist, especially around popular family tourist areas, such as Lake Garda and the Adriatic coast east of Venice. To book ahead, and to obtain a camping carnet and list of campsites, contact Centro Internazionale Prenotazioni Campeggio, *Casella Postale 23, 50041 Calenzano, Firenze; tel: 055 882 391, www.federcampeggio.it*. Local and regional tourist offices also offer illustrated directories of campsites or include them in their lodging guides.

The speed limit for caravans in excess of 3.5 tonnes and for camper vans is 100kph on *autostrade*, 80kph on highways and country roads and 50kph in towns. Remember that engine efficiency decreases by about 10% with each 3000 feet of altitude, so if you are driving in the mountains and towing a trailer, a non-turbo car may not be able to manage the incline.

Documents

Drivers from EU nations and the United States need only their own current driving licence; others should have an International Driving Permit in addition to their original permit. In practice, it is advisable to carry an international driving permit even if you are not required to do so, since it translates your own licence into Italian. You must get these in your own country, usually through an automobile club (you usually do not need to be a member). If driving your own car, you must have its registration and insurance documents in the car at all times. It is also important to get a card from your insurer to prove that you have third-party coverage.

Driving in the Italian Lakes and Mountains

Touring in Italy is a challenge to even the best driver. Italians drive at outrageous speeds, often whizzing in and out between cars with death-defying abandon. Roads range from state-of-the-art *autostrade* to winding mountain roads not quite two cars wide. The most nerve-wracking problem, apart from Italian drivers, is the number of mountain roads with precipitous drop-offs, some of which have no guardrails. Avoid these roads in the rain or in winter, and at night. In fact, it is wise to avoid night driving entirely, allowing enough time for daylight arrivals.

Traffic jams lasting several hours are not uncommon when an accident blocks an *autostrada* (which is a compelling reason to carry

Fines

An estimated 15% of drivers in Italy are stopped for speeding, which is a remarkably low number when you consider the disregard most Italian drivers show for speed limits. On-the-spot tickets are issued, and you should be prepared to pay. Although everything in Italy is flexible, the usual fines are €32–125 for speeds under 10 km/h over the limit (rarely even noticed except in especially hazardous places). Between 11 and 40 km/h above the limit, the fines are €125–500. Over 40 km/h in excess means a fine of €500–1250, plus loss of your driving permit. The good news is that drivers are not jailed for speeding in Italy.

both snacks and drinking water with you). Mountain roads can be narrow and the switchbacks over steep mountain passes will leave you breathless. When choosing a route, be sure to check the map for the tiny chevron marks or inverted brackets that indicate steep grades and passes. Don't be surprised to meet a car rounding a tight corner on a precipitous road with at least half the car in your lane, or to meet motorcycles entirely in your lane. Be alert and defensive at all times and if you want to look at the stunning mountain scenery, pull into a lay-by. The road needs your full attention at every instant.

The most immediate problem will be for those from left-hand drive countries, such as the UK and South Africa, since Italians drive on the right. In normal traffic, it will begin to seem natural as you follow other drivers. But at roundabouts or on dual-lane highways, it becomes more difficult, because your natural instincts give you the wrong signals. Be especially alert and continue to remind yourself of this danger.

The most difficult time for some is in starting out in the morning on a road without other traffic. You can drive for some distance without realising that you are on the wrong side. To solve this, attach a card to your keys, with the words 'Drive Right!' printed in large letters. Whenever you leave the car, and need to pocket your keys, remove it and tape it to your steering wheel. That reminds you as soon as you enter your car, at which time you return the card to your keys.

Driving rules

Traffic drives on the right in Italy. The most important rule of the road is to give way to the right. In the absence of a traffic light (*semaforo*), traffic officer or other indication, the vehicle on the right has the right-of-way, except at a roundabout, where a vehicle in the circle has right-of-way over entering traffic. This give-way-to-the-right rule does not apply to vehicles entering from driveways, lay-bys or parking spaces, although you should give way to buses leaving bus stops. It is also important to know that a green arrow indicating a left turn means only that the turn is allowed, not that oncoming traffic is stopped by a red light.

The left lane of an *autostrada* is only for passing. Slower vehicles are required to keep to the right. If a driver approaching from behind in the same lane flashes his or her high beams, you are expected to move to the right immediately. Do not pass on the right.

Pedestrians have the right-of-way on marked crossings, but it is not customary to stop for those on the kerb waiting to cross. To do so is to risk a rear-end collision, since other drivers will not anticipate this.

Fuel

Petrol = *benzina*
Diesel = *gasolio*
Unleaded = *senza piombo*
Full = *pieno*
Oil = *l'olio*
Water = *l'acqua*

Lights

Use headlamps at all times in rain, fog or poor visibility conditions. Right-hand-drive cars must have their headlight beams modified to prevent blinding oncoming traffic or be fitted with stick-on beam deflectors that make them dip to the right.

Mobile Phones

Drivers in Italy are permitted to use only those mobile phones equipped with ear-pieces for hands-free use. Hand-held phones may only be used by drivers who have pulled off the road and come to a full stop.

Petrol and diesel are sold by the litre, at fairly high prices. Many stations are self-service, and use credit cards at the pump, but the process can be very difficult to follow if you are not fluent in Italian. Some smaller stations take only cash. Many petrol stations, especially those in rural areas, close during the middle of the day and on weekends and holidays. It is wise to keep your tank as full as possible, especially on weekends. Be sure to check rental cars carefully when fueling them yourself, and tell attendants if you are driving a diesel car. The nozzles are not different and attendants may not bother to look at the warning before filling your tank.

Information

The best and most up-to-date road maps are issued by Michelin and Automobile Club d'Italia (ACI). Road maps disagree wildly, so it is best to carry several if you plan to do much exploring. One of your maps should show topography; an attractive-looking shortcut may be straight (or not so straight) over a mountain range.

When asking directions, remember to watch as well as listen: right, left, straight and roundabouts are all described with a wave of the hand. The most common answer is *sempre direto*, which translates as 'straight ahead' and usually means just that. But can also mean that the person you asked hasn't any more idea where your destination is than you have, so it's wise to check again before going too far.

Don't expect to always find route numbers on road signs. Instead, know the towns and cities on your route and follow signs from one to the next. Labelling is quite good, especially from major roads. *Autostrade* are usually labelled not by compass points but by the town or city at each end. This can be quite confusing, since the last point may be a tiny village on the Swiss or Austrian border. Before entering an *autostrada*, follow it on the map to know the names at each end.

Parking

Many parking areas (and streets where parking is allowed) have meter boxes which provide tickets when fed coins. These are quite simple to use, even without being able to read the instructions, although they are often not as easy to find. Put the ticket inside the windscreen, visible from the outside. You may find car parks where your stay is free, but limited to an hour or two. You can buy a paper 'clock' at news stands, or you can write the time you arrive on a piece of paper.

Parking garages usually have a cashier. Take a time-stamped ticket when you enter. Before leaving, pay for the ticket at the *cassa* (cashier window), drive your vehicle to the exit and insert the ticket to open the gate. Do not expect to find a cashier at the exit (and do expect to find irritated drivers behind you if you get there without the paid ticket).

Seat belts

Seat belts are mandatory for driver and all passengers, in front or back seats. Those under 12 must be in the back seat.

Speed limits

The speed limit on the *autostrada* is 130kph. Lower speed limits are posted when the road is dangerous or passes through an urban area (usually 100kph, but they vary between 80kph and 110kph) or when construction is underway (usually 60kph) – and you are required by law to slow down.

In towns, the limit is 50kph, and residential areas often post speed limits of 30kph. The maximum speed limit on country roads is 90kph, which may be faster than you would sensibly drive there. Often, they have no verge (shoulder) and you have no margin of error. They go through the centre of villages, where blind turns can hide anything from a parade or street market to a pair of local men discussing politics.

Security

Although Italy has a very high rate of car thefts and break-ins, the rate is not as bad in northern Italy, especially outside cities. But it is still high and precautions are wise. Try to park in a locked or guarded site or at least in a well-lit, busy place. Don't leave anything in the vehicle that you don't want to lose and don't leave anything at all in plain view when you leave your car. Choose vehicles with concealed luggage compartments and empty those when you stop for the night. When stopping for meals at roadside rest areas, try to park where you can watch your car from the table. Above all, don't leave anything visible that marks your car as belonging to a tourist – road maps, travel guides or brochures all lead thieves to believe that there will be luggage in the boot.

If car windows are open, be careful while stopped for a traffic jam or at intersections. Thieves work in teams, one drawing your attention by approaching the car as if to sell you something while another reaches into open windows to snatch purses and cameras – often right out of a passenger's lap. In case of theft, make a report at the nearest *questura* (police station) and ask for a *denuncia*, a stamped form that you must have for filing insurance claims.

Road signs

attenzione – watch out
bivio – crossroads
deviatzione – detour
divieto di accesso – no entry
gira a destra/sinistra – turn right/left
incrocio – crossroads
limite di velocità – speed limit
parcheggio – parking
pedaggio – toll
pericolo – danger
pronto soccorso – first aid
rallentare – slow down
sempre diritto – straight ahead
senso unico – one way street
senza uscita – no exit (cul-de-sac, dead-end)
sosta vietata/divieto di sosta – no parking
strada chiusa – road closed
strada senza uscita – dead-end/cul-de-sac
tenere la destra – keep right

traffico limitato – restricted access
uscita veicoli – exit
vietato il sorpasso – no overtaking/passing
vietato il transito – no through traffic
zona rimorchio – tow-away zone

Driving

il distributore – petrol station
il guasto – breakdown
il motore – motor
la benzina/il gasolio – petrol/diesel
l'accensione – ignition
l'acqua – water
la macchina – car
la pressione – air pressure
l'incidente – accident
l'olio – oil
non funziona – does not work
pieno – full
senza piombo – unleaded

ITALIAN ROAD SIGNS

RESTRICTION SIGNS

Maximum speed limit

No Entry,
one way street

No stopping at
any time

No honking

PRECEDENCE SIGNS

Give way

Crossroads with
right of way from
the right

Oncoming traffic
must wait

You have the
right of way

WARNING SIGNS

Roundabout

Signal lights ahead

Double bend,
first curving to
the right

Pedestrian
crossing

GENERAL SIGNS

Snow tyres
required

Stop for
police check

Border between
Italy & other
EU countries

Beginning of motorway (green
background),
or main road
(blue background)

Thanks to the following website for its kind permission to reproduce the above signs:
www.chianti-assistance.com

Getting to northern Italy

Airlines in the UK:

Alitalia tel: (0870) 544 8259; www.alitalia.it
British Airways tel: (0870) 850 9850; www.british-airways.com
KLM UK tel: (0870) 507 4074; www.klm.nl
Ryanair tel: (0871) 246 0000 (Mon–Sat), (0905) 566 0000 (Sun–premium rate number); www.ryanair.com
Virgin Express tel: (0870) 730 1134; www.virgin-express.com

Airline information in North America:

Air Canada tel: (in BC) 1 800 663 3721; (in central Canada) 1 800 542 8940; (in eastern Canada) 1 800 268 7240; www.aircanada.ca

Alitalia tel: (in US) 1 800 223 5730; (in Canada) 1 800 361 8336; www.alitalia.com

KLM tel: (in US) 1 800 374 7747; (in Canada) 1 800 361 5073; www.klm.com

TWA tel: (in US) 1 800 892 4141; www.twa.com

United Airlines tel: (in US) 1 800 538 2929; www.ual.com

The sooner you can begin planning your trip, the better deals you are likely to find. The best of these advance bargains require purchase 21 days ahead of travel, a stay of at least two weeks, return in 90–120 days and are not fully refundable. Conversely, you might also find deals on unsold seats a few days before leaving. On the Internet, visit *www.cheapflights.co.uk*, *www.lastminute.com* or *www.flightline.co.uk* for last-minute flights.

From the UK by car

Although it means hiring a car once there, it is much easier to fly from the UK than to drive to northern Italy. The advantages of having your own car there must be compared to the cost of getting it there and the two extra days it takes. Figure about 30 hours of driving, non-stop, to reach the Italian border from the UK, using the main north–south motorways. Add together the price of crossing the Channel, tolls, petrol and overnight stays en route and it quickly becomes expensive in both time and money; however, for a group of three or more, it might make good sense. London, as the European capital of discount flights, offers many alternatives. British Airways and Alitalia have flights several times a day to Milan and Pisa, along with cheap charter flights to these cities, Bologna and others. Many fly-drive packages are available from London, Manchester and Birmingham.

Right
Taverna al Ponte, Bassano del Grappa

Rail travel

The train offers no advantage in getting from the UK to Italy. Tickets, added to the cost of lodging and dining en route, are similar to flying and the trip requires at least another day each way. Contact **Eurostar** (*tel: (0990) 186186*) for trains to Paris, thence to Milan or other northern cities; **Citalia** (*tel: (0891) 715151, premium rate line*) for Italian rail tickets and passes; or **Rail Europe** (*tel: (0990) 848848*).

Car hire

It is rarely possible to rent a car spontaneously, except in mid-winter. By reserving well ahead, you will usually have the best rate and your choice of car. The best rates are often in a package with airfare, booked through the car rental company, airline or a reliable travel agency.

Major international rental companies are represented in Italy, with offices in Milan and Pisa, as well as other airports, for pick up and delivery. Auto Europe offers some of the most competitive rates and offers excellent air-auto packages that include mobile phones and other benefits. Contact them in the UK on *0800 169 9797*, in Ireland on *1 800 558892*, in Australia and New Zealand on *0800 169 6414* and in the USA on *1 888 223 5555*. Alternatively, visit them on the web at *www.autoeurope.com*. Most companies require a credit card when you claim the vehicle, even if the hire has been prepaid.

One problem with hiring a car in Italy is that you must nearly always purchase the collision damage waiver. Even though credit cards usually cover this, most do not in Italy, adding another expense to car hire. You can avoid this by leasing a car. Renault Eurodrive has a very smooth system for this, and will meet you with a brand-new car at Milan airport. The minimum lease period is 17 days, and the rate for additional days is quite inexpensive. Registration, insurance (without deductible) and all details are included and the rate compares very favourably with rentals (and without added VAT). Drivers over 70 are not banned, as they are by most rental agencies. Contact **Renault Eurodrive**, US *(800) 221 1052 (www.renaultusa.com)*, France *(0) 505 1515*. This plan is not available to residents of Europe.

Before leaving the car park, be sure you have all registration and insurance documents and that you know how to operate the vehicle. Don't plan a long day's driving after a long flight, especially if you are driving on the wrong side of the road.

From North America

Direct flights from several major gateways serve Milan's Malpensa airport. Many airlines fly daily to Bologna, Pisa, Venice and Verona from connecting hub cities in Europe.

Setting the scene

Geography

The Alps and the Dolomites form a tall, wide wall that separates Italy from its European neighbours. Most access from the north is over mountain passes or through highway tunnels that bore through at the base. Nestled at the foot of the mountains is a series of lakes, the largest of which are Como, Garda, Iseo, Lugano and Maggiore. South of the lakes and mountains, a flat plain stretches from Turin on the west to Trieste on the east and continues south to include the lower Adige, Mincio and Po valleys and their deltas on the Adriatic. South of Turin rises the Piedmont, blending into the Apuan Alps and Apennines – 'the spine of Italy' (*lo dosso d'Italia*) – that continues down through Tuscany and into the neighbouring province of Umbria. On the west, these mountains drop precipitously into the Mediterranean, forming the Riviera di Levante between Pisa and Genoa, and the Riviera di Ponente between Genoa and the French border. This steep coastline is punctuated by towns which have managed to find a foothold in the scant spaces between mountains and sea.

Below
Medieval pageantry, Mantua

Timeline

Above
Lion of St Mark, Udine

800–400 BC Etruscan settlements between the Tiber and Arno rivers, including Fiesole.

753 BC Latin and Sabine villages combine, the beginning of Rome.

*c.*600 BC Euganei and Veneti peoples occupy northeast Italy.

*c.*300 BC Rome conquers the Euganei and Veneti.

350–250 BC Rome conquers the Etruscans and Umbrians.

89 BC People of Verona, Padua, Vicenza, Este and Treviso gain full Roman citizenship.

*c.*87 BC Roman poet Catullus born in Verona.

59 BC Roman historian Livy born in Padua.

44 BC Julius Caesar appointed ruler of Rome for life.

AD 13–14 Romans create provinces of Umbria and Tuscia.

313 Christianity recognised by Emperor Constantine I in the Edict of Milan, which recognises freedom of religion.

330 Constantinople supplants Rome as capital of the Roman Empire.

395 Roman Empire divided into eastern and western parts.

410 The Visigoth Alaric invades from the north and sacks Rome.

421 Venice settled.

452 Attila the Hun invades the north but dies in 453.

455 Vandals sack Rome, then leave.

493–552 Ostrogoths under Theodoric seize control.

553 Byzantine emperor Justinian conquers Italy.

568–71 The Lombards conquer the northern region and are converted to Christianity. The Veneti begin to move to the lagoon islands.

697 Traditional date of founding of the Venetian Republic.

756 Peppin, King of the Franks, seizes Byzantine Umbria, giving it to the Pope and beginning the Papal State.

774 Charlemagne made king of the Lombards, conquers the region and Tuscany and Umbria become provinces of his empire.

800 Charlemagne crowned emperor by Pope Leo III.

828 Body of Saint Mark taken from Alexandria to Venice.

888 Berengar I crowned king of Italy at Verona.

*c.*1000 Holy Roman Empire breaks up, autonomous city states in Florence, Lucca, Pisa and elsewhere rise under the influence of the Pope. Guilds and the cloth industry rise, Europe's first banks created.

1095 Venice provides ships and supplies for First Crusade.

1125 Florence destroys Fiesole and fights wars with the Ghibelline cities of Pisa and Siena.

1028 Venice introduces first streetlights.

1155 Frederick Barbarosa crowned emperor of Holy Roman Empire, struggle with Popes continues.

1202 Venice uses the Fourth Crusade to conquer Constantinople, four bronze horses (and other treasure) brought to Venice.
1222 Founding of University of Padua.
1260 Scaligeri rule of Verona begins.
1271–95 Marco Polo journeys to China.
1301 Dante exiled from Florence, welcomed at Verona.
1309 Doge's Palace begun, following year Venetian constitution approved, creating Council of Ten.
1342 English loan default ruins the major banking houses of Florence, starting an economic crisis.
1348 Plague in Tuscany, Umbria and Venice kills half the population.
1380 Battle of Chioggia, Venice defeats Genoa for control of Adriatic.
1453 Constantinople captured by Turks, marking end of high point of Venetian Republic.
1489 Venice gains Kingdom of Cyprus by marriage.
1508 Palladio born at Vicenza.
1518 Birth of Tintoretto in Venice.
1528 Paolo Veronese born.
1559 Spain gains control over Milan region.
1571 Venice loses Cyprus to Turks, whose fleet is then defeated at Battle of Lepanto.
*c.***1595** Shakespeare writes *Romeo and Juliet*.
1630 Second major plague hits Venice, leads to building of Santa Maria Salute as offering.
1669 Venice loses Crete to the Turks.
1678 University of Padua awards doctorate to Elena Piscopia, the first woman in the world ever to receive a degree.
1708 Venetian lagoon freezes solid for the first time.
1718 Venice ceases to be a naval power after defeat by Turks at Morea.
1720 Caffè Florian opens on the Piazza San Marco in Venice.
1789 Dolomite mountains named after French geologist Diedonne Dolomieu.
1797 Napoleon Bonaparte conquers the Veneto, last Doge resigns, Venetian Republic ends.
1798–9 Napoleon occupies Tuscany and Umbria.
1805 Napoleon crowned King of Italy.
1805–14 Napoleon's sister Elisa rules the Duchy of Lucca.
1814 Napoleon banished to Elba, Papal state restored, Tuscany is ruled by the Austrians.
1831 Giuseppe Mazzini founds Young Italy movement, beginning resistance to Austria.
1848 The first Italian War of Independence. Italians under Mazzini rebel against Austrian rule and the Papal State. Daniele Manin leads

Guelphs and Ghibellines

During the Middle Ages, many of Italy's land-owning nobility chafed under the political authority of the Popes, which made them subservient to the clergy. It was also a time of rising influence for merchants, bankers and members of the trades guilds, who resented the authority of local lords to interfere in their lives and tax freely. This newly influential group favoured the Pope. The result was a contest between the Emperor's (and landed nobility's) authority and the political authority of the Pope.

Above
First World War Memorial at Villafranca

Venetian rebels, but the Austrians and Pope prevail.

1859 Second War of Italian Independence, Battle of Solferino leads to founding of Red Cross.

1861 Vittorio Emanuele II crowned King of Italy.

1865–70 Florence capital of Italy.

1866 Austrian rule ends throughout the Veneto.

1870 Completion of Italian unification as the Kingdom of Italy with Rome as its capital.

1902 *Campanile* of San Marco, Venice falls, reopens in 1912.

1915 Italy joins Allies in First World War against Austria.

1918 Austria invades Italian Dolomites, fierce fighting in the mountains.

1919 Istria/Trentino ceded by Austria, becomes part of Italy.

1922 Benito Mussolini becomes *Il Duce*.

1931 Venice first linked to the mainland by a road.

1937 Italy joins Germany and Japan in Anti-Comintern Pact: the Axis formed.

1939 Italy and Germany sign 'Pact of Steel'.

1940 Italy joins Second World War as German ally.

1943 Mussolini deposed, sets up Nazi puppet state at Salo on Lake Garda.

1944–5 Italy joins Allies, Italian partisans battle Nazis in the occupied areas. Livorno, Pisa, San Gimignano and other cities heavily damaged. July 1944 the Nazis blow up all the bridges in Florence, except Ponte Vecchio, and many medieval riverside buildings. All bridges in Verona destroyed.

1946 Vittorio Emanuele III abdicates, Republic of Italy declared.

1954 Trieste incorporated into Italy.

1957 Italy joins the European Economic Community, predecessor of the European Union.

1966 Catastrophic flood sweeps through Florence.

1969 Marxist terrorist group Red Brigade formed. Commit bombings, murder, assassinations and robberies throughout Italy into the mid-1980s.

1978 Two papal elections in one year.

1982 Italy wins soccer World Cup.

1984 Catholicism loses its status as the State religion.

1990 Italy hosts soccer World Cup and finishes third.

2002 Italy adopts the Euro.

2003 Massive power cut leaves most of Italy in darkness. Authorities blame a malfunction of supply lines from France.

2004 Premier Silvio Berlusconi's corruption trial collapses in Milan.

The label 'Guelph' applied to supporters of the Pope, who hoped to achieve greater control over public affairs at the expense of the nobility. 'Ghibellines' supported the Emperor and civil authority. For the Ghibellines, it was a matter of preserving feudal rights and authority over the fractious subjects in their city states. This tension spread throughout the Italian city states, as faction fought faction and intrigue pitted family members and city states against one another. Merchant fought nobleman and rival families fought one another with private armies.

Above
Portal, Santa Maria, Bergamo

Art and architecture

Roman

While few standing examples remain of the architecture of classical Rome, those few are worth visiting. These structures, or the remnants of them, date mainly from the 1st century BC through the 2nd century AD and are found primarily in Abano Terme, Aquileia, Brescia, Concordia Sagiteria, Sirmione, Trieste and Verona. In Aquileia are ruins of the riverside port, forum and other important structures (c. 1st-centuries BC and AD). Sirmione, on Lake Garda, has the large Grottoes of Catullus and a villa. In Trieste is the well-preserved Roman Theatre. The highest concentration, however, is in Verona and includes the Arena.(c. AD 30), Ponte Romano, also known as the Ponte Pietro (1st-century AD), Gavi Arch (1st-century AD), Scavi Archeologici (c. 1st-century BC), Porta Leone and Porta Borsari (c. 1st-century BC) and the Roman Theatre (1st-century BC).

Romanesque

Romanesque style, while it also applies to art, is best known in architecture. It flourished from the late-11th century until the 13th century, when it was gradually supplanted by Gothic. Romanesque features semicircular Roman-style arches over windows and doors, massive exterior walls and heavy internal columns resting on substantial bases. Ceilings are barrel-vaulted, forming groined junctions where structural segments meet. Sculptural elements were added to buildings, in a less formal and more stylised form than on the classical Greek and Roman buildings. In domestic structures, windows and doorways featured rounded simple arched tops. The Lombards had the greatest influence on the style, decorating the exteriors of their buildings with bands of colour and detached bell towers, and placing covered porticoes over the elaborately carved doorways. Pisan Romanesque was quite different, with layers of arcades decorating façades, more closely akin to the classical style. Florence had its own variant, using a simpler arched colonnade on the lower level and patterned walls of green and white marble. The best example anywhere of Lombard Romanesque is the church of San Zeno (1123–35), in Verona, closely followed by the city's *duomo* (1139). In Padua, see the Palazzo della Ragione (1218). Pisan Romanesque is epitomised by Pisa's *duomo* (1063–1180), with its baptistery (1152) and famous leaning *campanile* (1173–1350). In nearby Lucca, see San Frediano (1112) and San Michele in Foro (1143). Pistoia has its *duomo* (1108–1311) and Sant'Andrea (1180). Florentine Romanesque is best seen in the magnificent baptistery (1059–1128) and at the church of San Miniato al Monte (1050), both in Florence.

Gothic

While Gothic supplanted Romanesque, it did not happen overnight and the Gothic style did not reach full maturity until the 14th century. Buildings such as churches took decades to erect and later architects often imposed Gothic elements onto buildings that had started as Romanesque. Gothic structures in Tuscany follow this pattern, so are not pure, most containing Romanesque elements or having Gothic styles built on or around Romanesque buildings. The Gothic architectural style brought a more delicate grace. Rounded arches soared into pointed arches, often with pronounced ribbing. The arches themselves created the strength of the structure and walls became curtains in which great panels of stained glass could be hung. Church interiors reached skyward upon seemingly slender columns. Art and sculpture became more mystical and emotional, dwelling upon themes such as the birth and Passion of Christ. In Italy it took form in the use of fresco and mosaic. In Venice, Gothic took on a different look. The style was heavily influenced by exposure to eastern styles found in Constantinople and the eastern Mediterranean basin. Domestic architecture shows particularly the use of the pointed arch,

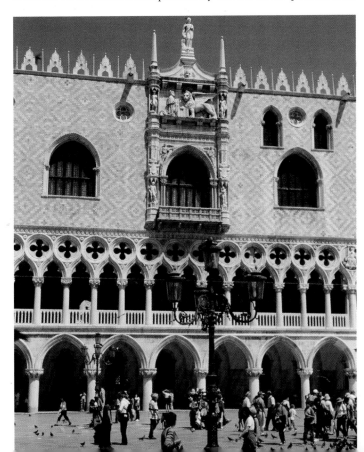

Right
Doge's Palace, Venice

ogee (reverse) curves and delicate tracery. The prime examples of Venetian Gothic are the Basilica San Marco and the Palazzo Ducale in Venice. Gothic is represented in Verona by San Fermo Maggiore (13th-century), Sant'Anastasia (late-13th-century) and San Fermo (13th-century), which shows a mixture of styles. The most outstanding Gothic church in Florence is the *duomo* (1294) and in Pisa the church of Santa Maria della Spina (1323).

Renaissance

From approximately 1400 until 1600, Europe witnessed a transformation in thinking, which was quickly reflected in all forms of art. Beginning in Italy, it spread across Europe, changing the focus of mankind from the perfection of man to assure redemption to the perfection of man as a civil being. Renaissance man began to see himself as a cognitive being and the real world crept into art. Architecture became appreciated as an art and architects became honoured professionals and not just craftsmen. Classical forms returned and in both art and in architecture perspective became important. The re-discovery of *De Architectura* by the Roman architect Vitruvius played a vital role. The sculptor Filippo Brunelleschi turned to architecture between 1412 and 1418, studying classical buildings and their mathematics. In 1418 he completed the dome of the cathedral of Florence, using, for the first time, a drum wall to support the dome. The Renaissance form developed rapidly as studies of classical remnants revealed their secrets. In art and architecture it became a matter of intellect and human individual endeavour to achieve balance. In architecture, the dome again became important and the familiar church floor plan of a cross with one elongated leg gave way to the Greek cross with equal sides and a domed centre. Stonework took on more sophisticated forms, such as at the Palazzo Medici-Riccardi in Florence where each level of the building received individual treatment. Classical forms were used in new ways. The orders of the classical world: Corinthian, Doric, Ionic, Tuscan and Composite, became important once again.

The real world began to show in the work of painters such as Piero della Francesca, Paolo Uccello and Masaccio. Perspective and realistic depiction became as important to art as the subject. In sculpture, Donatello and Ghiberti used the new principles to return their art to the classical ideal. Leonardo da Vinci, Michelangelo and Raphael – geniuses all – further developed the theory, creating some of the world's major masterpieces. In Florence, where the Renaissance

Below
Museo Cenedenze, Vittorio Veneto

gained its prime momentum, look for Spedale degli Innocenti (1419–24); Sagrestia Vecchia in San Lorenzo (1419); Cappella dei Pazzi in Santa Croce (1442); and San Lorenzo (begun in 1425), all by Brunelleschi. Also in Florence, see the Palazzo Medici-Riccardi (1444–59) and San Marco (1437–52), both by Michelozzo, and Sagrestia Nuova in San Lorenzo by Michelangelo (1520).

Mannerism and the Baroque

Toward the end of his life, Michelangelo had already begun to violate the rules of the Renaissance. Those artists that followed him were disparagingly referred to by the Tuscan artist Giorgio Vasari as trying to work 'in the manner of Michelangelo' and the label stuck. The title 'Mannerist' refers to those artists who followed Michelangelo's lead, breaking from the rules of the Renaissance. It was their work that led to the Baroque. From the logical realism of the Renaissance came the emotive world of the Baroque, where the subjects of paintings showed love, anger, fear and penitence in their faces and positions. Classical and mythical subject matter was introduced. Artists such as Bernini, Caravaggio, Tiepolo and Titian brought the form to Italian perfection. In architecture the classical forms appeared on a monumental scale, with embellished shields and other decorative detail. Classical forms also appeared in statuary and ceilings were painted with mythological themes. The forms were classical, but the architect and artist had greater freedom of expression. The result was an exuberance of creation. To see these styles in Venice, go to Santa Maria della Salute (mid- to late-17th-century), Ca'Pesaro (mid-17th-century), both by Longhena, and Santa Maria Assunta, also called Gesuiti (1715–28).

Festivals

With an entire calendar of saints' days, secular holidays, historical anniversaries, arts events and the harvest of locally grown produce, Italians seem never at a loss for something to celebrate. *Carnevale* in Venice (before Lent), Verona's summertime opera festival, Bolzano's Christmas marketplace, Marostica's biennial human chess game, Florence's *Calcio* (a ball-game and 16th-century procession) and Cortina's film festival are among the largest (and most crowded) of these. But don't be surprised to enter a small town and find a wine festival in full swing, or a celebration of the cherry or peach harvest, or a procession of the faithful bearing a statue through the streets. The one feature they all have in common is that visitors are welcome to join in the merriment – and sample the food, which is always a part of any festival.

Touring itineraries

While many of the routes described in the following chapters form loops, you can connect several of them into longer itineraries by travelling only one side of each to create larger loops, each a trip that would fill a holiday with a wide variety of sights and experiences. Italy's *autostrada* system makes it possible to connect even far-apart regions within a few hours of travel.

Venice and the East

Spend at least three days in Venice (*see page 172*), four if you want to explore its islands at leisure. Let it be the centrepiece of your visit if you have not been there before. From Venice head east to explore a part of Italy that even many Italians have not visited, described in 'The Borderland' route (*see page 170*). The Adriatic coast between Venice and Trieste is filled with Roman sites and lined with white sand beaches, and the fascinating area to the north bears visible evidence of the eastern hordes of Goths and Longobards that wrested the region from the Romans. A quick swing into the Dolomites adds another dimension, easy to do by following the 'Eastern Dolomites' route (*see page 160*) from Udine through mountain passes to Cortina d'Ampezzo. Return to Venice via some of the Veneto's most fascinating towns: Belluno, Conegliano, Vittorio Veneto and Treviso, described in the 'Eastern Alpine foothills' route (*see page 196*).

Below
Market, Bassano del Grappa

The Heart of the Veneto

If you have seen Venice, consider concentrating your attention on the trio of cities to its west – Padua, Verona and Vicenza. Each with its own distinct character, these cities (*see pages 222, 118 and 215*) provide focal points for trips into their surrounding regions. South of Padua and Vicenza lie the thermally active Euganean Hills. East of Padua is the Brenta Canal and its magnificent villas. North of Verona is the wine country of Valpolicella, the breathtaking road through the Pasubio Valley and the castellated town of Soave, described in the 'Valpolicella and Pasubio Valley' route (*see page 134*). That route blends easily into the very interesting group of towns in the 'Western Alpine foothills' route (*see page 208*). Distances are not great, but the variety is astonishing.

Mountains and foothills

For unmatched scenery and towns that capture the heart of the Dolomites and the Veneto's foothills, follow the 'Eastern Alpine foothills' route (*see page 196*) north from Venice, visiting the 'little Venice' towns. From Belluno, continue north through the Val di Cadore to Cortina d'Ampezzo, as described in the 'Eastern Dolomites' route (*see page 160*). Continue across the mountains, following 'The Dolomite Road' (*see page 152*) to Bolzano. Head south along 'The Alto Adige' route (*see page 144*) to Trento. Here you can head southwest to the northern tip of Lake Garda (*see page 104*), ending at the A4 *autostrada*, which takes you back to Venice or to Milan.

Highlights of the North

By taking full advantage of Italy's excellent *autostrada* system, you can combine the landmark cities of Florence, Pisa and Venice with mountain scenery, coastal towns and even a look at Italy's largest lake. Begin in Milan (*see page 76*), heading east past Bergamo (*see page 86*) to Brescia and following the southern part of the 'Brescia to Mantua' route (*see page 102*) to Mantua (Mantova). Travel south on the A22 to Bologna, following the 'Bologna to Florence' route (*see page 233*) across the Apennines to Florence (*see page 236*). Follow the 'Florence to Pisa' route (*see page 254*) west to the Mediterranean, then 'The southern Riviera di Levante' route (*see page 262*) north, past the Cinque Terre, and 'The northern Riviera di Levante' route *(see page 270)* to Genoa. From there it is a scenic, but straight return to Milan on the A7.

The Valle d'Aosta and Turin

Ratings

Castles	●●●●●
Geology	●●●●●
Mountains	●●●●●
Scenery	●●●●●
Nature	●●●●○
Outdoor activities	●●●●○
Walking	●●●●○
Historical sights	●●●○○

The wall of alps separating Italy and France includes the range's (and Europe's) highest peak, Mont Blanc – or Monte Bianco, as the Italians call it. The only way through the mountains was over steep passes, and today's roads follow essentially the same routes used by Neolithic travellers and the Celts. Roman legions used the valley carved by the Dora Baltea River to get to their colonies in Gaul, and the way-station they built at Aosta grew to a city so fine that it earned the nickname 'Rome of the Alps'.

Today the valley is popular with hikers and skiers. Forming its southern wall are Italy's own loftiest peaks, protected in the Gran Paradiso National Park. South of these, Turin flourished as capital of the Dukes of Savoy, and although now an important manufacturing centre, it is still easy to see why Italians called it 'Little Paris'.

AOSTA✧✧

ⓘ *Pza Chanoux 8; tel: 0165 236 627. Open daily 0900–1230, 1400–1800.*

ⓜ Museo Archeologico *Pza Roncas I; tel: 0165 238 680. Open 0900–1900 daily.*

Museo del Tesoro della Cattedrale € *Pza Giovanni XXIII. Open Apr–Sept, 0800–1130, 1500–1730; rest of the year by appointment.*

An ancient Roman post known originally as Augustus Praetoria, Aosta remains the core market town of the Valle d'Aosta region. Among its preserved Roman ruins are the sturdy stone **Arch of Augustus✧✧✧** built upon the town's founding in 25 BC, a well-preserved **theatre✧✧** also constructed by Augustus, **towers✧** and ancient **catacombs✧✧**. The town's good **archaeological museum✧✧** makes sense of many artefacts – bronzes, busts, tombstones, chalices, crosses, gemstones, even some bone art – from those heady times and its big piazza is a good place to watch the world go by. As impressive as Aosta's Roman remains is the ecclesiastical complex of **Sant'Orso✧✧✧**, where several centuries of art are packed into a church, belltower, crypts and cloister. The latter is Sant'Orso's highlight, with outstanding intricate stone carving. Almost lost in all this excitement is the fine local **cathedral✧✧**, featuring skilled mosaic and stained-glass work and the **Tesoro Museum✧✧**, holding icons, sculptures and other religious items of marble, wood and precious metals.

Le Cheval Blanc 3047
Le Mont Buet
Flaine 3099
Argentière
Le Brévent
Servoz 2526
E25
N506
Vallorcine
Aiguille d'Argentière 3900
Aiguille Verte 4122
Mont Dolent 3823
Chamonix-Mont-Blanc
Aiguille du Midi
Grandes Jorasses 4208
Mont Blanc (Monte Bianco)
4808
Champex
Orsières
21
E27
Rosablanche 3336
Lac des Dix
Val des Bagnes
Mauvoisin
Arolla
Dent Blanche 4357
Grand Combin 4314
Matterhorn (Cervino) 4478
Täsch
Zermatt
Monte Rosa
Macugnaga
Dufourspitze 4634
Lago di Campliccioli
Vanzone
Piedimulera
Pieve Vergonte
Ceppo Morelli
Carcoforo
Fobello
Lago Alpe dei Cavalli
Breuil-Cervinia
Grande Tournalin 3379
Great St Bernard Pass
2473
Bionaz
Valtournenche
Valpelline
Monte Faroma 3073
Grande Rochère 3326
St-Rhémy
Entrèves
Courmayeur
Morgex
La Salle
Pré-St-Didier
Etroubles
Gignod
Monte Fallère 3061
Aosta
Nus
Châtillon
E25
406
A5
27
Sarre
St-Pierre
Gressan
Brissogne
Fenis
Introd
Aymavilles
Monte Emilius 3559
St-Vincent
Montjovet
Monte Nery 3076
Gaby
Issime
Alagna Valsesia
Champoluc
Corno Bianco 3320
Gressoney-la-Trinite
Brusson
Evançon
Cravagliana
Balmuccia
Campertogno
Scopello
Sesia
Monte Barone 2044
Borgo
Coggiola
Trivero
Valle Mosso
26
La Thuile
Col du Petit St-Bernard 2188
Bonneval
Séez
N90
Isère
St-
Les Arcs
Ste-Foy-Tarentaise
D902
Mont Pourri 3779
Becca du Lac 3402
Valgrisenche
Lago di Beauregard
Rhêmes-St-Georges
Valsavarenche
Cogne
Rhêmes-Notre-Dame
Surier
Monte Glacier 3188
Issogne
Verres
Arnad
Fontainemore
Oropa
Donnas
Hône
Pont-St-Martin
Andorno Micca
Vigliano Biellese
Biella
Cossato
Settimo Vittone
Quincinetto
Campiglia Soana
Parco Nazionale del Gran Paradiso
Aiguille de la Grande Sassière 3747
Pont
Gran Paradiso 4061
Ronco Canavese
Monte Giavino 2766
Chiusella
Borgofranco d'Ivrea
Gaglianico
Candelo
Mongrando
Zubiena
338
232
230
Tignes
Barrage de Tignes
Lac du Chevril
Lago Serru
Noasca
Ivrea
228
Bollengo
Salussola
143
Balocco
Pointe de la Grande Casse 3852
Val-d'Isère
Col de l'Iseran 2764
Ceresole Reale
Lago di Ceresole
Orco
Locana
Pont-Canavese
565
E25
Cavaglià
A4
A4/5
Santhià
Carisio
D902
Bonneval-sur-Arc
Forno Alpi Graie
Groscavallo
Cuorgnè
Castellamonte
Strambino
Valperga
Borgo d'Ale
143
Tronzano Vercellese
Grand Roc Noir 3582
L'Albaron 3637
Uia di Ciamarella 3676
Ala di Stura
Cantoira
A5
E612
26
Lago di Candia
593
Lanslebourg-Mont-Cenis
Pointe de Charbonnel 3752
Col du Mont Cenis
Croix-Rousse 3541
Balme
Ceres
Rivarolo Canavese
Caluso
Cigliano
Bianzè
Livorno Ferraris
11
Canavese
Lanzo Torinese
Mathi
Ciriè
Rondissone
E64
Usseglio
Cafasse
460
Volpiano
2081
Lac du Mont Cenis
N6
Bramans
Aiguille de Scolette 3506
Margone
Punta Lunella 2772
Stura di Viù
Fiano
Caselle Torinese
Leinì
Chivasso
Saluggia
Crescentino
31bis
590
Mora
Valle di Susa
25
Susa
Bussoleno
Borgone Susa
Venaria
Settimo Torinese
Gassino Torinese
Casalborgone
Casale
A32
E70
Condove
24
Collegno
Turin (Torino)
Robella
590
458
Chiomonte
Exilles
Salbertrand
Sacra di S. Michele
25
Monte Orsiera 2878
Avigliana
Lago Grande
Rivoli
Beinasco
Grugliasco
Nichelino
Castelnuovo Don Bosco
Montiglio
Murisengo
Montechiaro d'Asti
Oulx
Monte Albergian 3043
Fenestrelle
Giaveno
Lago Piccolo
10
Chieri
Buttigliera d'Asti
Castell'Alfero
Pragelato
24
Chisone
Roure
Piossasco
Orbassano
Moncalieri
Sestriere
23
Cumiana
A21
Castagnole Monferrato
Montgenèvre
Punta Rognosa 3280
Perosa Argentina
Pinasca
589
23
23
20
393
Poirino
Villanova d'Asti
E70
10
None
Asti
Ripa
Bric Froid 3302
San Germano Chisone
Airasca
Carignano
Ferrere
Villafranca d'Asti
Pinerolo
Buriasco
Torre Pellice
Vigone
Pancalieri
29
San Damiano d'Asti
Isola d'Asti
Grand Pic de Rochebrune 3325
Bric Bouchet 3216
Abriès
Bobbio Pellice
Bricherasio
Pellice
Casalgrasso
Carmagnola
Monta
Aiguilles
Col de la Croix 2298
Luserna San Giovanni
Cavour
663
20
A6
Sommariva del Bosco
Canale
E74
Molines-en-Queyras
Bagnolo Piemonte
Moretta
Racconigi
Castagnole delle Lanze
Alzi Cozie
Col de la Traversette
Barge
Crissolo
661
Neive
Guil
Col Agnel 2914
589
Cavallermaggiore
E717
Bra
231
Grinzane Cavour
Alba
Monte Viso 3841
Tête des Toillies 2744
Chianale
Paesana
Po
Revello
Savigliano
La Morra
Diano d'Alba
29
Vesime
592
0 10 20km
10 miles
3015
Sanfront
Saluzzo
Cherasco
Monforte d'Alba
Cima delle Lobbie
Verzuolo
Genola
Narzole
Cortemilia
Casteldelfino
Sampeyre
Costigliole Saluzzo
E74
Varaita
Aigle de Chambeyron 3411
Monte Nebin 2510
Venasca
Fossano
Bene
Dogliani
Belbo
339
20

Sant'Orso V.
Sant'Orso, Aosta; tel:
0165 262 026. Open
Tue–Sat 0900–1900, Sun
1200–1900, winters
Mon–Sat 0930–1200,
1400–1730, Sun
1400–1730.

Aosta's market day:
Tue, when the city
market is held on Piazza
Cavalieri di Vittorio
Veneto.

Museo dall'Ospizia
tel: 417 871 236.
Open daily 0800–1930 mid-
Jun–mid-Oct.

Strung along the Val d'Aosta are small castles, each set on its own little hill or crag, many within sight of each other. Overlooking the vineyards of Sarre, 5km west of Aosta, **Castello Reale**✢✢ was the 'hunting lodge' of Italian King Umberto. To the east is **Fenis Castle**✢✢, with a lovely 15th-century courtyard from which a curved stairway rises to wooden balconies. The courtyard and chapel are painted in *freschi*, most in excellent condition. Another noteworthy castle close by is at **Aymavilles**✢.

From Aosta, it's a 35km trip (longer by the older, slower and more scenic road) north to the scenic top of the Gran San Barnardo Pass. Just over the Swiss border is the **Museo dall'Ospizia**✢✢, showing the history of the monk who built the first travellers' hospice and gave his name to the pass and the breed of rescue dogs (some of whom you may meet there).

Accommodation and food in Aosta

Hotel Europe €€–€€€ *Piazza Narbonne 8; tel: 0165 236 363; fax: 0165 405 66.* Very attractive hotel in the historic centre with friendly staff, free Internet access and covered parking.

Hotel Miage €–€€ *V. Ponte Suaz 137; tel: 0165 238 585; fax: 0165 236 355.* Small hotel with views, in-room TVs, parking and a restaurant. Breakfast is served, but extra.

La Cave de Tillier Brasserie €–€€ *Via de Tillier 40; tel: 0165 230 133.* Grilled steaks are delectable here, as is the gnocchi with fontina, the local cheese speciality.

Ristorante Praetoria €–€€ *Via San Anselmo 9; tel: 016 544 356.* The rabbit and polenta are good choices here, as are the pasta dishes.

COGNE AND THE GRAN PARADISO✢✢

TIC **AIAT**, Castello
di Sarre; tel: 0165 257
854; www.granparadiso.net.
Open Jul–Aug Mon–Sat
0830–1230, 1400–1800,
Sun 0830–1230, Dec–Jun
closed Wed pm, Sun.

Rising abruptly from the Val d'Aosta are the rugged, snow-capped mountains of **Parco Nazionale del Gran Paradiso**. Few roads penetrate this wilderness, following the valleys to end at remote villages. Beyond these are trails to rocky peaks inhabited by ibex and chamois. **Cogne**✢✢ is one of these villages, overlooking meadows of wild flowers in a panorama backed by craggy mountains. The town is a centre for woodcarving, which is sold in several studios and shops. **Cascata di Lillaz**✢✢ drops in a series of long falls, a short walk from the village of Lillaz, beyond Cogne. Hiking trails into the park begin here.

Accommodation and food in Cogne

Bellevue €€€ *Rue Grand Paradis 22; tel: 016 574 825; www.hotelbellevue.it.* The class act in town, with the best views and restaurant, along with an indoor pool.

Saint-Pierre €€ *V. Corrado Gex 61; tel: 0165 903 817; www.hotelsainepierre.it.* Located at the beginning of the road into Cogne's valley, this attractive modern hotel and restaurant is only 3km from the A-5 autostrada, but within easy reach of Cogne and the park.

MATTERHORN (CERVINO)✦✦✦

V. Carrel 29, Breuil-Cervinia; tel: 0166 949 136.

Few mountains are so universally recognised as the Matterhorn, called Cervino by Italians. But the usual view is from the Swiss town to its north. Much closer, and far more impressive, is the view from its Italian side, an almost sheer wall of rock rising overhead from the cul-de-sac village of **Breuil-Cervinia**. Unusual for mountains, the unique shape that makes this one so recognisable is the same on either side. The town itself is just plain ugly, but the best views of the mountain are from the breathtakingly beautiful foreground of **Lago Bleu**✦✦✦, a few km before town. Its clear Alpine waters mirror the mountain and a frame of dark larch trees complete a stage-set scene. The Alps don't provide a more perfect picnic site. Breuil-Cervinia provides hotels and the starting point for cable cars up the mountain.

Accommodation and food in Breuil-Cervinia

Hotel Bucaneve € *Pza Jumeaux 10; tel: 0166 949 119; fax: 0166 948 308; e-mail: info@hotel-bucaneve.it.* Small hotel with restaurant and sauna.

Hotel Hermitage €€€ *Srada Cristallo; tel: 0166 948 998; fax: 0166 949 032; e-mail: info@hotelhermitage.com.* Elegant mountain chalet featuring an exercise room, sauna, indoor pool and lush garden. There are TVs and data ports in all rooms.

Maison de Saussure €€ *V. Gorret 20; tel: 0166 948 259. Open Nov–May and July–Aug, closed on holidays.* This friendly restaurant serves the hearty French-influenced cuisine typical of the region.

MONT BLANC (MONTE BIANCO)✦✦✦

Pzle Monte Bianco 13, Courmayeur; tel: 0165 842 060.

Museo Alpina Duca degli Abruzzi *Pza Henry 2, Courmayeur; tel: 0165 842 064. Open daily except Mon, 0930–1830.*

Mont Blanc (**Monte Bianco** in Italian) forms a beautiful, but formidable, solid wall 50km long, 13km wide and 4800m high, separating Italy from France. Its tallest point lies just over the boundary, in France, and is the highest point in all Europe. It was once nearly impassable, but today can be traversed by auto, cable car, even – in places, if you're skilled enough – on foot or skis. The best base from which to visit the Italian side of the mountain is the pricey ski-resort town of **Courmayeur**. The town is actually half quaint despite the villas and shops, and there's a good little **Alpine museum**✦ to poke through and **San Pantaleone**✦, a parish church

Above
Monte Paradiso, Valle d'Aosta

dating from the late-14th century. It's only a few kilometres from here to **Entreves,** last town before the mountain and the French border and where you can board a cable car to the dramatic ridge-line dividing the two countries.

To press on into France by car, the 12km-long Mont Blanc Tunnel is the primary way, piercing the mountains to avoid the twisting, minor-road alternative. This was the longest such tunnel in the world when it opened in 1965. Some three-quarters of a million vehicles use it annually.

Accommodation and food in Courmayeur

Hotel Croux €€ *V. Circonvallazione 94; tel: 0165 946 644; fax: 0165 845 180; e-mail: info@hotelcroux.it.* This small hotel with a cordial staff makes a good base for excursions up to Mont Blanc. Opt for rooms with balconies from which you can see the mountain. Parking available.

Hotel Royale Golf €€€ *V. Roma 87; tel: 0165 831 611; fax: 0165 842 093; e-mail: info@hotelroyalgolf.com.* This large hotel dominates the cityscape and services a loyal – not to mention royal – clientele. Guests dine at the revered Grill Royal e Golf and can take dips in the heated outdoor pool. Parking available.

La Clotze €€€ *Planpincieux Nord; tel: 0165 869 720. Open July–mid-Sept and mid-Oct–May; closed every Wed.* Elegant restaurant located above the city and therefore offering splendid views from its outdoor terrace.

TURIN ❖❖

ℹ️ *Pza Castello 161; tel: 011 535 181.* There are also kiosks at both Porta Nuova Station *tel: 011 531 327* and the city airport *tel: 0115 678 124.*

Former centre of the Savoy dynasty's power, later a Communist hotbed and now Italy's fourth-largest city, Turin might not seem a likely candidate for a traveller's attention. But it is. Determined to make their capital a showplace that would gain them respect among the other courts of Europe, the Savoys lavished attention on their capital at Turin. The old Roman street grid provided the base for a well-designed city of broad avenues and spacious *piazze*. Its modern day prosperity has allowed the city to maintain and treasure its stately arcaded streets, Belle Epoch cafés, palaces, churches and public gardens. This might be one reason the city was the surprise winner – over Sion, Switzerland – of the right to host the 2006 Winter Olympic

Below
Café terrace, Turin

Duomo *Pza San Giovanni; tel: 0114 361 540. Open daily 0700–1200, 1500–1900.*

Museo Egizio € *Palazzo dell'Accademia delle Scienze 6; tel: 0115 617 776. Open Mon–Sat 0900–1900, Sun 0900–1400.*

Museo Nazionale del Risorgimento Italiano € *V. dell'Accademia della Scienze 5; tel: 0115 623 719. Open Tue–Sat, 0900–1900, Sun 0900–1300.*

Below
Sant'Orso cloister, Valle d'Aosta

Games, or it may be that there are so very many fine ski resorts so near at hand.

Among the city's attractions is its **duomo**✦✦, a typical 15th-century structure whose fame rests largely in the Sacra Sindone, the Holy Shroud. Displayed only rarely – the next time will be in 2025 – it is kept in a plain altar of a side chapel. A replica is displayed, however, and you can learn more about the continuing (and conflicting) tests for its authenticity at the small museum on Via San Domenica, the **Museum of the Holy Shroud**✦ (*tel: 011 436 5832*), which details some of these investigations. Piazza Castello is the largest in a city replete with grand-scale *piazze*, in which stands **Palazzo Madama**✦✦, enlarged in the 1400s from a fortifid Roman gate and renovated in the early 1700s to add the façade and a stunning staircase the width of the building itself. Overlooking the piazza is the **Palazzo Reale**✦✦✦, the Savoys' residence until the mid-1800s, resplendently over-decorated. Also off the piazza's southern end, the **Palazzo Carignano**✦✦, contains a museum detailing Italy's *Risorgimento* (Reunification) during the 19th century; appropriately so – this is the very building where the first

Palazzo Carignano
€ *Pza Carignano; tel:
0115 621 147. Open
Tue–Sun 0900–1900.*

Palazzo Madama € *Pza
Castello; tel: 0115 178 613.
Open daily except Mon
1000–2000, Sat to 2300.*

**Museo Nazionale del
Cinema** €
*V. Montebello 20;
tel: 0118 125 738; www.
museonazionaledelcinema.
org. Open Tue–Sun
0900–2000, Sat until 2300.*

Borgo Medioevale✝✝
Open Tue–Sun 0900–1900.

There's a huge open market each morning in the Piazza della Repubblica of fruit, flowers and other wares. Locals claim it's the largest open market in Europe. There's also a well-attended antiques market known as the Grand Balon one Sun each month behind the Porta Palazzo.

Italian Parliament met and where *Risorgimento* hero Vittorio Emanuele II (he of many squares throughout Italy) had been born. He would later become first king of the newly unified nation. Diagonally opposite this palace is another, the Science Academy Palace. This one holds the surprising and excellent **Egizio Museum**✝✝✝, an anthropology museum featuring the starring attraction of loads and loads of Egyptian artefacts from the time of Rameses and other ancient pharaohs. It's one of the world's finest second only to Cairo's, its holdings including statues, temples, fabric work, mummies, papyrus, burial items and much more. Best of all, these attractions all lie within perhaps a minute's walk of each other. There's an active, almost Viennese, café scene in the central city, as well.

Oh, and that famous Turin Shroud, which supposedly wrapped Christ's body? Well, it's kept under lock and key inside a special inner room of the *duomo* most of the time; but there's a replica on public show and on very special occasions the actual shroud is hauled out behind glass and carefully displayed. Forgive these folks if they neglect to mention that the cloth, tested by scientists, doesn't date from the proper time period to be considered genuine.

Tucked under the arcades are some splendid and historic places where the leaders of Italy's Risorgimento gathered to drink and plot. Some show their age, but others, such as the splendid **Caffè San Carlo**✝✝, in Piaza San Carlo, should be on any traveller's list.

Not far from the arcaded Via Po, is the peculiar **Mole Antonelliana**✝✝, which began as a synagogue, but when money ran out was turned into a monument to Vittorio Emanuele II. A glass lift speeds to the top for views to the Alps. Inside is the **Museo Nazionale del Cinema**✝✝, filled with screens for viewing classic movies and assorted mementoes of Turin's flourishing film industry.

Perhaps the city's most offbeat attraction is the faux Medieval village, **Borgo Medioevale**✝✝, alongside the Po river in the Parco del Valentino. Built for the Italian Exposition of 1884, the village is surprisingly authentic in architecture and decoration.

Accommodation and food in Turin

Boston €€ *V. Massena 70; tel: 011 500 359; fax: 011 500 359.* With a central location, car park and included breakfast, this medium-sized hotel is a good budget choice.

Hotel Luxor €€–€€€ *Corso Stati Uniti 7; tel: 0115 268 324.* Located near the train station, this independently-owned hotel is an affiliate of Best Western, and a reliable choice near the sights.

Victoria Hotel €€€ *V. Nino Costa 4; tel: 0115 611 909; fax: 0115 611 806; www.hotelvictoria-torino.com.* The quiet elegance and atmosphere of a Cotswold country house, set in the midst of the city centre; individually decorated rooms, free Internet access and bicycles. Included breakfasts are exceptional.

La Badessa €€ *Pza Carlo Emanuele II 17; tel: 011 835 940; www.labadessa.com*. Dining rooms are in a palazzo and the menu features specialities of the region's historic convents, updated by a talented chef.

Brek Ristoranti € *Pza Solferino; tel: 011 545 424*. At last a serious upscale, health-conscious, fresh-ingredient cafeteria! This place sparkles with just-picked berries and veggies and prepares them in traditional dishes; you can choose exactly what you want, and pay by plate size. Prices are low, quality high.

Caffè San Carlo €–€€ *Pza San Carlo 156; tel: 011 532 586*. Elegant décor, lots of history, genial service and good lunch dishes and pastries – the *carpaccio* is outstanding.

Idrovolante €€ *Viale Virgilio, Parco Valentino; tel: 0116 687 602; www.ristoranteidrovolante.com*. Inspired combinations, such as grilled swordfish sauced with limoncella and fresh oregano, served in a waterside setting.

Suggested tour

Total distance: 540km round-trip, 600km with detours.

Time: 6 hours driving one-way from Turin (Torino) to Mont Blanc (Monte Bianco) via the Valle d'Aosta, including the side trip to the Matterhorn (Cervino) and the town of Cogne. Allow 2 to 3 days without detours, 3 days with detours. Those with limited time can use the A5 toll road nearly the entire way. Skipping either the Matterhorn or Cogne saves considerable time as well.

Links: Turin (Torino), the beginning point for this route, is approximately 100km southwest of Arona on the Lake Maggiore route (*see page 61*) via the A4 and A26 toll *autostradas*.

Route: Leave **TURIN** (Torino) ❶, heading north on the A5 toll *autostrada* for 80km, exiting at **Châtillon** ❷ and crossing the river, then heading north along the R46 for 27km into the mountains to reach **Breuil-Cervinia** ❸, base camp for cable cars to the **MATTERHORN** (Cervino). Afterward, backtrack to Châtillon and proceed west on either the fast A5 or the more scenic S26 some 25km to **AOSTA** ❹. From Aosta, turn west on S26 to Sarre. Cross the valley, following R47 south, signposted **COGNE** ❺. Backtrack to the valley, turning west along the S26 for 35km to Pré-St-Didier, turning north for **Courmayeur** ❻ and **Entreves** – the base for cable cars over **MONT BLANC** (Monte Bianco) – and the 16km-long Mont Blanc Tunnel, of which approximately a third lies within Italian territory.

Above
Valle d'Aosta landscape

Detour 1: From Turin (Torino), cross the river going east and follow the S10 through an uneventful, ever-so-slightly rumpled 40km of terrain to reach **Asti ❼**. Though the town certainly isn't the most scenic in the Piedmont region, autumn brings an exciting *palio* (horserace) that rivals Siena's much more famous one. Spring brings the Feast of San Secondo, a festival of much parading, costumes, flags and eating, climaxing with, of all things, a bowl of soup. Asti is also the eponymous centre for Italy's Asti Spumante sparkling wine production – there are plenty of vintners in the surrounding area – and the town's impressive brick **cathedral**** is definitely worth a look, as well, for its elegant Gothic facing, trio of rose windows and careful stonework details. Strangely, there's no wine museum here in Asti; for that, head south an additional 30km along the SS231 to its rival town of **Alba ❽** – which holds an interesting horse race each summer – then follow signs south 8km to Diano d'Alba, turning west for **Grinzane Cavour**. The village castle here contains the **Enoteca Regionale Piemontese Cavour*** (*tel: 0173 262 159*), an entertaining little museum with wines for sale and a restaurant. It's perhaps another 5km across rugged little hills to little **La Morra**, boasting spectacular views from its village square, its own **wine museum*** and shops purveying the excellent local Barolo vintages.

Detour 2: Exit Turin (Torino) to the west, using Corso Vittorio Emanuele II (which becomes Corso Francia) for 15km to get to suburban **Rivoli ❾**. Ignore the A32 *autostrada* and keep to the secondary S25 another 15km. Just as you reach the dramatic foothills of the Alps, take the scenic left-turn to **Sacra di San Michele ❿**, a climbing road of a few kilometres to a fine little abbey (*tel: 011 939 130*) that was once a major stopping point for pilgrims coming south across the Alps. Among its spooky charms are a stairway whose walls contain the interred bones of priests; a door decorated with both Biblical scenes and signs of the zodiac; and 16th-century fresco work inside the inner church.

Also worth exploring

The southern portion of the **Parco Nazionale del Gran Paradiso** does not connect by road to the northern part, explored from the Val d'Aosta. The region is well worth discovering, for this is one of Italy's best national parks, a sprawling wilderness of remote river valleys, mountains (the peak of Gran Paradiso itself noses above 4000m) and exotic-seeming creatures like ibex and chamois. Founded in 1922, the park is interlaced throughout with rugged walking tracks; those on the lower slopes wind through Alpine wild flowers in spring, while the upper reaches pass mostly through pine and beech forests before moving above the treeline.

You can reach the park from Turin (Torino) by any number of indirect ways; but it's easiest, perhaps, to head north toward the city airport, then bear left onto the S460 until it gives way to an unnumbered road continuing onward north and west through **Courgnè ⓫** and beyond. Get a good map before attempting it.

Vernayaz · Saxon
Martigny · Charrat · Verbier · Evolène
Col de la Forclaz · Sembrancher
Champex · Val des Bagnes · Mauvoisin · Arolla
Orsières
Vallorcine
Argentière · Aiguille d'Argentière 3900 · Grand Combin 4314
Aiguille Verte 4122 · Mont Dolent 3823
Chamonix-Mont-Blanc · Aiguilles du Midi · Grandes Jorasses 4208 2473
Grande Rochère 3326 · St-Rhémy · Valpelline
Mont Blanc (Monte Bianco) 4808 · Courmayeur · Morgex · Monte Fallère 3061 · Gignod
Pré St-Didier · La Salle · Aosta · Sarre · St-Pierre · Introd · Charvensod · Fenis · Nus
La Thuile · Col du Petit-St-Bernard · Aymavilles · Monte Emilius 3559
Becca di Nona · Rhêmes-St-Georges · Valle d'Aosta
Valgrisenche · Cogne
Ste-Foy-Tarentaise · Rhêmes-Notre-Dame · Valsavarenche · Pont
Surier · Aiguille de la Grande Sassière 3747 · Gran Paradiso 4061 · Parco Nazionale
Tignes · Val-d'Isère 2764 · Ceresole Reale · del Gran Paradiso
Bonneval-sur-Arc · Noasca · Locana
Alpi Graie · Via di Ciamarella · Ala di Stura
L'Albaron 3637 3676 · Balme · Cantoira
Pointe de Charbonnel 3752 · Croix-Rousse 541 · Ceres
Col du Mont Cenis 2081 · Usseglio · Cafasse · Mathi
Margone · Punta Lunella 2772 · Lanzo Torinese · Fiano · Ciriè
Bussoleno · Borgone Susa · Caselle Torinese · Leini · Volpiano
Susa · Condove · Venaria · Chivasso
Chiomonte · Exilles · Sacra di S. Michele · Collegno · Settimo Torinese
Salbertrand · Monte Orsiera · Avigliana · Rivoli · Torino (Torino)
Oulx · Fenestrelle · Roure · Giaveno · Beinasco · Grugliasco · Nichelino · Chieri
Pragelato · Cumiana · Piossasco · Orbassano · Moncalieri · Castelnuovo Don Bosco
Sestriere · Perosa Argentina · Pinasca · None · Airasca · Poirino · Villanova d'Asti
San Germano Chisone · Torre Pellice · Pinerolo · Buriasco · Vigone · Carignano · Ferrere · San Damiano d'Asti
Bobbio Pellice · Villar San Giovanni · Bricherasio · Casalgrasso · Pancalieri · Carmagnola · Monta · Canale
Abriès · Bagnolo Piemonte · Barge · Moretta · Racconigi · Sommariva del Bosco · Castagnole delle Lanze · Neive
Molines-en-Queyras · Crissolo · Revello · Paesana · Cavallermaggiore · Bra · Alba
Chinanale · Sanfront · Saluzzo · Savigliano · Grinzane Cavour · Diano d'Alba · Vesime
Cima delle Lobbie · Sampeyre · Verzuolo · Genola · Cherasco · La Morra · Monforte d'Alba

BAGNES
Weisshorn 4505 · Saas Fee · Saas Grund · Bognanco
Matterhorn (Cervino) 4478 · Zermatt · Macugnaga · Vanzone · Pieve Vergonte
Breuil Cervinia · Grande Tournalin · Alagna Valsesia · Champoluc · Carcoforo · Fobello
Valtournenche 3379 · Gressoney-la-Trinite · Corno Bianco 3320 · Balmuccia · Varall
Châtillon · Brusson · Campertogno · Scopello · Monte Barone 2044 · Borgoses
St-Vincent · Montjovet · Gaby · Issime · Trivero · Valle Mosso · Coggiola · Borg
Verrès · Issogne · Arnad · Fontainemore · Oropa · Vigliano Biellese · Cossato
Hône · Donnas · Andorno Micca · Biella · Candelo
Pont-St-Martin · Quincinetto · Settimo Vittone · Borgofranco d'Ivrea · Mongrando · Zubiena · Balocco
Campiglia Soana · Ronco Canavese · Ivrea · Salussola · Cavaglià · Carisio · Sandigliano
Pont-Canavese · Castellamonte · Strambino · Borgo d'Ale · Tronzano Vercellese
Cuorgnè · Valperga · Caluso · Cigliano · Bianze · Livorno Ferraris · Desa
Rivarolo Canavese · Rondissone · Saluggia · Crescentino · Trino · Morano
Chivasso · Gassino Torinese · Casalborgone · Robella · Casale M
Leini · Settimo Torinese · Montiglio · Murisengo · Montechiaro d'Asti
Chieri · Buttigliera d'Asti · Castell'Alfero · Monte
Poirino · Ferrere · Villafranca d'Asti · Asti · Castagnole Monferrato
Monferrato · Niz

Lake Maggiore

Ratings

Gardens	●●●●●
Villas	●●●●●
Scenery	●●●●○
Architecture	●●●○○
Villages	●●●○○
Walking	●●●○○
Historical sights	●●○○○
Outdoor activities	●●○○○

Lake Maggiore's charms are subtle, rather than overpowering. A circuit of the lake – which juts a bit into Switzerland – soon brings one from the dull holiday villas of the southern shore into much more impressive geology, botany and history, with the lake's characteristic palm trees, colour-washed homes, steamer ferries and harbours to reinforce the sense of gently getting away from the rest of the world. There is a set of small, wonderful islands to explore, along with cutesy resort towns, cable cars and ridges from which to view the expanses of lake and mountains behind. Connecting boats link many of the lake's towns together. The suggested tour traverses the lake's western flank first, backtracks, uses a ferry to cross at the midpoint and then finishes with a tour of Maggiore's eastern shore.

ANGERA*

Rocca Borromeo
€ *V. alla Rocca; tel: 0331 931 300; www.roccaborromeo.it. Open Apr–late Oct 0900–1730, longer hours in summer.*

Museo dei Transporti
Off S629, Ranco. Open Tue–Sun 1000–1200, 1400–1800. Free.

Market day: Thur.

Angera crouches low on the lake's eastern shore under its amazingly well-preserved castle, **Rocca Borromeo***, guarding the strategic southern end of the lake as it has since the 13th century, reached by a steep access road. The Viscontis, bishops from Milan, added frescoes, towers, fortifications and other touches to the crude original structure. There's also a **Museo della Bambola** (doll museum) in the main castle showing more than 1000 dolls and a courtyard with views of the lake. The small stone palace on the same grounds reveals a further oddity: the **Children's Fashion Museum***, containing tiny examples of luxury children's clothing from the 17th century onward. Just north, in Ranco, is the thoroughly charming and quirky **Museo dei Transporti**, an open-air jumble of hundreds of cars, trains, funiculars, and other conveyances assembled in a maze of passageways. Some are historically significant – such as Pope Pius IX's railcar chapel – others just interesting. Tracks descend into a coalmine, an escalator into a subway station – all great fun.

Accommodation in Angera

Il Sole di Ranco €€€ *Piazza Venezia 5, Ranco; tel: 0331 976 507; fax: 0331 976 620; www.ilsolediranco.it.* One of the best reasons for visiting this part of the lake is to stay in this family-owned villa, whose elegant rooms overlook gardens and Lake Maggiore. Guests get preference for reservations at their highly acclaimed (two Michelin stars), extraordinary restaurant.

Dei Tigli €–€€ *V. Paletta 20; tel: 0331 930 836; fax: 0331 930 836.* Relatively simple hotel, open spring to autumn; breakfast is served, but there's no restaurant for dinner.

ARONA*

ⓘ *Pzle Duca d'Aosta; tel: 0322 243 601.*

ⓝ S Carlo Borromeo *€ Open daily Apr–Sept 0915–1230, 1400–1830, weekends only Oct & Mar.*

◖ Market day: Tue.

Arona is Maggiore's base camp and as such it does the heavy lifting: this is where you'll find many restaurants and tourist services. Parts of town can be predictably dull, but the village does redeem itself with an especially large supply of affordable hotel rooms. The singular monument here that can't be missed – it's 75ft (23.5m) tall – is a **statue of St Charles Borromeo**, which can be ascended via a set of interior stairs and is illuminated at night. The town's **Museum of Archaeology** in Piazza San Graziano (*tel: 032 248 294*) is worth a look as well.

Accommodation and food in and near Arona

Villa Carlotta €€ *V. Sempione 121/125, Belgirate; tel: 032 276 461; fax: 032 276 705; www.bestwestern.com.* Villa with terraced gardens, in-room Internet points, a few towns north along the lake; favourite of British coach groups.

Hotell Milano €€ *V. Sempione 4, Belgirate; tel: 032 276 525; fax: 032 276 295; www.bestwestern.com.* On the lake with its own dock and terrace restaurant; staff couldn't be nicer.

La Bruma dell Lago €–€€ *Corso Mazzini 65, Belgirate.* Lake fish is nicely grilled and pasta is served in inventive dishes.

Taverna del Pittore €€€ *Pza del Popolo 39; tel: 0322 243 366. Closed mid-Dec–mid-Jan and Mon.* Elaborate fish dishes and lake views make reservations absolutely necessary.

Ristoro Antico €€ *V. Bottelli; tel: 0322 246 482. Closed mid-July–mid-Aug and every Mon.* Good-value *trattoria*.

BAVENO*

Between busy Verbania and tiny Stresa, the lakeside road circles nearly all the way round to take in the little spur known as Golfo Borromeo.

ℹ Pza Dante Alighieri
14 Palazzo
Comunale; tel: 0323 924
632; fax: 0323 924 632.

🛒 Market day: Mon.

This flat portion of Maggiore is protected as a staging area for songbirds and waterfowl, and is only lightly developed. Round the bend, one emerges at the foot of pinkish Monte Crocino to find Baveno; once rather famous but now a slightly faded resort. It's quite a bit smaller than nearby Stresa, if fairly similar in character. The best church here in the village is **Santi Gervasio**✦✦; its **baptistery**✦✦ is wonderfully eight-sided and frescoed.

BORROMEAN ISLES✦✦✦

⊘ **Ferry information**
tel: 0322 233 200 or
0800 551 801. Or use one
of the many – and more
convenient – water taxis to
visit all three on a day ticket.

🏛 **Isola Madre** € Tel:
032 331 261. Open
Apr–Oct 0900–1730.

Palazzo Borromeo €€
Tel: 032 330 556. Open
Apr–Oct 0900–1730.

☾ **Hotel Verbano** €€
V. Ugo Ara 12, Isola
dei Pescatori; tel: 032 330
408; fax: 032 333 129; e-
mail: hotelverbano@tin.it.
Small and serene hotel on
the 'fisherman's isle'.
Breakfast is included and
half-pension is available,
though the restaurant is
only average.

Few sights on Lake Maggiore are as enjoyable as the Borromean Isles, a smattering of villa-covered rocks just off Stresa. Best of all, the three islands are connected to one another – and the lake shore – by frequent ferry runs. Each island's personality is distinct. **Isola Bella**, the most heavily visited of the islands, consists mostly of a palace and its gardens, plus some restaurants and just one simple hotel. The **Palazzo Borromeo**✦✦✦ and its associated **gardens**✦✦✦ are impressive enough – blooming fruit trees and colourful tropical flowers – but the constructions here pile architectural dazzle upon dazzle, all crests and Murano glass and intricate grottoes; Count Carlo III Borromeo began building the gardens in the 17th century. One ticket admits the traveller into both the palace and its gardens. Smaller **Isola dei Pescatori**, known for its associations with the American novelist Ernest Hemingway, remains a fairly quiet and pleasant place for a stroll – there are alleys, a tiny church and splendid views. The island's fishing industry isn't what it once was, but is still active. **Isola Madre**, the largest is halfway across the water to Verbania. This island is covered by a **palace**✦✦, especially interesting for its marionette theatres, and landscaped **gardens**✦✦ with terraces, lake views and peacocks.

Right
Boats at Isola dei Pescatori

CANNOBIO✦✦✦

ℹ️ *Vle Vittorio Veneto 4; tel: 032 371 212; fax: 032 371 212.*

🎪 Market day: Sun.

Very near the Swiss border, Cannobio is a genuine Italian treat, a little lakeside village that has taken full advantage of its position between lake and mountain without having sold its soul to the sprawl of inappropriate development that is encroaching on so many of northern Italy's lakes. There are good walks in town and the environs: walk, drive or cable car into one of the surrounding valleys. Those interested in historical churches should pop into the Renaissance-era **Santuario della Pieta✦**, an intriguing little structure with a typically Italian history of alleged miracles. Just outside the nearby village of **Cannero Riviera** – itself a fine place to bed down for the night – several ruined castles stand scenicly out of the lake water, though closed to the public.

Accommodation and food in Cannobio and Cannero Riviera

Hotel Cannero €€ *Pza Umberto 12; Cannero Riviera; tel: 0323 788 046; fax: 0323 788 048; e-mail: info@hotelcannero.com.* Serene property with wonderful views of lake and mountains; heated outdoor pool, tennis courts, parking and fine I Castelli restaurant **€€–€€€**.

Park Hotel Italia €€–€€€ *Vle delle Magnolie, Cannero Riviera; tel: 0323 788 488; fax: 0323 788 498; e-mail: parkhot-cannero@iol.it.* Lovely hotel with splendid views of Maggiore from garden terrace and pool. Covered car park and on-site restaurant **€€**.

Below
Isola Bella, palace gardens

Hotel Pironi €€ *V. Marconi 35, Cannobio; tel: 032 370 624; fax: 032 370 624; e-mail: hotel.pironi@cannobio.net.* Former 15th-century palace in medieval quarter, now comfortably housing guests and serving inclusive breakfasts.

Villa Belvedere €€ *V. Casali Cuserina 2, Cannobio; tel: 032 370 159; fax: 032 371 991; e-mail: hotel.villabelvedere@cannobio.net.* Eighteen rooms in a beautiful setting, plus a beautiful heated outdoor pool. Breakfast is included.

Scalo €€€ *Pza Vittorio Emanuele 32, Cannobio; tel: 032 371 480. Closed Jan, Feb and Aug.* The outdoor patio heightens the dining experience.

LAVENO✢

🛈 *Palazzo Municipale, Pza Italia 2; tel: 0332 666 666.*

⇄ **Ferry information** *tel: 0800 551 801.*

Laveno sits at the lake's narrowest point. An hourly auto ferry service shortens the driving distance round the lake considerably. Fine ceramics shops sprinkle throughout town and a little cable lift rises to Sasso del Ferro for a good overlook of the lake. Most impressive is the nearby 13th-century hermitage **L'Eremo di Santa Caterina del Sasso**✢✢ (*open daily 0830–1200, 1430–1800*), reached by car or small ferry, built into cliffs just outside the town between the villages of Cerro and Reno.

Accommodation and food in Laveno

Il Porticciolo €€ *V. Fortino 40; tel: 0332 667 257; fax: 0332 666 753; e-mail: ilportic@tin.it.* Exquisite views of the lake from a classy, ten-room hotel featuring in-room TVs and ample parking. The restaurant on the premises serves regional dishes such as *risotto* or scampi.

LUINO✢✢

🛈 *V. Piero Chiara 1; tel: 0332 530 019.*

◖ Market day: Wed.

Luino, snuggled on the cosy eastern shore of Lake Maggiore, makes a good stopping point while slowly exploring that shore on the way to the Swiss border. Both the **Madonna del Carmine**✢ church (15th-century) and the older **San Pietro**✢ (11th-century) are each worth a look; and, Wednesday, this is the site of the biggest market on the entire lake, at Piazza Garibaldi. Be aware that on Wednesday the market slows traffic to a snail's pace.

Accommodation and food in Luino

Camin Hotel Luino €€ *Vle Dante 35; tel: 0332 530 118; fax: 0332 530 118; e-mail: caminlui@tin.it.* Former villa featuring some rooms with whirlpool baths, a reasonably priced restaurant, a garden and parking.

Hotel Internazionale € *Vle Amendola; tel: 0332 530 193; fax: 0332 537 882. Closed Jan and Feb.* Good-value hotel with spacious rooms and amenities such as an elevator, in-room TVs and a car park.

STRESA✢

🛈 *V. Canonica 8; tel: 032 331 308. Open Mar–Nov 0900–1800.*

⇄ **Monte Mottarone cable car service** €€ *Tel: 0323 303 99.*

◖ Market day: Fri.

Make no make mistake about it: the resort town of Stresa exists by and for the moneyed tourist, and it always has. If you come expecting pretty squares, tour-buses from Switzerland and Germany, expensive shops and a row of luxury hotels elbowing for attention (one even found its way into Hemingway's *A Farewell to Arms*) you certainly won't be disappointed. Come in late summer and you'll even be treated to one of those classical music festivals that make European summers so glorious. The lone historical sight of note is actually a kilometre south of town. **Villa Pallavicino's**✧✧ various gardens and its expansive parkland populated with exotic animals from Africa and beyond, make it a good stopover for those travelling with children. The villa itself, however, cannot be toured.

A fascinating side-trip from Stresa involves taking a cable car from Lido Station (right on the waterfront) up to either **Alpino**, with its wonderful Giardini Alpina (Alpine Gardens), or the last station at **Monte Mottarone** – one of the best places to get a view of the lake before you, the Alps behind it and Milan lying amongst the flat plain to the south.

Accommodation and food in Stresa

Grand Hotel des Iles Borromees €€€ *Lungolago Umberto; tel: 0323 938 938; fax: 032 332 405; e-mail: borromees@stresa.net.* Ultra-luxury hotel, one of northern Italy's most renowned. Situated in a lush park, with a stunning view of the lake islands and fine gardens too.

Il Piemontese €€–€€€ *V. Mazzini 25; tel: 032 330 235. Closed Dec–Jan and every Mon.* Serving up great regional dishes such as *bollito misto*, a boiled meat plate. You can eat outside in the summer.

Triangolo €€ *V. Roma 61; tel: 032 332 736. Closed Nov–Dec and every Tue.* Tasty pizza served inside or on an outdoor terrace.

VERBANIA✧✧

ⓘ *Corso Zanitello 6/8, Pallanza; tel: 0323 503 249; fax: 0323 556 669.*

🏨 **Villa Táranto** € *Tel: 033 404 555. Open daily Apr–Oct 0830–1830.*

Linchpin for the lake because of the Verbania-Laveno Ferry, 'Verbania' is really an agglomeration of three towns (Intra, Pallanza and the true, tiny Verbania). The gardens at **Villa Táranto**, have thousands of exotic trees, flowers and shrubs in patterned beds. Some come from as far away as the Amazonian rainforest and thrive quite nicely here, in the shadow of the pre-Alps. Otherwise, the town is a typical lake resort, hopping with lots of tourists during summer – a summer which peaks with the big, well-attended Lake Maggiore Jazz Festival in July – but much slower out of season.

Accommodation and food in Verbania

Il Chiostro €€ *V. Fratelli Cervi 14; tel: 0323 404 077.* Former convent nicely transformed into large hotel on the lake.

Touring € *Corso Garibaldi 26, Intra; tel: 0323 404 040; e-mail: brusapignatt@mindless.com.* Five suites and nineteen rooms, many with air-conditioning. Hotel restaurant is only open to guests.

Ristorante del Sole €€€ *Pza Venezia 5, Ranco; tel: 0331 976 057; e-mail: soleranco@relaischateaux.fr.* Excellent regional restaurant just outside town, serving fish and seasonal dishes such as lasagne, scampi and lamb cutlets. Also offers five high-quality suites with all mod cons.

Suggested tour

Total distance: 220km; 305km with detours.

Time: 6–7 hours' driving. Allow 2 days without detours, 2–3 days with detours. Those with limited time should choose one shore of the lake on which to concentrate: the eastern shore is generally quieter, the western shore more scenic, historical – and developed.

Links: Milan (Milano) (*see page 76*), the starting point for this route, connects with Lake Como (*see page 64*) via the A2/E35 *autostrada*. Arona, near the end of this route, can be reached from the Valle d'Aosta and Turin (Torino) route (*see page 50*) via the A5, A4 and A26 *autostrade*.

Route: From Milan (Milano) **1**, drive the A8 toll road for approximately 55km, exiting for the S33 and Sesto Calende, then continuing west to the lake shore. The road soon turns north along the lake, running for some 50km and becoming progressively more scenic as it passes the magnificent fortress at **ANGERA 2**, the beaches of **Lido di Montvalle** and **Arolo**, the ferry connection at **LAVENO 3** and then lakeside towns such as **LUINO 4**. After passing a number of attractive side valleys, many worth a short detour, the road eventually reaches the Swiss border. To keep this a purely Italian journey, backtrack 30km to Laveno and catch the auto-bearing ferry to **VERBANIA 5**, then continue north through pretty **Cannero Riveria** and **CANNOBIO 6** to the Swiss border once again along the S33, a drive of perhaps 25km to the border post. Backtracking once more, return the 25km to Verbania and then drive an additional 35km south along the S33 through winding shore-side scenery and the resort towns of **BAVENO, STRESA 7** (jumping-off point for ferries to the BORROMEAN ISLES) and finally **ARONA 8**.

Detour 1: About 50km northwest of Milan (Milano) on the S233 lies **Varese 9**, the quiet lake of the same name and **Santa Maria del Monte** – one of the region's so-called *sacro monte* (sacred mountains). The walkway climbs past 14 chapels, most dating from the 17th century and each with terracotta statues symbolising the rosary. At the top, the original sanctuary looks out over a park and the lake. Small *auberges* in Santa Maria include the **Albergo la Samaritana** (*tel: 0332 225 035*) and the **Colonne** (*tel: 0332 244 633; fax: 0332 821 593*).

Detour 2: At Verbania, turn west from the lake shore to find pretty **Lake Orta****, which can be circled via a series of lake-shore roads. (To save time, simply head south on the S229.) The lake's highlight is the well-preserved town of **Orta San Giulio**** **10** and the island of **San**

Locanda dei Mai Intees €€–€€€ V. *Nobile Claudio Riva 2, Azzate (Varese); tel: 0332 457 223; fax: 0332 459 339.* Medieval frescoes decorate walls of this 1400s manor house above Varese, where guest rooms are filled with antiques. Hospitable owner Carla Promati advises guests on the day's choices from the outstanding kitchen – another reason to stay here.

Giardinetto €€
*V. Provinciale 1,
Pettensasco; tel: 032 389
118; fax: 032 389 219.*
A small hotel overlooking
the island.

Villa Crespi *V. General
Fava 8–10; tel: 0322 911
902; fax: 0322 911 919.*
A Moorish-style bonbon
with easy car access, but
somewhat outside of
Orta San Giulio.

Giulio** just across the water, with few tourists, a convent and a surprisingly fine **Basilica**** (*tel: 032 290 358. Open daily in summer and shorter hours Tue–Sun in winter*).

Also worth exploring

To make a complete circuit of the lake, you'll need to bring your passport and continue onward into Swiss territory for about 20km before re-emerging in Italy; the border post on Maggiore's eastern shore occurs just past little **Pino Lago Maggiore**. Halfway round the Swiss portion is the largest town on the entire lake, **Locarno ⓫**, a combination of tourist services, villas tacked to hillsides and attractions beneath often-sunny skies. You'll almost forget you've crossed a border, what with all the Italian being spoken in the compact streets, *piazze* and alleyways; summer brings a well-attended, important film festival, further heightening the relaxed sense of Italian cool that prevails here. It's also possible to day-trip to Locarno – though you'll have to leave your car behind – via hydrofoil from Arona, Baveno, Cannobio, Luino and Stresa, and other Lake Maggiore towns.

Below
Lakeside café, Stresa

To see some mountains a short distance from the lake, take the E62 *autostrada* or the slower S33 from Stresa or Verbania to reach **Domodossola ⓬** and its sacred mountain chapel **Sacro Monte di Domodossola** (*tel: 0324 241 976*), built in 1656. You can continue into Switzerland over the scenic **Simplon Pass ⓭**, over which Napoleon marched his army. Better yet, leave your car in Locarno to board the vintage cars of the Centovalli rail line to Domodossola and back. Among Europe's most scenic train rides, it passes high above the Centovalli (100 valleys) carved by the Melezza River and its tributaries, crossing 83 bridges in 52km. The route is included on a Eurail Pass.

Lake Como

Ratings

Boat trips	●●●●●
Mountains	●●●●●
Scenery	●●●●●
Gardens	●●●●○
Nature	●●●●○
Outdoor activities	●●●●○
Villages	●●●●○
Walking	●●●●○

Como's praises have been sung by centuries of admirers, from the time the Romans built the first villas on its shore. And no wonder. At nearly every point, the narrow lake is enclosed by steep mountainsides, rising to peaks often covered in snow. Pastel villages climb them in picturesque progression, lush foliage painting green all around them. It would be hard to find a prettier place to put a lake, or a more perfect mirror for such mountains. An astonishing array of villas catch these views and although few are open, you can often stroll in their gardens, designed to frame these vistas perfectly. Flowers bloom everywhere, especially in the Tremezzina Riviera, favoured with a mild year-round climate. Explore lakeside villages on foot to find narrow passages hung with flowering vines. Many buildings rise right from the water, often with arcaded watergates and tiny marinas of their own.

BELLAGIO◆◆◆

ⓘ IAT *Lungolago Mazzin; tel: 031 950 204; www.bellagiolakecomo.com. Open Apr–Oct daily 0900–1200, 1500–1800. Nov–Mar closed Tue and Sun.*

Ⓟ *Parking, though scarce, may sometimes be found along the shore near the boat landing.*

ⓜ Villa Melzi d'Eril € *South on S583; gardens open daily Apr–Oct 0900–1800.*

In an almost perfect lakeside setting, Bellagio stands at the tip of the peninsula that bisects the lake into a wide inverted Y. The land rises so steeply that the town is built in terraces. Narrow streets climb, lined by balconied yellow buildings with little shops and pleasant cafés at landings between flights of stone stairs. More cafés stretch languidly along an ample waterfront – the lake surrounds Bellagio on all but one side. The historic town centre sits high, around the 12th-century **Basilica di San Giacamo**◆, which has carved capitals and more fine stonework in the apse. Behind the church a long lane leads up to **Villa Serbelloni**◆◆, whose outstanding gardens are of 19th-century Italian design, with grottoes and fountains. The villa's interior frescoes are not on view. The surrounding park extends to the very top of the promontory and is landscaped to make the most of the views across the northern arm of the lake to the Alps. Neo-classical **Villa Melzi d'Eril**◆, with frescoes and stucco work from the early 19th century, sits

Villa Serbelloni €
*Tel: 031 950 204.
Open mid-Apr–mid-Oct
Tue–Sun 1100–1600.*

Boutiques, handicraft
and antique shops line
the streets, but don't
expect bargains in this
swish little holiday haven.

in splendid isolation on the shore south of town, surrounded by its own English-style gardens of exotic plants, azaleas and cypresses.

Walks from Bellagio include down the shore to **Pescallo** (20 mins), a fishing village with waterside cafés, and climbs to the Belvedere at **Mulini del Perlo** (1 hr) or **Makalle** (90 mins) for fine panoramas. Narrow mountain roads climb to the high town of San Primo and to the base of the cable car-ride up **Monte San Primo**, a ski area. At the centre of the lake, Bellagio is a good base for exploring, with boat connections to all three arms and car ferries crossing to either shore.

Accommodation and food in Bellagio

Be sure to sample the local cake, *mataloc*, made with nuts and dried fruits.

Camping Clarke € *Localita Visgnola; tel: 031 951 325.* Tent pitches on a small farm with horses, goats and small animals, directly south of Bellagio. You can buy farm-fresh eggs for your breakfast.

Nuovo Hotel Metropole €€ *Pza Pazzini 1; tel: 031 950 409; fax: 031 951 534.* With the best location in town, right on the water, the

Metropole's vine-shaded café is the place to be. Kids are welcome and there's parking for your car.

**Osteria Gaetan € ** *V. Prafilippo 28, Localita Prafilippo; tel: 031 964 762. Open mid-Jun–mid-Sept.* On a 500-year-old farm high above the lake, you can dine on *polenta* with cheese, farm sausages and other local specialities.

COMO❖❖

❶ APT *Pza Cavour 17; tel: 031 274 064. Open Mon–Sat 0900–1300, 1430–1800.*

❷ Brunate Funicular *€ Pza de Gasperi, on the lakefront; tel: 031 303 608; open daily 0600–1030.*

Navigazione Lago di Como *€–€€€ Pza Cavour; tel: 031 579 211.* Ferries and hydrofoils run all year. Day ticket €€€.

**❸ ** *€ Off Via Mazoni, in Piazza Volta, and at the western end of the lake front.*

❹ Museo Civico (Archeologico) *€ V. Vittorio Emanuele. Open Tue–Sat 0930–1230, 1400–1700; Sun 1000–1300.*

Sant'Abbondio *V. Regina,* which leads from the train station into a somewhat grubby neighbourhood. *Open daily 0800–1400.*

**❺ ** Como's main product is silk. Last Sat of each month, Como becomes a giant outdoor antiques market – and jammed with people. The market is on Via Mentana 15, Mon–Sat morning.

The provincial capital sits at the southern tip, where hills spill into the lake. The palm-lined shore **promenade**❖ past Piazza Cavour is its activity centre, where excursion boats and a regular passenger service leave several times daily. For good views, ride the funicular to **Brunate**❖, a hilltop resort and good place to begin hikes. Allow about 90 minutes to walk back to Como. The exuberant **duomo**❖❖❖, 14th-century, with a Gothic rose window and fine carvings, is considered the best transition in Italy from Gothic to Renaissance. Gothic pinnacles soar and the doorway in the highly decorated marble façade is flanked, not by the usual saints, but the Plinys, both native sons. An odd choice, in the light of Pliny the Younger's correspondence with Emperor Trajan about the reasons for executing Christians. The **Museo Archeologico**❖❖, part of the Museo Civico, has neolithic and Roman artefacts discovered in the lake region. **Museo Alessandro Volta**❖, named after another local boy, whose name we remember in the electric volt, has equipment used in his research. The white 'temple' by the lakefront was built to commemorate the centennial of Volta's death. The Romanesque church of **Sant'Abbondio**❖❖, created in the 11th century by the *maestri comacini*, Como's own and highly regarded school of architects, has cycles of bright Gothic frescoes in the apse. Its high naves are reminiscent of paleo-Christian churches. Other sights of architectural interest are **Casa del Fascio**❖, built 1932–6, behind the *duomo*, **Porta Vittoria**❖, the 12th-century gate to the city, and the neo-classical villas, **Villa Geno**❖ and **Villa Olmo**❖, each surrounded by a public park.

Accommodation and food in Como

Firenze €€ *Pza Volte; tel: 031 300 333; fax: 031 300 101.* Excellent location close to the shore and Piazza Cavour, with indoor parking.

Al Giardino €€–€€€ *V. Monte Grappa 52; tel: 031 265 016.* An *osteria* with good dining as well, on a garden terrace.

Terminus €€€ *Lungo Lario Trieste; tel: 031 329 111; fax: 031 302 550.* The stylish choice in Como is this *belle époque* grand hotel, recently refurbished to its old polish and right at the centre of the lakefront.

Ristorante Hosterietta €€ *Pza Volta 57; tel: 031 241 516.* Risotto is the speciality, especially with seafood or truffles.

ISOLA COMACINA AND SALA COMACINA✦✦✦

Villa Balbianello **€€** Lenno; tel: 034 456 110; fax: 034 455 575. Gardens open Apr–Oct Tue, Thur–Sun 1000–1230, 1530–1830. Guided tours of villa by appointment. Access by boat from Sala Comacina every 30 minutes during open hours.

A festival is held at the Oratorio di San Giovanni on Isola Comacina the Sun following St John's Day in late June.

Parking for boats to Isola Comacina is uphill, north of the dock above S340.

Reach the lake's only island, **Isola Comacina**✦✦✦, from Sala Comacina by boat €. Fortified and used by both the Romans and Byzantines, the island where the Lombard king Berengar II took refuge in 962 was razed by the citizens of Como in 1169. Only the Baroque **Oratorio di San Giovanni**✦ is intact, the rest are remains of medieval buildings. There are ruins of the pre-1169 **Basilica di San Eufemia**✦✦, a paleo-Christian **baptistery**✦✦ and eight ruined churches (they prayed a lot then), but the island is short on restaurants. Great for an atmospheric picnic. Between Sala Comacina and Lenno, to the north, is a peninsula ending in the stunningly located Baroque **Villa Balbianello**✦✦, reached by boat from Sala. Created by Cardinal Durini in the 1700s, the villa is set in grand gardens at the tip of a wooded point. Statuary and urns filled with bright flowers frame incomparable views. The best view of the villa and its setting is from the water, from a passing lake steamer. **Ospedaletto**, which seems to blend right into Sala, is easy to spot by the unusual late-Gothic *campanile* that sits below the road. At **Ossuccio**, just off the main road, is the **Santuario della Madonna del Soccorso**✦ and good views of the lake. A processional route leads up to it, past 14 chapels built in the 17th and 18th centuries, each with painted terracotta statues.

Accommodation and food in Isola Comacina and Sala Comacina

Lavedo € *V. Lavedo 9; Lenno; tel: 034 455 172, fax: 034 456 115.* Small hotel just south of the Tremezzina.

Crotto dei Platani €€–€€€ *V. Regina 73, Brienno; tel/fax: 031 814 038.* Dine on creative dishes in a medieval fort, in the winter in its vaulted cellar and in summer on a garden terrace overlooking Como's waters, 8km south of Sala Comacina.

Above
Waiting for the steamer at
Isola Comacina

LAKE LUGANO AND PORLEZZA✧✧

ℹ️ *V. Volta 16, Campione d'Italia; tel: 004 191 685 051. Open daily.*

🍴 **Carlo Gilardoni Farm** *V. Roccolo 1, Velzo, Grandola ed Uniti; tel: 034 432 671. Open daily year-round.*

Menaggio, a smart resort town with an attractive historic centre, is more lively than Tremezzo and the beginning of the road to **Lake Lugano**. Just north, in the shore village of Nobiallo, is the **Santuario della Madonna della Pace**✧, its setting idyllic in olives and cypresses. After a steep climb from **Menaggio** to a viewpoint high above Lake Como, the S340 makes its relatively level way west to Porlezza, via **Piano Porlezza**, at the shore of a small lake. **Porlezza** overlooks **Lake Lugano** and although there is a road along part of its shore, the best way to explore the lake towns of **Osteno** and **Valsolda** is by the lake steamer. These boats continue into the Swiss portion of the lake and are the only way from this side to reach the small Italian compound of **Campione d'Italia**, completely surrounded by Switzerland, on the eastern shore of Lugano. It is a lively place, filled with cafés and restaurants. A meandering back road travels through the hill towns of

Grandola ed Uniti, roughly paralleling S340 to Porlezza. The **Carlo Gilardoni Farm** in the little settlement of **Velzo** is a good source of picnic provisions, including farm sausages, ham and cheeses.

Accommodation and food in Lake Lugano and Porlezza

Royal €–€€ *Largo V. Veneto 1; tel: 034 431 444; fax: 034 430 161.* Views, parking and a restaurant, plus a prime location.

La Vecchia Chioderia €–€€ *V. ai Mulini 3, Grandola; tel: 034 430 152; fax: 034 432 937.* The rustic dining room specialises in trout, smoked, fresh, sun-dried and in delectable pâtés. Guest rooms, cottages and tent pitches encourage travellers to stay and enjoy riding, walking, cycling and fishing in the Sanagra River.

Below
Nesso lake front

NESSO**

P Parking in Nesso is alongside S583 below the castle, high above the lake.

Wholly unlike the towns across the lake, Nesso is visited by only a few of the lake steamers and is well hidden from the road high above it. Steep cobbled streets and stone stairs lined with **medieval stone houses**** cluster along the sides of a **deep ravine**** that cuts the town in two. Through this rocky cleft, which is spanned by a **Roman bridge****, drops a long **waterfall***, as the Nose River reaches Lake Como. It's a steep climb back up to the **ruined castle*** and road level, but this is a rare spot on the lake shore where you are likely to be the only visitor in town. It is at its most atmospherically mossy in the morning, but it photographs better when the afternoon sun penetrates the west-facing stone crevices. Just to its south, **Careno*** is another tiny moss-covered stone town nearly hidden in the steep lake shore. Like Nesso, it is reached by a path from the road above. At the shore is the Romanesque church of **San Martino***.

Accommodation and food in Nesso

Buy local honey at Locanda Mose.

Locanda Mose € *Localita Pian di Nesso; tel: 031 917 909*. Open all year, closed Wed. Almost 1000m above Lake Como, this farm has guest rooms and tent pitches and is a good base for walking and hiking. The restaurant specialises in the produce of the farm itself, filling *ravioli* with fresh *ricotta* and baking tarts with fresh-picked berries.

THE NORTHEAST: COLICO, BELLANO AND VARENNA**

Abbazia di Piona
Open daily 0830–1230, 1330–1900.

Orrido di Bellano € *Tel: 3383 257 117. Open Apr–Sept daily 1000–1230, 1400–2300; Oct–Mar Sat–Sun 1000–1230, 1400–1900.*

Villa Monastero € *Open daily 0900–1200, 1400–1900, 1700 off season.*

Neither of the small industrial towns of Colico or Bellano have much charm. Between them, the restored 13th-century abbey, **Abbazia di Piona****, stands at the end of a peninsula that almost encloses the little bay called Laghetto di Pione. The abbey, built by Benedictines, has a very fine **Romanesque cloister**** that shows the early transitions into Gothic style. Notice the columns, with their wide variety of carved capitals. Also at the abbey is the 11th-century **San Nicola**** church. North of Colico are what Napoleon's army left of **Forte di Fuentes**, a Vauban-style fort. **Orrido di Bellano*** is a steep gorge in Bellano, through which cascades a river, seen from walkways above. The cathedral, built in 1348, has a good Gothic façade. A former fishing village, built on its original Roman layout and fortified in the Middle Ages, Varenna is connected to both the western and central lake shores by car ferries. **Villa Monastero****, a Cistercian convent abandoned in the 16th century, has excellent views from the terraces of its formal gardens, less lush than the west shore, but rich in Mediterranean and exotic plants. The ruins of **Castello di Vezio***, north of town, offer fine views.

Accommodation and food in the Northeast

Agriturismo Memeo €–€€ *Localita Posol, Vestreno; tel: 0341 850 784. Open all year, closed Mon.* With panoramic views of the lake and mountains from a 500m elevation, this farm offers comfortable rooms and a restaurant that serves regional specialities, including duck, rabbit and *casoncelli*, the distinctive *ravioli* of Bergamo.

La Perla Verde €–€€ *Frazione San Rocco, Colico; tel: 0336 826 795. Open mid-Apr–Sept and winter weekends.* This farmhouse restaurant serves Bergamo-style *polenta*, smoked and grilled meats and sells its own sausages and cheese. Tent pitches are available.

La Sorgente €–€€ *Localita Pra'la Madona, Dorio; tel: 0341 930 114. Open all year.* An old farm, known for its pure springwater, sits high in the hills above the lake, with tent pitches and a restaurant. Cheeses and sausages are cured in the caves.

Below
View from Tremezzo

THE TREMEZZINA RIVIERA***

V. Regina 3, Tremezzo;
tel: 034 440 493;
www.tremezzina.com. Open
May–Sept Mon–Wed,
Fri–Sat 0900–1200,
1530–1830.

Villa Carlotta €€
V. del Paradiso, north
of Tremezzo. Open daily
Apr–Sept 0900–1800, Mar
& Oct 0900–1100,
1400–1630.

If Lake Como is the garden spot of Italy, then the Tremezzina is the garden spot of Como. The mild climate produces the lushest greenery and flowers, with palms, camellias and blooming trees in the spring. The Tremezzina begins with Lenno, whose 11th-century **Santo Stefano*** has an ancient crypt and octagonal baptistery, also Romanesque. **Mezzegra**, a short distance inland, is where a partisan leader dispatched Mussolini and his mistress in 1945, after their capture at Dongo. Just north of Tremezzo, **Villa Carlotta****, 18th-century palace of Prussian Princess Carlotta, is a museum with sculpture and paintings by masters of the Lombard School. But Villa Carlotta is best known for its **terraced gardens***, 14 acres (5.67ha) built in the 1850s. Camellias, rhododendrons, azaleas and exotic trees frame a never-ending series of lake views. **Cadenabbia** is just past Tremezzo and an easy, pleasant walk along the shore promenade, an alley of plane trees known as Via del Paradiso. Drive up the hill to **Griante*** and the little cone-towered church of **San Martino** for a matchless view. This is a good area for those who plan to see the lake by boat, since steamers to all parts of the lake stop here and both car and passenger ferries connect to Bellagio and Varenna across the lake. Lodgings are good, restaurants numerous – if a bit dull – and the atmosphere relaxed and pleasant.

Accommodation and food in the Tremezzina Riviera

Grand Hotel Tremezzo Palace €€€ *V. Regina 8; tel: 034 442 491; fax: 034 440 201.* The name says it all; it's both grand and palatial and even more so after a recent makeover. One of the finest views on the lake and a swimming pool that floats above its waters.

La Fagurida € *Rogro Ovest; tel: 034 440 676.* Informal *trattoria* with a blend of locals and tourists.

Suggested tour

V. Regina 33,
Cernobbio; tel: 031 510
198. Open daily.

Total distance: 117km, with detours 160km.

Time: 4 hours' driving. Allow 2 days for the main route, 3 days with detours. Those with limited time should concentrate on the Tremezzina and Belaggio, circling the southwestern arm only.

Links: From Milan (Milano) (*see page 76*) Como is a short distance north via A9. Bergamo (*see page 86*) is east of Como via S342.

Leave **COMO ❶**, heading north on S340, following signs to **Cernobbio**. (*See* **Detour 1** *on page 74*.) This is perhaps the most elegant of all the lakeside resorts, much to the credit of **Villa d'Este**, a late

International approaches: from Colico, S36 heads north for the Swiss border and San Moritz, and S38 goes east to Tirano, where it connects with S38A, and to the Bernina Pass, also to St Moritz.

Museo della Barca Lariana € *Fraz Calozzo, Pianello di Lario; tel 034 487 294. Open irregular hours; may be closed for renovations.*

Tip: The road from Bellagio to Como, while scenic, is so narrow and precipitous that it is difficult to focus on the scenery. An option to this tortuous trip is to cross the lake on the car ferry at Bellagio and return to Como along the western shore. Or you can visit this shore from Como by taking the northbound boat.

16th-century villa designed by Pellegrino Tibaldi. Formerly home of English Queen Caroline, it is now a posh hotel and still hosts royalty, who stroll in its Italianate garden. Not far north of Cernobbio is garden-studded **Moltrasio**, with the 11th-century church dedicated to **St Agatha***. The road borders the lake closely, with excellent views through **Brienno** to **Argegno ❷** (21km). (*See* **Detour 2** *on page 75*.) At the elbow-bend of the lake's western arm are fine views north across the lake to mountains. Even more panoramic are those from the village of **Pigra**, reached by a tramway on the north side of town. Leave Argegno, continuing north on S340 to **SALA COMACINA ❸**, stopping to take the boats to **ISOLA COMACINA** and **Villa Balbianello**. Continue north along the spectacular coast through **Tremezzo ❹** and **Cadenabbia** to **Menaggio ❺** (14.5km). In Menaggio, follow S340 to the right, leaving the lake shore and climbing steeply to the viewpoint at **Croce**. A diversion shortly past this leads up the Sanagra Valley to the several small villages of **Grandola ed Uniti**. S340 continues on its fairly level route to PORLEZZA **❻**, passing Lago di Piano on its way.

From Porlezza, return to Menaggio via S340, this time turning right before Lake Piano, on a road signposted **Bene Lario**, travelling along the other side of Lake Piano. Rejoin S340 before the descent into Menaggio (25km). In Menaggio, turn north (left) onto S340d, following the lake shore through a series of small towns. At **Pianello di Lario**, the **Museo della Barca Lariana** has an interesting collection of 150 fishing boats, work boats, sailboats and a Como gondola. In **Gravedona ❼**, the 13th-century church of **Santa Maria del Tiglio**** is one of the major Romanesque sites in the region, with an octagonal bell tower and outstanding early frescoes of St John the Baptist. Above Rezzonico is 14th-century **Castello della Torre**, in ruin except for its crenellated tower. The northern end of the lake is flatter, especially in the delta of the Adda and Mera Rivers. A sharp right turn after Sorico takes you over these and to S36, where you turn right, passing **COLICO** and **BELLANO**, before reaching **VARENNA ❽** (54km). At Varenna, take the car ferry to **BELLAGIO ❾**. Follow S583 southwest along the western arm of the lake, following signs to **Lezzeno**. Stop in **San Giovanni** to see the old church, with statuary by Canova. Pass through a succession of towns before reaching **NESSO ❿** and **Careno**. **Torno** is a medieval village, known for **Villa Pliniana**, built in the 16th century at one of Pliny the Younger's villa sites. The cascade of water there still flows at regular six-hour intervals, just as Pliny described. A path leads 1.5km from the village to the villa's grounds. The road continues along the shore to Como (31km).

Detour 1: Leave **Cernobbio**, continuing north on S340, watching for signs to **Monta Bisbino***, a 1355m mountain whose summit road offers a spectacular panorama. The international boundary with

(map of Lake Como region)

Arbedo
Lago di Mezzola
Mezzola
Verceia
sio Gordola
Bellinzona
13   8
Giubiasco
carno
Dubino
26
Gravedona   340
Dongo ❼
Colico
Talamona
38   13
Morbegno
Cadenazzo
Cavargna
28
Monte Legnone
Sta Maria   15
Rezzonico   Dervio   2609
Albaredo per San Marco
1962   2
17
Torricella
Taverne
Gerola Alta
Porlezza ❻   Menaggio
agno
Croce
Claino ❺
Agno   Lugano   340   Osteno Tremezzo ⓫
Mezzoldo   Bra
Bellano
8
Varenna
16   Cadenábbia ❹
Lago di Lugano   Lenno
Sala Comacina   Bellagio ❾
vena
Isola ❸   Introbio   Piazzatorre
resa   Argegno ❷   Comacina   Grigna
32   583   36   2409   Piazza Brembana
2   Nesso ❿   Barzio   Lenna
233   E35   340   Mandello del Lario
14   20   Careno   470
6   Ballabio
e   Mendrisio Torno   Asso   21
Cernobbio   San Giovanni
Varese   Valmadrera   Bianco   San Pe
Chiasso   Brunate   Lecco   Zogno
Malnate   Como ❶   32   Olginate   Calolziocorte
342   Erba   0   10   20km
10   Lago di Alserio   Lago di Pusiano
Castagliona   A9   342   Caprino   10 miles
Olona   41   Bergamasco   d'Almè
17   Cantù

If you choose this inland route over the next lakeside attractions, you can either make a short detour south from Menaggio to see the shore highlights, or can cross by passenger boat from Bellagio and Lezzeno, later in the itinerary.

Switzerland runs close to the mountain top. Return to S340 by the same road (34km).

Detour 2: For a slower, mountainous ride that leaves the lake's most crowded section, the **TREMEZZINA RIVIERA**, take the unnumbered road from **Argegno** up the valley of the Telo River. Follow signs to **Cerano d'Intelvi, Castiglione d'Intelvi** and **San Fedele d'Intelvi**. In Pellio d'Intelvi (10km), turn right to **Laino**. In Laino, bear left to **Claino-Osteno ⓫**, on the shore of **LAKE LUGANO**. Follow the lake shore to the right, to **Porlezza**, where you rejoin the main route, S340 (12km).

Also worth exploring

The other arm of the lake, known as Lake Lecco, is wilder, with fewer holiday resort towns. S583 hugs the narrow corniche between the steep mountains and the water. Several roads over the mountainous interior of the triangle connect the lake's two branches.

Milan

Ratings

Shopping	●●●●●
Food and drink	●●●●○
Art	●●●○○
Historical sights	●●●○○
Museums	●●●○○
Architecture	●●○○○
Children	●●○○○
Scenery	●○○○○

Milan is, quite simply, the centre of the New Italia. The nation's most prosperous, important – and self-important – city, Milan remains the home of the catwalk, where the world's fickle fashion decisions are first made. But it is so much more: a teeming manufacturing centre, an arts dynamo and the hub of the Italian sport and publishing industries. It is also an increasingly diverse place, as immigrants rush north to participate in this wealth. Yet visitors will probably do best to avoid the commercial glitter and endless suburbs, focusing rather on historical sights – most of them within a kilometre of the *duomo*, an over-the-top confection that must be Italy's splashiest cathedral. One can windowshop, sip coffee, view impressive art collections and tour a castle without ever straying terribly far from this unique church.

Arriving and departing

ⓘ *V. Marconi 1; tel: 0272 524 301, 0272 524 302 or 0272 524 303. Open Mon–Fri 0830–2000, Sat 0900–1900, Sun 0900–1700 summer, closes one hour earlier each day except Sun in winter.*

Stazione Milano Centrale; tel: 0272 524 360 or 0272 524 370. Open Mon–Sat 0900–1900, Sun 0900–1800.

Arriving in Milan is a snap. The city is served by two large airports, nearby Linate (*tel: 0274 852 200*) and more distant Malpensa (*tel: 0274 852 200*), which is often handier for beginning an excursion to the lakes and mountains. Both are connected to the city centre by regular transport connections: Linate by the No 73 bus to San Babila near the *duomo*, Malpensa by express trains and buses to Central Station. Once in the city, Milan's rail station is handy enough that one can reach the *duomo* and the other important sights with a short taxi trip or four-stop Metro ride on the M3 (yellow) line. The railway station neighbourhood and a few others, it should be added, are a bit rough around the edges; crime is on the increase and walking around the city isn't advisable at night except in heavily trafficked shopping or

Milan

Galleria d'Arte Moderna
Palazzo del Senato
Carlton Hotel Senato
Palazzo Serbelloni
Ufficio Postale SIT (P.O.)
Palazzo di Giustizia

Palazzo Centro Svizzero
Palazzo dei Giornali
Palazzo Bagatti Valsecchi
Ex Sem. Arcivescovile
Museo di Milano
Palazzo Melzi di Cusano
San Babila
Palazzo Bolagnos
Palazzo Durini
Jolly President Hotel
Palazzo Sormani

Archi di Porta Nuova
Palazzo Borromeo
Teatro Manzoni
M.te Napoleo
Museo Poldi-Pezzoli
Casa del Manzoni
Palazzo Belgioioso
Teatro Nuovo
Palazzo Spinola
Banca Popolare
Rosa Hotel

Palazzo del Risorgimento
Casa degli Omenoni
Palazzo Marino (municipio)
Museo d'Arte Contemporanea
Palazzo d. Capitano di Giustizia

Pinacoteca di Brera
Monte di Pietà
Casa Svizzera Hotel
Galleria Vittorio Emanuele
Duomo
Museo d'Arte Contemporanea
Palazzo Reale
Teatro Lirico
Palazzo Greppi
Università degli Studi di Milano

La Scala
Teatro d. Filodrammatici
Ufficio Postale (P.O.)
Ufficio Postale (P.O.)
Brunelleschi Hotel
Palazzo Acerbi
Palazzo Annoni
Torre Velasca
Palazzo Cusani
Centro Hotel
Palazzo Clerici
Palazzo Carmagnola

Bonaparte Hotel
London Hotel
Cairoli
Central Post Office
Palazzo della Borsa
Palazzo dei Giureconsulti
Spadari al Duomo Hotel
Gritti Hotel
Pinacoteca Ambrosiana
Dei Cavalieri Hotel
Miss
Zurigo Hotel
Palazzo Trivulzio

Palazzo dell'Arte
Castello Sforzesco
Pinacoteca
Rocchetta
Museo d'Arte Antica

Studio
Lan
Ufficio Postale (P.O.)
Ferrovie Nord Milano
Cadorna
Banco di Roma
Palazzo Borromeo
San Giorgio
Palazzo Stampa
Palazzo della Vetra
San Lorenzo Maggiore

Teatro Dal Verme
Palazzo Litta
Civico Museo Archeologico
Palazzo Stanga
Circo Romano
Colonne di San Lorenzo

Ufficio Postale (P.O.)
Tempio della Vittoria
Sant' Ambrogio
Università Cattolica
Pierre Milano Hotel

Santa Maria delle Grazie
Museo Nazionale della Scienza e della Tecnica Leonardo da Vinci

0   200m
0   200 yds

The M1 underground line does not run at night; at that time, it is replaced by buses.

tourist areas. The city's white taxis cruise the key areas day and night; there's a minimum charge of about €3 – more at nights and during holidays, and for luggage.

Getting around

Parking is very, very difficult in Milan's city centre and isn't recommended. If it must be done, however, there are car parks on Piazza Diaz (just south of Piazza del Duomo) and near Central Station (on Via Pirelli). Don't challenge the city's traffic patrols, either – you're likely to receive not just a ticket but a free tow to a distant lot as well.

Milan is board-flat, making transport easy; but, as Italy's largest commercial centre, there's a good deal of congestion in the central city. Thus, the Metropolitan underground system, which operates along two axes, is the swiftest form of public transport – reliable and inexpensive. Once here, travel to the Duomo Metro station from the central rail station, it's four stops in the direction of San Donato on the yellow M3 line; from San Babila, dropping-off point for the Linate airport bus, it's a one-stop ride on the M1 red line toward Bisceglie or a short walk – as this is where most of the major sights are concentrated.

Driving

Visitors claiming rental cars at the airport can drive into the city centre, but it's not advised – especially during morning and evening rush hours – as traffic is nearly always thick during these times and barely tolerable at others. For those who must, follow signs toward the Centro Historico. Note that Milan's city-centre street system is geared toward pedestrian traffic rather than auto traffic and funnels cars around a ring road and then into congested, narrow one-way streets; you must drive into one of six wedge-shaped sections, so choose carefully using a good map – if you've miscalculated, you'll need to double back out to the ring road to reach the adjacent wedge.

Milan's shopping is second to none in Italy. For high fashion, explore the Quadilatero district first – bounded by Via Monte Napoleone, Via Sant'Andrea, Via Borgospesso and Via della Spiga – but bring your wallet, things are pricey. For take-away snacks, produce and budget clothing, find the Sat morning market at Viale Papiniano, located south of the science museum and near the Porta Genova subway stop.

Trams and buses

Buses circulate slowly but regularly through the city; maps can be purchased for approximately €2 at stations and news stands. Ticket prices are the same for underground or overground transport; purchase them from tobacconists, news stands, or automatic ticket-vending machines on the street. Among the options are single-ride tickets valid for 75 minutes (costing approximately €1), 24-hour tickets (approximately €2.50) and 48-hour tickets (approximately €5).

Sights

Castello Sforzesco**
Once the exceptionally well-defended stronghold of the dukes of Milan, the city's blockish castle is today better known for the clutch of fine museums behind its walls. There are separate galleries here

Opposite
Duomo, Milan

Castello Sforzesco
Pza Castello; tel: 0280 463 054. Open daily 0930–1730.

Duomo € *Pza del Duomo; tel: 02 860 358. Open Mar–Oct 0900–1730; rest of the year 0900–1630.*

devoted to artwork, historical artefacts from all over the world, even ancient musical instruments. The sculpture area is probably the best of the lot, but the musical collection gives it a run for its money with an appropriately medieval collection of lute-like instruments.

Duomo***

The exterior of Milan's enormous cathedral is the gaudiest, most magnificent example of late-period Gothic architecture in Italy – it is also the nation's largest. Begun in the 14th century by the first duke of Milan, it took some five centuries to get just right. And no wonder! There were more than one hundred intricate (and quite tall) marble spires to contend with, thousands of statues sprinkled throughout its cruciform body, as well as carvings, stained-glass work and the 16th-century tomb of Gian Giacomo Medici. It's free to enter the massive church, though there's a charge to climb the stairs to the roof and gaze out over the *piazza* and city below. The in-house museum, which also charges a fee, describes the history and contains even more examples of religious artwork. Below is a paleochristian baptistery.

Galleria d'Arte Moderna**

Milan's modern art museum, housed inside an 18th-century palace, is well worth a detour if only for its holdings of paintings by the Impressionists and their kin. You'll find the work of Cézanne, Corot, Gauguin and Van Gogh – all the usual suspects and then some – in the Grassi collection. The PAC next door at No 14 displays revolving exhibits by contemporary artists.

Galleria d'Arte Moderna V. Palestro 16; tel: 0286 463 054. Open Tue–Sun 0930–1730; € for adjacent PAC complex at No 14.

Galleria Vittorio Emanuele**

There can't be any doubt what this cruciform, 19th-century complex is all about: it's the city's central mall, meeting place, eating place and *agora* all in one, domed in magnificent glass ceilings and touched up with mosaic work for good measure. Imagine a beautiful street preserved beneath glass and you've about got the idea. Rarely is a shopping centre such a major attraction. An *espresso* or *cappuccino* in one of the cafés can easily cost more than lunch.

Galleria Vittorio Emanuele Pza del Duomo. The Galleria's shops open daily, except Sun, from 0930–1300, 1530–1900.

La Scala**

The world's best-known opera house actually doesn't appear very impressive at first look. Its real treasures are within, reserved for those who have landed a precious (and pricey) ticket to an evening's performance. The interior of the opera house has just undergone a two-year restoration that reveals even more of its beauty, including long-hidden marble floors. Also returned to its original quarters to the side of the theatre, **Museo La Scala** contains stunning costumes worn by the great divas, models of stage sets and touching mementoes of Verdi and others, the museum is a must-see for any opera lover. An automated ticket sales point lets you choose seats and buy tickets by credit card.

Museo teatrale alla Scala € Corso Magenta; tel: 024 691 249; www.teatroallascala.it. Open daily 0900–1800.

Museo La Scala € Pzza della Scala; tel: 024 691 249; www.teatroallascala.it. Open daily 0900–1800.

Museo Nazionale Scienza e della Tecnica Leonardo da Vinci*

This sprawling museum just south of the historic centre focuses on Italy's considerable scientific and technical achievements, and while there is much to see here some of the exhibits might be lost on non-Italians. It's best to concentrate on the Leonardo da Vinci Gallery, with drawings, documents and exhibits which chronicle the great inventor's creativity.

Museo Nazionale Scienza e della Tecnica Leonardo da Vinci € V. San Vittore 21; tel: 02 485 551. Open Tue–Fri 0930–1630, to 1830 at weekends.

Pinacoteca Ambrosiana***

This art gallery – originally a palace built for the powerful Cardinal Borromeo – began as a home for his considerable collections, the works include those of Leonardo da Vinci and Caravaggio, as well as non-Italians such as Brueghel. The attached library contains more drawings by Leonardo.

Pinacoteca Ambrosiana € Pza Pio XI 2; tel: 02 806 91. Open Tue–Sat, 1000–1730.

Pinacoteca di Brera**

Milan's largest art museum is a sprawling complex on the northerly edge of the historic centre. Its art leans heavily toward Italian masters,

Pinacoteca di Brera € V. Brera 28; tel: 02 722 631. Open Tue–Sat 0830–1930, Sun 0900–1300.

Sant'Ambrogio *Pza Sant'Ambrogio 15; tel: 0286 450 895. Open Mon–Sat 0700–1200, 1400–1900; Sun 0700–1315, 1430–1945.*

Treasury € *Open daily 0930–1200, 1430–1800.*

Cenacolo, Santa Maria della Grazie €–€€ *Pza Santa Maria delle Grazie 2; tel: 0289 421 146 or 199 199 100 (within Italy only), 0289 421 146, from outside Italy +39 0289 421 146. Church open daily 0700–1200, 1500–1900.*

Cenacolo €€ *Open Tue–Sun 0815–1845. Timed Cenacolo tickets must be reserved in advance; operators speak English.*

both the well-known and the lesser-known; expect to find paintings by Caravaggio, Piero della Francesca, Raphael or Tintoretto alongside works of Veronese and the Bellinis. The modern rooms are good, though not quite up to the level of the Renaissance holdings. Equally interesting is the section of streets surrounding the Pinacoteca; they hold numerous smaller galleries, artists' studios and cafés, and convey the same exuberantly artistic feeling as, say, Paris' Left Bank – albeit in trim, elegant Italian clothing.

Sant'Ambrogio***

But for the amazing, wedding cake-like *duomo*, this oft-overlooked church would certainly be Milan's most fascinating. Its foundations were laid under the watch of none other than St Ambrose himself back in the 4th century AD and subsequent centuries of work have only rendered it more beautiful. Two bell towers frame the exterior. In its **treasury** (€) are some splendid bronze doors and a golden altar – both from the 9th century and well-preserved – as well as a chapel of exceptional mosaic work and the saint's remains.

Santa Maria della Grazie**

This small 15th-century Dominican friary would normally be drowned in a sea of better attractions, but it just happens to hold Leonardo da Vinci's singular painting *The Last Supper* and thus qualifies as an almost obligatory detour off the beaten Milanese track. The painting doesn't actually reside in the church itself, but rather in the attached refectory (*cenacolo*). Note that all tickets to the *cenacolo* must be reserved in advance by telephone; to compensate, however, its open hours are unusually long by Italian standards.

Accommodation and food

Be careful selecting a hotel in Milan; a one- or two-star hotel, normally a sure bet in Italy, is a risky gamble at best here. Pay more for a hotel with at least three stars, especially in neighbourhoods such as that surrounding the rail station. Remember that most of the city's restaurants close Sun and in August.

Hotel Ariston €€ *Largo Carrobbio 2; tel: 0272 000 556; fax: 0272 000 914.* An ecologically friendly place to lie down your head: all air is circulated and ionised, and building materials are recycled wherever possible. Bicycles are even available for touring the city once you've left your car in the car park.

Hotel Ascot €€–€€€ *V. Lentasio 3/5; tel: 0258 303 300; fax: 0258 303 203; e-mail: ascot.mi@bestwestern.it.* Part of the world-wide Best Western group, this is a pleasant hotel with covered parking and included breakfast.

Hotel Mediolanum €€€ *V. Mauro Macchi 1 (at Via Napo Torriani); tel: 026 705 312; fax: 0266 981 921; www.mediolanumhotel.com.* Contemporary hotel, well-decorated and with a hospitable staff; convenient to the Stazione Centrale.

Hotel Sanpi Milano €€ *V Lazzaro Palazzi 18, Milano 20124; tel: 0229 513 341; fax: 0229 402 451; www.hotelsanpimilano.it.* Stylish and spacious rooms, individually decorated. Quiet courtyard, close to Stazione Centrale.

Hotel Spadari al Duomo €€€ *V. Spadari 11; tel: 0272 002 371; fax: 02 861 184; www.spadarihotel.com.* Just off Piazza Duomo, with sleek modern rooms and original contemporary art.

Joia €€–€€€ *V. Panfilo Castaldi 18; tel: 0229 522 124. Closed weekends; also closed all of Aug, Dec and Jan.* Classy, top-quality vegetarian place whose Swiss chef dabbles inventively with aubergine, *zucchini* and *ravioli* – and also cooks some good fish dishes.

Savini €€€ *Galleria Vittorio Emanuele II; tel: 0272 003 433.* Well-loved city restaurant serving northern Italian specialities such as *risotto, osso buco* and all the rest. Expect to pay handsomely for the privilege.

Trattoria Il Carpaccio €–€€ *V. Palazzi 9 (opposite Hotel Sanpi); tel: 0229 405 982.* Warm, village-style trattoria right in the city, with outstanding *carpaccio* and *tortelloni*.

Trattoria Milanese €€ *V. Santa Marta 11; tel: 0286 451 991. Closed Tues and during Aug.* Typical Milanese favourites such as *osso buco* and veal cutlets.

Below
Pastry shop, Milan

Shopping

Italy's finest, most expensive shops are located in Milan; besides the **Galleria Vittorio Emanuele** (*see page 80*), the key district is the **Quadilatero**, a region bounded by four streets that contain most of the high fashion houses; of them, Via Sant'Andrea is perhaps most elegant of the four. Among the local stars – and there are so very many – **Giorgio Armani** (*V. Sant'Andrea 9*); **Trussardi** (*V. Sant'Andrea 5*); and **Prada** (*in the Galleria Vittorio Emanuele and also on V. Sant'Andrea*) are certainly worth visits. The most audacious recent addition to the picture must be the **Armani Megastore** (*V. Manzoni 31; tel: 0272 318 630*). This cavernous three-storey shop is a world unto itself, proffering books, clothing and household goods all bearing the well-known Armani label. For more modest prices, **La Rinascente** (*Pza del Duomo; tel: 02 88521*) is Milan's most famous department store, featuring well-made yet moderately priced goods; its chief competition is **Coin** (*Pza Cinque Giornate; tel: 0255 192 083*).

Entertainment

Milan's nightlife can be a pleasantly low-key or a high-energy experience depending on what you're after. For an interesting neighbourhood with lots of choice, head for the Navigli south of the city centre. **Bar Magenta** (*V. Carducci 13; tel: 028 053 808*) in that district is good for a drink or light meal amongst the jet-set and nearby **Scimmie** (*V. Ascanio Svorza 49; tel: 0289 402 874*) offers eclectic and well-loved jazz. **Propaganda** (*V. Castelbarco 11; tel: 0258 310 682*) – also in Navigli – is one of the city's most popualar discos; sometimes there are live shows and salsa nights. **Hollywood** (*V. Como 15; tel: 026 598 996*) is the dance club in the equally chic La Brera neighbourhood.

Walking tour

Total distance: 2–3km, 4–5km with detours.

Time: Allow one full day with or without detours, perhaps an additional day to more fully explore the *duomo* and all the churches and museums on this itinerary. If you're pressed for time, you can skip Sant'Ambrogio, Santa Maria della Grazie and the Leonardo da Vinci museum; from the Castello, it's a short (though crowded) walk back down busy Via Dante to the *duomo*.

Links: Milan is located approximately 50km south of Como (*see page 76*) – the A9 *autostrada* connects the city to the Como region – and approximately 50km southwest of Bergamo (*see page 86*), reached via the A4 *autostrada*.

Route: Begin at the always lively Piazza del Duomo, with its tourist information kiosk and awe-inspiring cathedral. Jump right in by visiting the elegant, over-the-top **DUOMO ❶**, one of Italy's very finest, making time to take in both the marvellously intricate exterior and the somewhat subdued (but obviously enormous) interior. The *piazza's* northern side is taken up by the **GALLERIA VITTORIO EMANUELE ❷**, a gorgeous shopping complex that's the nexus point of Milanese society and the perfect place to down an espresso or browse through every manner of wares. Thus fortified, proceed a short distance north to **LA SCALA ❸**, Italy's – indeed, the world's – best-known opera performance house, under reconstruction.

From La Scala, the walking begins in earnest. Head two blocks north along Via Brera to the large **PINACOTECA DI BRERA** ❹, Milan's biggest and most significant museum complex. Also take time to explore the surrounding area, a kind of bohemian Milan. It's a few blocks west – along the direct, busy ring road, Via Pontaccio, or smaller alleys that locals can show you – to the **CASTELLO SFORZESCO** ❺. This imposing edifice once defended the city's dukes from invasion and now holds a good concentration of several galleries in one place, some of them quite intriguing. From the Castello, busy Via Dante brings you smartly back to the city centre and the *duomo* in a few minutes' time if you so choose. If you've still the energy, however, there are churches and museums in the southern quarter of the city centre remaining to be explored. (*See Detour 2 below.*)

Detour 1: From La Scala, walk northeast along crowded Via Manzoni away from the city centre. Shortly you come to the **Museo Poldi Pezzoli**✦✦ (*open daily 1000–1800, €*) on the right, an old home containing a good selection of paintings, timepieces and whatnot, and then – again right, down the cross street called Via Napoleone – the atmospheric **Palazzo Bagatti Valsecchi**✦✦ (*open Tue–Sun 1300–1700, closed Aug, €*) which is full of rooms interestingly furnished in various themes. Continuing out on Via Manzoni past the ring road, you will reach the city's zoological gardens and two museums. Milan's U-shaped **GALLERIA D'ARTE MODERNA** ❻ contains the city's primary collection of modern art; its holdings include work by Cézanne and Van Gogh. Just adjacent and across Via Palestro, the city's Natural History Museum is not exceptional, but makes a child-friendly detour – it's a good idea to send half the family here while others are contemplating the artwork.

Detour 2: A few blocks south along the ring road (named Via Carducci at this point), one soon reaches the Corso. Turn right and continue to **SANTA MARIA DELLA GRAZIE** ❼, a small monastery with Leonardo da Vinci's great *The Last Supper* concealed within the attached **refectory**✦✦✦. The La Scala Museum is housed across the street. A bit farther south along Via Carducci, is the cross street called Via San Vittore. A left turn brings you to the church of **SANT'AMBROGIO** ❽, a fairly simple yet remarkable Romanesque structure whose origins go all the way back to St Ambrose himself in the 4th century. A right turn and you're soon at the entrance to the cavernous (and hard-to-say) **MUSEO NAZIONALE SCIENZA E DELLA TECNICA LEONARDO DA VINCI** ❾. As you might expect, it is heavy with exhibits tracing the scientific contributions of Italians, most notably Mr da Vinci.

Milan

Galleria d'Arte Moderna

Palazzo Serbelloni

Via Francesco Daverio

Palazzo di Giustizia

Palazzo del Senato

Carlton Hotel Senato

Palazzo Bolagnos

Palazzo Centro Svizzero

Palazzo dei Giornali

Ex Sem. Arcivescovile

San Babila

Palazzo Dunini

Postale SITO (P.O.)

Maggiore di Milano Hospital

Archi di Porta Nuova

Teatro Manzoni

Palazzo Bagatti Valsecchi

Museo di Milano

Piazza San Carlo

Piazza Liberty

Rosa Hotel

Jolly President Hotel

Palazzo Sormani

Palazzo Borromeo

Palazzo Reale di Cusano

Casa degli Omenoni

Museo Poldi-Pezzoli

Casa del Manzoni

Banca Popolare

Palazzo Spinola

Palazzo d. Capitano di Giustizia

Università degli Studi di Milano

M.te Napoleo

Museo del Risorgimento

Monte di Pietà

Palazzo Marino (municipio)

Casa Svizzera Hotel

1 Duomo

Palazzo Reale

Museo d'Arte Contemporanea

Teatro Lirico

Palazzo Greppi

Pinacoteca di Brera

3 La Scala

Ufficio Postale (P.O.)

Galleria Vittorio Emanuele

2 PIAZZA DEL DUOMO

Brunelleschi Hotel

Torre Velasca

4 Pinacoteca di Brera

Teatro d. Filodrammatici

Palazzo Clerici

Duo

Ufficio Postale (P.O.)

Dei Cavalieri Hotel

Palazzo Cusani

Centro Hotel

Ufficio Postale (P.O.)

Palazzo Carmagnola

Palazzo dei Giureconsulti

Spadari al Duomo Hotel

Gritti Hotel

Palazzo Sant' Alessandro

Palazzo Trivulzio

Bonaparte Hotel

London Hotel

Palazzo della Borsa

Central Post Office

Banco di Roma

Pinacoteca Ambrosiana

S. Giorgio

Palazzo Stampa

5 Castello Sforzesco

Rocchetta

Cairoli

Teatro Dal Verme

Palazzo Borromeo

San Lorenzo Maggiore

Pinacoteca

Museo d'Arte Antica

Palazzo Litta

Civico Museo Archeologico

Palazzo Stanga

Circo Romano

Colonne di San Lorenzo

Ufficio Postale (P.O.)

Tempio della Vittoria

Università Cattolica

Pierrer Milano Hotel

Ferrovie Nord Milano

Cadorna

8 Sant'Ambrogio

Palazzo dell'Arte

7 Santa Maria delle Grazie

9 Museo Nazionale Scienza e Tecnica Leonardo da Vinci

200m
200 yds
0

Bergamo and Lake Iseo

Ratings

Architecture	●●●●
Art	●●●●
Scenery	●●●●
Boat trips	●●●
Food and drink	●●●
Historical sights	●●●
Mountains	●●●
Outdoor activities	●●

High on a rocky promontory, Bergamo's old city is a charming warren of stone buildings that wear their centuries well. Its cobbled streets are lively with cafés and restaurants, and art treasures abound. Yet Bergamo is not on every traveller's list. It ought to be, along with the most overlooked of Italy's larger lakes, Iseo. Sheer limestone cliffs drop straight from tiny medieval villages, a cone-shaped island rises out of the middle, its shores busy with fishermen, its heights crowned by castles. Along the eastern shore are a remarkable string of medieval churches decorated with frescoes that are hardly ever mentioned. To the north is the Valle Camonica, where prehistoric peoples carved hundreds of pictographs onto the valley's rocks. So rich are these finds that a National Park surrounds them. It's a part of Italy well worth exploring.

BERGAMO❖❖❖

ⓘ APT *Vicolo Aquila Nera 2 off Pza Vecchia; tel: 035 232 730. Open daily 0900–1200, 1400–1730.*

ⓟ Parking € is limited, but available in the Città Alta at Piazza Mercato Fieno, off Via San Lorenzo.

High above Bergamo's newer city is the walled **Città Alta**, the old upper city, where Bergamo's treasures are concentrated. The Venetian Lion of St Mark above the Città Alta's entrance gate, **Porta Sant Aostino** (1592), on the east, leaves no doubt who built the 5km of walls that surround the old town. To the north is the least pretentious gate, **Porta San Lorenzo**, through whose single passage Garibaldi entered with his troops and liberation in 1859. At the centre of the old city is the beautiful ensemble of **Piazza Vecchia❖❖❖**, bounded by **Palazzo del Podesta**, the tall **Torre Communale❖❖** and the **Pallazzo della Ragione**, with its columned staircase, triple-arched *loggia*, Gothic arches and a definite Venetian flavour complete with lion. In the centre of the *piazza* is the **Contarini Fountain** with its friendly-looking lions and serpents. Tucked into the corner by the *loggia* is a café, a prime spot for seeing the *piazza* at night – a highlight of

Bergamo. Through the *loggia* is **Piazza Duomo**, with the Romanesque **Santa Maria Maggiore**** and the Renaissance **Colleoni Chapel****, mausoleum of *condottiere* Bartolomeo Colleoni, designed by Giovanni Amadeo. Built onto Santa Maria Maggiore, its Renaissance polychrome marble and embellishment jars with the Gothic simplicity of the church. Inside, however, is some of the finest Lombard art. The centrepiece is the tomb of Colleoni, topped by a gilt equestrian statue. The tomb of Medea, his daughter, is graceful and serene.

Outside, the unusual **baptistery**** (*open by appointment; tel: 035 210 311*) faces the *duomo* from across the *piazza*. It was originally inside, removed in 1659 and stored, re-erected in 1856, again torn down and rebuilt. Eight 14th-century statues of virtues surround the roof. **Santa Maria Maggiore**** was begun in 1137 and, aside from the Colleoni Chapel and a vestry, retains its original exterior. Inside, the church has lost its Gothic past to the Baroque, but 13th-century frescoes survive on the left side and by the south door is an exquisite fresco from 1347. The walls are hung with nine 16th-century Tuscan tapestries. Of interest to music lovers are the tombs of Simone Mayer and Gaetano Donizetti. On the backs of the benches in the Presbytery is outstanding marquetry of biblical scenes. Behind Piazza Duomo is the

Gallery of Modern and Contemporary Art V. San Tomaso 53; tel: 035 399 527. Call for exhibition dates and times.

La Rocca Viscontea V. Rocca; tel: 035 247 116. Open daily 1000–1200, 1500–1900, closed major holidays.

Museo Donizetti V. Arena 9; tel: 035 237 374. Open Tue–Sat 1430–1800.

Santa Marie Maggiore Pza Duomo; tel: 035 222 327. Open daily 0900–1200, 1500–1800; Apr–Oct until 1900. Hours may vary seasonally.

Torre Comunale Pza Vecchia; tel: 035 262 565. Open May–Sept daily 0800–2200, Oct Sat–Sun 1000–1800, Nov–Feb Sat–Sun 1030–1600, Mar–Apr Tue–Fri 1000–1230, 1400–1800.

Shopping for gourmet foods is a highlight of Bergamo, especially at Mangili Angelo (V. Gombito 8; tel: 035 248 774), where you will find cheeses from local farms, sausage, cured meats, dried pasta and the ingredients for the local polenta.

Tempietto di Santa Croce**, from the 9th and 10th centuries (*open by appointment; tel: 035 237 279*). Leading back to Piazza Duomo is a passage through the **Aula della Curia****, the ancient entry hall to the diocesan offices. Inside are splendid 13th- and 14th-century frescoes, including one of Christ Judging the Damned, showing Christ with a dagger between his teeth. On the same street is **Museo Donizettiana****, the home where the composer wrote many of his operas. The town's castle, **La Rocca**, was probably the Roman Capital. Access it through Remembrance Park. The outstanding **Carrera Gallery****, in the lower town, houses Italian and European art covering several centuries. One of Europe's major collections, it has over 1600 paintings, plus prints, bronzes and sculptures. Artists include Titian, Tiepolo, Dürer, Velasquez, the Bellinis, Mantegna, Canaletto, Longhi, Carpaccio, Pisano, Botticelli and more. Opposite is the new **Gallery of Modern and Contemporary Art*** in a 16th-century monastery.

Right
Café on Via Gombita, Bergamo

Accommodation and food in Bergamo

Hotel Agnello d'Oro €€ *V. Gombito 22; tel: 035 249 883; fax: 035 235 612.* This comfortable and attractive hotel is in the centre of the Città Alta, only a few steps from Piazza Vecchia and the main attractions. Its restaurant serves local specialities.

Best Western Premier Cappello D'Oro €€–€€ *Viale Pappa Giovanni XXIII 12; tel: 035 232 503; fax: 035 242 946; www.bestwestern.it.* Easy to reach by car and with covered parking, in the centre of the lower city, near the funicular station to the upper town. Full English breakfast.

San Lorenzo €€ *Pza L Mascheroni 9a; tel: 034 237 383; fax: 035 237 958.* Within an easy walk of Piazza Vecchia, in an historic building with parking available, the hotel is handicapped accessible.

Caffè del Tasso € *Pza Vecchia 3; tel: 035 237 966.* In a corner of the *piazza* next to the *loggia*, a good place for breakfast, coffee or for evening drinks in their piano bar.

da Franco Ristorante €€ *V. Colleoni 8; tel: 035 238 565.* A good choice for dining in the Città Alta, serving beautifully prepared local specialities.

Trattoria Tre Torre € *Pza Mercato del Fieno, south end of V. San Lorenzo; tel: 035 244 366.* Try the *gnochetti* with cream and *arugola* and don't miss their *polenta* with *porcini* and *Taleggio*.

CAPO DI PONTE❖❖

ⓘ *At Darfo Boario Terme tel: 0364 531 609; at Edolo tel: 036 471 065: at Ponte di Legno tel: 036 491 122.*

Ⓟ Parking for the National Park is signposted from S42, in a large car park in town. A footpath climbs to the park. In quiet seasons, you can drive to a higher point, parking in the few spaces at the entrance.

Ⓗ **Monasterio di San Salvatore** € *Capo di Ponte. Open daily 0900–1200, 1500–1800.*

History records human settlements in the **Valle Camonica** from the Rhaetians, then the Cenomani tribe of Celts, as early as 400 BC. But even earlier prehistoric peoples provide the valley's highlight, **Parco Nazionale delle Incisioni Rupestri**❖❖❖ at **Capo di Ponte**. Here hundreds of prehistoric images are carved into the rock of the hillsides. Incisions include deer, shovels, labyrinths, hunters and ladders, as well as 'northern Etruscan' alphabets. A descriptive map in English is available. A small museum has dioramas, tools and information on the lives of prehistoric peoples. Close by is the **Monasterio di San Salvatore**❖, from the 11th and 12th centuries, in Burgundian Romanesque style with beautifully carved capitals. Capo di Ponte's parish church of **San Siro** is of 8th-century Longobard origin, but the present church is 11th-century Romanesque, with good stone carving. Two parks, **Parco dell'Adamello** and the **Parco Nazionale dello Stelvio**, provide opportunities for getting out of the car and hiking.

Parco Nazionale delle Incisioni Rupestri € *Capo di Ponte; tel: 036 442 140, signposted from S42. Open Mar–mid-Oct Tue–Sun 0830–1930.*

Accommodation and food in Capo di Ponte

Bressanelli € *V. Medaglie d'Argento 2, Sellero, just north of Capo di Ponte; tel: 0364 637 307.* Cottages and rooms by reservation in an inviting *agriturismo* inn, hidden in the forest close to hiking trails and the Parco Rupestri. They also have a restaurant € that serves good lamb stew or rabbit with *polenta*.

Iseo✤

Azienda Promozione Turistica *Lungolago Marconi 2; tel: 030 981 361. Open Mon–Sat 0900–1230, 1530–1830; Sun 0900–1230.*

Parking is available along the lakefront.

Castello Olfredi *V. Mirolte. Open Mon–Fri 0900–1200, 1400–1700.*

San Pietro in Lamas *Amici del Monastero c/o Batista Simonini, Provaglio d'Iseo; tel: 030 983 477.*

The long Lake Iseo, at the end of the Camonica Valley, was from prehistoric times an important highway for the products of the entire region and **Iseo** was its major trading post. With the building of a shoreline road and a railroad in the 19th century, lake traffic declined, but Iseo remains an important community for the lake's tourism. On Piazza Garibaldi is its **Town Hall**, built in 1830 at the height of the town's power. On nearby Via Mirolte is the **Castello Olfredi**✤ dating from the 11th century, burned by Frederick I of Swabia (The Redbeard) on his campaign to suppress the Guelphs. Rebuilt in the 14th century, it has served as a monastery and presently as the town library. The church of **Sant'Andrea**✤, from the 12th century, shows its Lombard Romanesque heritage on the outside, particularly in its notable bell tower, but the interior was 'modernised' in the 19th century in the neo-classical style. On the exterior is the **tomb of Giacomo Olfredi**. **Lungolago Marconi**✤ is a promenade with beautiful views of the lake, toward **Monteisola** island. At **Provaglio d'Iseo**, on the main road south of Iseo, is the 12th-century monastery of **San Pietro in Lamas**✤ with fine frescoes dating from the 15th century.

Accommodation and food in Iseo

L'Albereta €€€ *V. Vittorio Emanuele 11, Erbusco; tel: 0307 760 550; fax: 0307 760 573; www.terramoretti.it.* A 19th-century villa hotel with beautifully decorated guest rooms, sumptuous baths, gardens and a elegant restaurant with a creative chef – delicate pasta may enclose scallops touched with ginger. The villa is south of Iseo, close to the A4 *autostrada.*

Hotel Milano € *V. Lungolago G Marconi 4, Iseo 25049; tel: 030 980 449; fax: 0309 821 903; e-mail: hotel.milano@tmz.it; www.lakeiseo.it/HM.* The hotel looks out across the lake and several of its 15 rooms have lakefront balconies. The restaurant €–€€, with a terrace, serves trout, grilled duck and several veal dishes.

Above
Vello, from upper
terrace, Lake Iseo

LAKE ENDINE✤✤

ⓘ APT *Vicolo Aquila*
Nera, Città Alta,
Bergamo; tel: 035 232 730.
Open daily.

ⓟ Parking is available
along the lake shore,
in a large lay-by apart from
hotels or other facilities,
whose purpose seems to
be for enjoying the scenery
and picnicking.

Even few Italians choose quiet **Lake Endine**, one of the prettiest and least developed of the Italian lakes. Long and very narrow, it winds along the base of a mountain to its east. On the valley floor and along the shore are farms. Unlike other lakes, it has almost no development along its shore, despite the fact that a well-travelled road borders it on one side and a smaller one on the other. An ochre-coloured farmhouse is about all you'll see along its tree-lined banks. The town of Endine Gaiano spreads along the western side, providing traveller services, but doesn't quite touch the shore itself.

Accommodation and food in Lake Endine

Hotel Bruxelles € *V. Pura 12, Endine Gaiano 24060; tel: 035 827 362.* Ten rooms, handicapped accessible, close to the lake and with restaurant and bar.

Hostaria la Trisa €€ *V. IV Novembre 2, Valmaggiore, Endine Gaiano; tel: 035 825 119.* Expect the likes of quail breast or *ravioli* filled with *porcini*.

LAKE ISEO✦✦✦

ℹ️ In Monte Isola **Municipal Tourist Office** tel: 030 982 226; in Peschiera **Maraglio Ufficio Turistico Peschiera** tel: 0309 825 088.

🚢 **Ferry service to Peschiera Maraglio** and Sensole operates from Sulzano on the east side road. Ferries to Carzano leave from Sale Marasino. Both ferries are frequent but hours vary.

🎫 **Barcaioli Piccola Soc. Co-op** Monte Isola. By appointment; tel: 0347 819 9172 Mario or 0335 844 0916 Emanuele.

Castello Olfredi Monte Isola, west of Peschira Maraglio on the road to Sensole.

Gestione Navigazione Lago d'Iseo V. Ariosto 21, Milano 20145; tel: 024 676 101; fax: 0246 761 059. Reservations: V. Nazionale 16, Costa Volpino; tel: 035 971 483; fax: 035 972 970. Boat tours and ferries on the lake.

Rocca Martinengo Monte Isola, near Menzino, north of Sensole.

Santa Maria delle Ceriola Monte Isola, on the top of the mountain outside Cure, accessible by bus in summer.

Santa Maria delle Neve on the road toward Fraine, Pisogne; tel: 036 487 032. Open Tue–Fri 1500–1700, Sat–Sun 0945–1150. If closed enquire at Romanino Bar, next door.

Lake Iseo, not far west of Lake Garda, has much of the same beauty, but far fewer visitors. For more than a millennium it has been a place of fishermen, traders, merchants and of nobles from Brescia and Bergamo who summered in palaces along its shore. In the middle of the lake is **Monte Isola**✦✦, the largest freshwater lake island in Europe. The church of **Santa Maria delle Ceriola**✦ has a venerated wooden statue of Mary and an *Ecce Homo* fresco. **Rocca Martinengo**, from the beginning of the 14th century, and **Castello Olfredi**, outside Peschiera Maraglio, are the island's castles. Fishing and the curing of fish are still important occupations on the island and you can see the curing houses and watch people making or mending fishing nets. **Barcaioli**✦✦, a local co-operative, conducts private tours of Monte Isola and two other islands, that include visits to a fishing-net-making shop and a wooden-boat builder. Monte Iseo has good hiking trails and bicycling, but the roads are narrow. While a road encircles Lake Iseo, you can also tour it by boat and by train. **Gestione Navigazione Lago d'Iseo**✦✦ operates ferries and touring boats with dining facilities.

The region is especially known for its frescoes. From the town of **Marone**, a narrow road winds uphill to **Zone**. On the way, **Santa Maria delle Rota**✦ has several frescoes by Giovanni da Marone and there are more at **San Giorgio di Cislano**✦ in Zone. Along the lake road, at the **Chiesa Cimiterio**✦ (Cemetery Church) on the right just as you enter the village of Vello, are more da Marone works. At the head of the lake on the east shore is **Pisogne**, a small town at the entrance to the Camonica Valley, where **Sant Maria della Neve**✦✦, a former monastery, had an outstanding series of frescoes by Girolamo Romani, called Romanino. The parish church of **Santa Maria in Silvis** (1485) also has interesting restored frescoes by Giovanni da Marone. For wild scenery, head uphill to the old centre of **Riva di Solta**, called **Zorzino**✦✦, to see the vertical limestone cliffs that drop into the lake. The old town of **Castro**✦✦, built on Roman foundations, has another vertical cliff.

Accommodation and food in Lake Iseo

La Foresta €€ *Peschiera Maraglio; tel: 0309 886 210: fax: 0309 886 455.* Has rooms and a good restaurant, *closed Wed.*

Albergo/Ristorante La Foresta € *Peschiera Maraglio; tel: 0309 886 210.* A modest lodging on the lake, with a restaurant and bar.

Suggested tour

Total distance: 178km, with detours 188km.

Time: 6 hours' driving. Allow 3 days for the main route with or without detours. Those with limited time should concentrate on Bergamo.

Links: A4 connects Milan (Milano) (*see page 76*) to Bergamo from the west and to Brescia (*see page 96*) on the east. From Iseo, it is only a few kilometres to Brescia on S510.

Route: Leave **BERGAMO** ❶ heading east on A4, exiting at **Cazzago San Martino**. Head north on P11, following signs to **ISEO** ❷. Follow the eastern side of **LAKE ISEO** ❸ on the shore road, avoiding S510, which does not access the lake as well. Continue through **Solzano**, **Marone** and past Vello, bearing right onto S42 before reaching **Pisogne** (64km). Follow S42 along the Val Camonica past **Darfo** and **Brenno** to **CAPO DI PONTE** ❹. Backtrack to Darfo, bearing right onto S42, signposted **Lovere**, by-passing that city (70km). (*See Detour 1 below*.) From Lovere, at the north end of Lake Iseo, S42 leaves the lake's steep west shore and after passing through a series of tunnels it emerges at the town of **Endine Gaiano** near the head of **LAKE ENDINE** ❺. (*See Detour 2 below*.) From the lake, continue south on S42, following signs back to Bergamo (44km).

Detour 1: Instead of by-passing **Lovere**, take the local route through it, following the lake shore and signs to **Castro** and **Riva di Solto**. Follow the scenic shore to the less than scenic industrial city of **Sarnico**. Continue south, following signs to **Credaro** and **Palazzolo**, turning west at the A4 and following it back to Bergamo (55km).

Detour 2: For an even more rustic view of **Lake Endine**, before reaching Endine Gaiano, bear left at the head of the lake, following signs to **Monasterolo del Castello**. The road follows the wooded shore, past a few farms. Stop for views of the castle before rejoining S42 in **Casazza** (8km).

Getting out of the car

You can reach Lake Iseo from Bergamo via the **Treno Blu***, a tourist railroad that runs to Sarnico, where it links with the boats of Navigazione del Lago for a water tour of the lake and Monte Isola. Contact **Treno Blu** *tel: 0354 243 937; www.ferrovieturistiche.it.* Buy tickets on board or at **Clio Viaggi** *V. G d'Alanzo, Bergamo; tel: 035 233 031; fax: 035 248 023.* A day excursion includes train, boat to Monte Isola and lunch.

Right
Lungolago Marconi, Iseo

Opposite
Monte Isola, Lake Iseo

Also worth exploring

ⓘ Ask at any APT office
for a copy of the
Agriturismo booklet for
Lombardy. It will list places
that welcome visitors to
buy, dine or spend the
night.

The **Val Bremabana** is the valley of the Brembo River, as it flows through the mountains on a route that traders have followed for centuries. This rural area is filled with small farms, many of which welcome visitors to buy their cheese, sausage, fresh baked goods, wines and fruit. Follow the Brembo to the spa town of **San Pellegrino** ❻, whose *belle époque* grand hotel is sadly closed, but whose art deco cafés and spas still thrive.

Brescia to Mantua

Ratings

Art	●●●●
Food and drink	●●●●
Historical sights	●●●●
Museums	●●●●
Architecture	●●●
Nature	●●●
Outdoor activity	●●●
Castles	●●

The hills at the foot of Lake Garda soon melt into the low plain of the Po and the Mincio, rich alluvial farmlands, but flat. What could be a boring landscape is not, because of the lakes and rivers, and because of the green farms and rice fields spreading on all sides. Add little farming villages, the appealing ducal seat of one of the great families of Italian history and a major Roman centre in the first centuries BC and AD, well-preserved. This is a far from boring route, and the driver will appreciate a break from mountain roads. It is prime birding, boating and biking country, and tourist offices offer an excellent cycling guide detailing several routes. As you might expect in a land so filled with farms, abundant *agriturismo* establishments sell fruits, vegetables, honey, farm cheeses and a wide variety of pork sausages and hams.

BRESCIA✦✦✦

ⓘ *Pza Loggia 6; tel: 0302 400 357; fax: 0303 773 773; www.bresciaholiday.com. Open Mon–Sat 0930–1830. Shorter hours Mar–Oct.*
APT *Corso Zanardelli 34; tel: 030 43 418; fax: 030 293 284; www.gardanet.it/aptbs*

ⓟ *Parking € for the Castello is at Via della Rocca and Via del Castello. There is also parking at Piazza Vittoria (close to the TIC) and close to Piazza Mercato.*

By the 1st century AD, Romans were building grand, classic buildings in Brixia and a surprising number survive. Today's visitor can stand in the forum, **Piazza del Foro✦✦**, and see the **Capitolium✦✦** temple with four of its six columns and much of its pediment. Remnants of the 1st-century **basilica** are integrated into a wall on Piazza Labus. To the right of the Capitolium is the 3rd-century **Teatro Romano✦✦**, built to hold 15,000. On the left are remnants of the **Roman East Gate✦**, while part of the Roman main road, the **Decumanus Maximus✦**, remains below. On Decumanus Maximus is the **Civici Musei d'Arte e Storia Santa Giulia✦✦✦**, a newly-created museum of art and history that brings together the riches of the city's past in a former Benedictine monastery. In the complex are Roman homes with mosaic floors, an outstanding Winged Victory, *stelli*, altars and architectural fragments spanning from the 1st century BC to the 5th century AD. The Treasury contains exceptional jewellery and gold-work, including the jewelled

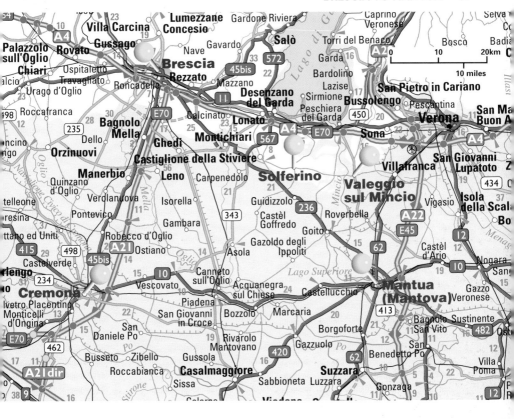

🕈 **Civici Musei d'Arte
e Storia Santa
Giulia** €€ V. Musei 81b;
tel: 1800 762 811;
tel: 0302 977 834;
www.comune.brescia.it/musei
or
www.bresciaholiday.com.sant
agiulia.
Open Jun–Sept Tue–Sun
1000–1800; winters
Tue–Sun 0930–1730. Park
at Piazza Tebaldo Bruscato.

gold **Cross of Desiderio**. The medieval periods, the commune and Venetian era are shown in art and architectural artefacts, providing a complete picture of the late-Gothic and Renaissance periods. Few museums have this range, so well displayed.

At the **Piazza Paolo VI** (named after native Brescian Pope Paul VI) stands the 13th-century tower and buildings of the **Broletto** and the nearby 11th-century **Duomo Vecchio** (*Pza delle Loggia*), called **Rotonda** for its unusual round shape. Inside are a carved red marble sarcophagus and carved wooden choir stalls. Shades of Renaissance Venice haunt **Piazza Loggia's** 15th-century colonnades by Sansovino and Palladio. Topping the clock tower are two *Macc de le ure* ('crazy time keepers') made of metal-covered wood, at work since 1581. **Galleria d'Arte Tosio Martinengo** (*V. M da Barco*) has a collection by 13th- to 18th-century Brescian painters. **Museo d'Arte Moderno e Contemporario** (*V. Monti 9*) has fine collections, with works by Picasso, Dali, Chagall and Matisse. The hilltop **Castello**, fortified since the 13th century, is today surrounded by quiet gardens, although its contents recall its defensive past in museums of ancient arms and the *Risorgimento*.

Accommodation and food in Brescia

Ambasciatori €€ *V. Crocifissa Rosa 92; tel: 030 399 144; fax: 030 381 883; www.bresciaholiday.com/ambasciatori.* Well-located hotel with parking and a restaurant € serving local specialities.

Hotel Industria €–€€ *V. Orzinuovi 58, 25125; tel: 0303 531 431; fax: 0303 347 904; www.hotelindustria.it.* Just off Tangenziale Ovest, close to the Piazza Republica, the hotel has parking and a restaurant €.

Trattoria Al Fontanone €€ *V. Musei 47; tel: 030 405 54.* Near the Giulia Museum (you can leave and return), with good service and excellent house wine.

Trattoria Labirinto €€ *V. Corsica 224; tel: 0303 541 607.* Beautifully prepared local specialities with a contemporary twist.

La Piazzetta €€ *V. Indipendenza 87; tel: 030 362 668.* This well-known restaurant features local seafood, such as fish-filled *ravioli*.

CREMONA✤

ⓘ APT *Pza del Commune 5, Cremona; tel: 037 221 722 or 037 223 233. For guides tel: 037 237 970; www.cremonaturismo.com. Open daily.*

ⓟ Parking € is around Piazza Cadornaat (near Piazza Commune), Piazza Marconi or nearby Piazza San'Angelo; on the east at Piazza Lodi on Via Amati, at Piazza del Liberta and in the north along Via Dante.

ⓝ Baptistery € *Open Tue–Sun 1000–1300, 1430–1800.*

Il Torazzo € *Open Tue–Sun 1000–1300, 1430–1700.*

Although its name is synonymous with violin-making, Cremona has a lot more. The **Duomo**✤✤ is filled with art: its arches and vaulting painted in fresco of enormous detail, as is the crypt beneath the altar. The high altar and both pulpits are faced in relief-carved marble. In the left trancept is a magnificent 15th-century **silver cross**✤✤✤ with 160 miniature figures of saints. You can climb **Il Torazzo**✤✤, Europe's tallest stone bell tower at 111 metres, and visit the **Baptistery**✤, opposite the Palazzo Comunale, where there is an exhibit of priceless **violins** (€€). Look into workshops as you pass, to see violin makers at work. Cremona is well known for its restaurants and food emporia; behind the Duomo, visit **Formaggi d'Italia di Losi Pietro**✤✤ (*V. Boccaccino; tel: 037 223 270*) for cheese, salami, torrone and other local specialities.

Accommodation and food in Cremona

Continental €€ *Pza Liberta 26, 26100; tel: 0372 434 141; fax: 0372 454 873; www.continental.it* Hotel in the centre of town, with many extras, a restaurant €–€€ with local specialities, and parking.

Hotel Duomo € *V. Gonfalonieri 13, 26100; tel: 037 235 242; fax: 0372 458 392.* Central, but with quick access to the *autostrada*, it has a restaurant € and parking.

Hosteria Il 700 €€ *Pza Gallina 1; tel: 037 236 175. Closed Tues.* Elegant restaurant with local dishes, such as Cremonese *marubini*, local ravioli-filled with chicken and salami.

Palazzo Comunale Collezione di Violini Antichi € *Pza del Commune; tel: 037 222 138.* **Palazzo Fodri** *Corso Matteotti 17; tel: 037 221 454.*

La Sosta €–€€ *V. Sicardo 9; tel: 0372 456 656.* Local dishes with a nod to newer styles, and delectable potato *gnocchi.*

MANTUA✦✦✦

ⓘ Ufficio Informazioni *Pza Mantegna 6; tel: 0376 328 253; fax: 0376 363 292; www.aptmantova.it. Open Mon–Sat 0930–1230, 1400–1800; Sun 0900–1230.*

ⓟ Parking € areas are well marked close to the centre.

🏛 Palazzo Ducale €€ *Pza Sordello. Open Tue–Sun 0845–1915. Last entry 1830.*

Palazzo Te €€€ *Vle Te; tel: 0376 323 266. Open Tue–Sun 0900–1830.*

San Andrea *Open daily 0800–1200, 1500–1900,* **Crypt** € *open Tue–Sat 1030–1130, 1530–1800 (1730 Sat), Sun 1530–1730.*

Archaeology Museum *Tel: 0376 329 223, open Tue–Sat 0830–1830, Sun, hol 0830–1330.*

⊖ Antiques Market 3rd Sun each month. Market day: Thur.

◍ Antica Fiera dei Mangiari *end May–mid-June, Sat–Sun 1100–2000.* A colourful celebration of local produce, with medieval dress and flag-throwing.

Lying between three lakes, Mantua combines the pleasures of a small city with the nature and outdoor pursuits a water-setting provides. Mantua was the town of the Gonzagas, a strong but enlightened and public-spirited family. The **Palazzo Ducale**✦✦✦ was their home for centuries. Their palace, a sombre pile of grey-brown stone, houses splendid rooms filled with paintings by Rubens and Tintoretto, among others. The Spouses' Room is done in frescoes by Mantegna. In the same *piazza* is the mid-15th-century **duomo**✦, its façade neo-classical, its *campanile* Romanesque. Inside, Corinthian columns support an ornate coffered ceiling. Behind, opera-lovers should seek **Casa di Rigoletto**✦, with a statue of the jester in its walled garden. Opposite, a bakery makes typical local sweets. **Palazzo Te**✦✦, built for later Gonzagas, is more Renaissance in flavour. **Sala dei Cavalli** features the family's favourite horse and in the startling **Sala dei Gigantei** the painted walls give the impression that the world is falling down; an Egyptology museum is tucked into its upper levels. **Basilica di San Andrea**✦✦ dates from 1472, baroque in flavour, with coffered vaulted ceilings and an 80m dome. Adjacent is **Piazza Erbe**✦, with the market, a splendid **Torre Orologio**✦ (clock tower) and **la Rotonda di San Lorenzo**✦✦, a small round church from 1083 that was discovered among later buildings. A small, but growing, free **Archaeology Museum**✦✦ is inside the Mercato Bozzoli building beside the ducal palace, detailing local settlements from Paleolithic times; ask for descriptive papers in English.

Accommodation and food in Mantua

Hotel ABC € *Pza Don Leoni 25; tel: 0376 322 329; fax: 0376 322 329.* A comfortable hotel, breakfast included, dining room, bar/café, parking available.

Casa Margherita €–€€ *V. Broletto 44; tel/fax: 0376 222 392; www.lacasadimargherita.it.* A B&B a few steps from the Ducal Palace.

Palazzo Costa €€ *V. Freatelli Grioli 46; tel/fax: 0376 362 357; www.palazzocosta.it.* Frescoed walls are in restoration at this antique-furnished Renaissance palazzo, just 5 min from Palazzo Te. Breakfast and parking are included and rooms have internet points.

Above
Cafés on the Piazza
Sordella, Mantua

Il Girasole € *Pza delle Erbe 16*. In the centre of town, a good place for a glass of *prosecco* and excellent *bruscetta*.

Osteria delle Erbe €–€€ *Pza delle Erbe 15; tel/fax: 0376 225 880*. Tables in the market square, with pizza and light meals.

Osteria delle Vecchia Mantova €€ *Pza Sordello 26; tel: 0376 329 720*. Their location opposite the Ducal Palace has not turned this local favourite into a typical tourist stop; the *gnocchi* with *porcini* is divine.

Ristorante Cortaccia Biocucina €–€€ *Corte dei Sogliari 6; tel: 0376 368 760. Closed Mon & Tue afternoon*. Specialises in Mantovese dishes: pumpkin *tortellini* with local sausage, *bigoli* (pasta) with *porcini*, also vegetarian dishes.

SOLFERINO⁜

ⓘ Associazione Turistica Colline Moreniche del Garda
Pza Torelli 1, Solferino; tel: 0376 854 360 or 0376 854 001; e-mail: colline.moreniche@dsmnet.it; www.dsmnet.it/ collinemoreniche

ARPT *V. Francese; tel: 376 854 068.*

ⓜ La Capella Ossaria and Museo Storico
€ Pza Ossaria, Solferino; tel: 0376 854 019. Open daily 0830–1230, 1400–1830, closed Mon.

◔ Antiques Market 2nd Sun of each month, Mar–Nov. Market day: Sat afternoon.

In 1859, as Italians fought for independence from Austria, this was the scene of some of the heaviest losses on both sides. A Swiss, Henry Dunant, was so moved by the aftermath of the Battle of Solferino – more than 40,000 troops dead or injured and without medical care or burial – that he began a campaign that resulted in the Geneva Convention and later, the International Red Cross. Today the hill town is marked by the solemn **La Capella Ossaria**⁜, its walls lined row-on-row with skulls of the dead from that battle. Below, **Museo Storico**⁜ contains artefacts from the battle including cannon and uniforms. Farther up the hill is the lovely enclosure of the **castle**⁜ that was the seat of the Gonzaga family. Houses line two sides, a church stands in the middle next to a tiny walled garden. Below spreads a view of mountain-framed Lake Garda. Above, the **Rocca di Solferino**⁜ tower (1022) was used by Italian forces as an observation point for its wide views. On the lane to the tower is a memorial to Henry Dunant, the **Red Cross Monument**⁜.

Accommodation and food in Solferino

Albergo Ristorante Vittoria € *V. Ossario 37; tel/fax: 0376 854 051.* A friendly hotel with a restaurant featuring home-style cooking, opposite the Museo Storico.

La Barche € *V. Barche 6; tel: 0376 854 113 or 8545 262. Closed Jan & Tue.* The restaurant serves regional dishes including *bigoli* (a wide, fresh pasta), pigeon, grill of mixed meats and braised beef. Rooms and cottages available, and they sell their own produce and wines.

Ristorante/Pizzeria al Castello € *Pza Castello; tel: 0376 855 255.* Local specialities, such as *I capunsei*, made of bread, egg, cheese and parsley. Fantastic views of Lake Garda from the terrace dining area.

Ristorante/Pizzeria Vecchia Fontana € *Pza Marconi 3; tel: 0376 855 000.* In the middle of the old town.

VALEGGIO⁜⁜⁜

ⓘ Turismo *tel: 0457 951 880; e-mail: valleggio@tin.it; www.valeggio.com. For restaurants: www.valeggio.com/ristoratori*

Snatching success from adversity when the local silk industry failed, local women did what they knew – they made the best pasta in the valley. Little restaurants opened, word spread and Valeggio put *tortellini* on the map. Now the once-abandoned mill village on the river, **Borghetto**⁜, is devoted entirely to tourists, with cafés and craft studios in the picturesque restored buildings, sitting over the water.

Castello Scaligeri
€ *Open daily, tower Sun & holidays 0900–1200, 1430–1900.*

Parco Giardino Sigurta
€€ *Valeggio sul Mincio, signposted; tel: 0456 371 033; e-mail: sigurta@sigurta.it; www.sigurta.it. Open daily 0900–1800.*

Antiques Market
4th Sun each month.

Market day: Sat.

Crossing the Mincio above Borghetto is a long, heavily fortified bridge, **Ponte Visconteo**✦✦, which has guarded the town since 1393. Overlooking it is the restored **Castello Scaligeri**✦✦ with outstanding views to the Dolomites. In the valley, **Parco Giardino Sigurta**✦✦, beautifully landscaped flower garden, stretches over 1 125 acres (455.62ha).

Accommodation and food in Valeggio

Ristorante Albergo San Giorgio € *V. Cavour 12; tel: 0457 950 125; fax: 0457 370 555.* Comfortable rooms above a centrally located restaurant €, with parking.

Ristorante Lepre € *V. Marsala 5; tel: 0457 950 011. Closed Wed, Thur evenings.* One of the original restaurants; a third generation is now enjoying their *tortellini in brodo.*

Ristorante San Marco €€ *Borghetto; tel: 0457 950 018. Closed Mon, Tues.* Lots of jovial Italian families on Sun, quieter weekdays.

Suggested tour

Tour Mantua's three lakes with Motonaves Andes €€
Pza Sordello 8; tel: 0376 322 875; www.amerigo.it/ANDES

Total distance: 182km, with detours 185km.

Time: 4–5 hours' driving. Allow 3 days with or without detours. Those with limited time should concentrate on Brescia and Mantua (Mantova).

Links: From Bergamo (*see page 86*) A4 leads directly to Brescia. To reach Peschiera for the Lake Garda route (*see page 115*), follow S249 north from Valeggio. To Verona, travel north via S62 from Mantua (Mantova).

Route: Leave **BRESCIA** ❶ heading east on S236, following signs to **Castiglione**, but continuing past it about 9km to the left turning where signposted **SOLFERINO** ❷. Leave Solferino on the unnumbered road signposted **Valeggio sul Mincio** (or simply **VALEGGIO**) ❸. (*See Detour on page 103.*) On arriving in Valeggio, turn right, but before following the road across **Ponte Visconteo**, divert to the right, alongside the river, to visit **Borghetto**. Returning to cross **Ponte Visconteo, Castello Scaligeri** will be straight ahead. To reach it, turn left at the end, then go right, following signs to the castle (41km). From Valeggio, head south on S249, through Roverbella until its intersection with S62, where you turn right, following signs to **MANTUA** (Mantova) ❹ (28km). Leave Mantua travelling west on S10 to **CREMONA** ❺. Return to Brescia on S45b, or the faster A21 (113km).

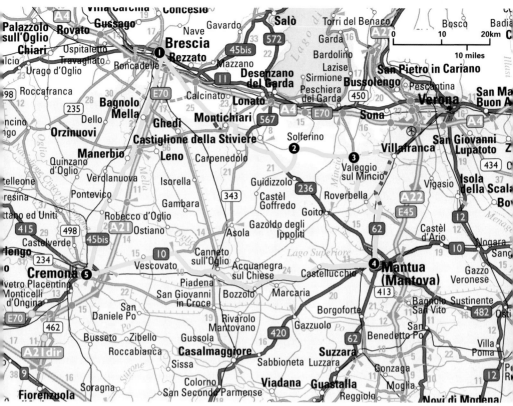

Turismo *Pza d'Armi 1, Sabbioneta; tel: 0375 221 044. Guided tours €€.*

Detour: History enthusiasts can leave **Valeggio** on the unnumbered road east, signposted **Villafranca**. The town centre is dominated by a large castle, scene of the 1859 Conference where Hapsburg Austria lost its Italian provinces. Follow S52 south to Mantua (Mantova) (25km).

Also worth exploring

The failed 16th-century Utopia of **Sabbioneta** still stands, although its monumental buildings seem as oddly out of place in the agricultural Po plain as they did when built. You must take a tour, organised by the AAST, which includes two palaces, a church with a surprising *trompe l'oeil* ceiling, and a copy of Vicenza's *Teatro Olimpico*. To reach Sabbioneta, travel southwest from Mantua on S420.

Lake Garda

Ratings

Scenery	●●●●●
Boat trips	●●●●○
Castles	●●●●○
Children	●●●●○
Mountains	●●●●○
Outdoor activities	●●●●○
Markets	●●●○○
Beaches	●●○○○

The largest lake in Italy, Garda covers more than 350sq km, its water in places as deep as 346m. It is 84km long, narrow at its northern end, widening out at the south. Palms, agaves and olive trees adorn the slopes that cradle it, growing north of their usual range because of the mild year-round climate. Mountains rise steeply from its northern portion, making stunning scenery from nearly any vantage. La Gardesana, the 50km road that hugs the lake's western shore from Riva del Garda to Salo, is wilder than the more developed eastern shore route. The road pops in and out of tunnels, and tiny towns cling to the steep hillside above or below it. Nearly every town on the shore can be easily reached by boats that circle the lake and shuttle from point to point throughout the day.

BARDOLINO**

ⓘ **APT** Pzle Aldo Moro; tel: 0457 210 078; www.info-bardolino.it

APT V. Fontana 14; tel: 0457 580 114; www.info-lazise.it. Open daily summer.

ⓟ Parking € just north of town, signposted from S249.

↪ A cycling and walking path follows the lake shore from Bardolino to Torre del Benaco.

Bardolino's shaded benches invite visitors to enjoy the view of the tidy little marina and lakefront. Olive trees grow on the shores of the lake, some distance north of their usual range. Locally-pressed olive oil is highly prized and at **Museo dell'Olio d'Oliva*** visitors can compare the flavours of various oils and purchase them in the shop. Two churches are of special interest: the 9th-century Carolingian **San Zeno** and the 11th-century Romanesque **San Severo**, with a frescoed interior. South of Bardolino, the beautiful little enclosed harbour of **Lazise**** is bordered by ochre buildings and a venerable stone church. A Scaligeri castle guards the southern edge, its 11th-century walls wrapping around the core of the old town.

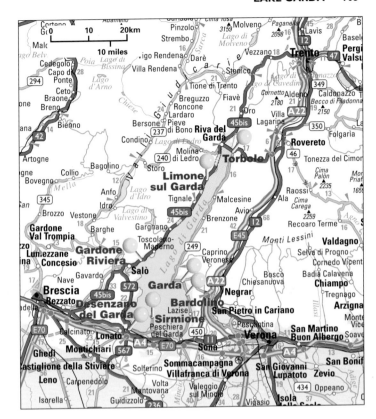

Accommodation and food in Bardolino

Museo dell'Olio d'Oliva V. Peschiera 54, S249, Cisano di Bardolino. Open Mon–Fri 0900–1230, 1500–1900, morning only Sun, hol.

Antiques Market 3rd Sun of each summer month.

Market day: Thur.

Restaurants and tavernas line the waterfront.

Albergo Alighieri € V. Dante Alighieri 48; tel: 0457 211 988; fax: 0456 228 283. Open mid-Mar–Oct. Studio apartments in the centre of the old town, on a walking street, parking garage available.

Hotel Capri €€ V. Mirabello 21, 37011; tel: 0457 210 106; fax: 0456 212 088; e-mail: info@hotel-capri.com; www.hotel-capri.com. Open Apr–Oct. Contemporary rooms with balconies, safes, satellite TV, handicapped access. Dining room €€.

DESENZANO DEL GARDA❖❖

ARPT Porta Vecchia; tel: 0309 141 510; www.info-decenzano.it. Open daily.

While it is not as 'cute' as some of Garda's other shore towns, Desenzano is hard to beat as a base for exploring the lake. Hotels are plentiful and well-located, it has both bus and boat connections to every town on the lake and is the only one with train access. Abundant restaurants, cafés and shops, as well as a pretty marina and stunning views of the lake and mountains, add to its attraction.

Parking € in a secured garage is on Via Scavi Romani, off Via Antonio Gramsci, the main route from the A4, signposted.

Museo Archeologico Rambotti € *Vle T da Molin; tel: 0309 144 529. Open Tue–Sat 0930–1230, 1430–1730.*

Villa Romana € *V. Scavi Romani; tel: 0309 143 547. Open Tue–Sat 0930–1230, 1430–1730.*

A small Roman villa with some excellent mosaics, **Villa Romana✦✦**, has been excavated and nicely interpreted. The **Museo Archeologico Rambotti✦** has finds from Roman and earlier eras and the parish church has a painting by Tiepolo.

Accommodation and food in Desenzano del Garda

Palazzo Arzaga €€€ *Carzago; tel: 030 680 600; fax: 0306 806 168; www.palazzoarzaga.it.* A 15th-century monastery turned luxury hotel with a Saturnia spa, Jack Nicklaus- and Gary Player-designed golf courses and fine dining. Guest rooms and public areas are decorated in 18th-century Venetian furniture.

Hotel Piroscafo € *V. Porto Vecchio 11, 25015; tel: 0309 141 128; fax: 0309 912 586.* On the small boat harbour, this family-run hotel has

● Market day: Tue.

been recently renovated. Rooms are bright, some have balconies. The restaurant €€ offers indoor or arcade dining. Parking available.

Hotel Vittorio €€ *V. Porto Vecchio 4, 25015; tel: 0309 912 245; fax: 0309 912 270.* Almost every room of this art deco hotel has views of the lake or small marina, while most have balconies. Room 410 has the best view. Friendly and helpful staff, breakfast included in the room price, garage parking 200m.

Bagatta alla Lepre Ristorante/Wine Bar €–€€ *V. Bagatta 33; tel: 0309 142 313. Closed Tue.* Mediterranean cuisine with emphasis on fish, mushrooms and truffles. The wine bar is a less expensive option, serving *risotto* inside a *grana* cheese and fresh pasta.

Trattoria La Biocca €–€€ *Vicolo Molino 6; tel: 0309 143 658. Closed Thur.* Our favourite place in Desenzano, serving local specialities with flair. Reservations suggested high season. Try the pumpkin *ravioli* or *carpaccio*.

Ristorante la Villetta €–€€ *V. del Colli Storici 8–10; tel: 0309 110 618. Closed Mon.* The speciality is *porcini* mushrooms, featured in several dishes.

Opposite
Hotel Vittorio, Desenzano

GARDA❖❖

❶ **APT** *V. Don Gnocchi 25; tel: 0456 270 384; www.aptgardaveneto.com. Open daily.*

Ⓟ Parking € in a large car park at the east side of S249, limited 1-hr spaces € at the lakefront in front of Casa de Commune.

Ⓜ **Museo del Castello Scaligero** € *Tel: 0456 296 111. Open daily Jun–Sept 0930–1300, 1630–1930; Apr–May, Oct 0930–1230, 1430–1800.*

San Vigilio *S249, 2km west of Garda, parking in summer along S249, rest of year at point.*

It's hard to find a pleasanter lakeside town to laze about in than Garda, which makes no pretence of being anything else. Benches face the lake from a fringe of shade trees, a walking and cycling path borders the shore, while behind sprawls an assortment of cafés where no one minds if you sit for hours over one *espresso*. There's no must-see sight except the lake, open 24/7. Evening brings music, alfresco dinners and the general air of people relaxing and enjoying life. Those who feel guilty without visiting a museum can take comfort in the **Museo Civico**, featuring prehistoric inscriptions at **San Vigilio**❖❖, a scenic point of land overlooking the lake. Although its pebble beach is very crowded in the summer, the point is particularly beautiful, with its 16th-century palace framed by tall cypresses. Just north is **Torri del Benaco**, with its 14th-century castle, built by the ubiquitous Scaligeri of Verona. **Museo del Castello Scaligero**❖ overlooks a little marina of fishing and pleasure boats. A ferry carries cars across the midpoint of the lake, to Gardone Riviera.

Accommodation and food in Garda

Hotel-Ristorante Gardesana €€ *Pza Calderini 20, Torre del Benaco; tel: 0457 225 411.* Beautiful view over the marina, and a restaurant that is part of the Buon Ricordo group: chefs committed to offering traditional regional dishes. Here it's delicate, white, lake fish *lavarello*.

Hotel Roma €–€€ *Lungolago Regina Adelaide 8, 37016; tel: 0457 255 025; fax: 0456 270 266; e-mail: info@hotelromagarda.it; www.hotelromagarda.it. Open Mar–Oct.* You couldn't have a more central location, right on the lake, next to a *loggia* and with cafés at its feet. Parking is available.

Locanda San Vigilio €€€ *Punta San Vigilio; tel: 0457 256 688; fax: 0457 256 551; e-mail: sanvigilio@gardanewa.it; www.gardanews.it/sanvigilio. Open Apr–mid-Oct.* The peninsula and villa are equally lovely and the hotel has an excellent restaurant €€€. Sporting activities are available.

Caffè Bar Taverna € *Pza Catullo.* An old favourite updated, an enjoyable place to spend an evening sampling local wines.

Taverna Fregoso €–€€ *Corso Vittorio Emanuele 39; tel: 0457 256 622. Closed Wed.* A cosy restaurant/taverna/pizzeria where you can sit outdoors and watch the world go by, live music summer, nightly 2100–0200.

GARDONE RIVIERA✤✤

ARPT *Corso Republica 8, Gardone; tel: 036 520 347; www.info-gardone.it. Open daily.* ARPT *V. Lungolago Zanardelli 52, Salo; tel: 036 521 423; www.info-salo.it. Open daily in summer.*

Hruska Botanical Gardens € *V. Roma. Open daily Mar–Oct.*

Il Vittoriale degli Italiani €€ *V. Vittoriale; tel: 036 520 130. Open daily Apr–Sept 0800–2030, Oct–Mar 0900–1230, 1400–1730.*

Market day: Wed.

Gardone is elegantly turned out around public gardens, which cascade in terraces of stately trees. Plants from all around the Mediterranean and from as far away as Africa grow in the **Hruska Botanical Gardens✤✤**. The mild lake climate favours plants that would ordinarily not survive this latitude, and made Gardone a popular site for villas. Lake Garda's most famous villa overlooks the lake, built for the eccentric poet Gabriele d'Annunzio. **Il Vittoriale degli Italiani✤✤** eschews the usual villa architecture for art deco, and is filled with proof of the poet's unusual tastes: a coffin-shaped bed, black-covered windows and a ship imbedded in the extensive gardens. Although neighbouring **Salo✤** is best known for Mussolini's puppet Salo Republic, in the final years of the Second World War, the town has much more to be remembered for. Its pastel buildings form a nice frame for the lake, and its *duomo* has a fine wooden altarpiece and Renaissance portal. Salo also has a small archaeological museum.

Accommodation and food in Gardone Riviera

Grand Hotel Gardone €€€ *V. Zanardelli 84, 25083; tel: 036 520 261; fax: 036 522 695; e-mail: ghg@grangardone.it; www.grangardone.it.* Its pink art deco façade adorns the shore, with poodle-cut trees and palms. It is, of course, full service with a restaurant €€€, beach and gardens.

Opposite
Lakefront, Garda

Locanda Agli Angeli € *Pza G Garibaldi 2, 25083; tel: 036 520 832; fax: 036 520 746; e-mail: angeli@mail.phoenix.it. Open all year.* Attractive guest rooms in an older, well-kept, building, with parking. It has its own restaurant €.

Hotel Monte Baldo, Villa Acquarone € *V. Zanardelli 110, 25083; tel: 036 520 951; fax: 036 520 952, e-mail: info@hotelmontebaldo.com; www.hotelmontebaldo.com. Open Apr–late-Oct.* An attractive hotel facing onto the lake, with a restaurant serving local specialities.

Villa Del Sogno €€€, *V. Zanardelli 107; tel: 0365 290 181; fax: 0365 290 230; www.villadelsogno.it.* The gracious – and spacious – villa overlooks the lake; the restaurant is outstanding, with creative preparations of local ingredients, and an excellent wine list.

Agli Angeli €–€€ *Pza G Garibaldi 2, 25083; tel: 036 520 832. Closed Mon & Wed mid-Oct–mid-Mar, Mon mid-Mar–mid-Apr.* Good local cooking at attractive prices.

Ristorante Laurin €€–€€€ *Vle Landi 9, Salo; tel: 036 522 022.* A stylish menu that does not overlook its local roots, featuring traditional trout dishes rarely found elsewhere.

Ortofloricoltura Agriturismo in Serra €–€€ *V. del Pozzo 19, San Felice del Benaco Cisano district; tel: 036 562 301.* The menu of this *agriturismo* restaurant is based on fresh, locally grown produce and meats, mostly grilled.

LIMONE SUL GARDA✦✦

ⓘ **ARPT** *V. Combone 15; tel: 0365 954 720; www.info-limone.it*

◒ Market days: 1st and 3rd Tue each month.

◐ **St Peter's Day** 29 June, brings a fair and fireworks.

The climate on the steep, east-facing slopes is even milder than on the opposite shore, making Limone an ideal place for the groves of lemon trees that give it its name. Terraces were cut into the hillside for the trees, some of which still thrive above the picturesque old town that clusters around the port. Despite the onion-shaped domes of the churches, Limone is a classic little Italian town, a patchwork of pastel stucco buildings ascending the mountainside. While it has no 'sights' in particular, it is a relaxed and pleasant town for browsing in shops and lazing in cafés.

Accommodation and food in Limone sul Garda

Hotel la Gardenia € *V. IV Novembre 47, 25010; tel: 0365 954 178; fax: 0365 954 214.* The hotel sits in a wooded garden setting on the west side of the highway above the town and lake. It has a well-respected restaurant with vegetarian offerings.

MALCESINE✦✦✦

ARPT *V. Capitanato 6; tel: 0457 400 555; www.info-malcesine.it. Open daily.*

Parking € *is in the tiered garage on the hillside above S249.*

Funivia €€ *Tel: 0457 400 206. Open daily 0800–1800 Apr–Oct, until 1900 mid-May–mid-Sept.*

Museo de Castello Scaligero € *Tel: 0456 570 333. Open daily 0900–2000 last admittance 1930.*

Artists' studios and boutiques line several of the narrow streets leading to the castle.

Market day: Sat.

Below
Castello Scaligero, Malcesine

It's hard to be this handsome and unaware of it, so if Malcesine is a bit too tarted up and tidied, it can – like Sirmione – be forgiven. Its narrow streets wind upward from the boat-landing to the castle, passing under arches and past artists' studios, restaurants and boutiques. The German poet Goethe had much to say of Malcesine, where he was arrested as a spy for drawing a picture of **Castello Scaligero✦✦**, on one of the finest settings in all Italy. Lake views are splendid from the terrace just below the entrance, which overlooks a tiny beach (reached by stairs from Via Posterna). On a clear day, the 10-minute ride by ultra-modern revolving funavia (cable car) to an elevation of more than 1700m on **Monte Baldo✦✦** rewards with views to distant Dolomite peaks and access to scenic walking trails.

Accommodation and food in Malcesine

Hotel Alpi €€ *Campograngе; tel: 0457 400 717, fax: 457 400 529.* A modern hotel, on the main highway and an easy walk to the centre of town. Restaurant €€.

Hotel Garni Diana €€ *V. Scoisse 8, 37018; tel: 0457 500 192, fax: 0457 400 415, www.malcesine.com/diana, e-mail: diana@malcesine.com.* On the hill overlooking the medieval town, a 5-minute walk below; modern and bright with a pool and restaurant €€.

Osteria alla Rosa €–€€ *V. Cerche. Polenta* dishes with salami, sausage or fish from the lake.

Ristorante Taverna Agli Scaligeri €–€€ *V. Monti at V. Dossa; tel: 0457 401 382. Risotto* is served with game birds, perch fumed with Prosecco and chicken cooked in brandy.

PESCHIERA**

APT *Pzle Bettoni 15; tel: 0457 551 673; www.info-peschiera.it.* Open daily.

Parking € is along the lakefront at the port, opposite the TIC.

La Rocca € *Complesso Monumentale.* Open daily 0900–1230, 1430–1800.

Market day: Mon.

Anniversario della Liberazione *Apr 25,* the town celebrates the anniversary of its liberation in 1945.

Where the River Mincio flows from the southern end of Lake Garda, the Austrians fortified the fine **Port of Peschiera**** to defend the position during Italy's war for independence in the mid-19th century. Italy won, and kept the fort, now more scenic than defensive, a fine backdrop for the colourful little boat basin. The romantically crumbling old *palazzo* was German command headquarters during the Second World War, which explains the town's enthusiastic celebration of Liberation Day. You can tour the whole fort complex, **La Rocca**** , whose grass-topped walls form a bridge over the end of Peschiera's river-mouth harbour. Peschiera is in two parts, and it is the western, fortified section you should head to. Coming from the A4, bear left and pass through the impressive main gate, **Porta Verona*.**

Accommodation and food in Peschiera

Camping Cappuccini € *Localita Cappuccini, Peschiera del Garda 37014; tel: 0457 551 592; fax: 0457 551 592; e-mail: info@camp-cappuccini.com; www.camp-cappuccini.com. Open Mar–Sept.* Showers, caravan and tent pitches, shelters, beaches, swimming and other sports, no campfires.

Hotel Bell'Arrivo €–€€ *Piazzetta Benacense 2, 37019; tel: 0456 401 322; fax: 0456 401 311.* This small hotel has been completely refurbished and is right on the marina, at the Port of Peschiera, which its café overlooks.

Ristorante al Fiore €€–€€€ *Lungolago Garibaldi 9; tel: 0457 550 113.* A reliable standard menu, well prepared.

La Vela €–€€ *Pza Benacense.* Along with a full dinner menu, La Vela offers an excellent selection of sandwiches (ask for *Carta Paninoteca*), which you can eat on the terrace overlooking the pretty boat basin. The menus have English translations.

Vecchio Viola €€ *V. Milano 7; tel: 0457 551 666. Closed Tue.* Local dishes are a speciality, with lake fish and traditional filled *ravioli*. Guest rooms are also available.

Opposite
Via Posterna, Malcesine

RIVA DEL GARDA AND TORBOLE✧✧

ⓘ ARPT *Giardina di Porta Orientale 8; tel: 0464 554 444; www.inforiva.it. Open daily.*

Ⓟ Parking **€** is at the eastern entrance to Riva, connected to the lakefront by a walking path. Limited parking **€** is also at Piazza Cesare Battista.

◯ Market days: 2nd and 3rd Wed, summer months only.

ⓘ Arco Arboreto *V. Lomego. Open Apr–Sept daily 0800–1900, Oct–Mar 0900–1600.*

Castel Drena € *Drena S45B; tel: 0464 541 220. Open Apr–Oct Tue–Sun 1000–1800, Nov–Mar Sat–Sun 1000–1800.*

Cascata de Varone € *Tel: 0464 521 421. Open May–Aug daily 0900–1900; Apr, Sept daily 0900–1800; Mar, Oct daily 1000–1230, 1400–1700; Nov–Feb Sun 1000–1230, 1400–1700.*

Museo Civico, Rocca di Riva € *Pza Cesare Battista; tel: 0464 573 869. Open Sept–Jun Tue–Sun 0900–1730; daily Jul–Aug. The castle museum is accessible to people with disabilities.*

Museo delle Palafitte € *Molina de Ledro; tel: 0464 508 182. Open mid-Jun–mid-Sept 1000–1300, 1400–1800; mid-Sept–mid-Jun 0900–1300, 1400–1700.*

Riva's palm-lined hotel grounds spread eastward around the head of the lake, extending right to Torbole, because they have very little room to grow to the west. The sheer face of Monte Brione rises above the town on that side, overlooking the attractive old town centre. **Museo Civico, Rocca di Riva✧✧** sits behind its moat, a solid castle built by the Scaligeri, now housing a very good museum. Featured are finds and interpretive displays on the prehistoric settlement here, and armour. Follow brown signs from Riva to find **Cascata de Varone✧✧✧**, one of Europe's most dramatic waterfalls, plunging out of a lake suspended almost directly overhead. The falls have carved a swirling corkscrew tunnel through the mountain and created a ecosystem all their own, so cool and wet that you will need a waterproof jacket. Excellent signage in English. The area is a centre for water sports, especially in Torbole, a favourite of the younger set where windsurfing is king. Rental equipment is plentiful in both towns, and sailing-boat hire establishments line S249 to the south.

North of Riva in Arco, **Arco Arboreto✧** contains mature trees from all over the world, which flourish in the micro-climate of a large park created by a Hapsburg duke in the 1800s. Walk from the attractive little village up to **Castello di Arco✧**, high on a rock cliff, with good views all along the way. Perched over the Salagoni Gorge in nearby Drena, the tall single tower and curtain walls of **Castel Drena✧✧** date at least to the 1100s and its museum includes Bronze Age archaeological finds and later historical artefacts. In Molina di Ledro **Museo delle Palafitte✧✧** shows a remarkable collection from the archaeological excavations of Bronze Age lake dwellings from the second millennium BC. One of these dwellings has been reconstructed nearby to complete the picture.

Accommodation and food in Riva del Garda and Torbole

Cafés and pastry shops line the lakefront, many of them serving sandwiches.

Albergo Ancora € *V. Montanara 2, Riva 38066; tel: 0464 522 131; fax: 0464 550 050; www.rivadelgarda.com/ancora.* A small, cosy hotel with a nice restaurant and roof terrace, in the centre of town.

Hotel Europa €€ *Pza Catena 9, Riva 38066; tel: 0464 555 433; fax: 0464 521 777; www.rivadelgarda.com/europa.* Perfectly located on the quay in the old town centre, where the boats arrive. It has been completely renovated.

Ristorante Picolo Mondo €€–€€€ *V. Matteotti 7, Torbole; tel: 0464 505 271.* Along with its innovative dishes, the restaurant is known for its rendition of a traditional local meat and bean salad.

Sirmione✦✦✦

ARPT Vle Marconi; tel: 030 916 114; www.info-sirmione.it. Open daily in summer.

Parking € is on the mainland side of the moat; only foot traffic is allowed inside the gates.

Market day: Fri.

Grotte di Catullo tel: 030 916 157. Open Tue–Sun 0900–dusk.

Rocca Scaligeri and Museo dei Castello € Tel: 030 916 468. Open Apr–Oct Tue–Sun 0830–1530, Nov–Mar Tue–Sun 0900–1600.

To many travellers, Sirmione is the highlight of the lake, as it certainly was to the Romans. To others it is a Hollywood set overflowing with boutiques and tourists. However you see it, you will not deny that it has a perfect setting, at the end of a long narrow point of land, water whichever way you look. **Rocca Scaligeri✦✦**, a 13th-century moated castle, fairly begs for at least one photograph. You can cross its drawbridge for a tour, as well. Its harbour inside the castle's defensive walls provided safe refuge for fishing boats and the Scaligeri ships. At the end of the scenic point, reached via a lakeside promenade, is **Grotte di Catullo✦✦**, a retreat built by Roman poet Catullus in the 1st century BC. More than a villa, it was a full-scale resort, with the Roman equivalents of apartments, a spa and shopping mall. Artefacts discovered here are in the small **Antiquarium✦**. **San Pietro✦** is built on a rise, and preserves 12th-century frescoes.

Accommodation and food in Sirmione

Amid Sirmione's swish boutiques and cafés, don't expect to find budget dining.

Hotel Broglia €€ V. G Piana 34–6, 25019; tel: 030 916 172; fax: 030 916 586. Open late Mar–late Oct. A full-service, upscale hotel with a restaurant €€, bar, parking and gardens.

Hotel Marconi €–€€ V. Vittorio Emanuele II 51, 25019; tel: 030 916 007; fax: 030 916 587. Open May–Sept. A good location right on the lake in the town centre, with parking.

Osteria al Pescatore €–€€ V. Piana 18, has reasonably-priced seafood.

Suggested tour

Total distance: 161km, with detours 288km.

Time: 6 hours' driving. Allow 2 days for the main route, 3 days with detours. Those with limited time should tour the lake on a day-trip by boat, stopping at Sirmione and Malcesine.

Links: To reach Lake Garda from Brescia (see page 96), take the A4, which also leads on to Verona (see page 118). To connect to the Alto Adige route (see page 144), follow S45b north from Riva to Trento, or S240 east from Torbole to Rovereto.

Route: Leave **DESENZANO DEL GARDA ❶** headed east on S11 to Colombare, turning left to visit **SIRMIONE ❷**, return to Colombare and continue on S11 to **PESCHIERA ❸**. Continue to follow the lake shore along S249, north to **Lazise, Bardolino** and **GARDA** ❹. (*See Detour 1 below.*) From Garda the road swings west to round the beautiful point of **San Vigilio**, turning north again to **Torri del Benaco** (54km). The various little settlements that make up **Brenzone** and its northern neighbours all blend together as they line the shore. The prettiest of these is easy to spot from S249 by the little river that cascades through it. Parking is scarce, but worth finding to follow this stream on foot to the beautiful little port at its mouth. A charming ensemble of brightly-painted houses, an arched bridge and a round stone tower surround the basin. There are few prettier vignettes on the lake. The road continues to border the lake closely with a succession of glorious views of the western shore and its steep mountain slopes. At **MALCESINE** ❺ these views are framed by a medieval castle on a wooded point. S249 continues north, hugging the lake shore and through a series of tunnels, before emerging at **TORBOLE** and **RIVA DEL GARDA** ❻ (39km). (*See Detour 2 below.*) Go south from Riva on S45B again closely following the shore through a series of tunnels to **LIMONE SUL GARDA** ❼. Several small towns cling to the shore north of **GARDONE RIVIERA** ❽ and **Salo** (47km). South of Salo S572 continues south travelling inland but with fine views all the way to your starting point at Desenzano del Garda (21km).

Detour 1: From **Garda**, follow the signposted road east to **Caprino Veronese**, then north to **Spiazzi**. Here the sanctuary of **Madonna della Corona** overlooks the Adige Valley. Continue to **Ferrara di Monte Baldo** to visit **Orto Botanica del Monte Baldo**. The gardens display the plants indigenous (and many endemic) to this pre-alpine mountain range, including edelweiss, alpine lilies and wild roses. Backtrack through this high valley to Garda (45km).

Detour 2: From **Riva del Garda** S45B heads north past the castellated towns of **Arco** and **Drena**, both worth visiting. North of Drena the road becomes increasingly scenic as views of the surrounding Dolomites open out in all directions and continues to be scenic all the way to **Trento** (*see page 140*). For a different series of views of the same area, backtrack to Riva (82km).

Getting out of the car

Boat options range from slow and scenic 'steamers' to fast hydrofoils and catamarans. The problem, of course, with touring by boat is that the time in each town is limited (or extended) according to the departure of the next boat. In general, towns on the southern end of the lake are more easily explored by boat, since there are many options without having to wait for the next round-the-lake steamer.

Orto Botanica.
Open daily May–mid-Sept 0900–1800.

Navigazione Lago di Garda €–€€
Tel: 0309 149 511; www.navigazionelaghi.it.
Operates Jun–mid-Sept. Schedules and connections for boat travel on Lake Garda.

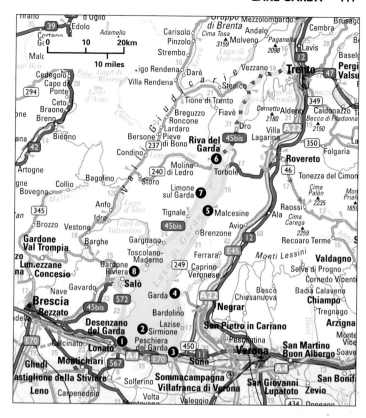

Ristorante Miralago
€€ *Pia A Cozzaglio 2,
Tremosine; tel: 0365 953
001; www.miralago.it.* Those
with acrophobia might not
appreciate the setting,
suspended above 300
metres of thin air, but the
lake views are unmatched.
A hotel adjoins, with an
equally good prospect.

Also worth exploring

From **Limone** a narrow, but very scenic, mountain road climbs to the village of **Vessio** and winds along a high terrace to **Tignale** before rejoining S45B north of **Gargnano**. This road gives a different set of views down over the lake, and passes the sanctuary of **Monte Castello**, just beyond **Gardola**.

Right
Limone sul Garda

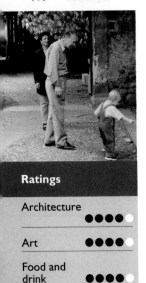

Verona

Ratings

Architecture	●●●●
Art	●●●●
Food and drink	●●●●
Historical sights	●●●●
Museums	●●●
Walking	●●●
Castles	●●
Children	●

'There is no world without Verona walls' lamented Romeo in Shakespeare's Romeo and Juliet. While that's not quite true today, the traveller will find many of the city's attractions in the historic centre the walls enclose. Others – a Roman theatre and the church of San Zeno – lie within a pleasant walk along the Adige's banks. Although Shakespeare never set foot in Verona, he set two plays there, and gave Verona's tourism officials an icon that they have not failed to exploit. You will hear of the mythical Juliet everywhere, and be shown her tomb and her balcony in a courtyard now trashed by graffiti. Latter-day legends surround both. Far more interesting are Verona's Roman, medieval and Renaissance relics, which include the best preserved Roman arena in Italy, still in use for everything from grand opera to rock concerts.

Getting around

ⓘ APT V. *Alpini 9, off Pza Bra; tel: 0458 068 680; fax: 0458 003 638 weekdays.* Good for lodging recommendations, but not much else. **IAT** *Scavi Scaligeri, off Pza dei Signori. Open Tue–Sun 0900–1900, shorter in winter.* Virtually useless except for its good selection of books for sale.

The old city, which is also today's busy centre, lies between the huge Piazza Bra, where the arena is, and the river, which describes a large, graceful curve through Verona. Via Mazzini, the main shopping street, leads from the arena to Piazza Erbe, the former Roman forum, now a lively morning vegetable market. Most streets between the two are closed to traffic, unless you are staying at one of the hotels, in which case you can unload baggage and park, if the hotel has permits. North from Piazza Bra, historic Castelvecchio stretches along the river, which is spanned by a graceful medieval castellated bridge. Verona's historic centre is small enough to explore on foot.

Venezia

Verona

300m
300 yds

Museo Archeologico
S. Giovanni in Valle
Teatro Romano
Giardino Giusti
VIA SANTA MARIA IN ORGANO
VIA CARDUCCI
VIA S. PAOLO
S. Paolo
Santa Maria in Organo
VIA SANTA MARIA IN ORGANO
Scaligeri Tombs
INTERRATO DELL' ACQUA MORTA
Palazzo Pompei
VIA S. FRANCESCO
Università
LUNGADIGE PTA. VITTORIA

Sant' Anastasia
Casa di Romeo
Torre dei Lamberti
Palazzo de Ragione & Lamberti Tower
PONTE NUOVO
PONTE NAVI
Ponte Romeo (Ponte Pietra)
Duomo di Santa Maria Matricolare
VIA DUOMO
PIAZZA DUOMO
PONTE GARIBALDI
VIA GARIBALDI
VIA EMILEI
Casa di Giulietta
Piazza Erbe
Piazza dei Signori
VIA S. STELLA
VIA MAZZINI
VIA CAPPELLO
Scavi Archeologici & Roman Gates
San Fermo Major (Maggiore)
PONTE ALEARDI
GALTAROSSA
Adige

S. Eufemia
Porta Borsari
CORSO PORTA BORSARI
VIA CATULLO
S. Nicolò
LUNGADIGE G. MATTEOTTI
PONTE D. VITTORIA
VIA MAMELI
VIA MARSALA
L'Arena di Verona
Municipio
PIAZZA BRÀ
Palazzo d. Gran Guardia
V.D. ALPINI
PALLONE
VIA DELLO ZAPPATORE
VIA MACELLO
VIA SS. TRINITÀ
SS. Trinità
Tomba di Giulietta e Museo degli Affreschi
VIA DEL PONTIERE
PONTE FRANCESCO
LUNGADIGE
Ponte Francesco
VIA DEL FANTE

Vittorio Veneto
VIA F. ANZANI
VIA ASPROMONTE
VIA IV NOVEMBRE
BORGO TRENTO
VIALE DELLA REPUBBLICA
VIA DEL RISORGIMENTO
CANGRANDE
V. PRATO SANTO
LUNGADIGE
Adige
Piazza Arsenale
Arco dei Gavi
VIA ROMA
CORSO CAVOUR
Museo Lapidario Maffeiano
V. MANIN
V.S. ANTONIO
V.S. CATERINA
VIA BATTISTI
VIA BERTEGONI
VIA DON BERTONI
VIA MONTANARI
CORSO PORTA NUOVA
CIRCONVAL. RAGGIO DI SOLE
MINATORE
CIRCONVAL - ALFRED ORIANI
Porta Nuova
VIA FRANCO FACCIO
VIA S. FRANCESCO

Ponte Scaligero
Castelvecchio
PORTA PALIO
VIA SCESA
DON STEEB
MARCONI
VIA VALERDE
VIA SCALZI
S. Teresa d. Scalzi
Verona's Walls
VIA D'ACQUISTO
VIA LOCATELLI
VIA DELLA

REGASTE S. ZENO
VIA PICCOLO
STRADONE
Porta Palio
Giardino Zoologico
VIALE LUCIANO
DAL CERO
VIALE "B." CARDINAL
Stazione FS. Porta Nuova
VIA COSTA

BARBARANI
VIA SCORSELLINI
DA VICO
PONTIDA
Piazza S. Zeno
San Zeno Major (Maggiore)
VIA SPAGNA
VIA RATERIO
VIA P. TA. S. ZENO
VIA LEGA VERONESE
TOMMASO
San Bernardino
VIA TRASIMENO
ROSMINI
CIRCONVALLAZIONE MARONCELLI
VIA DALLA BONA
VIA DA CAMPONE
BETTELLA A22

Piscina
VIA V. MERIGHI
COL.
GALLIANO
VIA V. MERIGHI
VIALE
VIA B. LONGHENA
VIA GIULIO
CAMUZZONI
VIA NASCIMBENI
VIALE PALLADIO
VIA DA GRIGIONE
VIA GIOCONDO
VIALE ALBERE

VIALE
VIA DORIA
VIA CABOTO
VIA APPOLLONI
VIALE COLOMBO
ORSO
MILANO
VIALE
B. LONGHENA

Mantova

Sights

ℹ **Turismo** *Ponte Aleardi at V. Pallone and V. Macello. Open Mon–Fri 0900–1800, Sat–Sun 0900–1230, 1400–1730.* More useful than APT, and adjacent to a new complex of handy facilities for travellers, including a café, lockers, public conveniences and shops selling local products.

🏠 **Casa di Giulietta,** house €, courtyard free. *Open Tue–Sun 0800–1900.*

Castelvecchio € *Corso Castelvecchio 2, end of Corso Cavour. Open Tue–Sun 0900–1900, last entry 1800.* Get the room-by-room guide.

Duomo € *Pza Duomo. Open Mar–Oct Mon–Sat 0930–1800, Sun 1330–1800, Nov–Feb Mon–Sat 1000–1300, 1330–1600, Sun 1330–1700.*

Arco dei Gavi*

Close to Castelvecchio, between the river and Corso Cavour, sits a 1st-century AD arched gateway from a Roman road. It was moved in 1933, complete with the stone pavement bearing chariot tracks.

The Juliet connection

The story of the young lovers Romeo and Juliet comes to us from Vicenza, where Luigi da Porto chose names from two local families for his characters. English poet Arthur Brooke took up the tale in 1562, drawing the attention of William Shakespeare, whose play is considered the best version. Although entirely fictional, the story draws tourists, and the city has obliged by creating homes for the pair and a tomb for the heroine.

Casa di Giulietta*

The setting was once sweetly romantic, a restored medieval building with stone balcony (added in the 1930s) facing a quiet courtyard. Today it's a mob scene crammed with young tourists who have turned the walls into a polychromed madness of graffiti. The delicate bronze statue of the heroine is disfigured by the rubbing of thousands of hands.

Casa di Romeo*

Not well marked (*V. Arche Scaligere 4*), not open and bearing no apparent relationship to the young hero who has been lost in the Juliet hubris, this house is nevertheless an interesting walled medieval building.

Castelvecchio and Ponte Scaligero***

The castle was built by Cangrande II (1355–75), as was the adjoining Ponte Scaligero, a castellated bridge. The castle has been converted into one of Italy's finest museum spaces, housing a remarkable art collection, most of it from city palaces, churches and monasteries. Most are from the 13th–19th centuries and include works by Bellini, Pisano, Francheschi, Rubens, Falconetti, Montagna, Tintoretto, Tiepolo and Guardi.

Duomo di Santa Maria Matricolare**

The cathedral, on the site of a 5th-century church built over a Roman temple, was begun in 1139, combining Gothic, Romanesque and Renaissance styles. The two-storey Romanesque portal shows the knights Roland and Oliver surrounded by stern-faced saints, created by

Giardino Giusti €
V. Giardini Giusti 2.
Open daily daylight hours.

L'Arena di Verona €
Pza Bra. Open daily
0800–1900, opera days
0815–1530.

medieval sculptor Nicolo. In the first chapel (*left*) is Titian's *Assumption*.

Giardino Giusti**

An easy walk from the Roman Theatre, Giusti Gardens are among the finest Renaissance gardens in Italy, designed in the 15th and 16th centuries. On the lower level are formal parterres of clipped hedges, walkways, cypress trees and grottoes. The steep hillside above is a more natural setting. It's a cool, shaded place to wander or picnic under the eyes of Renaissance statues.

L'Arena di Verona***

The arena has been part of Verona life since about AD 30, when its 22,000-plus seating capacity could accommodate the city's entire population. It was used for combat between gladiators and wild beasts and for grand expositions; St Fermo may have been martyred here. A place of refuge during barbarian invasion, it was also used for executions. It is the third largest Roman arena and the best preserved. Since 1913, each August it has been home to a world-class opera festival.

Museo Lapidario
Maffeiano € Pza Bra
28. Open daily 0900–1400.
Buy tickets at
Castelvecchio.

Lamberti Tower € Pza
dei Signori. Open Sun–Sat
0900–1800, first Sun free.

Throughout Verona you
will see a shield with a
ladder on the escutcheon.
This is the symbol of the
della Scala family (scala
means ladder), rulers of
the city and immediate
area during medieval
times (1263–1390).
Collectively they, and
their works, are referred
to as Scaligeri and their
style dominates the city.
It is recognised
particularly by the fish-tail
crenellations along the
tops of castle walls.

San Fermo
Maggiore Stradone
San Fermo, near Ponte Navi.
Open Mar–Oct Mon–Sat
0930–1800, Sun
1330–1800, Nov–Feb
Mon–Sat 1000–1300,
1330–1600 & Sun
1300–1700.

Museo Lapidario Maffeiano*

The stones here are from Roman Verona, a reliquary of architectural fragments that show the city of 2000 years ago.

Palazzo de Ragione and Lamberti Tower**

Rising above Piazza Erbe, the 275-ft (83.82m) Lamberti Tower marks the location of the medieval palace used as law courts. The palace and the lower courses of the tower are of striped layers of pink brick and white tufa. Look into the courtyard for the fine Renaissance staircase to the courtrooms. Climb the tower or use the elevator for views of the Dolomites.

Piazza Bra**

At the centre of old Verona lies this large open square, which has the huge Roman arena as a focal point. On the east is the large neo-classical municipal building, while opposite is a row of colourful 19th-century buildings housing cafés, from whose tables the Veronese enjoy the wide promenade. The 14th-century Palazzo delle Gran Guardia and the arched gateway, **Portone della Bra** complete the southern side. Look for Shakespeare's quote inscribed on the Portone.

Piazza dei Signori**

Palaces of the medieval della Scala family surround this elegant square. At its centre stands an 1865 statue of Dante (always with a pigeon on his head), who stayed here during his exile from Florence. Behind Dante the **Loggia del Consiglia** has frescoes on the upper façade and statues of Veronese notables. On the wall of the Palazzo de Ragione is a denunciation box, a good way to get even with enemies.

Piazza Erbe**

For more than 2000 years a market has filled this spot, which once adjoined the Roman forum. It is still a vibrant marketplace with cafés spreading into it in the evening. In the centre is the **Madonna of Verona**, actually a Roman statue given a new persona in 1368. At the end is a column surmounted by the Lion of St Mark, erected in 1528 when La Serenissima ruled. Behind the lion rises **Palazzo Mafei**, 17th-century palace of the Mafei family, its façade topped by a balustrade of Roman gods. Now a hotel and restaurant, it occupies the site of the Roman Temple to Jupiter, excavated beneath.

San Fermo Maggiore**

Erected in the 8th century to honour SS Fermo and Rustico (alleged to have been martyred in the Arena), the church was covered in the 11th century by a new one of pink brick and white tufa. The original church remains as the crypt. Originally Romanesque, San Fermo has 14th-century Gothic elements superimposed. Above the Brenzoni mausoleum are Pisanello frescoes and the ornate pulpit is also

Right
Piazza Erbe

surrounded by frescoes. Statues of saints sit in niches. Alessandro Turchi's *Adoration of the Shepherds* is in the St Joseph chapel.

San Zeno *Pza San Zeno, west of the centre, near Porta San Zeno. Open daily.*

San Zeno Major✦✦✦

San Zeno, 1123–35, is one of the finest examples of Italian Romanesque churches to be found, built of alternate layers of pink brick and white tufa. You see San Zeno's first artistic masterpiece as you enter: 48 bronze door panels, some dating from an earlier 1039 church, depicting biblical scenes and the life of San Zeno, first bishop of Verona. The portico roof is supported by columns resting on lions, below a 12th-century Wheel of Fortune rose window. The outstanding wooden, arched, polychromed ceiling of the nave dates from 1386. On the main altar is a fine triptych: *Virgin and Child with Saints* by Andrea Mantegna. A crypt contains the tomb of San Zeno, and the cloister has Romanesque and Gothic columns.

Sant'Anastasia €
Pza Sant'Anastasia.
Open Mar–Oct Mon–Sat
0930–1800 & Sun
1330–1800, Nov–Feb
1000–1300 & 1330–1600,
Sun 1300–1700.

Santa Maria in Organo
Pza Isolo Sorge, V. San
Chiara, north of the Roman
Theatre.

Santa Marie Antica € V.
Arche Scaligeri, behind Pza
dei Signori. Open daily
0730–1230, 1500–1900.
The tombs are outdoors
and always visible.

Teatro Romano €
Regaste Redentore 2; tel:
0458 000 360. Open
Sun–Sat 0900–1830, until
1500 winter and
performance nights.

Tomba di Giulietta € V.
Shakespeare off
V. del Pontiere. Open
Tue–Sun 0900–1900.

Sant'Anastasia**

The late 13th-century Gothic church has a portal carved with scenes from the life of St Peter, surmounted by 15th-century frescoes. Just inside, a pair of marble hunchbacks support holy water fonts; the one on the left (1495) is by Gabriele Caliari, father of painter Paolo Veronese. A highlight is the Pisanello fresco *St George and the Princess*.

Santa Maria in Organo*

The highlight of the 15th-century church is the 1477–1501 wood marquetry by Fra Giovanni da Verona. The inlay in the choir stalls, lectern and sacristy is outstanding for its precision and realistic perspective. Some panels appear to be shelves of books or display cupboards, others show lifelike chickens and rabbits.

Scaligeri Tombs**

The ornate pinnacled tombs of Verona's leading military family are just behind Piazza dei Signori, outside tiny **Santa Marie Antica**. The church, consecrated in 1185, became the family church of the della Scala princes. Their tombs are topped by fully armoured effigies.

Scavi Archeologici and Roman Gates**

Verona has recently uncovered more of its Roman past, and integrated them skilfully into its busy shopping district. In Via Cappello, off Piazza Erbe, are part of the Roman forum and a Roman city gate, **Porta Leoni**. On the opposite end of Piazza Erbe, Via Corso Porta Borsari leads west to the other remaining Roman gate, **Porta Borsari**.

Teatro Romano, Ponte Romano (Ponte Pietra) and Museo Archeologico**

Dating from the 1st century BC, the stage is gone but the semicircular seating area overlooking the Adige River is substantially intact. Shakespeare plays are performed here as well as other plays, ballet and jazz concerts. Above, in a converted monastery, is the **Archaeological Museum**, showing Roman statuary, mosaics, architectural fragments, pottery and glassware. Nearby, the five-arch span of **Ponte Pietra** was painstakingly restored after destruction in 1945.

Tomba di Giulietta e Museo degli Affreschi*

The heroine's 'tomb' is in a crypt of San Francesco al Corso, its stone sarcophagus empty but in atmospheric surroundings. The museum exhibits the convent frescoes. Again, a somewhat carnival atmosphere prevails outside, exemplified by the recent addition of a tree covered in paper messages.

Verona's Walls**

Verona has always been in the path of invaders, so its rulers reinforced the natural protection of the river with substantial walls. Unusually

The main shopping street is Via Mazzini, a double row of smart shops filled with the latest fashions. Around the corner, at the foot of Piazza Erbe, another walking street has more practical shops, including a department store. Look especially for gloves and fine leather goods. Each morning the vegetable market fills Piazza Erbe.

The Arena is the scene of one of Italy's major opera festivals each summer, as well as other festivals and special events. Teatro Romano is a smaller venue, perfect for Shakespeare and more intimate concerts and ballet. For arena schedules and tickets contact *Fondazione Arena di Verona, Pza Bra 28; tel: 0458 051 811; tickets: V. Dietro Anfiteatro 6/b; tel: 0458 005 151; fax: 0458 013 287.* The TIC has schedules for other venues.

Below
Veronese courtyard

complete, these date from the 12th and 13th centuries. Five 16th-century gates provide monumental entrances. These are **Porta Nova** in white marble; **Porta Pailo** in brown tufa and **Porta San Zeno**, in white tufa and brick, all three designed by Michele Sanmicheli. Across the river are **Porta San Giorgio** (also called Porta Trento), of tufa faced in white stone, and **Porta Vescovo**, enlarged in 1860, site of the liberation of Verona from Austria in 1866.

Accommodation and food

Hotel Aurora €€ *Pza Erbe; tel: 045 594 717 or 597 834; fax: 0458 010 860.* Recently renovated rooms and a terrace bar overlook the market. All rooms have en suite baths, satellite TV and air-conditioning. Parking nearby.

Due Torre Hotel Baglione €€€ *Pza Sant'Anastasia 4; tel: 0455 950 444.* The city's finest, this former palace is furnished with period antiques, each room unique. Service is impeccable, as is the restaurant.

Catullo € *V. Valerio Catullo 1, 37100; tel: 0458 002 786.* A good, basic 3rd-floor walk-up, in the centre of the old town with nearby parking. Private and shared bathrooms.

Hotel Mazzanti €–€€ *V. Mazzanti 6; tel: 0458 006 183; fax: 0458 011 262.* In the centre on the city's main shopping street, simple and clean, and with a history spanning 700 years.

Dodici Apostoli €€–€€€ *Piazzetta Tirabosco; tel: 045 596 999. Closed Sun evenings & Mon.* Verona's best-known restaurant, holding its pre-eminent position for decades with a generous list of local dishes and fine classic Italian cuisine. The wine cellars are exceptional.

Ristorante Greppia €–€€ *Vicolo Samaritana 3 off V. Mazzini; tel: 0458 004 577, closed Mon.* This family-owned restaurant overflows into the adjacent *piazzetta*, serving pasta stuffed with pumpkin, almonds and nutmeg in a light cheese sauce or tender *tortellini mascarpone* with thinly sliced *radicchio*.

Ristorante Maffei €€€ *Pza Erbe 38; tel: 0458 010 015. Closed Mon.* In the beautiful Palazzo Maffei, serving traditional dishes with flair, in an elegant setting.

Trattoria alla Pigna €–€€ *V. Pigna 4; tel: 045 800 0492.* A secret the Veronese rarely share, La Pigna serves creative dishes such as steelhead trout sauced in brandied courgette flowers, or creamy white *pancotta* with a purée of woodland berries. The atmosphere is elegant, the service personal, the menu translated.

Walking tour

P Metered parking is along the river on Lungoadige Capuleti, beyond the Ponte Aleardi bridge. A 24-hr car park is at Piazza Cittadella, just south of Piazza Bra. Some hotels in the historic centre have parking permits, but you should ask when reserving a room.

Time: 1¹/₂ hours, 3 hours with detours.

Route: Begin at PIAZZA BRÀ ❶ and the ARENA ❷, following Via Alpini, on the south side of the *piazza*, and walk east. Turn left onto Via Maffei, which becomes Stradone San Fermo. Near the river, the church of SAN FERMO ❸ is on the right. Continue toward Ponte Navi turning left on Via Leoni, which becomes Via Cappello, looking into the courtyard of CASA DI GIULIETTA ❹ before reaching PIAZZA ERBE ❺, with the **Madonna de Verona** in the centre and **Palazzo Maffei** at the opposite end. There are good **frescoes** on the buildings along the side. Follow the passageway under the LAMBERTI TOWER into PIAZZA DEI SIGNORI ❻. Opposite Dante is the entrance to the **Palazzo de Ragione** and the tower. Return to Piazza Signori, turning right and through the arch to the SCALIGERI TOMBS and **Santa Maria Antica**. Past the tombs turn left to Corso Sant'Anastasia, taking it to the right to the church of SANT'ANASTASIA ❼, opposite the **Hotel Due Torre**. (*See Detour 1 below.*) Follow Corso Sant'Anastasia back to Piazza Erbe, past Palazzo Maffei, where the street becomes Corso Porta Borsari. This was the main street of Roman Verona, and you will pass through Roman **Porta Borsari** ⓫. Here the name changes to Corso Cavour which you follow past ARCO DEI GAVI ⓬ to CASTELVECCHIO ⓭ and PONTE SCALIGERO. (*See Detour 2 below.*) Opposite the castle gate, Via Roma will return you to Piazza Brà ❶, where you can visit the MUSEO LAPIDARIO MAFFEIANO ⓮.

Detour 1: To see the DUOMO ❽, take Via Duomo from the small *piazza* in front of Sant'Anastasia, walking north three blocks. Follow the street behind the *duomo*, crossing PONTE PIETRA ❾ to the ROMAN THEATRE and MUSEO ARCHEOLOGICO ❿. Backtrack to Sant'Anastasia ❼.

Detour 2: From the gate of Castelvecchio ⓭ turn right and follow the building around to the right, onto Regaste San Zeno, following it along the river. Follow Via Barbarini when it angles off to the left. This long but pleasant walk takes you to SAN ZENO ⓯. Follow Corso Milano a short way to see **Porta San Zeno**. Backtrack to Castelvecchio ⓭.

Verona

300m
300 yds

↑ Venezia

Museo Archeologico
S. Giovanni in Valle
Giardino Giusti
Teatro Romano
S. Paolo
Palazzo Pompei
Università

Santa Maria in Organo
Casa di Romeo
Santa Anastasia
Palazzo de Ragione & Lamberti Tower
Scaligeri Tombs
Casa di Giulietta
Piazza dei Signori
Piazza Erbe
Scavi Archeologici & Roman Gates
San Fermo Major (Maggiore)
Ponte Romeo (Ponte Pietra)
Santa Maria Matricolare
S. Eufemia
S. Nicolò
L'Arena di Verona
Municipio
SS. Trinità
Tomba di Giulietta e Museo degli Affreschi

Duomo
Porta Borsari
Piazza Brà
Palazzo d. Gran Guardia
Porta Nuova

Arco dei Gavi
Museo Lapidario Maffeiano
S. Teresa d. Scalzi

Vittorio Veneto
BORGO TRENTO
Piazza Arsenale
Ponte Scaligero
Castelvecchio
Verona's Walls

Giardino Zoologico
Porta Palio
Stazione F.S. Porta Nuova

San Zeno Major (Maggiore)
Piazza S. Zeno

Piscina

↗ Mantova

Valpolicella and Pasubio Valley

Ratings

Castles	●●●●●
Scenery	●●●●●
Vineyards	●●●●●
Geology	●●●●○
History	●●●●○
Mountains	●●●●○
Nature	●●●●○
Architecture	●●●○○

The region along the great sweeping curve of the River Adige has been inhabited since prehistoric times, with neolithic settlements followed by those of the Etruscans and later Romans. The Ostrogoths and Longobards also left their mark, as did the Scaligeri of Verona, the Venetians and even, briefly, Napoleon. The Valpolicella region, formed by the valleys of the Fumane, Negrar and Marano rivers as they flow south from the Lessini mountains, is home to some of the most popular Italian red wines. Along with its vineyards are natural attractions and some surprisingly rugged terrain. Few more dramatic roads challenge the driver than that through the Pasubio Valley, to the north. The Adige Valley opens the main route from the Mediterranean through the Dolomites to Bavaria, via the Brenner Pass; its rich history evidenced in the towns of Avio and Ala.

ALA❖❖

ⓘ Informazione *tel: 0464 671 001. Open seasonally.*

ⓟ Park in Largo Guiseppi Vicentina, as the road enters the old town.

ⓗ Cantina Sociale *V. Bolzano; tel: 0464 671 168. Open Mon–Fri.*

ⓒ Unusual painted ceramics are sold at **Il Coccio** *V. Carerra 11.*

The Romans saw immediately that Ala's location controlled the narrow valley, the only passage north through the Dolomites. It was the Venetians, however, who launched the industry that brought Ala its fortune and its fame. This was the production of silk, which led in turn to high-quality velvet, a necessity to the courts and nobility of all Europe. Eight silk spinning mills, three dye works and other manufactories lay along the short Roggia River, where it dropped into the Adige. The palaces of the velvet merchants still grace Ala's streets, several with good stonework, some with frescoes, many with fine wooden doors. More frescoes are inside **San Giovanni❖**, which also has ceramic stations of the cross. At the foot of Via Santa Catarina is the baroque **Palazzo de Pizzini❖❖**, housing a piano museum, rarely open except for concerts. In the summer, actors and musicians in period costume recreate scenes from Ala's history and lead tours of the palaces. The **Cantina Sociale** winery is open for tastings. North of

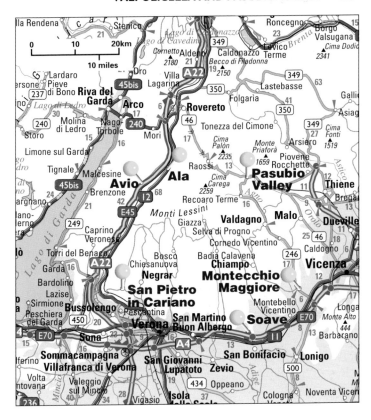

Below
Balcony and door, Ala

town, along the old Roman road, stands a shrine to **St Anthony***, an onion-domed Baroque church.

Accommodation and food in Ala

Viennese € *S12 near Ala turn-off; tel: 0464 672 530; fax: 0464 672 312.* A plain, but pleasant hotel with access for guests with disabilities and parking.

Bar Di's Club €–€€ *Piazzetta Erbe 2; tel: 0464 674 106. Open Tue–Sun 0700–0100.* The best lunches in town, with delectable *bruschetta* and *focaccia* sandwiches; full dinner menu, as well.

Trattoria La Luna Piena € *V. Carera 7. No reservations. Closed Mon, Sun evening, Tue lunch.* The wide variety on the menu may include hearty country fare, such as sausage and beans or more sophisticated dishes like *scallopini* in balsamic vinegar.

AVIO✦✦✦

Cantina Sociale
V. Dante 14; tel: 0464
684 008. Open Mon–Fri
0800–1200, 1400–1800.

Castello di Avio €
Tel: 0464 684 453. Open
Tue–Sun 1000–1300,
1400–1800, Oct–Dec closes
1700, closed Jan.

**Maresi Guerrieri
Gonzaga** Borghetto; tel:
0464 689 004. Open
Mon–Fri 0800–1200,
1400–1700.

**Buy local cheeses at
the co-operative,**
V. Al Parco 10, Sabbionara
d'Avio; tel: 0464 684 641.

Castello di Avio✦✦✦ guards the town and valley from a majestic mountainside perch, posing for photos with its tall tower and vineyards enclosed by a ring of well-preserved walls. It makes the transition from a medieval fortress to the more liveable palace-castles of the early Renaissance. Frescoes are in the main tower and guard room, the latter cycle a rare view of 13th-century men-at-arms. A short, steep path back to the car park leads past a small cascade. The local **Cantina Sociale** is open for wine tastings, as is **Maresi Guerrieri Gonzaga✦**, in nearby Borghetto. The latter winery has an interesting museum of old farm equipment.

Food in Avio

Ristorante Castellum Ava €–€€ Avio Castle; tel: 0464 684 299. No views from inside the castle walls, but a pleasant arbour-covered terrace and good veal and lamb choices.

Dai Menegheti € V. Morielle 37; Sabbionara d'Avio; tel: 0464 684 646. Closed Mon, Tue. Antonelli Gianni presents the freshest and best of local produce.

Trattoria Castelbarco € V. Castelbarco, Sabbionara d'Avio; tel: 0464 684 134. Traditional local dishes, in an informal setting.

MONTECCHIO MAGGIORE✦

Informazione Pza
San Paolo, Alta
Montecchio; tel: 0444 696
546.

**Castello di
Giulietta and
Castello di Romeo**
V. Castelli; tel: 044 496 172.
Open Wed afternoon, Mon
0930–2330. Interiors open
occasionally.

**Villa Cordellina-
Lombardi €** V. Lovara 36;
tel: 0444 696 085. Open
mid-Apr–mid-Oct Tue–Fri
0900–1300, Sat–Sun
0900–1200, 1500–1800.

Opposite
Avio Castle

Travellers following the trail of Juliet should stop at the two castles that local lore hold to be the homes of the supposed rival families. They are named accordingly, **Castello di Giulietta✦** and **Castello di Romeo✦**. Legend or no, they are pretty castles on their vineyard-green hills, with views to the north from the terrace. Just east in a garden park is the Palladian-style **Villa Cordellina-Lombardi✦✦**, built in the early 1700s, with large Tiepolo frescoes in the central reception hall. A 6km trip northward leads to **Arzignano✦** and an interesting black stone castle.

Accommodation and food in Montecchio Maggiore

Castelli €€–€€€ Vle Trieste 89; tel: 0444 697 366; fax: 0444 490 489. A full range of services and amenities, as well as a restaurant €€–€€€, open evenings only.

PASUBIO VALLEY❖❖

ℹ Informazione V. Roma 25, Recoaro Terme; tel: 044 575 070.

Monte Pasubio was one of the hardest fought battle lines of the First World War, and the traces of war are still found along its heights. Defensive positions carved out by the Italian and Austrian armies still pockmark the mountainsides. The route through the Pasubio Valley is misleading on a map. Although it follows the river, don't picture a serene valley road; instead, the narrow (but well-surfaced) road is carved out of the steep bank, hundreds of metres above the river. The trip is much less hair-raising if travelled from southeast to northwest, on the inside of the S46. The scenery (which the driver must use a lay-by to enjoy) is splendid throughout. Above the top of **Passo Pian di Fugazze** (1159m) is a war memorial, the **Ossuary Pasubio**❖. The remains of gun emplacements and fortifications are also visible, and a ruined fort is above **San Antonio**. **Recoaro Terme**❖ is an old spa town laid out in well-kept parks and gardens. It is also an active winter sports centre, with a tramway, ski-lifts and cross-country trails centred at **Recoaro Mille**❖.

Accommodation and food in the Pasubio Valley

Carla €€ V. Cavour 55, Recoaro Terme; tel: 0445 780 700; fax: 0445 780 777. A modest hotel with good local dishes in its restaurant **€€**, closed Sun evening & Mon.

SOAVE❖❖❖

ℹ IAT Pza Antenna 2; tel: 0457 680 648; www.comunesoave.it. Open summer only.

🅿 Parking **€** outside the town gates, in the large piazza, also at the castle.

🏰 La Rocca € V. Castello Scaligero; tel: 0457 860 036. Open Tue–Sun.

One of the finest of the several castles that dot the countryside around Verona, Soave's **La Rocca**❖❖❖ commands and encircles the town. Crenellations march in neat rows down the hillside and around the cluster of stone buildings. The castle, sometimes inaccurately called 'Rocca Scaligeri', actually predates that Verona family, who enlarged it in the 1200s. Inside the rooms are furnished to the early Renaissance. Soave, first settled by the Romans, but built by the Longobards, has several distinguished buildings within the walled town. On the way into town, you cannot miss the huge plant whence Bolla's popular white wine makes its way around the world.

Accommodation and food in Soave

Al Gambero € Corso Vittorio Emanuele; tel/fax: 0457 680 010. Closed Tue evening, Wed, late Aug. A pleasant restaurant serving local dishes, with 12 comfortable guest rooms **€**.

VALPOLICELLA WINE TOWNS✦✦✦

APT *Pza delle Erbe 38, Verona; tel: 0458 000 065.*

Vivere Molino *V. Bacilieri 1; tel: 0457 702 185; www.cascatemolina.it*

Casa Vinicola Sartori *V. Casette 2, Negrar; tel: 0456 028 001; www.sartoriwinery.com*

Museo Botanico della Lessinia *Parco delle Cascate; tel: 0457 720 145.*

Tommasi *V. Ronchetto 2, Pedemonte; tel: 0457 701 266.*

Villa Mosconi-Bertani *Novare (Negrar); tel: 0456 011 211. Open Mon–Fri 0900–1200, 1400–1800, Sat 0900–1200.*

Palio del Recioto *festival, mid-Apr, Negrar; tel: 0457 500 033.*

Those who enjoy wines will find many vineyards in the Valpolicella region where they can sample the product; others will enjoy the scenery, villas, churches and natural attractions. The primary town is **San Pietro in Cariano**, and the whole area is scattered with distinguished villas. **Villa Mosconi-Bertani**, in Novare, was built by a follower of Palladio; Bertani wines, sold at the villa, are among the Valpolicella's finest and you can schedule a tasting €€€, with accompanying food. You can dine and spend the night at the Renaissance **Villa da Quar**, in Pedemonte, listed as an Italian National Monument (*see Accommodation below*). The 18th-century **Villa Rizzardi**✦✦, in Negrar, has particularly fine Italianate and English gardens. Nearby, at **Casa Vinicola Sartori**✦✦, you can visit the gardens and taste the wines. Quarries at **Sant'Ambrogio di Valpolicella** are the source of the most prized building stone used in Verona's churches and even the arena. **San Giorgio**, just to the north, is known for the Longobard Romanesque **Pieve San Giorgio**✦✦, with a fine cloister and a museum showing Roman and earlier finds, along with fossils. Inside the church is the rare 8th-century Longobard **ciborio**✦✦. **Molina Falls Park**✦✦, in the Fumane valley, includes several waterfalls, with nature trails along a wooded brook. The **Museo Botanico della Lessinia**✦ identifies the many indigenous plants. The most remarkable natural site is the huge **Ponte di Veja**✦✦✦, a natural bridge that formed the entry to a cave where prehistoric artefacts were found. The entire area is filled with fossils, and the **Museo dei Fossili**✦✦ in Sant'Anna has a 7m shark, 70 million years old.

Accommodation and food in the Valpolicella wine towns

Villa del Quar €€€ *V. Quar 12, Pedemonte (Verona); tel: 0456 800 681; fax: 045 680 0604; www.hotelvilladelquar.it.* Well-appointed guest rooms in a beautifully maintained Renaissance villa. The Michelin-starred Arquade €€€ restaurant is among the finest in northern Italy.

Ai Parcheggi € *Parco della Cascate; tel: 0457 720 078.* Right at the entrance to the park, this bar/restaurant is a good refreshment stop after walking the trails to waterfalls.

Trattoria da Nicola € *V. Valle 41, Monte, Sant'Ambrogio di Valpolicella; tel: 0457 760 180.* Try the local *sopressa* salami as a starter.

Trattoria dalla Rosa Alda € *Strada Garibaldi 4, San Giorgio di Valpolicello; tel: 0457 701 018.* Friendly *trattoria* with local dishes, such as wild rabbit or pheasant with *polenta*.

Suggested tour

Informazione
Vle Trento, Valdagno;
tel: 0445 401 190.

A road tunnel connects Valdagno with Schio and S46, a faster but less scenic route to the Pasubio Valley.

Villa Trissino Marzotto €€
Trissino; tel: 0445 962 029.
Open Mon–Fri by appointment.

Total distance: 202km, with detours 342km.

Time: 5 hours' driving. Allow 3 days for the main route, 4 days with detours. Those with limited time should concentrate on Valpolicella.

Links: The Lake Garda route (*see page 115*) begins a few kilometres west of Verona, via A4. The Alto Adige route (*see page 144*) begins on S12 in Rovigo. Vicenza (*see page 215*) is close to Montecchio Maggiore via S11 or A4.

Route: Leave Verona ❶ (*see page 118*), heading east and following signs to **Venice** (Venezia), on the A4 *autostrada* (thus avoiding frequent traffic tie-ups on S11), exiting at **SOAVE** ❷. (*See Detours 1 & 2 below and on page 135.*) Follow S11 east, turning north (left) on S246, following signs to **MONTECCHIO MAGGIORE** ❸ (44km). Continue north on S246, signposted **Valdagno**. Although visits require advance booking, **Villa Trissino Marzotto**✦✦ is worth the effort of a 2km sidetrack, left, signposted to **Trissino**. Two villas, one an atmospheric ruin, are set in a splendid Italianate garden park. Continue north on S246 to **Valdagno** (20km). Just northwest, follow signs to **Montaga Spaccata**✦✦✦, with a 100m-deep gorge and waterfall. From Valdagno, follow the scenic valley north to **Recoaro Terme**, where you turn right to climb the 671m **Passo Xon**, following signs to **Valli del Pasubio** (23km). Here you enter the historic **PASUBIO VALLEY** ❹, and, after turning west (left), begin climbing immediately up the **Passo Pian delle Fugazze**. As the road levels out on the western side, the river valley lies hundreds of metres directly below. This scenery continues all the way to the outskirts of **Rovereto** (*see page 139*), where you reach the old Brenner Pass road, S12 (39km). Head south (left) on S12, to **ALA** ❺, whose historic centre lies just east of the main road. From Ala, continue south on S12 to **AVIO** ❻, following brown signs up winding narrow streets to the castle. Returning to S12, continue south through the Adige valley to **Domegliara**, turning north (left) to **Sant'Ambrogio di Valpolicella**, and the vineyards of **VALPOLICELLA WINE TOWNS** (49km). Continue on the unnumbered road east to **San Pietro in Cariano**, past **Pedemonte** and back to S12 just outside Verona, your starting point (25km).

Detour 1: To explore the **Monti Lessini plateau**, follow the unnumbered road west from the north side of Soave, beyond the castle, or take S11 west, in either case following signs to **Colognola ai Colli**. Turn north (right) following signs to **Tregnago** and **Giazza**✦✦, in a beautiful setting along a valley. It is one of several in Monti Lessini plateau that were settled by Bavarian farmers in the 13th century. The local **Museo Etnografico**✦ (*V. dei Boschi 62, open daily summer, Sat–Sun winter, €*) tells their story. Backtrack south to S11 and **Soave** (80km).

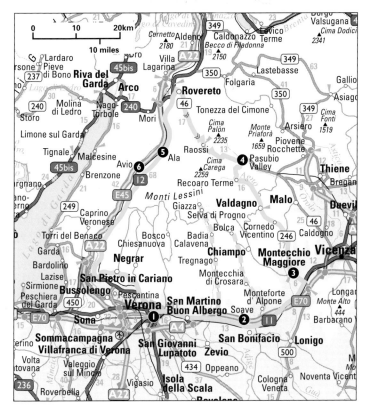

Museo di Fossili €
V. san Giovanni
Battista. Open Tue–Sun.

La Terrazza €€€
V. Cesare 1,
Montecchia di Crosara; tel:
0457 450 940. The
panoramic view vies on
even terms with the food
– look for the speciality:
scallops with black truffles
in port.

IAT Pza della Chiesa
34, Bosco Chiesanuova;
tel: 0457 050 088. Open
year round.

Detour 2: To explore another of the long valleys that drop from the Monti Lessini plateau, follow S11 east from Soave to a turning north (left) signposted **Monteforte d'Alpone**. Head north along the river through **Monteccia di Crosara** to **Bolca**✦✦, on the plateau. This entire area is a fossil centre (many are in Verona's Museo Civico) and **Museo di Fossili**✦✦ has a large collection of reptiles, fish and plants. Ask at the museum for directions for the 3km loop to quarries where fossils were found. Return by the same road to S11 (60km).

Also worth exploring

Any one of the valleys that stretch between the Lessini plateau and S12 between Verona and Vicenza bear investigation. In **Grezzana**✦ is the 13th-century church **Santa Maria**✦ with Romanesque font and *campanili* of multi-coloured limestone. At **Cuzzano**✦, nearby, is baroque **Villa Allegri-Arvedi**✦, built in the 1600s (*tel: 045 907 045, open Tue morning only*). South, **Santa Maria in Stelle**✦✦ is a Roman *nymphaeum*, beside a church. **Bosco Chiesanuova**✦✦ is a popular ski resort with downhill lifts and cross-country trails. East of Bosco, near **Camposilvano**, is **Valle delle Sfingi**✦✦, filled with large rock formations.

The Alto Adige

Ratings

Castles	●●●●●
Geology	●●●●●
Scenery	●●●●●
Vineyards	●●●●●
History	●●●●○
Mountains	●●●●○
Architecture	●●●○○
Villages	●●●○○

The Adige's valley was for centuries the main route from northern Europe to the Mediterranean. Its strategic and commercial importance was tremendous, and its history is filled with the movements of traders, travellers and armies. The legacy of that history is the astonishing string of castles that seem to crown every crag. Although today's traveller sees many of these – the great white walls of Besano and elegant towers of Avio are hard to miss – dozens more hide in side valleys, or simply blend into the rocky landscape. Mountains rise on every side, and on their lower slopes and protected valleys grow vineyards that produce outstanding wines: red and white, dry and sweet, still and *frissante*. Even without the dinosaur footprints, the medieval frescoes, the hiking trails and the magnificent views, the traveller could spend a very pleasant holiday here just seeking its wines and castles.

BOLZANO✦✦✦

ℹ **APT** *Pza Walther 8; tel: 0471 307 000, www.bolzano-bozen.it. Open posted hours Mon–Fri 0900–1830, in reality closed 1230–1400, Sat 0900–1230.*

Club Alpino Italiano *Pza Erbe 46, has information on hiking and climbing.*

Ⓟ *Parking € is plentiful in underground car parks at Piazza Walther and the bus terminal nearby.*

Ringed by mountains, Bolzano looks more Austrian than Italian – not surprising, since the city spent its formative centuries under Austrian and Bavarian rulers. The eye-catching patterned roof and carved spire of the **duomo**✦ overlook spacious **Piazza Walther**, Bolzano's lively centre of everyday life. Inside, the *duomo* is soaring Gothic, with fine polychrome and gilt carving in the ambulatory chapel. At nearby **Chiesa dei Domenicani**✦✦, the Dominican cloister is decorated in 15th-century frescoes; those in Capella di San Giovanni are from the Giotto school. Follow Via Goethe from the Dominican church, through **Piazza delle Erbe**✦✦, bounded by an assortment of architectural styles and enlivened by a morning market. Directly beyond, Via dei Francescani leads to **Chiesa de Francescani**✦, a 14th-century church with a fine Gothic wooden altarpiece and frescoed cloisters.

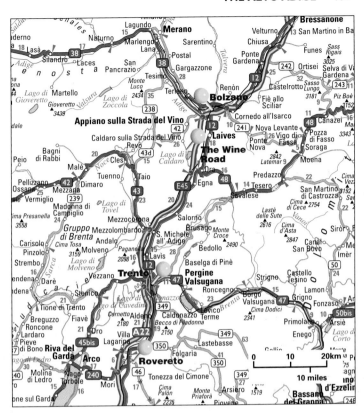

Across the river in **Parrocchiale di Gries**✣✣ is an exceptional polychrome carved altarpiece from the 15th century, along with a Romanesque wooden crucifix, dating from the 1200s. The museum exhibit few visitors can resist seeing is 'Frozen Fritz', the 5300-year-old man found on a nearby glacier. The Ice Man and his equipment are displayed, along with other pre-medieval finds, at the **Museo Archeologico**✣✣. Opposite, at the **Museo Civico**✣, you can learn about local life through arts, costumes and furnishings. **Castel Roncolo**✣✣ presents a rare picture of 13th-century life, with the largest collection of medieval secular frescoes in existence. Details of dress, jousting tournaments and court life cover the walls of several rooms. For many, the greatest pleasure of Bolzano is simply wandering the streets and squares of its old town, with their ornate buildings, cafés and shops. **Via dei Bottai, Piazza del Municipio** and **Via dei Portici** all have frescoed façades, balconies and plasterwork.

Accommodation and food in Bolzano

Albergo Figli €–€€ *Pza del Grano 9; tel/fax: 0471 978 412; e-mail: info@figl.net; www.figl.net.* Starkly modern, the hotel is centrally

🄝 **Chiesa dei Domenicani** *Open Mon–Sat 0930–1730.*

Duomo *Open Mon–Fri 0945–1200, 1400–1700, Sat 0945–1200.*

Museo Archeologico € *V. Museo; www.iceman.it. Open Tue–Sun 1000–1800, Thur until 2000.*

Museo Civico € *V. Cassa di Risparmio. Open Tue–Sat 0900–1200, 1430–1730.*

Parrocchiale di Gries *Corso Liberta. Open Apr–Oct Mon–Fri 1030–1200, 1430–1600.*

located in a pedestrian area, parking € at nearby Garage Walther 3. Café with outdoor seating.

Hotel Greif €€€ *Pza Walther; tel: 0471 318 000; fax: 0471 318 148; e-mail: info@greif.it; www.greif.it.* The stylishly designed rooms may be traditional or modern in decor, all have computer workstations, some whirlpools. Excellent restaurant €€€ serves both Italian and German dishes, including smoked venison.

Ristorante Argentieri €€–€€€ *V. Argentieri 14.* Smart restaurant with pavement tables and an upscale menu.

Vogele € *V. Goethe 3; tel: 0471 973 938.* Small restaurant popular with local people serving home-style regional specialities.

Right
Piazza Erbe, Bolzano

Rovereto*

APT *V. Dante 63; tel: 0464 430 363, www.apt.rovereto.tn.it. Open daily.*

Parking *is at Largo Posta, and at the foot of Viale de Colli at the base of the old town; limited parking behind the castle.*

Castel Beseno € *Besenello; tel: 0464 834 600. Open Apr–Oct Tue–Sun 0900–1200, 1400–1730.*

Museo Civico € *Borgo S Caterina 41. Open Tue–Sun 0930–1200, 1500–1800.*

Museo Storico, Castello de Rovereto € *Open Jul–Sept Tue–Sun 0830–1830, mid-Mar–Jun, Oct–Nov Tue–Sun 0800–1230, 1400–1800.*

Santa Maria Assunta *Villa Lagarina. Open Mon–Sat 0900–1300, 1500–1900, Sun for worship.*

Vini Vallagarina *V. Brancolino 4, Nogaredo; tel: 0464 412 073. Open Mon–Fri 0800–1200, 1400–1800.*

St Mark's lion on the old city gate reminds travellers that they are back in the lands of *La Serenissima* – the Venetian Empire. Crowning a hill, 13th-century **Castello de Rovereto**** gives views over the red-roofed town to mountains that rise steeply from the Adige valley. Inside is an extraordinary history of the impact of the First World War on the whole of northern Italy. Artefacts, photographs and posters are so graphic and well-arranged that you don't need to read Italian. Look especially at the racks of photographs showing the liberation of towns you might visit – Trento, Gorizia, Riva and Udine. **Strada degli Artiglieri*** is named after the First World War artillery that Italian forces dragged and pushed up this steep route, literally digging their defensive positions into the mountainside. Memorials to the men lost here, among them a Count of Savoy, line the road. Following signs to the dinosaur tracks (*see below*), almost under the power line, a short trail leads to one of the defensive caves. Each evening Rovereto remembers the thousands of lives lost, with the ringing of the **Maria Dolens**, a huge bell cast from cannons contributed by both sides.

Greek and Roman archaeology, local dinosaur finds and silk manufacture are themes of the **Museo Civico***, much of it donated by archaeologist Paolo Orsi. To see the **dinosaur tracks**** on a mountainside south of town, follow signs for the **Ossario di Castel Dante** (war memorial), then follow Strada degli Artiglieri to the car park, clearly marked. The first footprint is about a 15-minute walk from the road. Along with distinct imprints of single tracks are entire paths of footprints – about 350 – dating back 200 million years. Although it may seem presumptuous for tiny Villa Lagarina, across the Adige, to bill itself as 'Little Salzburg', its church of **Santa Maria Assunta**** was designed by the same artists who created Salzburg Cathedral. The fine baroque interior has elaborate stuccowork and a high altar of coloured marble. To its south are several wineries, including **Vini Vallagarina***, where you can taste and purchase all the local varieties. A short distance north of Rovereto; **Castel Beseno***** covers an entire hilltop, a magnificent sight from the valley below. One of the largest castles south of the Alps, it was owned by the Trapp family until 1973. Fortifications enclose three medieval compounds, 'modernised' to reflect Renaissance refinements. After seeing Palazzo dei Mesi's 15th-century frescoes and the inner courtyards, you can walk the defensive walls surrounding a large tournament field.

Accommodation and food in Rovereto

Leon d'Oro €€ *V. Tacchi 2, 38068; tel: 0464 437 333.* Located in the centre of town, all rooms are comfortable, well furnished and have private bath. Parking available.

Above
Old town, Rovereto

Hotel Rovereto €–€€ *Corso Rosmini 82d, 38068; tel/fax: 0464 439 644.* Traditional hotel, well located between highway and centre, with indoor car park.

Al Borgo €€€ *V. Garibaldi 13; tel: 0464 436 300. Closed Sun evening & Mon.* Pricey, but known as one of the region's best, serving dishes such as quail roasted in acacia honey and balsamic vinegar.

Novecento €€–€€€ *Corso Rosmini 82; tel: 0464 435 222. Closed Sun.* The *canederle* *(gnocchi)* with three cheeses is excellent, as are *tortellini* and freshwater fish.

Vecchia Trattoria Scala della Torre 7 €–€€ *Scala della Torre 5, off Pza della Erbe; tel: 0464 437 100. Open 1200–1430, 1930–2100.* Veal *tonato*, wild boar with *polenta*, and a nod to its northern clientele with goulash.

TRENTO❖❖

ⓘ APT *V. Manci 2; tel: 0461 983 880; www.apt.trento.it. Open Mon–Sat 0900–1800, Sun 0900–1300.*

Ⓟ Parking € is at Piazza della Mostra, opposite Castello Buonconsiglio. A combination ticket €€ includes Castello Buonconsiglio museums and Castel Beseno.

Ⓗ Basilica di San Vigilio € *Pza Duomo. Open Mon–Sat 1000–1200, 1430–1800.*

Castello Buonconsiglio❖❖ houses several museums in a walled complex that includes the 13th-century **Castelvecchio**, 16th-century **Palazzo Magno**, the **Torre Grande** and the **Torre dell'Aquila**. Once the residence of the prince bishops, the buildings not only contain their considerable art collections, but are themselves works of art, especially the richly frescoed Castelvecchio. Frescoes also adorn the rooms throughout the Palazzo Magno, but the most remarkable are in Torre dell'Aquila, a beautiful fresco cycle dating 1400–1539, known as the *Ciclo dei Mesi*, or Cycle of Months, hard to find without asking. Also at the castle is **Museo Storico**❖, covering local history from Napoleon to the Second World War, when Trento was a centre for the resistance.

Trento is best known for the Council of Trent, which took place in the castle and **duomo**❖❖ 1545–1563, and began the Counter Reformation. Its decrees were announced from before the large wooden crucifix in the side chapel. Unusual are the colonnaded stairs in this Lombard Romanesque church. In the 13th century, it replaced the earlier **Basilica de San Vigilio**❖❖, still beneath the present *duomo*. Enter from the north transept to see fragments of mosaics and the tombs, including that of San Vigilio. Adjoining the *duomo* is the

Castello Buonconsiglio €
V. B Clesio 5. Open Oct–Mar
0900–1200, 1400–1700
summer, Apr–Sept
0900–1200, 1400–1730,
actual hours may vary.

Giardino Botanico Alpino € Rifugio Viote,
Monte Bondone. Open
Jun–Sept 0900–1200,
1430–1700.

Museo degli Usi e Costumi € V. Edmondo
Mach 1; tel: 0461 650 314;
www.delta.it/mucgt. Open
Tue–Sun 0900–1230,
1430–1800.

Museo dell'Aeronautica Gianni Caproni €
V. Lidorno 3, Mattarrello at
the airport; tel: 0461 944
888. Open Tue–Sun
0900–1300, 1400–1800,
handicapped accessible.

Museo Diocesano €
Pza della Duomo. Open
Mon–Sat 0930–1230,
1430–1800.

Museo Storico €
V. B Clessio 3;
www.museostorico.tn.it.
Open Oct–Mar 0900–1200,
1400–1700 summer,
Apr–Sept 0900–1200,
1400–1730.

Museo Tridentino di Scienze Naturali €
Via Calepina 14;
www.itc.it/mtsn.
Open Tue–Sun 0900–1230,
1430–1800.

Palazzo Pretorio, a 13th-century Episcopal palace housing the **Museo Diocesano***. The diocesan treasury includes 15th–19th-century goldwork and outstanding 16th-century Belgian tapestries, hung in the cathedral during the council meetings. In the centre of Piazza della Duomo is the baroque **Neptune Fountain**, and facing the square are façades with 16th-century frescoes. Wall frescoes are also along Via Manci and Via Belenzani. On nearby Via Cavour another Council of Trent venue, **Santa Maria Maggiore**, has good frescoes in the ceiling and over-altar dome.

Museo Tridentino di Scienze Naturali* contains minerals, fossils, dinosaur footprints, local reptiles, birds, mammals and botanical displays, mostly relating to the Dolomite region. Look for the 16th-century frescoed ceilings in rooms flanking the entrance hall. **Museo dell'Aeronautica Gianni Caproni**** contains a remarkable collection of 20 planes built 1910–80, nine of which are the only surviving examples in the world – the personal collection of pioneering aircraft designer Gianni Caproni. Multi-media exhibits show the history of flight using early flight movies with English captions. On Monte Bondone, high above the Adige west of Trento, is **Giardino Botanico Alpino***, near Rifugio Viote. The garden displays over 2000 species of Alpine flora, with eco-system signage in English. In San Michele all'Adige, north of Trento, **Museo degli Usi e Costumi della Gente Trentina**** is housed in a 12th-century Augustinian monastery that was once a hospice for Rome-bound pilgrims. One of the most important ethnographic museums in all of Europe, it contains displays and artefacts that show the farming, wine-making, metal-working, weaving, wood carving, pottery, costumes and many other facets of local culture over several centuries, with English signage.

Accommodation and food in Trento

Hotel America €€ V. Torre Verde 50, 38100; tel: 0461 983 010; fax: 0461 230 603; e-mail: hotel_america@iol.it. Close to the cathedral and to the castle, rooms are pleasant and the staff welcoming. The hotel has a good restaurant €–€€ with local specialities. Parking available.

Hotel Buonconsiglio €€–€€€ V. Romagnosi 14–16; tel: 0461 272 888; fax: 0461 272 889; e-mail: hotelhbtin.it; www.kompassitalia.com. A fine and genial hotel, well situated, with many services and enclosed parking.

Antica Trattoria due Mori € V. San Marco 11; tel: 0461 984 251. Closed Mon. Innovative dishes, such as risotto with arrugola and gnocchi with pumpkin blossoms. It's near the castle.

Rifugio Viote € Viote, Monte Bondone; tel: 0461 948 162. A pleasant bar and restaurant at an altitude of over 1500m.

Ristorante la Cantinota € *V. San Marco 22/24; tel: 0461 238 527. Closed Thur.* Venison marinated with lavender and served with *polenta*, courgette blossoms filled with herbed *ricotta* – not your ordinary chef.

Ristorante Le Tire-Bouchon €€ *V. Milano 148; tel: 0461 261 456. Closed Sun. Open 1830–0100.* You might find goat cheese *gnocchi* with a salad of fresh herbs and an entrée of loin of rabbit with *pignoli* and thyme.

THE WINE ROAD❖❖

❶ APT *Caldaro sul Strada del Vino, Pza Principale 8; tel: 0471 963 169. Open Mon–Sat 1930–1200, 1430–1700.*

❶ Gewürztraminer tasting May, Termeno. A chance to compare this wine from around the world, in the town of its origin.

The road west of the Adige below Bolzano is designated 'Strada del Vino' (the Wine Road), for good reason. Vineyards cover entire landscapes, broken only by picturesque towns clustered around onion-domed churches. The attractions are the scenery, the castles and the wineries, where you can taste and often dine, under leafy arbours. About midway is **Lake Caldaro**, the warmest lake for swimming in all the Alps, and well-equipped with lakefront amusements and walking trails. A wine museum, at **Caldaro**, traces the history of wine growing here from Roman times. At nearby **Castelvecchio** (Altenburg) are the ruins of the 4th-century church of **St Peter**, and a view of the lake and the Sud Tyrol peaks.

Castles overlook every valley: in **Appiano** there are 12 and in **Missiano** you can stand on the terrace of **Castel Corba**❖ (Schloss Korb) and see two others along the same slope. A trail connects the three. From Castel Corba's terrace is one of the region's loveliest panoramas, dropping away to vineyards that stretch across the broad valley to the tree-clad foothills. Beyond, as though standing on tiptoes to see, are the snow-covered Dolomites; and in the middle, where the mountains break for the Adige, lies Bolzano, compressed into a tidy red and white mosaic. **San Paolo**❖ is a typical village, its rural Renaissance buildings surrounding a parish church with a melodious peal of bells. The cloister churchyard seems more like a garden, with fresh flowers decorating graceful iron crosses.

Accommodation and food on the Wine Road

Hotel Schloss Korb €€€ *Missiano, Appiano; tel: 0471 636 000; fax: 0471 636 033.* Surrounded by vineyards, with views over Bolzano and the Dolomites, the setting doesn't get better. The charm of a medieval castle, with all mod cons and an outstanding restaurant.

Opposite
Piazza Duomo,
Trento

Suggested tour

 A mountain lift climbs from **Caldaro** to the summit of **Passo di Mendola** for a 360-degree panoramic view, saving a tortuous climb via S42.

Total distance: 96km, with detours 154km.

Time: 2½ hours' driving. Allow 3 days for the main route, 4 days with detours. If time is limited concentrate on Bolzano and Trento.

Links: From Verona (*see page 118*), follow the Valpolicella and Pasubio Valley route (*see page 134*) to Rovereto. To Cortina d'Ampezzo, follow the Dolomite Road route (*see page 152*) from Bolzano.

Route: Follow S12 north from **ROVERETO** ❶, continuing to **TRENTO** ❷, along the historic Adige Valley. Mountains rise dramatically on either side, more scenic than the valley floor's industry (21km). (*See Detour 1 below.*) North of **San Michele all'Adige**, at Salorno, follow brown signs for the **THE WINE ROAD** ❸ (*Strada del Vino*) left over the river, turning right to **Termeno** and **Lago di Caldaro**. Continue north to the town of **Caldaro**. Continue north to **Appiano** and follow the small road left, signposted **San Paolo**. At the church, bear right to **Missiano**. Backtrack to S42 which leads left into **BOLZANO** ❹ (75km). (*See Detour 2 on page 145.*)

Detour 1: For a more challenging and scenic drive, circle the slopes of **Monte Paradiso**, between Rovereto and Trento. On a map the road looks like a plate of spaghetti as it twists through the mountains. At **Besenello**, turn east (right) onto S350, which winds to **Folgaria** and

Below
Vineyards and church, San Paolo

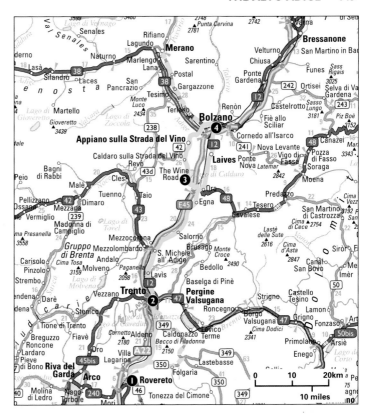

over the **Passo di Sommo**. Turn north (left) on S349 through **Centa San Nicolo** to **Trento** (48km).

Detour 2: Before entering **Bolzano**, turn left onto S38, signposted **Merano**. The road follows the Adige to the spa town favoured by Austrian empress Elisabeth. The town is a centre for winter sports and Alpine walking, and for garden lovers, who stroll the flower-bordered promenades and visit the new botanical gardens at **Castel Trauttmansdorff**. Backtrack on S38 or follow the unnumbered local road on the Adige's west bank back to Bolzano (52km).

Also worth exploring

East of Trento is a beautiful area of mountains and lakes reached via S47 or the smaller S349. S347 leads to the **Val Sugana** and eventually to **Bassano del Grappa** (*see page 203*). In Lavarone on S349 is a rare remaining highland Austrian fort, **Forte Belvedere**, a three-storey pillbox from the First World War. Its interior is largely intact, as are the deep tunnels which were dug into the bedrock.

The Dolomite Road

Ratings

Geology	●●●●●
Mountains	●●●●●
Nature	●●●●●
Outdoor activities	●●●●●
Scenery	●●●●●
Walking	●●●●●
Villages	●●●●○
Architecture	●●○○○

Although this route from Bolzano to Cortina is designated 'Strada delle Dolomiti', its views are typical of those seen from nearly any road in this remarkable mountain massif. It begins with a bang, leaving Bolzano along the Ega River through a dramatically carved gorge, whose convoluted rock walls rise on both sides. The whole of the Val d'Ega is scenic, and mountain views begin almost immediately. The route crosses three passes, first the Passo di Costalunga, then the higher Passo Pordoi, under the magnificent Gruppo di Sella, one of several such clusters of peaks to come. The third is Passo di Falzarengo, near Cortina. All along the way, side roads beckon with tempting signs pointing to other passes. Adventurous travellers, who are not timid of narrow and winding mountain roads, could spend weeks exploring these – until their supply of film ran out.

ARABBA AND THE CORDEVOLE VALLEY✢✢

🛈 **APT Arabba**; *tel: 0436 791 30.* A hotel connection board in the centre of Arabba assists with lodgings.

By contrast with the passes on either side, the road along the Cordevole Valley between mountain villages seems almost straight. **Arabba**, an attractive resort town, stretches along S48 with views from every window. A funicular climbs **Col Burz✢✢**, the 1943m mountain north of town, for even more panoramic views. Towns dot the valley below, its bright green slopes looking like well-kept – but quite vertical – lawns, its houses and churches like toys. **Pieve di Livinallongo** is a typical Dolomite town filled with Tyrolean-style buildings, but it is larger than most, with restaurants and cafés. Tiny **Andraz**, with its onion-domed church, has fewer services for travellers, but takes the prize for its ruined **Castello di Andraz✢✢**, built in the 14th century. From its picturesque perch on a rocky crag, it controlled access to the pass ahead, and helped protect it from bandits. **Falzarego Pass✢✢** was the scene of bitter fighting as Italy struggled against Austria in the First World War. Several sites are marked by memorials.

Bressanone

Marebbe

t

10   20km

10 miles

13 San Martino in Badia

La Valle

Lago di
Braies

14

Chiusa

244

Croda
Rossa

51

Funes

Sass
Rigais

Badia

3146

C

Ponte
Gardena

242 Ortisei

3025

Selva di Val 7
Gardena

e

18

Cristallo 9

3221 M

25

32 *Sasso*
Lungo

243 11

Corvara
in Badia

Le Tofan

2150 3243

Renòn

Castelrotto

7

2150 3243

Cortina
d'Ampezz

Fiè allo
Sciliar

3181

Arabba

h

Passo di
Falzarego

Boite

Cornedo all'Isarco

11

c

11

San Vito di Cadore 3C

Nova
Levante

Canàzei

Passo
Pordoi

Monte Pelmo Piev

26

Pozza
di Fassa

Marmolada

3343

Alleghe

3168

Laives

Ponte
Nova

Passo di
Costalunga

Soraga

Lago d'Alleghe

Monte
Civetta

C

18

Latemar 2842

203

3220

Zoldo Alt

o di Caldaro

9 48 Moena

t

Falcade

Cencenighe
Agordino

Forno

Ora 16

Preda zo

22

Cima della
Vezzana

Tegnàs

Taibòn
Agordino

Lago di
Pontesei

gna 48

14 Tesero

San Martino
di Castrozza

3192 *Pala di*
San Martino

Agordo

39

Monte
Schiara

Cavalese

Cima
di Cece

2754

e

22 2982

15

Laste

Fiè allo

lano

olzano

Laives

Ora

Accommodation and food in Arabba and the Cordevole Valley

Hotel rates are higher during winter than in summer.

Hotel-Ristorante Al Forte €€ *V. Pezzei 66, Pieve di Livinallongo; tel: 043 679 329; fax: 043 679 440; e-mail: alforte@rolmail.net; www.alforte.com.* Contemporary Alpine-style hotel near ski slopes, with whirlpool baths and playground. Accessible for guests with disabilities.

Hotel Evaldo €–€€ *V. Arabba 1, Arabba; tel: 043 679 109, 79 281; fax: 043 679 358; e-mail: hotel.evaldo@rolmail.net; www.hotelevaldo.com.* Chalet near the slopes, with wooden balconies and après-ski luxuries, including whirlpool baths. Restaurant serves local and continental dishes.

Cesa Padon €–€€ *V. Sorau 62, Livinallongo; tel: 0436 7109; fax: 0436 7460. Closed mid-Oct–Nov.* Local specialities include sausage and Tyrolean ham.

CANAZEI AND PASSO PORDOI✦✦✦

ⓘ APT *V. Roma 34,*
Alba; tel: 0462 601
113. Open Mon–Sat
0830–1215, 1500–1830,
Sun 1000–1230, at the
southeastern end of
Canazei.

ⓝ Col Rodella (and
other cable cars) €
Open daily 20 Jun–20 Sept.

La Sia (sawmill) *Penia di*
Canazei. Open mid-Jun–mid-
Sept, Mon–Sat 1000–1200,
1500–1900.

Museo degli Sci
Col Rodella cable car
departure station. Open daily
0800–1830 Dec–Apr.

Canazei is an attractive ski and mountain climbing resort, whose
profile – unlike neighbouring Cortina's – has remained low enough
that mountains can be seen even from the village centre. A waterfall
drops almost directly into town, and many houses are painted with
lively Tyrolean frescoes. For those who prefer a slightly less jet-set
atmosphere, Canazei is an excellent alternative to Cortina as a centre
for exploring the Dolomites. In neighbouring Campitello di Fassa is
the family-owned **Museo degli Sci**✦ which shows ski and winter sports
equipment spanning the entire 20th century, plus even older wooden
skates. A 16th-century Venetian sawmill, **La Sia**✦, which provided
lumber for building the Venetian navy, is the last of its type existing
in this region. The restored mill is not just a museum, but is used by
local residents. North of Canazei, **Passo de Sella**✦✦✦ leads north to the
Val Gardena and the town of **Ortesei**, heart of the Ladino country,
where remnants of the Roman legions settled. The road must climb to
an elevation of 2239m to scale **Passo Pordoi**✦✦✦, the lowest point
between the Gruppo di Sella (3152m) to the north, and the Gran
Vernal (3210m) to the south. Views stretch in every direction at the
top, although the foreground is less photogenic than the backdrop:
walls of jagged rock rising vertically like teeth on every side. La
Funivia, a cable car, carries skiers and hikers from here to **Sass Pordoi**,
where **Refugio Maria** perches on a terrace at 2950m.

Accommodation and food in Canazei and Passo Pordoi

Easter–mid-June and mid-Sept–Nov, many hotels and restaurants close
for maintenance.

Albergo Stella Alpini €–€€ *V. Antermont 4; tel: 0462 601 127; fax: 0462*
602 172; e-mail: stella.alpina@softcom.it. This beautifully restored
Alpine home offers a rare chance to see a traditionally decorated
interior, with hand-painted furniture, antiques and fine woodcarving
in the breakfast room. Corner room 204 has good mountain views.

Lupo Bianco Hotel €€ *Pian Frataces; tel: 0462 601 330; fax: 0462 602*
755. In little glen on the road to Ortesei, the hotel has a dining room
and lounge.

Hotel Miramonti € *V. Costa 229, Alba; tel: 0462 601 325; fax: 0462*
601 066. A small hotel with good views and a dining room €–€€
serving hearty mountain dishes.

Enoteca Balentina € *V. Antermont 4; tel: 0462 601 127. Open summer &*
winter only, 1530–1930. A cosy wine bar for après-ski.

La Bolp € *V. Costa 51, Alba; tel: 0462 602 313.* One of the few
restaurants open off-season, serving a fixed menu. In season La Bolp
serves dishes such as Tyrolean ham, *polenta* with venison and the local
sausage, *luganegahe.*

Above
Alpine decoration in Canazei

La Stalla Ristorante €€ *V. Col da Ronch 43; tel: 0462 600 173.* In the centre of Canazei; the choice for fine dining.

La Stua dei Ladins € *V. Pareda 35; tel: 0462 601 052.* Near the lifts, serving simple, good food; noted for their *bruschetta*.

CORTINA D'AMPEZZO❖❖❖

ⓘ **APT** *Piazzetta San Francisco 8; tel: 0436 3231; www.apt-dolomiti-cortina.it. Open daily.*

The 1956 Winter Olympics put Cortina on the jet-set map and turned a secret hideout of serious skiers into an international resort to rival the Swiss Alps. The only unfortunate result of all this attention is that Cortina is now crowded, both with visitors and with buildings that sometimes obscure the stunning scenery. But a few steps from nearly any place in town will bring an opening to the Cinque Torri, the five peaks that tower above. The scenery from the ski slopes is so breathtaking that it's difficult to concentrate on skiing. Along with the

P Parking is plentiful at the Apollonio Stadium below the Tondi di Faloria lift, and in several places in the town centre.

Shop for smart ski-wear and local woodcarving.

Market days: Tue, Fri.

Below
Cortina d'Ampezzo

downhill thrills are many kilometres of cross-country trails through equally spectacular snowscapes. Bobsleighing (the run ends at Via Ronco) joins sports such as skating in the Olympic rink, **Stadio del Ghiaccio**. Lifts lead from the town to mountains in all directions, used in summer by walkers to access high mountain trails, and by those who just wish to look at the **views**✦✦✦.

Accommodation and food in Cortina d'Ampezzo

Miramonte Majestic Grand Hotel €€€ *V. Pexie 103, above S48, Cortina; tel: 043 642 01; fax: 0436 867 019; www.geturhotels.com.* It really is grand, on a hillside with a golf course, stunning views and a good dining room.

Hotel Natale €€–€€€ *Corso Italia 229; tel: 0436 861 210; fax: 0436 867 730; e-mail: meublenatale@libero.it.* A small hotel with fine views over the town and mountains from its carved wooden balconies.

Hotel Parc Victoria €€–€€€ *Corso Italia 1, Cortina; tel: 0436 3246; fax: 0436 4734; www.victoria.dolomiti.com.* Five-storey chalet-style, most rooms with balconies overlooking town. Fine dining in their restaurant.

Savoia Grand Hotel €€–€€€ *V. Roma 62, Cortina 32043; tel: 0436 3201; fax: 0436 2731; e-mail: ghsavoia@sunrise.it.* A freshly renovated hotel in the heart of the town, it has a friendly, English-speaking staff and fine dining.

Da Beppe Sello €€–€€€ *V. Ronco 68; tel: 0436 3236. Closed Tue.* Across the river from the centre, the speciality of its talented chef is a well-seasoned loin of venison.

Leone e Anna €–€€ *V. Alver 112, Cortina; tel: 0436 2768. Open Wed–Mon, Dec–Apr, Jul–Oct.* A comfortable little restaurant that serves mountain food with a Sardinian twist.

Ra Stua € *V. Grohmann 2, Cortina; tel: 0436 868 341.* A good place for good simple food, well prepared.

MARMOLADA***

APT V. Roma 15, Rocca Pietore; tel: 0437 721 319.

Museo della Guerra € Refuge Passo Fedia. Open daily Jul–Sept 1000–1230, 1400–1830.

While snow on the surrounding ski trails lasts only Nov–May, the high slopes of **Marmolada***, the Dolomites' highest at 3343m, offer year-round skiing. Access is easy via several tramways, which leave from S641. At the **Fedaia Pass**** is **Museo della Guerra***, a small private collection including a field kitchen, for those with a particular interest in the First World War. On the other side of Marmolada, at the terminal of the **Malga Ciapela** cable car, is a monument zone with machine-gun postings, trenches, artillery posts and huts intact.

Accommodation and food in Marmolada

Rosalpina €–€€ V. Bosco Verde, Rocca Pietore; tel: 0437 722 004; fax: 0437 722 049; e-mail: rosalpina@marmolada.com. Open Dec–Apr, Jun–Sept. A cosy inn with mountain views and a restaurant €–€€ serving hearty Tyrolean food.

Refugio alla Seggiova € Passo Fedia; tel: 0462 601 181. Open summer & winter only. This rustic lodging for hikers and skiers has a small café.

PASSO DI COSTALUNGA AND VAL DI FASSA***

APT V. Carezza 21, Nova Levante; tel: 0471 613 126, www.welschnofen.com Open daily, good information on hiking and skiing.

Molin de Pezol (watermill) V. Jumela 6, Pera de Fassa. Open mid-Jun–mid-Sept, Mon–Sat 1000–1200, 1500–1900. Shorter hours off season.

Museo Ladino di Fassa € San Giovanni Vigo di Fassa; tel: 0462 764 267; www.tqs.it/ladin. Open Mon–Fri 0845–1200, 1400–1800 (may change with completion of new museum).

The summit of **Passo di Costalunga*** is one of the loveliest on the route, wooded rather than open, with two attractive stone hotels clad in wooden Alpine balconies. Tall pine trees frame views of surrounding peaks. To the west of the pass, nestled in a wooded vale, is the bright blue **Lake Carezza***, at the village of Carezza al Lago. Nearby is **Nova Levante** with a tiny historic **onion-domed church**** below the road level. A number of walking trails lead into the surrounding hills, past green meadows filled with wildflowers. A few tiny villages perch high above, overlooking the river and valley. **Chiesa Santa Elena****, in Nova Ponente, has extensive 14th-century frescos. The **Val di Fassa**, east of the pass, is a centre for the Ladino culture, and the **Museo Ladino di Fassa****, in Vigo di Fassa, looks at the traditions of this unique ethnic group. Restored rooms show how people lived and worked, as well as their religion, music and festivals. A watermill, **Molin de Pezol***, in Pera di Fassa has millstones for grinding cereals, powered by three large paddlewheels.

Accommodation and food in Passo di Costalunga and Val di Fassa

Golf Hotel €–€€ Passo di Costalunga 38030; tel: 0471 612 462; fax: 0471 612 477. The best views at the top of the pass. Restaurant €–€€.

Hotel Pension Diana € *V. Carezza 94, Nova Levante; tel: 0471 613 160; fax: 0471 614 403; e-mail: info@diana-hotel.it; www.pensiondiana.com.* Modern Alpine hotel known for its wine cellar and its restaurant.

Hotel Savoy €–€€ *S48, Passo di Costalunga 5, 38039; tel: 0471 612 124; fax: 0471 612 132.* Wooded mountain setting and panoramic views. Restaurant €€ with a cosy atmosphere.

Tscheinerhutte €–€€ *Nigerstrasse, Nova Levante; tel: 0471 612 152.* Serves home-style Tyrolean specialities, including dumplings.

Suggested tour

Total distance: 100km, with detours 130km.

Time: 3 hours' driving. Allow 2 days for the main route, 3 days with detours. Those with limited time should concentrate on the scenery instead of the towns.

Links: From Lake Garda (*see page 104*) the Alto Adige route (*see page 144*) leads to Bolzano. Continue to Udine to reach the Borderlands route (*see page 170*) via the Dolomite Road route from Cortina d'Ampezzo.

Route: Leave Bolzano ❶ on 241, along the Ega River through a deep, narrow gorge that the river has carved through the rock, forming undulating curves, caves and walls on both sides. A waterfall pours unexpectedly from a cave into the river. Be sure to pull into the small lay-by to look back – and almost straight up – at **Castel Cornedo**, perched on solid rock. The road climbs to **Nova Levante** and continues climbing past the beautiful **Lake Carezza**. The lake is surrounded by majestic evergreens which continue to line the road as it climbs **PASSO DI COSTALUNGA** ❷, which, unlike the other passes on this route, has summit views framed by trees. From the pass, the road plunges sharply into the **VAL DI FASSA**, meeting S48 in Pozza di Fassa, where you turn left, following signs to **CANAZEI** ❸. (*See Detour on page 153.*) Look for waterfalls dropping through the lower forested slopes and from rock ledges high above (47km). Continue east from Canazei on S48 climbing the 2239m **PASSO PORDOI** ❺. From **ARABBA** ❻, the road drops suddenly to the valley floor, bordering the river before rising to **Pieve di Livinallongo**. At **Andraz** the narrow road (poorly signposted) to **Castello di Andraz**, which you can see on the left at the head of the valley, offers the only views of the castle from a safe stopping place. It leaves S48 to the left at a dangerous curve, so you might wish to continue to a safe turning point and approach it from the other direction. S48 ascends to yet another panoramic viewpoint at **Pocol** before arriving at **CORTINA D'AMPEZZO** ❼ (53km).

Map labels: Bressanone, Marebbe, San Martino in Badia, La Valle, Lago di Braies, Croda Rossa 3146, Chiusa, 10 / 20km / 10 miles, tino, Funes, Sass Rigais, 244, Badia, Ca, Ponte Gardena, 242, Ortisei, Selva di Val Gardena, 3025, Corvara in Badia, Le Tofane, Cristallo 3221, Mi, one, 12, 25, Castelrotto, Sasso Lungo, 243, 2150 3243, Cortina d'Ampezzo, Renòn, ano, 32, Sasso Lungo 3181, Passo Pordoi, Arabba, Passo di Falzarego, olzano, Fiè allo Sciliar, Canazei, Marmolada 3343, San Vito di Cadore, Cornedo all'Isarco, Nova, Monte Pelmo Pieve 3168, 241, Levante, Pozza di Fassa, Alleghe, Laives, Ponte Nova, Passo di Costalunga, Soraga, Lago d'Alleghe, Monte Civetta 3220, Zoldo Alto, Latemar 2842, 48, Moena, 203, Forno d, Ora, Predazzo, Falcade, Cencenighe Agordino, Tesero, San Martino di Castrozza, Cima della Vezzana, Taibòn Agordino, Lago di Pontesei, Cavalese, Cima di Cece 2754, Pala di San Martino 2982, Agordo, Monte Schiara, Lastè, Cristallo 3146

Detour: For wild, open scenery along the shoulder of **MARMOLADA** ❹, leave Canazei on S641, through the settlement of Alba, climbing 2057m **Passo di Fedaia**. Continue through **Sottoguda** and **Rocca Pietore** to a junction with S203. Turn north (left), signposted to **Andraz**, there you rejoin S48, turning right (41km).

Also worth exploring

The area south of Vigo di Fassa along the Aviso River is reached by turning south (right) on S48 toward **Moena**, instead of left to **Canazei**. This craggy mountain area has a very interesting geology and is rich in minerals. The **Museo Civico** in **Predazzo** displays some of the more famous minerals and thousands of fossils, some as old as 270 million years. It offers a number of walking itineraries, interesting even to those without a background in geology. A chair lift from Predazzo climbs the 2264m **Doss Capel**. To the south is the particularly scenic **Paneveggio-Pale Nature Park** in **San Martino**.

Eastern Dolomites

Ratings

Mountains	●●●●●
Outdoor activities	●●●●●
Scenery	●●●●●
Walking	●●●●●
Nature	●●●●○
Villages	●●●●○
Architecture	●●●○○
Historical sights	●○○○○

Scenery is what this region is all about, and it doesn't get any better. Traditional tourist sights are rare, but the Dolomites more than compensate with stunning panoramas, walking paths, cable car rides and ski trails. In the spring, Alpine meadows are dotted with bright wildflowers. Driving the winding, steep and often narrow roads is a full-time job, as they weave through tiny villages and zigzag over high mountain passes. The roads are often abuzz with motorcycles (often in the wrong lane), which seem to operate on a blend of petrol and testosterone. Although tourism is newer to the ski resorts on this eastern side of the Dolomites, much of the lodging and the mountain tramways are aimed at skiers and summer climbers, closing spring and autumn. Many of the mountain passes are closed in winter, when snowfall becomes too great for maintenance.

THE CADORE VALLEY✦✦✦

ⓘ **APT** *Pza Venezia 22, Pieve di Cadore; tel: 043 531 644; e-mail: infotai@apt-dolomiti-cortina.it. Open daily summer.*

Tourist Service
V. Nazionale S52, San Vito di Cadore; tel: 043 699 240; e-mail: touristservice @sanvitocadore.com. Open Wed–Sun 0930–1230, 1600–1900. Lodging information and assistance.

A long string of towns with 'Cadore' ending their names, are all located on or above the River Piave and its tributary, the Boite. Each stands at between 800 and 1100m elevation, and all around them soar peaks topping 3000m. Each has its charms, with Alpine architecture and a different set of stunning mountain views. **Pieve di Cadore✦✦** has the greatest claim to fame, as the birthplace of the artist Titian, whose house, **Casa di Tiziano✦**, and the **Museo Archeologico✦** make interesting stops. The parish church has a Titian painting of the Madonna. Between **Pieve di Cadore** and **Vigo di Cadore**, the Piave's course is through a steep, narrow ravine. From **Venas di Cadore** to **Cortina d'Ampezzo** (*see page 149*), the road lies along the north slope of a deep valley, with **views✦✦✦** to Monte Pelma and others. **San Vito di Cadore** is a ski resort, less crowded than nearby **Cortina**.

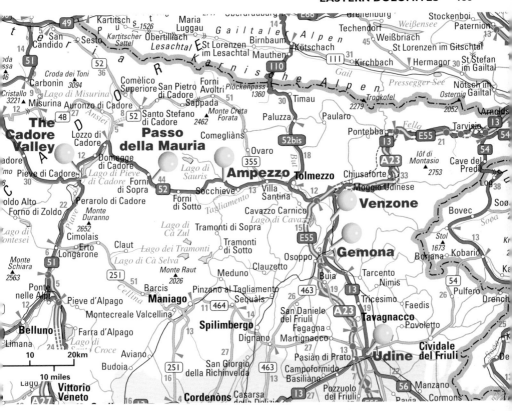

Accommodation and food in the Cadore Valley

Casa di Tiziano €
V. Arsenale 4. Open
Jun–Aug Tue–Sun,
0930–1230, 1600–1900.

Museo Archeologico €
Pza Tiziano. Open Jun–Aug
Tue–Sun, 0930–1230,
1600–1900.

Market day in Pieve di
Cadore: Mon.

Hotel Cima Belpra €–€€ V. Calvi 1, San Vito di Cadore; tel: 0436 890 441; fax: 0436 890 418; www.hotelcimabelpra.com. Easy to find, this modern hotel has balconies on some rooms, good views from all.

Italia € V. IV Novembre 39, Vigo di Cadore; tel: 043 577 643; fax: 043 577 764. A well-kept chalet-style hotel with balconies and a restaurant.

La Scaletta €–€€ V. Calvi, San Vito di Cadore; tel: 0436 890 441. Local dishes with a Germanic accent.

GEMONA AND VENZONE**

ℹ **Informazioni**
V. Caneva 15; tel/fax:
0432 981 441. Open
weekdays.

🅿 Parking is available at
the *duomo* in
Gemona, and outside the
walls of Venzone.

🌀 **Agosto medievale**
a Gemona, *first*
weekend Aug. Gemona's
citizens re-enact life in the
14th century.

On 6 May 1976, an earthquake registering 6.4 struck the upper Tagliamento Valley. When the dust had settled, the 14th-century **duomo**** in the historic centre of Gemona lay in ruins. Only one wall of its bell tower remained, the entire west side of the church was collapsed and open, and the apse wall was gone. Around the church, the medieval centre lay in rubble, with 400 lives lost. A quarter of a century later, the *duomo* stands again, the gigantic **St Christopher statue**** – one of the few things left undamaged – dwarfing its portal, both original to the 1300s. To the same period belong the large central **rose window**** and the two smaller ones at each side. Inside, original features include sections of the gilded, carved 14th-century **altarpiece****, to the right of the main door. The rest of the town centre has been as carefully restored, and the streets are well worth exploring to see the fine arcaded buildings, especially **Palazzo Boton***, at the far end of Via G Bini. A short distance north of Gemona is **Venzone****, a rare 13th-century fortified town. The walls are intact, as are several of the gates. The small church of **Santa Caterina*** stands atop a crag, the road to which offers good views of the wall-enclosed town.

Accommodation and food in Gemona

Hotel Pittini € *Pzle della Stazione, Gemona; tel: 0432 971 176; fax: 0432 971 380; www.italiaabc.com.* Convenient to the historic centre and easy to find from S13.

Da Si-Si € *V. Piovega 15, Gemona; tel: 0432 981 158.* Serves local dishes and Friulian wines.

PASSO DELLA MAURIA AND TAGLIAMENTO VALLEY***

ℹ **APT** *V. Cadore 1,*
Forni di Sopra; tel: 043
886 767.

🌀 Villa Santina is a
centre for mushroom
growing, and you can buy
bags of these dried *funghi*
in most shops (closed Sat
afternoon).

Before dropping into the Tagliamento Valley, S52 climbs out of the Cadore Region, over the 1300-metre **Passo della Mauria*** and through the **Friuli Dolomites National Park***. The road falls steeply from the pass, then levels out somewhat before winding its scenic way down through a land of Alpine meadows and spruce forests. The backdrop of limestone crags retain their white colour even when not covered in winter snow. The wide, pale-blue Tagliamento River loops back and forth under the road through its valley, east of the Passo della Mauria. In **Enemonzo**, not far from the town of **Ampezzo**, the 13th-century church of **Santilario e Taziano*** was reconstructed after an earthquake in 1700, and has a Domenico Fabris fresco of the Ascension of Christ. A brook runs below its stone bell tower and a chestnut tree shades a nice picnic spot.

Opposite
Valle de Cadore

Accommodation and food in Passo della Mauria and Tagliamento Valley

Albego al Pura € *Strada Esterna Corso 7, Ampezzo; tel/fax: 043 380 056.* Fine views of Ampezzo, below, from this Alpine hotel and its restaurant.

Cridola € *V. Mauria 6, Forni di Sopra; tel/fax: 043 388 015.* Inexpensive rooms, with a million-euro view.

Edelweiss € *V. Nazionale S52, Forni di Sopra; tel: 043 388 016; fax: 043 388 017.* On the western edge of town, has a good restaurant.

UDINE✦✦✦

🛈 *Pza I Maggio, northeast of the castle; tel: 0432 295 972. Open Mon–Fri 0900–1300, 1500–1700.*

🅿 Parking € is available in Piazza I Maggio, Piazza Duomo and several other places close to the historic centre.

🛈 **Galleria d'Arte Antica** € *Castello. Open Tue–Sat 0930–1230, 1500–1800.*

Museo Archeologico € *Castello. Open Tue–Sat 0930–1230, 1500–1800.*

Palazzo Arcivescovile € *Pza Patriarcato. Open Wed–Sun 1000–1200, 1530–1830.*

⬤ The main shopping street is Via Mercatovecchio, near Piazza Matteotti, where a morning market brings vendors of cheese and local sausages.

Reminders that this was once part of the Venetian Empire fill **Piazza della Liberta**✦✦✦ – in the three bibliophilic lions, in the Moors that strike the bells on the **clock tower**✦, and in the beautiful (and freshly restored) façade of the 15th-century **Loggia del Lionello**✦✦. The oldest part of town – where most of the attractions are – lies below the **castle**✦, whose walls surround a broad park. Inside the castle is the **Galleria d'Arte Antica**✦✦ and the **Museo Archeologico**✦✦. The former has works by several of the great Venetian painters, including Carpaccio, Caravaggio and Tiepolo. The climb to the castle from **Piazza della Liberta**, through a gate designed by Palladio and along an ascending stone arcade, passes the lovely **Santa Maria del Castello**✦✦. Built in the 13th century, it is decorated with frescoes of the period. Behind the *loggia*, narrow streets lead to **Piazza Matteotti**✦✦, the busy market square. Surrounding it are tall, arcaded buildings in fascinating architectural variety. South (downhill) from the **Piazza della Liberta** is the **duomo**✦✦, looking a bit crowded in its small *piazza*. Its portals are especially fine, and inside are frescoes by Tiepolo. The most unusual is in the chapel on the right, nearest the altar. Over the tabernacle is a painting of the Resurrection, also by Tiepolo, who lived for many years in Udine. Nearby is the **Palazzo Arcivescovile**✦✦, with Tiepolo frescoes of scenes from the Old Testament.

Accommodation and food in Udine

Hotel Cristallo €€ *Pzle d'Annunzio; tel: 0432 501 919; fax: 0432 501 673.*

Hotel Principe €€ *Vle Europa Unita 51; tel: 0432 506 000; fax: 0432 502 221.* Well-appointed rooms and off-street parking, a five-minute walk

Right
Market,
Piazza Matteotti, Udine

How the Dolomites were formed

In the Triassic Period – 250 million years ago, give or take a few – a seabed of coral, shellfish, seaweed and fish was slowly thrust upward by the collision of the African and European tectonic plates. The land cracked, folded and was further disrupted by volcanic eruptions as it rose. In the millennia since, water, weather and glaciers – once more than 1500m thick here – wore and eroded the soft limestone, which was compacted into layers alternating with calcium carbonates. These layers eroded at different rates, accounting for the rough, jagged and uneven textures of the rock, and the mountains they form.

from the historic area, but right on the circumferential street for easy access.

Villa Coren € *V. Cividale 1, Siacco di Povoletto; tel/fax: 0432 679 078; no credit cards*. An old winery, which has been converted into guest rooms and two apartments, with kitchens. Ask for a vineyard tour.

Trattoria Le Maddalene Sporcje €–€€ *V. Pellicerie 4, off Pza Matteotti; tel: 043 225 211. Closed Sun evening & Mon*. Dine street-side or upstairs in this smart wine bar, whose inspired daily menu may include ravioli with asparagus and walnuts, toothsome *tagliatelle* with *pesto* and fish cooked to the moment of perfection.

Osteria Cappelo € *V. Sarpi, at the Fish Market*. A popular and noisy wine bar that spills out onto the street.

Vitello d'Oro €€–€€€ *V. Valvason 4; tel: 0432 291 982. Closed Tue evening, Wed, July*. Seafood and lamb are specialities, or opt for the full-course regional menu, with local wines. A vine-draped terrace overlooks the street.

Shortly before reaching **Forni di Sopra**, a cable car climbs the southern slope of the 2865m Monte Tudaio di Razzo.

International Access: In **Tolmezzo**, S52 intersects with S52B, which heads north over the **Passo di Monte Croce Carnico** (Plockenpass) into Austria, and on to **Lienz**. Just to the east, near **Amaro**, the A23 *autostrada* heads east to the border town of **Tarviso**, and on to **Villach**, also in Austria. To reach the Slovenian resort of **Bled**, leave the A23 at **Tarviso** and follow the signs to the frontier and **Jesinice**.

Al Plan Paluz €–€€ *V. Malignani, Tarcento; tel: 0432 784 120. Closed Mon.* This *agriturismo* restaurant, on a farm about 3km from S13 via S356, serves local specialities, such as *gnocchi* with *ragu*, at lunch and dinner.

ATP *V. Misurina; tel: 0436 390 16. Open daily summer.*

Hotel Lavaredo €–€€ *V. Monte Piana; tel: 043 536 227; fax: 043 539 127.* A modern hotel and restaurant on the lake shore.

Suggested tour

Total distance: 159km, with detours 188km.

Time: 5 hours' driving. Allow 2 days for the main route, 2–3 days with detours. Those with limited time should concentrate on Udine and the route over the mountains to Cortina.

Links: The Dolomite Road route (*see page 152*) ends in Cortina. Cividale and Gorizia (*see pages 164–5*) are a few kilometres east of Udine via S54.

Route: Leave Cortina ❶ on S51, following signs to **San Vito di Cadore**. As you descend from Cortina, you'll see ahead the pyramidal Antelao, 3263m high ahead, forming a backdrop for San Vito. To the south along this entire route through THE CADORE VALLEY, mountains tower above the Valle d'Ampezzo, and towns string out along the hillside road to **Tai di Cadore** (30km). (*See Detour 1 below.*) At Tai di Cadore, head north (left) on S51B to **Pieve di Cadore** ❷. Leave Pieve di Cadore travelling north on S51B to **Lozzo di Cadore** (12km). Just past Lozzo, turn east (right) onto S52, signposted to **PASSO DELLA MAURIA** and Ampezzo. Follow this scenic road through a series of panoramic views, over the 1298-m pass and down the other side to **Forni di Sopra**. Continue through the mountain scenery, through **Forni di Sotto** dropping suddenly into **Ampezzo** ❸ (47km). (*See Detour 2 below.*) Leave Ampezzo, on S52, following signs to **Tolmezzo** (17km). Make your way through the confusing roundabout, following signs to **Tarviso**, but at **Carnia**, turn south (right) onto S13, signposted **Udine**. Follow S13 south, stopping in **VENZONE**, to **Ospedaleto**, there turning left on a road signposted **GEMONA** ❹ (26km). Leave **Gemona** via the southern approach, returning to S13 and on south to **UDINE** ❺ (27km). Alternatively, enter the A23 *autostrada* here for a quicker trip through this flat countryside.

Detour 1: Shortly past **Vito di Cadore**, turn south (right) on S347, signposted to **Passo Cibiana**. After a steep, winding climb, stop in **Cibiana di Cadore** to admire the unique paintings on the walls of traditional local stone and wood *tabia*. All created since 1980, several of the paintings are works of internationally known artists. Return to S51 by the same road (10km).

Detour 2: If you are up for more mountain driving, on even narrower and steeper roads, make the scenic loop from just west of **Ampezzo**, turning north (left) on an unnumbered road signposted Passo del Pura. After topping the 1425m pass, descend to the crystal waters of **Lago di Sauris**. Continue to the right, looping back south into Ampezzo (18km).

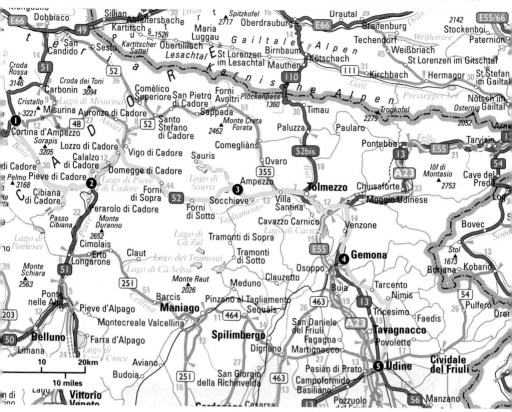

Malga Misurina
€–€€ *Cella de dan Innocente; tel: 043 592 88.*
Local meats and cheeses are featured in dishes such as *gnocchi ricotta* or *polenta* with cheese.

Also worth exploring

The waters of **Lake Misurina***, north of Cortina, reflect the peaks of the Tre Cime di Lavaredo and Cristallo, a photographer's dream. High above the town, reached by a steep mountain road past **Lake Antorno**, at the **Refugio Auronzo*** is a simply splendid panorama of jagged peaks. Travellers come here for the views and to walk along the high trails. The trip to Misurina from Cortina is short, about 14km over the **Tre Croce Pass**, a particularly scenic route. From Misurina, continue north on S48B, turning south (left) onto S51 to return to **Cortina**. On S51, about 6km north of Cortina, a small car park sits at the head of the walking trail to **Fanes Waterfall**, where a long stream of frothy water pours off a ragged rock wall. The walk is about 30 minutes, and a perfect venue for a picnic.

The Borderlands

Ratings

Historical sights	●●●●
Architecture	●●●
Beaches	●●●
Food and drink	●●●
Museums	●●●
Nature	●●●
Scenery	●●●
Geology	●●

The part of the Veneto known as Friuli-Venezia Giulia is seldom visited by foreign travellers, except those bound for its fine-sanded Adriatic beaches. But this land had its fill of other invasions since the Romans first built their towns here, long before the Venetian lagoon was settled. Travellers with a nose for history can almost see the successive eastern hordes that swept through during the Dark Ages, and get a rare glimpse of their civilisation. Just as visible is the process of their Christianisation, as they built their basilicas, interpreting Christian/Roman forms through their own Eastern eyes. The architecture of the Austro-Hungarian Empire overlays the Roman, but has an almost Slavic touch. The influence of Venice is clear in Portogruaro, which lies east of Friuli. Museums give vivid accounts of the First World War, hard-fought among the limestone hills.

AQUILEIA✦✦✦

ⓘ APT Pza Basilica; tel: 0431 919 491. Open Mon–Wed, Fri 0930–1900, Sat–Sun 0930–1340.

ⓟ Parking is free at the basilica.

ⓗ A winery, **Vini Catullio**, and the Botega della Grappa distillery welcome visitors with samples.

St Mark is believed to have spread Christianity to the Roman town of Aquileia, and although greatly altered over the years, the 9th-century **basilica✦✦✦** is impressive. This church replaced the one that Attila the Hun burned in AD 425. **Mosaic floors✦✦✦**, discovered in 1909, are from the 4th century, the largest paleo-Christian mosaic floor known in Western Europe. Below the sanctuary is a 9th-century **crypt✦✦**, whose walls and ceiling are covered in Byzantine-style frescoes from the 12th century. To the left of the entry is another remarkable series of **mosaic floors✦✦✦**, their bird and animal designs intricate (even to facial expressions on animals) and condition near perfect. After admiring the **baptistery✦** and perhaps climbing the 73m **campanile✦**, walk around back to see the **First World War cemetery✦**, with rows of iron crosses and gripping memorial statuary. Follow the path behind the walls to the ruins of the city's former port, once washed by the Natisone. Later constructions overlay it somewhat, built of bits and

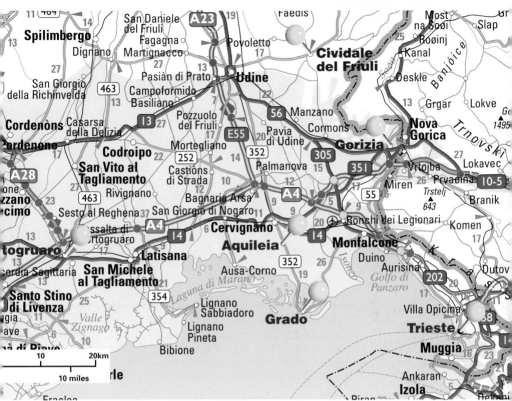

Basilica of Aquileia € *Open daily 0900–1850 summer, 0900–1230, 1430–1750 winter. Closed for mass Sun 1030–1115. An excellent brochure is available in English.*

Campanile € *Open Mon–Sat 0930–1300, 1430–1800; Sun & holidays 0900–1300, 1500–1830.*

Museo Archeologico € *V. Giulia Augusta; tel: 043 191 016. Open daily 0900–1850 summer, 0900–1230, 1430–1750 winter.*

Several *agriturismo* farms along S352 have restaurants serving their products.

pieces of Roman stonework. Remains of a **Forum** stand along S352, as does the **Museo Archeologico**∗, with excellent sculptures, mosaics, glass and other Roman artefacts.

Accommodation and food in Aquileia

Ai Patriarchi €€ *V. Giulia Augusta 12; tel: 0431 919 595, fax: 0431 919 596.* In the town centre, close to the basilica, with a restaurant serving fresh seafood and grilled meats.

Trattoria Al Morar €–€€ *V. Beligna 66; tel: 0431 919 340.* Friendly little place with good fresh seafood.

CIVIDALE DEL FRIULI✦✦✦

ℹ️ **ARPT** *near Ponte del Diavolo; tel: 0432 731 461. Open daily.*

🅿️ Limited free parking near the Tempietto Longobardo, and by timed ticket (ticket machines are well hidden) around the market square.

🔑 **Ipogeo Celtico** *V. Monastero Maggiore.* Ask for key at Bar al Ipogeo, around the corner near the bridge.

Museo Archeologico € *Pza del Duomo. Open Mon–Fri 0900–1330, Sat–Sun 0900–1230.*

Museo Cristiano *Pza del Duomo. Open Mon–Sat 0930–1200, 1500–1800, Sun 1500–1800.*

Tempietto Longobardo € *Off Pza San Biagio, open Apr–Sept daily 0930–1230, 1500–1830, Sun & holidays 0930–1300, 1500–1930; Oct–Mar 0930–1230, 1430–1830. Actual hours vary.*

Cividale hangs on the edge of a ravine carved by the final efforts of the Natisone to burst out of its rocky confines into freedom on the Friulian Plain. The city was founded by Julius Caesar in AD 50 and was a Longobard capital 500 years later, reaching its apex in the 8th and 9th centuries as the seat of the bishop of Aquileia. **Ponte del Diavolo** (Devil's Bridge)✦✦ spans the chasm, with views of houses crowning the convoluted limestone cliffs. Cividale's streets climb and twist among buildings straight from the Middle Ages – and before. The **Tempietto Longobardo**✦✦✦, a gem of 8th-century construction, was rebuilt after a 13th-century earthquake. Look especially for the saints' statues and the stucco arch – rare surviving examples of Longobard art. To appreciate even further the degree of civilisation these conquering tribes had achieved, see the 5th- and 6th-century jewellery and weaponry at the **Museo Archeologico**✦✦. In the **duomo**✦, along with a masterful silver altarpiece and an octagonal baptistery, is the small **Museo Cristiano**✦, with the 8th-century Altar of Ratchis and newly discovered fresco panels. Perhaps the most unique attraction in town is its least known, hidden behind an unremarkable door, just around the corner from the Ponte Diavolo. The 4th- or 3rd-century BC **Ipogeo Celtico**✦✦✦ is a Celtic burial chamber, with graves set into the walls of a series of caves in the cliff above the river. Access to this spooky crypt is down several flights of narrow stairs.

Accommodation and food in Cividale del Friuli

Frasca di Gianni €€ *V. Valli del Matisone 38; tel: 0432 732 319.* Serves lunch and dinner (except Thur) of locally cured meats, a Friulian speciality, and other local farm produce.

Locanda al Castello €€ *V. del Castello 20; tel: 0432 733 242; fax: 0432 700 901; www.infotech.it/castello.* About 2km from the centre, this former monastery stands on a hillside with fine views. A terrace restaurant serves local specialities and continental dishes.

Roma € *Pza Picco; tel: 0432 731 871; fax: 0432 701 033.* On a quiet square in the centre of Cividale, the Roma is handy for sights and dining.

Osteria Alla Terrazza €–€€ *Street C Gallo 2; tel: 0432 700 288; www.laterrazza.it.* Excellent sandwiches and full meals featuring local products. Opening onto the street opposite, a wine bar gives samples of local cheeses, smoked meats and pastries.

Opposite
River view, Cividale

GORIZIA✧

ⓘ ARPT *V. Roma 9; tel: 0481 386 222. Open daily.*

ⓑ Castello € *Borgo Castello. Open Apr–Sept Tue–Sun 0930–1330, 1500–1930; Oct–Mar Tue–Sun 0930–1800.*

Museo de Storia e Arte € *Borgo Castello. Open Tue–Sun 1000–1200, 1500–1800.*

Sant'Ignazio *Pza della Vittoria. Open daily 0900–1230, 1530–1800.*

Looking more like part of Austria, which it was until the First World War, Gorizia sits on the Slovenian border. The former Yugoslavia built Nova Gorizia on its side of the line after the Second World War. You can visit the Slovenian town, although there's not much to see there. Gorizia's main sight is the medieval **Castello**✧, on a hill with good views. Around the castle, which was fortified during a short Venetian rule, is **Borgo Castello**✧, a quarter also built by the Venetians. Here you will find **Chiesa di Santo Spirito**, a small 14th-century church, and the **Museo de Storia e Arte**✧, with local crafts, a costume collection and good WWI exhibits. The best of the churches, however, is **Sant'Ignazio**✧, replete with onion domes and clearly a product of the Austrian years. Over in Nova Gorizia, Francophiles will want to visit the **Castagnavizza**✧, called Kostanjevica in Slovenian, the crypt of the last of the French Bourbons. The family spent its final years here in exile.

Shopping is geared mostly to the Slovenians who throng across the border for western goods.

Accommodation and food in Gorizia

Golf Hotel Castello Formentini €€€ *V. Oslavia 2, San Floriano del Collio (6km from Gorizia's centre); tel: 0481 884 051; www.golfsanfloriano.it.* Contessa Isabella Fiorentini makes guests feel at home in her castle with a complimentary 24-hour buffet of local food and drink specialities. The view from the hilltop golf course makes it hard to concentrate on the game.

Euro Palace Hotel €–€€ *Corso Italia 63; tel: 048 182 166; fax: 048 131 658.* Centrally located, this large hotel has parking and bicycles.

Osteria Korsic €–€€ *S Floriano del Collio; tel: 0481 884 248.* Almost on the Slovenian border, this osteria serves excellent grilled lamb; sample three local pastas in *tre pasti*.

Ristorante Alla Transalpina €€ *V. Caprin 30; tel: 0481 530 291.* Specialises in local dishes and wines, they have rooms € as well.

GRADO❖❖

APT *Vle Dante 72; tel: 0431 899 111.* Open daily Mar–Nov 0800–1900, Mon–Fri winter.

P Parking € is available around the fishing port.

Duomo and baptistery Open daily 0900–1200, 1400–1900.

Motonave Christina €€€ *Riva San Vito; tel/fax: 043 181 412; Mon–Sat 1030–1230 lagoon tour, 1530–1830 islands.*

Perdon First Sun July. A colourful votive procession of boats.

Above
Doorway, Grado

When the barbarian hordes made life too dangerous for the Romans in Aquileia, they decamped hastily to the more easily defended tip of the peninsula. Grado, the town they built there, is still a pleasant one, for all the holiday crowds that flock to its beaches. In the centre of its old quarter, several blocks of narrow lanes, is the 6th-century Romanesque **duomo**❖❖, with outstanding columns topped by Byzantine capitals. Its mosaic floor, although not as impressive as the one in Aquileia, is well worth seeing, and you can look through a hole in the floor to see more from the 4th century. The Venetian silver **altarpiece**❖ is also interesting. More capitals, plus a collection of ancient **stone carving**❖❖ (many of the intertwined designs have a distinctly Celtic look), are displayed in a stone courtyard, with good identifying signs. Next to the *duomo* is a 6th-century **baptistery**♦♦, also with mosaics, and facing the same square is **Santa Maria della Grazie**♦♦, a basilica from the period. Close by is the very picturesque **fishing port**♦♦, where **Motonave Christina**♦ leaves for excursions around the lagoon, with refreshments on board.

Accommodation and food in Grado

Lodging is scarce in summer, and booked well in advance. Many hotels insist on full board; many close Nov–Mar.

Ambriabella €€ *Riva Slataper 2; tel: 043 181 479; fax: 043 182 257.* In the centre, and open all year, this small hotel has a garden and pleasant restaurant serving local dishes.

Serena € *Riva Sant'Andrea, Fraz. Isola della Schuisa; tel: 043 180 697; fax: 043 185 199.* Quieter than the busy centre, located on a close-by island in the lagoon. The hotel has a restaurant.

Trattoria al Marinaio €€ *Campo Porta Nova.* Has a covered patio and serves a mixed grill of fish, grilled shrimp and *calamari*.

Trattoria Santa Lucia €€ *Campo Porta Nova. Closed Tue.* Dine outdoors or inside, choosing from a full menu of fresh fish.

PORTOGRUARO AND CONCORDIA SAGITTARIA♦♦

ⓘ APT *Borgo S Agnese 57; tel: 042 176 00.*

Ⓜ Museo Nazionale Concordiese € *V. Seminario 22; tel: 042 172 674. Open daily 0900–2000.*

Palaeo-Christian Excavations *Pza Duomo, Concordia Sagittaria. Open daily 0900–2000. Free.*

Ⓜ Market day: Thur.

Ⓕ Festival delle Citta *Mid-Aug–Sept; tel: 042 171 352.* Brings music groups of local and international repute.

One of the several 'little Venices' that grace the region, Portogruaro sits along a river that is often visible only through the gateways of the 15th-century **palazzi**♦ that line its main street. These reflect the graceful lines of the Venetian palaces in their arched windows and Gothic doorways. Many of them are arcaded, one supported by columns with carved capitals. When a view of the river does open out, it's worth waiting for. Behind the **duomo**, whose tall leaning bell tower follows the design of St Mark's *campanile*, is as pretty an ensemble of architecture and water as you will find in the Veneto. The **fish market**♦ is under a *loggia*, and a medieval building overlooking the river has a tiny votive chapel tucked into its lower floor. A pair of old **mills with large waterwheels**♦♦ are connected by a footbridge to the other bank, and the whole is framed in weeping willows. The best views are from the path through a tiny linear garden that borders the river's opposite bank. Before Portogruaro was founded in medieval times, Concordia Sagittaria, just south of SS14, was a thriving Roman city. Beside and under its **duomo** (with an 11th-century **baptistery**♦) is the excavation of **Roman and palaeo-Christian buildings**♦♦, including a porticoed burial chamber and mosaic floors. Descriptive

⊘ Festa della
Madonna della
Pescheria *Mid-Aug; tel:
042 171 399.* A colourful
event along the river.

signage is in English. Ask there for a brochure showing other Roman sites, such as a **stone oven*** and **Roman bridge***. The many finds from the various Roman sites in Concordia are in the **Museo Nazionale Concordiese****, in Portogruaro. This impressive collection includes statuary, capitals, mosaics and bronzes.

Accommodation and food in Portogruaro and Concordia Sagittaria

Antica Locanda Campanile €–€€ *V. Roma 13; tel: 042 174 997. Closed Mon.* Right under the leaning *campanile*, with a full menu of stylish and casual dishes, including luncheon sandwiches.

Antico Spessotto € *V. Roma 2; tel: 042 171 040; fax: 042 171 053.* In the town centre, with few frills, but a friendly staff.

Right
Fish market and
campanile, Portogruaro

TRIESTE✦✦

ℹ **APT** *Stazione Centrale, Pza della Liberta*, at the northern approach to the city and *V. San Nicolo 20; tel: 040 679 611. Pza dell'Unita; tel: 0463 478 312.*

🅿 Parking € is at Piazza dell'Unita d'Italia and on either side of it along the port. There is also parking at the castle.

🚌 Bus No 24 goes to the castle.

🏛 **Castello and Museo Civico** € *Open Wed–Mon 0900–1900, later in summer.*

Museo di Storia e d'Arte € *V. Cattedrale 1. Open Tue–Sun 0900–1300, 1900 Wed.*

🛒 The daily market is in Piazza Ponterosso, beside the Canal Grande.

🎭 **Teatro Verdi** *Pza Verde 1; tel: 0406 272 111.* The opera house.

Even more telling for Trieste than its location at the far edge of Italy, it is also at the point where Slavic east meets Latin west. The city has been fought over since the Illyrians and Celts tussled for it, and as late as 1954 it was not a part of Italy. The city has a distinct Eastern feel to it, quite different from its Italian neighbours. While the Romans left their mark, it's the imprint of Maria Theresa and the Austro-Hungarian Empire that you see today, in its baroque and neo-classical buildings, and in the **Piazza dell'Unita d'Italia**✦. This square, bounded by three elegant buildings and the sea, is a natural focal point, as is the elevation which rises inland. This **Capitoline Hill**✦✦ was the heart of Roman Trieste, and continued to be so through medieval times. Beside the remains of the **Forum**✦ stands the 11th-century **Basilica di San Giusto**✦✦, featuring mosaics and early medieval frescoes, set in a melange of architectural styles and periods. Also crowning the hill is the **Castello**✦✦, built when the Venetians were in residence, in the 15th century. Walk its high walls for fine views. **Museo di Storia ed Arte**✦ has old stone work displayed in its garden. Two other churches are of particular note: **Chiesa di Santa Maria Maggiore**✦✦, a baroque gem about halfway between the castle and Piazza dell'Unita, and **Chiesa di Santo Spiridone**✦, near the end of Canal Grande. Below, a Roman amphitheatre is set into the steep hillside.

Accommodation and food in Trieste

Try to avoid Trieste at weekends, when cars from Belgrade flood the city to shop.

Antica Trattoria Suban €€€ *V. Comic 2; tel: 040 543 68.* Possibly the city's oldest restaurant, its been a favourite since 1865.

Caffè San Marco € *V. Cesare Battisti 18.* A traditional Austrian-style café with generations of Trieste tradition.

Continentale €€€ *V. San Nicolo 25; tel: 040 631 717; fax: 040 368 816.* Overlooking the Canal Grande, close to restaurants and sights.

Grand Hotel Duchi d'Aosta €€€ *Pza dell'Unita d'Italia; tel: 0407 600 011; fax: 040 366 092.* Stay in a style that Empress Maria Theresa would have enjoyed, with all the extras from whirlpool tubs to a parking garage, all in a prime location.

Suggested tour

Castello Miramare
€€ *Open daily*
0900–1800 until 1600 winter.

Villa Manin € *Passaiano, 3 km south of Codroipo. Open Tue–Sun 0930–1230, 1500–1800 hours variable.*

Castello Duino €€ *Open Mar–Sept Tue–Sun 0930–1730, Oct Tue–Sun 0930–1700, Nov Sat, Sun, hols 0930–1600.*

Al Mulina del Conte € *V. Tagliamento 268, Cisterna di Coseano; tel: 0432 862 240; www. agriturismodelconte.3000.it.* North of Codriopo, with modern rooms and an outstanding restaurant, both at unbelievably low prices.

Dal Diaul €€– €€€ *V. Garibaldi 20, Rovignano; tel: 0432 776 674. Open lunch except Thur–Fri, and dinner daily.* Six km north of Latisana, this rustic restaurant has a garden terrace for alfresco summer dining on dishes such as *risotto* with truffled pigeon.

Borgo Grotta Gigante €€ *Open daily summer 0900–1200, 1400–1900, shorter hours in winter.*

Total distance: 251km, using detours 248km.

Time: 5 hours' driving. Allow 2–3 days with or without detours. Those with limited time should concentrate on Aquileia and Cividale.

Links: Udine (*see page 158*) is connected to Cortina via the Eastern Dolomites route. Venice (Venezia) (*see page 172*) is only a few kilometres west of Portogruaro, via S14 or A4.

Route: Leave Udine ❶ on S54, following signs to **CIVIDALE DEL FRIULI** ❷ (17km). Head south from Cividale on S356, turning east (left) upon reaching S56 in **Cormons** and continuing on to **GORIZIA** ❸ (30km). From Gorizia, head south on the scenic S55 until it intersects with S14 at **San Giovani**, on the Adriatic coast. Head south (left), stopping at the beautifully located **Castello Duino** and at **Castello Miramare***, a white confection of a Hapsburg palace set in gardens overlooking the sea. Continue south into **TRIESTE** ❹ (41km). (*See Detour 1 below.*) Leave Trieste by retracing your route north on S14 to **Monfalcone** (17km). (*See Detour 2 below.*) From Monfalcone follow S14 west to **Cervignano del Friuli** (18km). Turn south (left) on S352 to **AQUILEIA** and **GRADO** ❺ (19km). Leave Grado travelling north on S352. On returning to Cervignano, turn west (left) on S14, through **Latisana** and on to **PORTOGRUARO** ❻ and **CONCORDIA SAGITTARIA** (52km). Take S463 north from Portogruaro to **Casarsa**, turning east (right) on S13 to **Codroipo**: worth a stop to see the gigantic **Villa Manin***, built for the last Doge of Venice, and continuing on S13 back to Udine (57km).

Detour 1: At 4.5km north of **Trieste**, turn left onto S58, signposted to **Villa Opicina***, where there are views, then bear left again following signs to **Borgo Grotta Gigante*** *, billed as the world's largest accessible cave (13km). Return to the coastal S14, following signs to **Prosecco** and head north to **Monfalcone**.

Detour 2: For a shorter, slower, and more interesting ride, from **Monfalcone** follow the unnumbered road south, signposted to **Grado** (24km). Bird spotting is especially good in the delta marshlands and lagoon.

Getting out of the car

An excellent brochure, *In Bici 165km de Percorsi Ciclabili*, is available from local TICs. It maps 165km of cycling routes between Grado and Palmanova, with good details on sights en route.

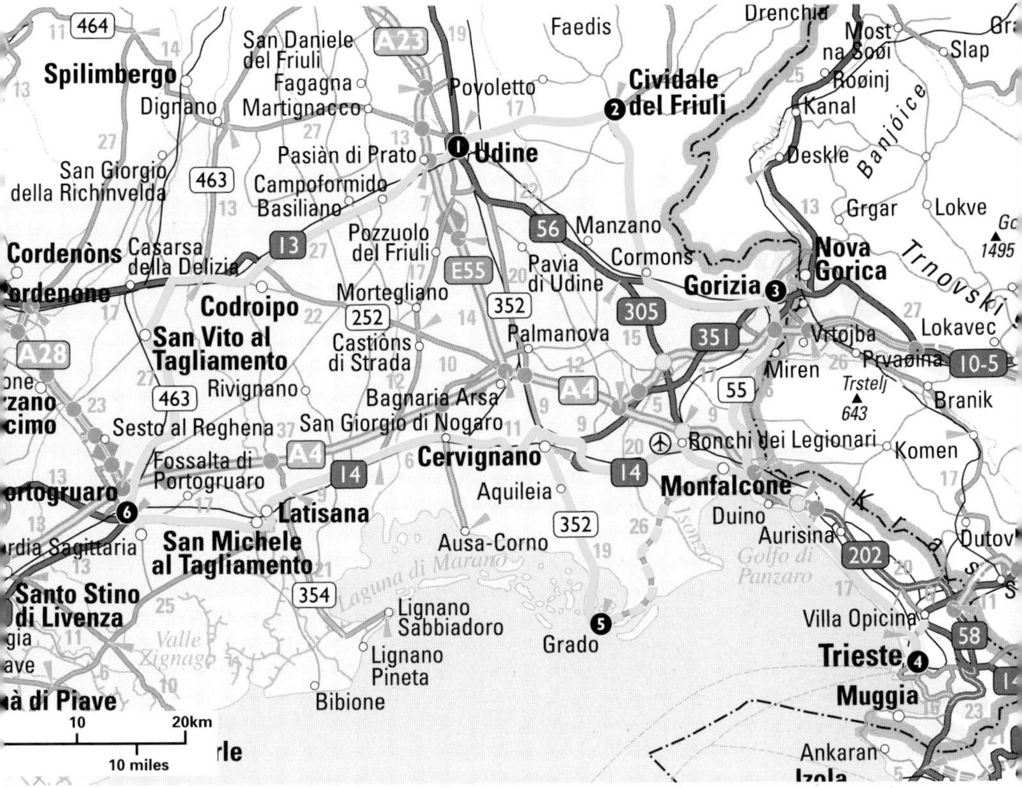

Also worth exploring

APT V. Maia 37,
Bibione;
www.bibionecaorle.it

From Jesolo's 15km-long beach to Bibione's 6km of wide beach backed by pine forest, nearly any road you follow southward will lead to a beach. Forming the barrier for the Venetian lagoon is the Litoriale del Cavallino; Punta Sabbione at its end has regular boat access to Venice and its islands. The fine-sand beaches slope gently, with no sudden drop-offs, and bird-life is abundant in the reedy marshlands bordering the lagoons.

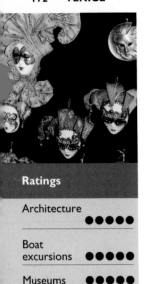

Venice

Ratings

Architecture	●●●●●
Boat excursions	●●●●●
Museums	●●●●●
Art and craft	●●●●○
Scenery	●●●●○
Children	●●●○○
Historical sights	●●●○○
Walking	●●●○○

Venice is unique. In the span of 1100 years this tiny city state at the edge of the Adriatic Sea rose to become the Serene Republic, *La Serenissima*, conqueror of Constantinople. Long a magnet to European royalty, it also drew artists, poets and writers. The centre, heart and soul of the empire was Piazza San Marco. Here were Palazzo Ducale, home of the ruling Doges, and the basilica of San Marco, the spiritual centre of the city. Even today, a café on San Marco is the place to be. The Accademia, museums and churches of the city are the repository of the best of 12th–19th-century art. Works by Tintoretto and other Venetian masters are almost commonplace and even the smallest church has its masterpiece. But it is the city itself that charms, for its canals, bridges, passageways and *campos* have no match.

ℹ **APT** *Pza San Marco; tel: 0415 225 150*. At the foot of Piazza San Marco: crowded but not especially useful. Ask for *Un Ospite di Venezia* for current events, opening times and gondola rates. The TIC at the train station is more helpful with lodging.

Transport information: *www.hellovenizia.it* includes transport and hours of museums and attractions. *www.actv.it* has vaporetto lines, and *direzione@actv.it* will give specific directions between points.

Getting there

International flights arrive at Marco Polo airport, small and easy to navigate. Boats to the city are pricey, but a bus to Porta Roma *vaporetto* stop is cheap. Buy a ticket at the news stand near the door. Those arriving by car can park at Porta Roma (expensive) or at one of the car parks near Marco Polo airport (free shuttle to the airport bus stop). In any case, leave nothing in your car.

Getting around

Venice spreads across several islands, and the only ways to get from one place to another are by boat or on foot. Depend on getting lost. That's part of the fun, and locals will point you on your way cheerfully. *Vaporetto* boats ply the Grand Canal and around the edges of the islands, encircling the entire city on route No 52. Maps,

A very useful website, packed with information and links, all updated frequently, is *www.veniceforvisitors.com*

available at the TIC, are easy to follow. Be sure the boat is going in the right direction or you'll have to circle the whole route. If you plan to use the *vaporetto* more than twice within 24 hours, an all-day pass saves money. It includes all the islands and Porta Roma car park. Venice also has picturesque gondola ferries crossing the Grand Canal. *Traghetto* rides are so cheap you will want to cross just for fun. Romantic rides in your own gondola are pricey, but rates are regulated and published.

Sights

Finding an address
Venice is divided into six *sestieri* or neighbourhoods, so it is important to know which *sestiere* an address is in. From there, if you cannot locate an address on the map, ask someone. Directions and addresses often include the nearest church as a landmark. The sights below are divided alphabetically into the six *sestieri*, which can be reached on foot from one another. The gazetteer concludes with a selection of the best of the out-lying islands, which can only be reached by boat. Streets have many designations, including *fondamenta* and *riva* (paved waterside paths) and *sottopassagio* (a tunnel passageway). These wander into *campi* (singular *campo*), often little more than courtyards, but sometimes large squares. Venice has only one *piazza* – San Marco.

CANNAREGIO
Beyond the usual tourist path, Cannaregio forms an arch across the north side of the Grand Canal. It is one of the quieter quarters, with a more measured pace. On the east and south it abuts Castello.

Museo Ebraico € *Campo del Ghetto Nuovo. Open Jun–Sept Sun–Fri 1000–1730, Oct–May 1000–1700. Guided tours hourly.*

Santa Maria dei Miracoli € *Campo dei Miraculi. Open Mon–Sat 1000–1200, 1500–1800.*

Ghetto and Museo Ebraico✦
The Venetians called the foundry here *geto* and in 1516 it was decreed that all Jews in the city would live on this islet, the original use of the word. While their numbers have dwindled, the area still bears the tone of their culture with Jewish libraries, food stores and synagogues. The museum has artefacts of 17th–19th-century Jewish life and schedules tours of three synagogues.

Santa Maria dei Miracoli✦✦
This early Renaissance jewel box has a three-part façade faced in pink, green and white marble. The lower has Corinthian columns with panels of coloured marble between, the second level Ionic columns with arched windows and the third a marble lunette with rose windows. Interior walls are geometric patterns of coloured marble.

CASTELLO
Immediately east of San Marco, bordered also by Cannaregio and Canale di San Marco on the south and Canale delle Fondamente Nuove on the north.

S.GIROLANO

Ricovero
Penitenti

S. Alvise

Madonna
dell' Orto

CANNAREGIO

S. Giobbe

Museo
Ebraico

GHETTO

Tempio
Israelitico

Ex Conv. S.M.
dei Servi

S.Marziale

Parco
Savorgnan

Pal.
Labia

S. Geremia

S.
Marcuola

Pal. Vendramin-
Calergi

Stazione Ferrovie
dello Stato
Santa Lucia

Gli
Scalzi

Fondaco dei
Turchi

S. Zan
Degolà

S. Stae

Ca'
Pesaro

S. Simeone
Grande

Galleria
d'Arte
Moderna

S. Simeone
Piccolo

Pal.
Mocenigo

S. Giacomo
dell' Orio

S. M.arie
Mater
Domini

Pescheria

S. Cassiano

Fabbriche
Nuove

Giardino ex
Papadopoli

Fabbrich
Vecchie

Scuola di
S. Giovanni
Evangelista

S. Giovanni
Elemosinario

San
Aponal

PIAZZALE
ROMA

S. Nicolò
dei Tolentini

S. Giovanni
Evangelista

SANTA CROCE

Archivio di Stato

SAN POLO

Scuola
San Rocco

Santa Maria
Gloriosa dei Frari

San
Polo

Pal.
Dandolo

Scuola Grande di
San Rocco

Museo
Goldoni

Pal.
Loredan-
Ca' Farsetti

S.Tomà

S. Pantalon

Palazzi
Mocenigo

Pal.
Foscarini

Palazzi
Contarini

Pal. Contarini
d. Bovolo

Scuola Gr. di
S. Maria d
Carmini

Palazzi
Foscari

Ca'
Rezzonico

S.Fantin

S. Maria
dei Carmini

Campo
San Barnaba

S. Barnaba

DORSODURO

Angelo
Raffaele

SAN MARCO

Teatro
La Fenice

S. Nicolò
dei Mendicoli

S. Maria
Zobenigo

San
Sebastiano

Stazione
Marittima

Accademia

Galleria dell'
Accademia

Santa Maria
della Salute

San
Trovaso

Peggy Guggenheim
Collection
(Pal. Venier)

Squero di
San Trovaso

(Grand Canal)

Gesuati

GIUDECCA

Spirito
Santo

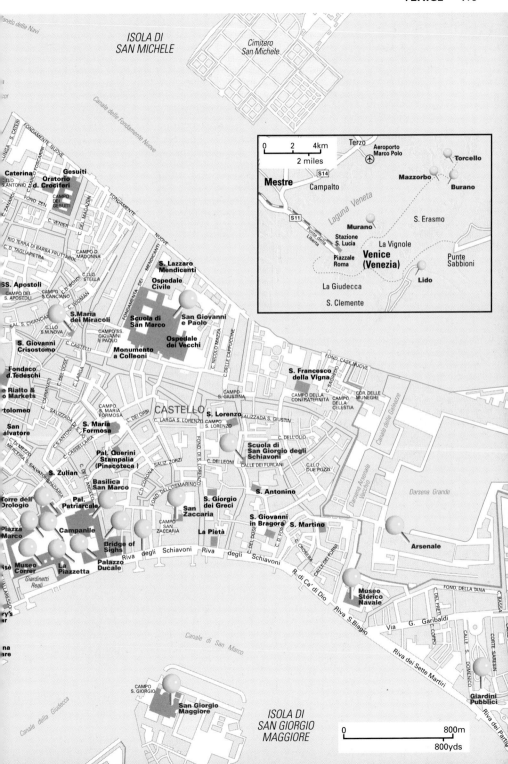

ISOLA DI
SAN MICHELE

Cimitero
San Michele

Canale delle Navi

Canale delle Fondamente Nuove

Inset map:

0 2 4km
2 miles

Terzo
Aeroporto
Marco Polo

S14

Mestre
Campalto

Torcello

Mazzorbo
Burano

Laguna Veneta

S11

Ponte della Libertà

Murano

S. Erasmo

Stazione
S. Lucia

La Vignole

Piazzale
Roma

**Venice
(Venezia)**

Punte
Sabbioni

Lido

La Giudecca

S. Clemente

FONDAMENTE NUOVE

LUNGA S. CATERI

FONDAMENTE NUOVE

C. ZAN C. TREV. TOSCARINI

FOND ZEN

Caterina
C.LLO
S.ANTONIO

Gesuiti
Oratorio
d. Crociferi

CAMPO DEI GESUITI

C. VENIER

C. DEL MAGAZEN

RIO TERRA DI BARBA FRUTTAROL

C. D. TAGLIAPIETRA

CAMPO D.
MADONNA

SS. Apostoli
CAMPO DEI
S. APOSTOLI

CAMPO
S. CANCIANO

C.LLO
BONDI

C.D.

C.LLO
STELLA

S.Maria
dei Miracoli

C.LLO
S.M.NOVA

S. Giovanni
Crisostomo

AL. S. CHIANCIAI

C. CASTELLI

C. DEL FORNI

C. LARGA

Fondaco
d.Tedeschi

e Rialto &
o Markets

rtolomeo

C. CARMINATI

C. SALIZZADA

San
alvatore

MERCERIA

C. SALVATORE

SPADARIA

C. DI MEZZO

S. Zulian

C. ANTONIO

C. CASSELLARIA

S. Maria
Formosa

CAMPO
S. MARIA
FORMOSA

C. DEI ORBI

Pal. Querini
Stampalia
(Pinacoteca)

SALIZ. ZORZI

C. ANGELO

C. CORONA

Basilica
San Marco

Torre dell'
Orologio

Pal.
Patriarcale

Piazza
Marco

Campanile

Ise
Museo
Correr

Giardinetti
Reali

La
Piazzetta

CAMPO
SAN
ZACCARIA

Bridge of
Sighs

Palazzo
Ducale

Riva

degli

Schiavoni

CAMPO
SAN
GIORGIO

FONDAMENTA DEI MENDICANTI

MENDICANTI

NUOVE

FONDAMENTE

C. WIDMAN

CAMPO SS.
GIOVANNI
E PAOLO

S. Lazzaro
Mendicanti

Ospedale
Civile

Scuola di
San Marco

San Giovanni
e Paolo

Ospedale
dei Vecchi

Monumento
a Colleoni

C. NICOLO MAZZA

C. DELLE CAPPUCCINE

FOND. CASE NUOVE

S. Francesco
della Vigna

CAMPO
S. GIUSTINA

CAMPO DELLA
CONFRATERNITA

CAMPO
DELLA
CELESTIA

COR DELLE
MUNEGHE

Canale di Santa Giustina

CASTELLO

C. LARGA S. LORENZO

S. Lorenzo

CAMPO
S. LORENZO

SALIZZADA S. GIUSTIN

C. DELL'OLIO

Scuola di
San Giorgio degli
Schiavoni

CALLE DEI FURLANI

C.LLO
DUE POZZI

FOND. DI S. LORENZO

C. DEI LEONI

Darsena Grande

Darsena Arsenale Vecchio

FOND. DELL'OSMARINO

S. Antonino

S. Giorgio
dei Greci

San
Zaccaria

S. Giovanni
in Bragora

S. Martino

Arsenale

La Pietà

R. DI CA' DI DIO

C. DEL DOSE

C. CROSERA

CALLE DEI FORNI

Riva

degli

Schiavoni

Riva S. Biagio

Museo
Storico
Navale

FOND. DELLA TANA

C. DEI PIETRI

C. BASSA

Canale di San Marco

Canale di San Marco

Via G. Garibaldi

Riva dei Sette Martiri

CORTE
SARESIN

CALLE S. DOMENICO

Giardini
Pubblici

na
are

ry's
ar

Canale della Giudecca

San Giorgio
Maggiore

ISOLA DI
SAN GIORGIO
MAGGIORE

0 800m
800yds

Riva dei Partig

Museo Storico Navale € *Campo San Biagio, at Fondamenta dell'Arsenale. Open Mon–Sat 0845–1330, closes 1300 Sat.*

San Zaccaria € and chapels *Campo San Zacccaria. Open Mon–Sat 1000–1200, 1600–1800, Sun 1100–1200, 1600–1800. San Zaccaria vaporetto: through the Sottopassagio San Zaccaria on the Riva degli Schiavoni.*

Santi Giovanni e Paolo *Campo Santi Giovanni e Paolo, Vaporetto Fondamente Nuovo. Open Mon–Sat 0900–1200, 1500–1800, Sun 1500–1730.*

Scuola San Giorgio degli Schiavone € *Ponte dei Greci at Rio de San Lorenzo. Open Apr–Oct Tue–Sat 0930–1230, 1530–1830, Sun 0930–1230; Nov–Mar Tue–Sat 1000–1230, 1500–1800, Sun 1000–1230.*

Arsenale**

The great navy of the Venetian Republic was born here, using one of the first production-line techniques in history. Unfortunately it is not open, but you can see much of it from the high bridge over the Riva dell'Arsenale. Ships were moved from station to station (the recesses along the canal) during construction. The arched gate dates from 1460, and in front are a pair of lions snatched from Piraeus and a strange-looking lion, thought to be Scandinavian in origin, from a 1040 war with Byzantium.

Giardinni Pubblici, Bienniale*

The tree-shaded gardens are a cool getaway from sun-warmed buildings and pavements. Summers of odd-numbered years fill the pavilions with an international art show, the Bienniale.

Museo Storico Navale**

Bringing together artefacts of Venice's glory days of naval power, the fascinating collection is user-friendly, with good English signage. It includes original ship models created and used in the Arsenale (*see above*), a model of the Doge's ceremonial barge *Bucintoro*, as well as equipment and uniforms of the Italian Navy into modern times.

Riva degli Schiavoni**

The Riva is the High Street and front window of Venice, a long quay extending from Piazzetta San Marco to the Rio Ca'di Dio. The Schiavoni always seems packed with people, walking and talking. The colourful buzz is most intense near Piazza San Marco, where people go to promenade. Artists sell their paintings (some quite good), others hawk souvenir trinkets. The waterfront is a constant hubbub of gondolas, *vaporetti* and *motoscafe*.

San Zaccaria*

Begun as a Gothic building, by the time San Zaccaria was completed in 1515 it included classical elements of the Renaissance, a mix that continues inside. The second altar to the left has a fine Madonna and Saints, by Giovanni Bellini and opposite is an early Tintoretto, *The Birth of Saint John the Baptist*. Eight Doges are entombed, two of whom died here. More treasure fills the adjacent chapels.

Santi Giovanni e Paolo (San Zanipolo)**

From the mid-13th to the late 18th century, 25 Doges were buried here. The cross-vaulted interior, more than 91m long, is supported by ten stone columns. Tombs flanking the entrance are by the three Lombardos. On the right side in the chapel closest to the front is a unique ceiling, *The Glory of Saint Dominic*, by Giovanni Piazzetta, who influenced the young Tiepolo. Veronese decorated the Capella del Rosario.

Scuola San Giorgio degli Schiavone*

Venice colonised the Dalmatian coast and many Slavs (*schiavoni*) became Venetians. In the 15th century they were numerous and

wealthy enough to build this meeting house, commissioning Vittore
Carpaccio to paint the life cycles of the Slav saints George, Tryphone
and Jerome. Of his three Venetian cyclic paintings, this is considered
the finest.

DORSODURO
West of the San Marco district, Dorsoduro is bounded by the Canale
della Giudecca on the south, the Grand Canal on the east, Santa
Croce/San Polo on the north and the cruise port district on the west.

Campo San Barnaba✛✛
This charming square faces Rio San Barnaba, close to the Grand Canal,
but worlds away. Moored alongside Fondamenta Gherardini is usually
a barge loaded with fruit and vegetables. On the bridge look for
footprints in the white stone, memorialising furious fist fights here in
the 1600s. On a more civilised note, look for **Pasticceria Colussi**,
locally popular for its sweets.

Ca'Rezzonico✛✛
This is a rare opportunity to see the interior of one of the major
Venetian residential palaces. Begun in 1667 and finished at staggering

Ⓝ Ca'Rezzonico €
Fondamenta Rezzonico; tel: 0415 204 036. Recently under restoration, check for current hours.

Gallerie dell'Accademia €€
Grand Canal at Accademia Bridge. Open Tue–Sun 0815–1915, Mon 0900–1400.

Peggy Guggenheim Collection €€
Fondamenta Venier dei Leoni. Open Mon & Wed–Sun 1100–1800.

Most museums do not accept credit cards; keep a supply of paper notes. Admission prices are low, usually under €4, and several have combined admissions schemes.

Basilica San Marco €
(€ Treasury, € Pala d'Oro) Pza S. Marco. Open 0945–1700 Mon–Sat, 1400–1700 Sun Apr–Oct, from Nov–Mar closing is at 1630. Expect long lines. Private worship through the Piazzetta dei Leoncini portal before 0945.

Opposite
Canal scene, Burano Island

expense in 1758, it is now the museum of 18th-century Venice. Poet Robert Browning lived here. It is filled with frescoes, paintings by Guardi, Tiepolo, Canaletto and Longhi, and period furnishings. The ballroom ceiling is in *trompe l'oeil*, other rooms are by Tiepolo.

Gallerie dell'Accademia✦✦✦
The Accademia's 24 galleries house the largest collection of Venetian art in the world. Spanning the 14th–18th centuries, much of it was brought from monasteries and churches suppressed during the Napoleonic period. Artists include Longhi, Carpaccio, Giorgione, Tintoretto, Veronese, Veneziano, and Jacopo, Giovanni and Gentile Bellini, and scores of others.

Peggy Guggenheim Collection✦✦✦
This museum is an exciting counterpoint to the Renaissance art elsewhere. Collector Peggy Guggenheim lived here from the late-1940s until 1979, gathering works of modern artists such as Pollock, Picasso, Ernst, Miro, Kandinsky and Mondrian. Sculpture is displayed throughout the house and gardens.

Squero di San Trovaso✦✦
One of very few gondola construction and repair shops remaining, this *squero* behind the Accademia always seems busy. While you can't go on tour, you can see the gondolas in progress and watch the work across the narrow canal from the Fondamenta Maravegie. The workers who built the shop were from the Dolomites, hence the Alpine-style buildings.

SAN MARCO
In the centre of Venice, its borders are the Grand Canal and the waterfront, except on the east, where Rio di Palazzo, San Zulian and della Fava border it.

Basilica San Marco✦✦✦
Even those who 'don't do churches' marvel at this one. Whether reflecting the midday sun or floodlit at night, the sight is magical, especially when high tides flood the *piazza* to reflect the lighted façade. Built 1063–94, San Marco is Romanesque with a strong Byzantine accent. Five lower arches support a portico for replicas of the famed **bronze horses** from Constantinople (the originals are inside). The whole is topped off with five domes, each with its own parachute-like minidome. To the left, in **Piazzetta dei Leoncini**, are two porphyry lions, more spoils of war, worn smooth by children posing for photographs. Inside, the basilica overwhelms with gold; glittering mosaics dating from the 12th century cover domes, columns and walls. Behind the alabaster high altar is the **Pala d'Oro**, a 250-panel altarpiece created by 10th-century goldsmiths, set with precious stones. The **Treasury** is filled with more silver and gold objects, many collected in conquest.

Bridge of Sighs*

This sad landmark derives its name from the prisoners passing from the Palazzo Ducale to the dank cells of the adjacent prison. The best view of it is from Ponte d'Paglia along the Riva degli Schiavoni, in morning light.

Campanile € *Pza S. Marco.* Open 0930 until 30 minutes before sunset, Apr–Oct, 0930–1630 Nov–Mar. Note that there are usually queues for the ascent.

Campanile**

Rebuilt following its dramatic collapse in 1902, the *campanile* offers views over the entire archipelago, and to the Dolomites on clear days. Originally erected as a lighthouse in 1153, it was also used to suspend prisoners in cages. Contemplate this during a ride to the top in the 14-passenger lift.

During the heyday of the Republic the Piazzetta was called the *broglio*. In the morning it was limited to the use of scheming nobles, hence *imbroglio*.

La Piazzetta***

Joining Piazza San Marco at the campanile, this was the great formal entrance from the sea, at the beginning of the Grand Canal. It is marked by two columns, San Marco and San Teodoro. The focal point is the quintessentially Venetian façade of Palazzo Ducale, the Doges' Palace, beside the basilica of San Marco.

Museo Correr €€€ *Pza S. Marco.* Open daily Apr–Oct 0900–1900, Nov–Mar 0900–1700. Last admission 1hr before closing.

Palazzo Ducale €€€ (combined ticket) *Piazzetta S. Marco.* Open Daily Nov–Mar 0900–1700, Apr–Oct 0900–1900. Last admission 2 hours before closing.

Museo Correr**

Designed by Napoleon as a grand ballroom, the building now houses Venice's civic museum with bits and pieces of its long history. The story of the Republic is on the first floor. You can watch Venetian art blossom on the second, in a fine collection of works by Paolo Veneziano, Cosmè Tura, Antonello da Messina, Gentile Bellini and Vittorio Carpaccio.

Palazzo Ducale***

The candy-coloured marble confection, built throughout the 1400s, was the home of Venice's elected noble rulers. Its Byzantine-influenced Gothic epitomises the Venetian style, which influenced architecture throughout the Veneto. Above the street-level arcade is an arched *loggia*, surmounted by a solid wall of pink and white marble in geometric shapes, with fine carvings on the capitals and corners. Enter through the 1442 **Porta della Carta** into a Renaissance courtyard. The first level above the courtyard was the **Doge's apartments**, with paintings by Bellini, Bosch and Tiepolo. Above were the official government chambers, with Veronese's masterpiece, *The Rape of Europa*, a ceiling also by Veronese and several works by Tintoretto. The **Grand Council Chamber** is spectacular both for its size – 52m long – and its rich decoration. Over the throne is Tintoretto's immense *Paradise* and on the ceiling *The Apotheosis of Venice*, by Veronese. Cross over the **Bridge of Sighs** to see the prison.

To reach Piazza San Marco, take *vaporetto* 1, 52 or 82 to S. Marco or S. Zaccaria.

Piazza San Marco***

Once the seat of power, today San Marco is the cultural and social centre of Venetian life. The basilica of San Marco commands the east end of the square, while the other three sides are formed by three exquisite colonnaded Renaissance buildings, built at different times.

Above
Basilica of San Marco and
Piazza San Marco

On the north is the **Procuratie Vecchie**, anchored at the east end by the **Torre dell'Orologio** (clock tower). The south wall is the colonnaded **Procuratei Nuove**, home to **Caffè Florian**, favoured by Byron, Dickens, Proust and countless others. **Ala Napoleonica**, built in the same style during the Napoleonic occupation, forms the end wall. The **campanile** punctuates the square.

San Giorgio Maggiore

🛈 **San Giorgio Maggiore**
Open Apr–Sept Mon–Sat,
0900–1230, 1430–1830
Sun 0930–1030,
1430–1630; Oct–Mar
Mon–Sat 1000–1230,
1430–1700, Sun
0930–1030, 1430–1630.
Campanile € same hours.

San Giorgio Maggiore✦✦
A masterpiece of Andrea Palladio, San Giorgio sits across the lagoon from the Piazzetta, pure Renaissance with a façade of superimposed classical temples. Inside, Corinthian columns support arches, which in turn support the gallery. Two of Tintoretto's late paintings, *The Last Supper* and *The Gathering of Manna*, are on the chancel side walls. His last, *The Deposition*, is in the Chapel of the Dead. He and his son Domenico painted the *Martyrdom of Saint Stephen* in the left transept.

Torre dell'Orologio✦✦
Calle Mercerei leaves Piazza San Marco, passing under the 15th-century clock tower. The gilt-and-blue clock face shows phases of the moon and the zodiac, surmounted by a statue of the Madonna. Ascension Week brings figures of the Magi from side doors to pay homage. Atop the tower a pair of Moors, *Due Mori*, strike the large bell each hour.

Ca'Pesaro €
Canal Grande, Santa Croce. Open Tue–Sun 0900–1400. San Stae vaporetto stop.

Frari Santa Maria Gloriosa dei Frari €
Campo dei Frari, vaporetto to San Toma. Open Mon–Sat 0900–1800, Sun 1400–1700.

Scuola San Rocco
€€ Campo San Rocco. Open daily Apr–Oct 0900–1730, Nov–Mar 1000–1300 Mon–Fri, Sat–Sun 1000–1600. Last entrance half hour before closing.

SAN POLO and SANTA CROCE

Located on the west side of the Grand Canal, which forms their boundary, except in the south where the boundaries are the Rio Nuovo and the Rio di Ca'Foscari.

Ca'Pesaro, Galleria d'Arte Moderna✦✦

The Pesaro family were prominent Venetians, and their 1710 *palazzo* was given to the community to exhibit works by unknown artists. It now displays works of Klimt, Klee, Bonnard, Matisse and Miro, along with works of lesser-known Italian painters of the last two centuries.

Ponte Rialto✦✦✦

Since 1591 this graceful bridge has been one of only two ways of crossing the Grand Canal on foot. The single arch span has balustraded staircases of 42 steps rising along each side. In the centre are two rows of shops, now largely selling souvenirs. It's a fascinating place for watching water traffic on the canal as gondolas, *motorscafe*, rowboats, *vaporetti* and work-a-day barges and delivery boats perform a water ballet vying for space. Watch housewives and chefs in the **Rialto markets✦** choose from the myriad fish and fresh produce from lagoon farms to learn what the evening's menu specials will be. Barges loaded with *radicchio*, artichokes, sole, squid and sardines begin to arrive at dawn. The colourful spectacle is all over and closed up by noon. Cross the Rialto bridge from San Marco and take the first right along the Grand Canal.

Santa Maria Gloriosa dei Frari✦✦✦

When the Franciscans built this brown brick Gothic church in the mid-15th century, they made it big. The 97m nave was big enough to accommodate some of the finest art in the city. At the centre of the high altar is a magnificent *Assumption of the Virgin*, by Titian; his *Madonna di Ca'Pesaro* hangs by the side entrance. Pietro Lombardo's exquisitely-carved **rood screen** hides an unusual set of relief-carved **choir stalls** of Venetian scenes and saints. Flanking the main altar are the tombs of two doges and in the first chapel to the right of the altar is a fine carved wooden Saint John the Baptist by Donatello. Tombs and monuments commemorate Titian, Canova, Monteverde and other greats. The former monastery has two cloisters, one by Sansovino, the other by Palladio.

Scuola San Rocco✦✦✦

The 16th-century Scuola in tribute to San Rocco was a hedge against the return of the plague. Tintoretto was commissioned to decorate, and reached new heights in the treatment of light, colour and perspective. Ceilings and walls in three large chambers are covered with his work. In Venice, a *scuola* was a building housing charitable organisations for the city's poor or a meeting place for a minority population. Their ornate décor shows the attention that was lavished on them.

Right
Gondolas at S. Zaccharia,
Riva degli Schiavoni

THE ISLANDS

While most of the lagoons have been filled, leaving only canals to separate them, a few islands still exist and they make a delightful day excursion. Boats leave from San Zaccaria, but before setting out, verify the return schedule so you will not be stranded.

Museo del Merletti
€ *Pza Galuppi. Open Apr–Oct Wed–Mon 1000–1700; Nov–Mar Wed–Mon 1000–1400.*

Trattoria da Gatto Nero €–€€
Da Ruggero. Sits along the canal with views of bright coloured houses and the tilting campanile.

Burano and Mazzorbo❖❖

Smaller than Murano Island, but far more colourful and interesting, Burano is famed for its lace. **Museo del Merletti**, in the former lace-making school, has demonstrations and historic examples of the art and a school where lace making is taught. The small houses that line Burano's canals are painted in brilliant colours, as are its fishing boats. Somewhat startling is the dramatic tilt of the **Campanile di San Martin**, which seems ready to topple into the lagoon. Cross to the island of **Mazzorbo**, for a nice walk through a garden and along a *fondamenta*, where you can catch the ferry.

Lido❖

Lido was the favoured beach of the crowned heads of Europe; everyone who was anyone came to try the new sport of sea bathing on its 11km of beach. Although past its social prime, Lido still draws crowds to its casino, film festival and hotels. To explore its quiet roads and canal, hire a bicycle opposite the *vaporetto* quay.

Museo Vetrario €
Fondamenta Giustinian.
Open Thur–Tue
1000–1700, 1600 winter.

Museo dell'Estuario €
Open Mar–Oct Tue–Sun
1030–1730, Nov–Feb
Tue–Sun 1000–1700.

Santa Maria Assunta €
Open same hours as
museum.

Murano*

Famed for glass-blowing, Murano is thronged by tourists. Beware of people touting free tours: they will lead you to places of inferior quality. Leave the main *fondamenta* to see the real Murano, and visit **Museo Vetrario** to see the glass-blowers' art in a 17th-century *palazzo*. When the shops close, the island shuts down.

Torcello**

When the Veneti escaped into the lagoon in the 5th century they first set up shop at Torcello, but soon outgrew it. The highlight of the marshy island is their basilica, **Santa Maria Assunta**, parts of which date from 638. Its tall *campanile* stands out above the lagoon. The church has an exquisite 9th- to 12th-century floor and wall mosaics, including a Madonna on a gold ground and a frightening rendition of the Last Judgement. The small church nearby is **Santa Fosca** (11th-century). In the *piazza* is the **Museo dell'Estuario**, with an excellent collection of ancient artefacts from around the lagoon and, in a second building, mosaics, Byzantine and Medieval art.

Accommodation and food

Nearly every *campo* of any size has at least one restaurant, and they cluster in droves along the Grand Canal near the Rialto and in the streets close to San Marco. But those in heavy tourist areas are not necessarily the best. Better to browse in the narrow streets away from the Grand Canal.

Hotel Alex €€ *Friari, S Polo 2606; tel/fax: 0415 231 341; www.hotelalexinvenice.com.* A short walk from the S Toma *vaporetto* stop, this new hotel has attractive rooms at budget prices for Venice.

Hotel Caneva €€ *Castello 5515; tel: 0415 228 118; fax: 0415 208 676.* Hospitable, clean and inexpensive hotel perfectly located on the shortest route between the Rialto and San Marco.

Above
Scallops and fish at the
Rialto market

Hotel Gallini €€ *Calle della Verona 3673, San Marco; tel: 0415 204 515; fax: 0415 209 103; www.hotelgallini.it.* Near La Fenice theatre, with a friendly staff.

Pensione Accademia-Villa Maravage €€–€€€ *Fondamenta Bollani 1058 Dorsoduro 31023; tel: 0415 237 846; fax: 0415 239 152.* San Trovaso and the Accademia are just a few steps away from this fine small hotel facing the Grand Canal over gardens.

Trattoria Casa Mia
€–€€ *Calle de L'Oca.*
Closed Tue. An inviting
dining room with wainscot
and stucco walls; Venetian
specialities are marked on
the menu and include *sarde
in saor* (marinated
sardines).

Fiaschetteria Toscana €€–€€€ *Salizzada San Giovanni Crisostomo 5719; tel: 0415 285 281.* Near the Marco Polo house, this restaurant serves regional specialities. Look for scallops with almonds or more traditional *frito misto*.

Bar alla Toletta € *Calle Toletta; tel: 0415 200 196.* Delicious *pannini* near San Trovaso and the Accademia. Very popular with locals.

Osteria Alberto € *Calle Giacinto Gallina, near Santa Maria dei Miracli; tel: 0415 238 153.* Menu includes aubergine *parmegian*, gnocchi with four cheeses, *fegato Venetiana* (veal liver). It's popular, so expect a wait.

Signor Blum *Campo San Barnaba, Dorsoduro; tel: 0416 226 367.* Captivating, intricate wooden puzzles in natural finishes and bright colours.

Tragie Comica *Calle dei Nomboli 2800, San Polo; tel: 041 721 102; www.tragicomica.it.* Maker of outstanding masks and costumes.

Osteria alla Botte €€ *Calle de la Bissa, off Campo San Bartolomeo; tel: 0415 200 623. Closed Wed.* Small and cosy, with dark panelling and friendly service. Good *cicchetti* (traditional snacks) include creamed salt cod with grilled white-corn *polenta*.

Osteria Vivaldi €€ *Calle de la Madoneta, S Polo; tel: 0415 238 185.* The menu changes daily and always includes local seafood dishes. Cash only.

Trattoria alla Madonna €–€€ *Calle della Madonna 594; tel: 0415 223 824. Closed Wed.* The big, unpretentious dining room is known for the high quality of its seafood; try *risotto*, fried baby whitefish or *anguilla frita* (eel).

Shopping

Among the warren of streets are excellent shops and craftsmen's studios. Streets called *Ruga* are good places to look, since the word indicates that the street is lined with shops.

Franco Furlanetto *Calle dei Nomboli, corner of Rio Terra Nomboli; tel: 0415 209 544; e-mail: ffranco01@libero.it.* Wood carver makes *forcola*, the oar supports for gondolas, and gondola details. A fascinating place to visit.

Il Pavone *Campiello dei Meoni, Calle de Mezzo 1478, between the Rialto and Campo San Polo; tel: 0415 224 296.* Some of the finest paper goods in the city.

Karisima *Rio Terra de Nomboli 2752, at the corner of Calle dei Saoneri.* Speciality papers including botanicals, blank books and leather-bound books, at excellent prices.

La Bottega dei Mascareri *San Polo 80, near the Ponte Rialto; tel: 0415 223 857, and Calle Saoneri; tel: 0415 242 887.* A fine mask shop with two locations.

Moro Giovanni, Il Mondo in Miniatura *Calle della Toletta 1193, near the Ponte della Marevegie between San Barnaba and Accademia; www.morogiovanni.com.* Colourful and beautifully executed miniatures of every major Venetian building fill the walls of this small shop.

Punto Arte *Calle dei Saonere 2721, S Polo; tel: 0415 227 979; www.etchingvenice.com.* Hand-printed etchings in the traditional technique capture Venice's unique light refractions with aquatint.

Walking Tour – San Marco and Castello

Time: About 3 hours.

Route: Start at **PIAZZA SAN MARCO ❶** in front of **PALAZZO DUCALE ❷** and head towards the water, turning left onto **RIVA DEGLI SCHIAVONI ❸**, created 600 years ago. Cross a bridge over the Rio del Palazzo, looking left to see the **BRIDGE OF SIGHS ❹**. Just before the next bridge is the former **Palazzo Dandolo**, now **Hotel Danieli**. Cross the bridge and directly ahead is the monumental statue of **Vittorio Emanuele II**, the first king of a united Italy. On the left opposite the San Zaccaria *vaporetto* stop, a *sottopassagio* through a building leads to the *campo* and church of **SAN ZACCARIA ❺**.

Leave the **Campo San Zaccaria** at the top left corner, passing through the **Campo San Provolo** and along the **Fondamento dell'Osmarin**, look for the pink **Palazzo Pruili** on the opposite side. Turn left, crossing **Rio San Provolo** at **Rio dei Greci**. While crossing it, look to the right, at the precariously leaning *campanile* of **San Giorgio dei Greci**. Follow **Fondamento di San Lorenzo** along the canal to **Calle dei Leoni**, going right across the canal and continuing across **Rio della Pieta** to the SCUOLA SAN GIORGIO DEGLI SCHIAVONI ❻. Backtrack across Rio dei Greci on Calle dei Leoni and turn right onto **Fondamento di San Lorenzo** along the canal to the second left, **Calle Larga San Lorenzo**. Follow it, turning right at the **Palazzo Cavagnis** and following **Calle Ospedale** as it twists to the left and right crossing three canals on the way. At the **Salizzada SS. Giovanni and Paolo** go left and the extraordinary mounted statue of **Colleoni** is ahead when you reach **Campo SS. Giovanni and Paolo**. In this square you will find the **Scuola di San Marco ❼** and SANTI GIOVANNI E PAOLO ❽.

Leave by the northwest corner of the campo and cross **Rio dei Mendicanti** on **Calle Larga G Gallina**, which leads into the beautiful **Campo Santa Maria Nova**, a good place for a café break. Across the bridge and **Rio dei Miracoli** is SANTA MARIA DEI MIRACOLI ❾. From its front door, take **Calle dei Miracoli** across **Rio dei Miracoli** to **Salizzada San Canzian**, turning left and following it to **Campo di San Giovanni Crisostomo**. Here follow **Salizzada San Giovanni Crisostomo** to the left to **Campo San Bartolomeo**, an active place at any hour. Follow **Salizzada Pio X** right to PONTE RIALTO ❿ for a good vantage point over the busy **Grand Canal**. At the foot of the bridge follow the shore a few feet right on **Riva di Ferro** to **Via Mazzini**, following it to **Merceria San Salvatore**, **Merceria San Zulian** and **Merceria di Orologio**, shopping streets, all signposted, back to Piazza San Marco ❶.

This is a map of Venice showing the Castello area and surrounding landmarks.

Labels on map:

S. Lazzaro Mendicanti

Ospedale Civile

SS. Apostoli

CAMPO DEI S. APOSTOLI

CAMPO S. CANCIANO

C.D. BONDI

C.LLO STELLA

C. WIDMAN

Santi Giovanni e Paolo

SAL. S. CANZIAN

Santa Maria dei Miracoli ❾

C.LLO S.M.NOVA

CAMPO SS. GIOVANNI E PAOLO

Scuola di San Marco ❼

Ospedale dei Vecchi

S. Giovanni Crisostomo

C. CASTELLI

Monumento a Colleoni

C. NICOLO MAZZA

C. DELLE CAPPUCCINE

Fondaco d.Tedeschi

C. DEL DOSE

C. LARGA

❿ Ponte Rialto & Rialto Markets

C. CARMINATI

CAMPO S. GIUSTINA

CASTELLO

S. Bartolomeo

SALIZZADA S. LIO

CAMPO S. MARIA FORMOSA

C. DEI ORBI

C. LARGA S. LORENZO

S. Lorenzo

CAMPO S. LORENZO

San Salvatore

C. DI MEZZO

MERCERIA S. SALVATORE

C.S. ANTONIO

S. Maria Formosa

C. CASSELLARIA

FOND. DI S. LORENZO

Scuola San Giorgio degli Schiavoni ❻

C. DEI LEONI

Pal. Querini Stampalia (Pinacoteca)

SALIZ. ZORZI

C.D. CORONA

FOND. DELL'OSMARIN

S. Zulian

C. DELL' ANGELO

COR. D. FORNO VECCHIO

COR. ZORZI

Torre dell' Orologio

Pal. Patriarcale

San Zaccaria ❺

S. Giorgio dei Greci

CAMPO SAN ZACCARIA

Basilica San Marco

Campanile

MERCERIA S. SPADARIA

Palazzo Ducale ❷

❹ Bridge of Sighs

La Pietà

Campanile ❶

PIAZZA SAN MARCO

❸ Riva degli Schiavoni

S. Moisè

Museo Correr

LA PIAZZETTA

C. VALLARESSO

C. DEL RIDOTTO

Giardinetti Reali

Harry's Bar

Canale di San Marco

Venice

0 — 100m

100yds

Eastern Alpine foothills

Ratings

Architecture	●●●●○
Food and drink	●●●●○
Mountains	●●●●○
Scenery	●●●●○
Vineyards	●●●●○
Art	●●●○○
Markets	●●○○○
Villages	●○○○○

At the height of the Venetian Republic, *La Serenissima*, as it was called, spread its influence over most of northeastern Italy. St Mark's lion gazed benevolently over places far from the Adriatic lagoons, bringing art, culture and – for its time – an enlightened civil government. That influence is still so evident that many of the cities are known as 'little Venices' and today's visitor will recognise them first by their architecture. Graceful curved windows and balconies, often traced in delicate stonework, recall the *palazzi* that overlook the Grand Canal. Along with the physical signs, these small cities bear a cultured grace that makes them exceedingly pleasant places to be. They are rarely crowded, except by a festival celebrating a local harvest or the day of a patron saint. The rich farmlands of the Treviso province assure a varied seasonal cuisine.

BELLUNO❖❖

❶ APT *V. Rodolfo Pesaro 21; tel: 0437 940 083; www.dolomiti.it/apt or www. bellunocentrostorico.com. Open Mon–Sat 1000–1230, 1430–1730.*

❷ *Arriving from the south, cross the river and enter a tunnel under the city, which you can see directly above. Immediately out of the tunnel is the entrance to a car park, **Parcheggio Lamboi €**, and to the steep stair-lift that takes*

Belluno's setting, high above the confluence of the Piave and the Ardo, surrounded by mountains, is reason enough for a visit. The steep stair-lift from the car park deposits you in front of Belluno's most elegant building, the Venetian **Palazzo Rettori❖**. Now governmental offices, this *palazzo* was built between 1491 and 1536, with a nine-arch colonnade and clock tower. Next to it is the 12th-century **Torre Civica❖**, the battlemented remnant of a medieval castle. Opposite is the **duomo❖**, designed by Lombardo, with a tall *campanile* which you can ascend for splendid mountain views. Construction began on the cathedral in 1517 in a combination of both the Renaissance and baroque styles. The unfinished bronze doors honour Bellunese Albino Luciani who became Pope John Paul I.

Facing the *duomo* is the **baptistery❖❖**, with a magnificent carved font cover. Also facing the *duomo* is the **Museo Civico❖❖**, which has archaeological artefacts and paintings by the master, Montagna. Just

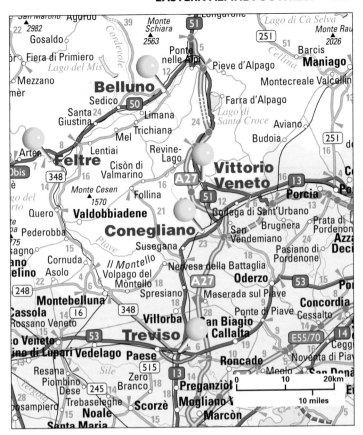

you to the old town. Take a token from the machine on entering the car park and take it with you to the lift. As you leave the lift on your way back, put the token into the machine at the door and it literally tells you what to pay (in English). If you drive into the upper town, parking is on Piazza di Martiri.

Duomo *Pza Duomo.*
Open daily
0700–1200, 1500–1900.
Baptistery *open daily*
0800–1200, 1500–1900.

beyond is the **Piazza del Mercato** (also called the Piazza Erbe), faced by the **Loggia dei Ghibellini**, dating from the 15th and 16th centuries. A barely discernible Lion of St Mark is on the wall, put there when the Venetians were in control and defaced in 1797. In the centre is an early 15th-century fountain. Along Via Rialto is **Porta Dojona**, a gate whose southern side was built in 1289 and north side in 1533. Attractive **Piazza dei Martiri** with its cafés and public gardens is north of the *duomo*. The streets in old Belluno are well worth wandering as they wind between and under Renaissance buildings. The church of **San Pietro** has altars carved by Brustolon, who did the font cover in the baptistery, and a side chapel with a fresco cycle by Ricci. The church of **San Stefano** also has some of Brustolon's carving, and sits in a pleasant shaded garden not far from Piazza dei Martiri.

Accommodation and food in Belluno

Hotel Alle Dolomiti € *V. Carrera 46, Belluno 32100; tel: 0437 941 660; fax: 0437 941 436; www.dolomiti.it/alledolomiti.* Well located between the Piazza dei Martiri and San Stefano. Comfortable, attractive and bright, with a restaurant; rate includes breakfast.

Museo Civico € *Pza Duomo. Open Tue–Sat 1000–1200, 1600–1900, closed Sat Oct–Apr.*

San Pietro *Pza San Pietro, east of V. Mezzaterra. Open Mon–Sat 0900–1230, 1600–1900.*

San Stefano *V. Roma at Pza San Stefano. Open Mon–Sat 0900–1200, 1600–1900.*

Market day: Sat.

Hotel Astor €–€€ *Pza dei Martiri 26E; tel: 0437 942 094; fax: 0437 942 493.* Nicely located in a modern building on the historic *piazza*.

Enoteca Mazzini € *Off Pza Mazzini.* A good place to sample local wines in a very traditional atmosphere.

Ristorante Taverna € *V. Cipro 7; tel: 0437 25 192.* A good menu and pleasant patio for alfresco dining, plus bar.

Trattoria Moretto € *V. P Valeriano 8; tel: 0437 943 476.* Simple surroundings and simply delicious food. Pasta with smoked cheese filling may be on the menu, which changes daily.

CONEGLIANO

APCT *V. XX Settembre 61; tel: 043 821 230; fax: 0438 428 777. Open Mon–Fri 0900–1230 (Tue, Thur, Fri also 1500–1800), Sat–Sun 0930–1230, 1500–1800.*

Parking is plentiful at the castle, less so in the lower town.

Casa di Cima € *· V. Cima; tel: 043 822 660. Open Sat–Sun 1500–1900.*

Galleria Civica dell'Arte € *V. XX Settembre. Open Mon 1430–1830, Tue–Fri 0900–1200, 1430–1830.*

Museo Castelvecchio € *Pzle Castelvecchio; tel: 043 822 871. Open Tue–Sat 1000–1230, Sun & holidays 1000–1230, 1530–1900.*

Scuola di Santa Maria dei Battuti € *V. XX Settembre. Open Sun & holidays 1500–1830, or enquire at the duomo.*

Market day: Fri.

Conegliano rolls down a hillside in three terraces, crowned at the summit by **Castelvecchio**✧✧✧, a walled enclosure with a square tower, shown in some of the paintings of Cima de Conegliano. Inside the tower, **Museo Castelvecchio**✧ contains frescoes and 16th-century paintings, among other works of art. This castle's walls are a good place to get an up-close look at the unique 'fishtail' crenellations that are the hallmark of castles built by the Scaligeri family of Verona. Here they frame views of the town and the beautiful rolling countryside of vineyards, where Prosecco, one of Italy's finest sparkling white wines, is produced. Views from the castle's terrace extend over a vineyard-filled valley to the Dolomites, best savoured from a table at **Bar Ristorante Al Castello**, designated as the first stop on the *Strada del Vino Bianco*, the 'White Wine Road' (maps at tourist offices en route).

The castle is connected to the town below via a cobbled walkway, Calle Madonna della Neve, bordered by the arcaded wall of a monastery, under restoration. It passes the appealing little **Oratorio Madonna della Neve**✧. Conegliano's middle terrace is its heart, the curving and arcaded Via XX Settembre. Here are the best of the town's *palazzi*, many from the 15th century. Some are decorated in fresco, some have distinctive windows in the Venetian style. Opening onto this street under a deep *loggia* is the **duomo**✧✧, which is highlighted by the only major work to remain in the city by its most noted artist, Cima da Conegliano. This **altarpiece**✧✧✧, of the Virgin and Child, was created by commission of the brotherhood of flagellants, the *Battuti*, whose headquarters is next door. Reached from a passageway beside the cathedral, the **Scuola di Santa Maria dei Battuti**✧✧✧ is at the top of a flight of stone stairs. It is lined with a most unusual cycle of 15th- and 16th-century frescoes, in which the Dolomites are recognisable. Listen for the *duomo* bell, which clearly rings out 'Figaro, Figaro, Figaro'.

On the opposite side of Via XX Settembre is the **Galleria Civica dell'Arte***, where you should at least step into the courtyard to see the unusual wooden statue of the Madonna, with a door enclosing the infant Christ. Although it has no originals, Cima's birthplace, **Casa di Cima***, has reproductions of many of his works, in which it's easy to recognise the landscapes of his hometown region. At its centre, Via XX Settembre opens out into a terraced plaza, in front of the **Accademia**, a neo-classical theatre guarded by two buxom and oft-photographed sphinx. Below is a wide passageway leading down to the town's business area, much of which lies along Corso G Mazzini, bordered by·a swathe of greenery with cafés overlooking it.

Right
Accademia, Conegliano

Accommodation and food in Conegliano

Canon d'Oro €–€€ *V. XX Settembre 129, Conegliano 31015; tel: 043 834 346; fax: 043 834 249; e-mail: canondoro@sevenonline.it*. Beautifully and recently renovated, the rooms in this historic frescoed building are very nicely furnished. Enclosed parking and a secluded garden terrace.

Cristallo € *Corso G Mazzini 45; tel: 043 835 445; fax: 043 824 434*. A full service hotel with restaurant and bar, and with parking for guests.

Caffè Centrale € *Piazzetta XVIII Luglio 8; tel: 043 822 488*. Good for sandwiches, light meals and people-watching from a terrace above Corso G Mazzini.

Restaurante Canon d'Oro €–€€ adjoining the hotel, but separately owned, is excellent, serving starters such as *risotto* with shellfish and mixed grilled fish *en brochette*, along with several good veal dishes.

Osteria/Trattoria Citta di Venezia €–€€ *V. XX Settembre 77/79; tel: 043 823 186. Closed Sun night, Mon & late Aug*. Although the speciality is seafood, they usually have four options including pasta and meat dishes, all well prepared.

Tre Panoce €€ *La Vecchia Trevigiana 50 S13; tel: 043 860 071. Closed Sun evening & Mon*. Wooden ceiling beams and warm lighting create an inviting atmosphere. A speciality is duck with Prosecco.

Trattoria Stella €–€€ *V. Academia 3; tel: 043 822 178*. No menu, but genial host will describe the day's specials, which might be veal, or crepes with asparagus.

FELTRE♦♦

ⓘ ARPT *Piazetta Trento; tel: 0439 2540. Open daily.*

Ⓖ Galleria Rizzarda *€ V. del Paradiso 8. Open Jun–Sept, Tue–Sun 1000–1300, 1600–1900.*

Museo Civico *€ Pza Maggiore; tel: 0439 885 241. Open Apr–Oct, Tue–Sun 1000–1300, 1600–1900, earlier afternoon hours in winter.*

Ⓜ Market days: Tue, Fri morning.

The steeply-roofed 16th-century houses that line the streets of Feltre reflect the shapes of the mountains that rise behind it. The homogeneous architecture results from Feltre's rebuilding by Venice after it was sacked by enemies of the empire. This, of course, accounts for the Lion of St Mark, prominent on a column in the central square. Only a part of the medieval castle is left of the earlier city, also found on **Piazza Maggiore♦♦**, along with a Lombardo **fountain♦**. A row of Renaissance *palazzi* lines one side of the square. The **Museo Civico♦** tells the town's tumultuous history since the Romans and Etruscans, in addition to paintings by arch-rivals Bellini and Cima da Conegliano and local artist Lorenzo Luzzo. More palaces lie along the main street, **Via Mezzaterre♦♦**, many with frescoed walls by Luzzo. In the lower part of the town, reached by arcaded steps, is the **duomo♦**, which has an outstanding **Byzantine cross♦♦** carved in the 6th century, showing 52 New Testament scenes. **Galleria Rizzarda♦** exhibits modern art and wrought iron work by the local master Carlo Rizzarda.

Accommodation and food in Feltre

Hotel Nuovo € *V. Fornere Pazze 5, 32032; tel: 043 92 110; fax: 043 989 241.* Located near the historic centre, this full-service hotel is comfortable and has a bar; parking is available for guests.

Osteria Novacento € *V. Mezzaterra 24; tel: 043 980 193. Closed Mon.* Sample local wines with well-prepared seafood.

TREVISO✦✦✦

APT *Pza della Signori 41; tel: 0422 547 632; www.provincia.treviso.it. Open Mon–Fri 0900–1230, 1400–1800, Sat–Sun 0930–1230, 1500–1800.*

Below
Houses along one of Treviso's canals

Descriptions of Treviso that bill it as a mini-Venice don't do it justice. While it does have a river and two canals running through its centre, it looks and feels very little like Venice. It is quite pretty in its own right, with flower-draped balconies and graceful willows overhanging the water and wide, tree-lined streets. In addition to the trees, it differs from Venice in that it is a completely walled town, entered over a moat and through monumental gates. It's clear who built the protective walls, however: lions look down from the gates. Small enough to explore easily on foot, Treviso is level, compact and a pleasure to walk in.

The Lion of St Mark

Wherever you go in the Veneto, you are likely to find the symbol of *La Serenissima*, Venice's name for its republic. The lion, often standing atop a column, but also found in *bas-relief* on a prominent wall overlooking a square, holds a book in one paw. If the book is open, Venice is at peace. When the book is closed, Venice is at war. Many of these lions are gone, victims of war, neglect or development, but a careful search will turn them up, even in such unexpected places as carved on a pulpit.

P Parking is in Piazza Duomo € Piazza Matteotti €, just inside the north town wall € and along most of the broad streets with entrance gates.

A Sunday antiques market is set up along Via Liberale.

Market days: Tue, Sat morning.

Duomo *Pza Duomo. Open daily 0900–1200, 1500–1800.*

San Nicolo *V. San Nicolo. Open 0900–1200, 1500–1800.*

The **duomo**⁕⁕ has been rebuilt several times since its beginnings in the 1100s. In the chapel to the right of the high altar is a Titian painting, and the church also has an excellent Pordenone fresco and a Lombardo tomb. At the church of **San Nicolo**⁕⁕ and chapterhouse of the adjacent Dominican monastery, are paintings by Thomas of Modena as well as a number of frescoes, decorated columns and monumental tombs. The chapterhouse wall friezes and frescoes are particularly notable, as is the Byzantine crucifix. Modena frescoes decorate several other Treviso churches.

Treviso is the home of an Italian family business success story: **Benetton**. To see what's new in the Kingdom of United Colours, visit their store, prominently located next to the fine old **Palazzo dei Trecento**⁕⁕, built in the 13th century. It was severely damaged in Second World War bombings, and you can see the line of rebuilding. Behind the *palazzo* is the colourful arcaded **Pescheria**⁕⁕, a daily food market on an island in the canal. Behind that is the rebuilt 13th-century church of **San Francesco**⁕, with more Modena frescoes in a chapel adjacent to the chancel.

Accommodation and food in Treviso

Hotel Campeol € *Pza G Ancillotto 8, 31100; tel: 042 256 601; fax: 0422 540 871.* A good, comfortable, hotel in the town centre, behind the Palazzo dei Trecento, but without guest parking.

Al Fogher €€ *Vle della Republicca 10; tel: 0422 432 950; fax: 0422 430 391; e-mail: htl@alfogher.com.* A full-service hotel with restaurant, serving local specialities. Parking available for guests, handicapped accessible. Outside the town walls to the west.

Hotel Al Giardino € *Strada di Sant Antonino 300/a, 31100; tel: 0422 406 406; fax: 0422 406 406.* Out of town a bit, but with easy access and plentiful parking. Inexpensive comfortable rooms, a restaurant and bar.

Above
Clock tower with Lion of St Mark, Treviso

Antica Osteria al Cavallino €–€€ *Borgo Cavour 52 at town gate, Porta Quaranta; tel: 0422 412 801. Closed Tue.* The fish is delectable, the owners good-natured and the atmosphere cosy. Sun afternoon favourite of local families, who fill the vine-draped terrace with laughter.

Il Cascinale € *Strada Torre d'Orlando 6/B, Sant'Angelo; tel/fax: 0422 402 203. Restaurant open Fri–Sun and by advance booking.* A bright new *agriturismo* lodging and restaurant, 3km south from the centre of Treviso. The *gnocchi* with local red endive, fresh asparagus or other seasonal vegetable is delectable.

Osteria alla Pasina €€ *V. Peschiere 15, Dosson di Casier, 2km from Treviso; tel: 0422 382 112. Closed Mon evening & Tue.* In season, try the *zucchini* blossoms filled with fresh fish.

VITTORIO VENETO✦✦

ⓘ ARPT *Pza del Populo 18; tel: 0438 572 43. Open Mon–Sat 0900–1300, 1500–1800.*

ⓟ *Parking is difficult in old Serravalle, and nearly impossible on Mon; park well south of town and walk to the old centre.*

ⓖ Duomo *Off Pza Marcantonio Flaminio. Open Mon–Sat 0900–1300, 1500–1900.*

Museo del Cenedense € *Pza Marcantonio Flaminio 1; tel: 0438 571 03. Open May–Sept Tue–Sun 1000–1200, 1630–1830, Oct–Apr Tue–Sun 1000–1200, 1500–1700.*

Museo della Battaglia € *Pza Giovanni Paolo 1, Ceneda; tel: 0438 576 95. Open May–Sept Tue–Sun 1000–1200, 1600–1830, Oct–Apr Tue–Sun 1000–1200, 1400–1700.*

Really two towns, Serravalle and Ceneda could not be more different, despite their close proximity. Apart from the **Museo della Battaglia**✦, of particular interest to those questing First World War history, there is little in the southern Ceneda worth stopping for. Serravalle, however, is a delight to explore, with slightly lopsided stone buildings, venerable wooden doors beneath low arched arcades, and frescoes decorating its walls. At the northern end, just before the town ends abruptly at a sheer rock face, is one of the Veneto's loveliest squares, **Piazza Marcantonio Flaminio**✦✦. At one end is the **Museo del Cenedense**✦, worth a visit, but more notable for its elaborately decorated exterior than for the mixture of archaeology, sculpture and frescoes inside. Other buildings around the square are adorned with frescoes and balconies and a Lion of St Mark surveys it all from his customary pillar. Occasional market stalls sell local sausages and cheeses from nearby farms. Just across the bridge from the *piazza*, the **duomo**✦ has a Madonna by Titian. The **Oratorio di San Lorenzo dei Battuti**✦✦ is decorated by a remarkably well-preserved cycle of mid-15th-century frescoes.

Accommodation and food in Vittorio Veneto

Al Ben Star €–€€ *V. Piandera, Nogarola village just west of Vittorio Veneto; tel: 0438 583 659.* Two guest rooms on a lovely farm just west of town, with a restaurant open on weekends or with advance notice. Specialities are farm-fresh vegetables and grilled meats. Children are welcomed with a full playground.

Oratorio di San Lorenzo dei Battuti *Open Tue–Sun 1400–1500. Tour begins at Museo del Cenedense.*

Market day: Mon.

Hotel Diana €–€€ *V. Roma 49, Valdobbiadene 31049; tel: 0423 976 222; fax: 0423 972 237.* Comfortable accommodation in town with a restaurant and bar, garage parking. Disabled accessible. Breakfast €.

Casa Caldart €€ *V. Erizzo 165, Valdobbiadene; tel: 0423 980 333.* Dine indoors or out on their terrace. Well-prepared local dishes.

Hotel Flora € *V. Cavour 8, 31029; tel: 043 853 142; fax: 0438 941 440; e-mail: hotelflora@libero.it.* Close to the rail station and in the centre of town, this is a comfortable and convenient venue from which to explore. Breakfast is included in the rate and the hotel has a restaurant, bar and garage.

Trattoria alla Cerva € *Pza Marcantonio Flaminio.* In the centre of town on a square that looks like a stage set. Serves well-prepared local specialities.

Suggested tour

Total distance: 140km, with detours 143km.

Time: 3½ hours' driving. Allow 3 days for the main route, 3 days with detours. Those with limited time should concentrate on Treviso.

Links: From Venice (Venezia) (*see page 172*), S13 leads north to Treviso. Connect to the Western Alpine foothills route (*see page 208*) through Asolo via S248 from Montebelluna.

Opposite
Piazza Marcantonio, Vittorio
Veneto

Right
Museo Cenedense, Vittorio
Veneto

Route: Leave **TREVISO** ❶ heading north on S13, crossing the wide
River Piave before arriving at **CONEGLIANO** ❷. Return to S13 and
continue north a short distance, turning north (left) onto S51. Follow
it to **VITTORIO VENETO** ❸. Note that the *autostrada* A27 bypasses

Da Nani *V. Maseral Fabri 14, Solighetto di Pieve di Soligo; tel: 0438 842 078. Open Fri–Sun, Mar–Dec.* A pleasant, rustic restaurant, where you can sample Prosecco with your sausage or grilled chicken.

the town of Vittorio Veneto (41 km). Continue north from Vittorio Veneto on S51 through a scenic valley past the lake of Santa Croce to **Ponte nelle Alpi** where you again cross the Piave and immediately turn left on S50 signposted for **BELLUNO** ❹ (39km). Leave Belluno heading west on S50 to **FELTRE** ❺ (31km). Backtrack from Feltre as far as **Busche**, turning south (right) on S348 which parallels the Piave River. At **Fener** turn left to cross the Piave, following signs to **San Vito** and **Valdobbiadene**. (*See Detour on page 199*) From Valdobbiadene backtrack through San Vito and across the Piave to S348, turning south (left). Follow S348 past **Montebelluna** and back to **TREVISO** ❶ (60km).

> This region is the centre for *Cartizze*, a DOC (*denominazione di origine controllata*) of Prosecco, a sparkling white wine, which you can taste and buy at vineyards along the way from Valdobbiadene to Conegliano. The area has a number of *agriturismo* farm restaurants, open only on weekends, most of which specialise in grilled meats, sausages and fresh vegetables and fruit from their farms – and of course, the local white wines.

Right
Café, Castello, Conegliano

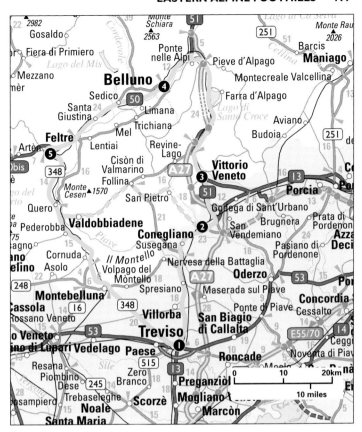

ARPT *V. Roma 10, Forno di Zolda; tel: 0437 787 349.*

Detour: From Valdobbiadene, the *Strada del Vino Bianco*, the 'White Wine Road', should be easy to follow, but is not. Signs lead in all directions, much to the traveller's confusion; but the detour is enjoyable, and if you get lost, simply follow signs or ask directions to Conegliano. Instead of following the wine road signs, it's best to follow town signs east from **Valdobbiadene** to **Miane** and **Follina**. In **Follina** turn south (right) to **Solighetto**, then left to see the Romanesque frescoes in the parish church at **San Pietro di Foletto**. From **San Pietro** follow signs south to **Conegliano**. You can return to **Treviso** by heading south on S13 (39km).

Also worth exploring

The **Valzoldana** is the valley north of Belluno, formed by the Zolda River as it flows from the Dolomites into the valley of the Piave. Its principal resort centre is **Forno di Zoldo**. Villages are distinctly Tyrolean in appearance, with balconied chalets in wood and stone, wayside shrines and wood-carving shops. A benign foreground of green meadows dotted with wildflowers is set against a background of rock cliffs and jagged peaks.

Western Alpine foothills

Ratings

Architecture	●●●●●
Castles	●●●●○
Art and craft	●●●○○
Children	●●●○○
Historical sights	●●●○○
Scenery	●●●○○
Villages	●●●○○
Mountains	●●○○○

This short route packs some very interesting towns into a tight circle. The landscapes through the two walled southern towns – Castelfranco and Cittadella – are flat, while the northern loop is along the foothills of the Dolomites, which rise quite suddenly from the plain. Steep streets of Asolo and Marostica lead to castles, from which are splendid views over the towns and across the hilly landscapes. Behind lie the mountain towns, and nearly any road headed north will climb immediately into a jagged terrain of steep slopes dotted with secluded valleys. This route combines some of the most interesting and visual elements of northern Italy: castles, walled towns, Palladian villas and medieval pageantry. Signs of Venice's empire, which once spread its influence here, are legion: a Venetian balcony, a wall of the characteristic windows, or St Mark's lion looking down from a pillar or façade.

ASOLO❖❖

ⓘ APT *Municipio, Pza Gabriel d'Annunzio 2; tel: 0423 524 192. Open Mon–Fri 0900–1230, 1500–1800, Sat–Sun 0930–1230, 1530–1800.* A rare TIC where they let visitors browse racks of information rather than having to beg for each scrap.

The climb from the lower car park is a steep one, and seems steeper on a hot afternoon, but that doesn't discourage throngs of locals, for whom it is a favourite Sunday outing. One suspects that it was a bit less crowded and precious when Robert Browning fell in love with it. The main activity is strolling the arcaded streets, admiring the frescoed walls and views of surrounding hillsides. That and stopping at the many *osterie* to sample Prosecco.

Two women feature prominently in Asolo's story, one a queen of Cyprus and the other a queen of the stage. Queen Caterina, a Venetian married to the king of Cyprus, was given Asolo in exchange for Venetian control of the island, and lived here until the Austrians claimed Asolo. Elenora Duse, an early 20th-century dramatic actress, sought quiet here between tours. A **Museo Civico❖**, in the elegant 15th-century **Loggia della Ragione**, has personal mementoes of the

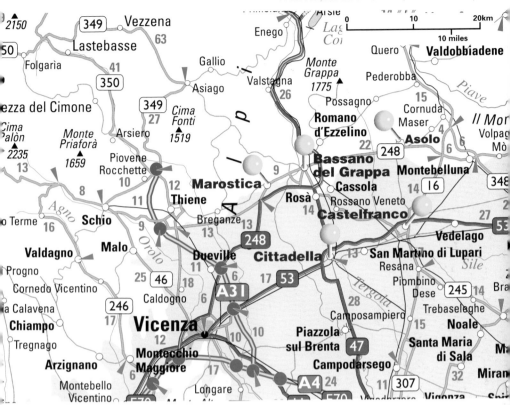

actress, the queen and the poets and artists who made their homes here, plus paintings and sculpture. Follow signs to Bar Castello, to reach Queen Caterina's **Castello della Regina**◆◆, from whose walls are good views over the town, at their best bathed in afternoon light. At the top of the hill opposite is **Rocca di Asolo**◆, a solid fortress shaped like a ship. Stairways lead to its ramparts, for another set of views over the town, *Sat–Sun, €*.

In nearby Maser, clearly signposted, is **Villa Barbaro**◆◆◆, perhaps the most perfect marriage of painting and architecture of any villa. Palladio worked with Veronese, and the result highlights the genius of each. The interior's 'architectural' details are actually *trompe l'oeil* frescoes, adding a playful touch to the sense of light and air and spaciousness. To many, this is the pinnacle of perfection in the Veneto's villas. On the grounds are the **Tempietto**◆, Palladio's only church outside of Rome, and a carriage museum. An equal distance north of Asolo is the birthplace of the neo-classical sculptor Canova, whose plaster casts are in the elaborate **Gipsoteca**◆ and whose remains rest in an outsized mausoleum.

Pricey boutiques, antiquaries and studios line the streets. In summer, buy fresh, sweet cherries from the *agriturismo* farm below the gate.

Market day: Sat. On the second weekend of each month (except Jul–Aug) the main square is filled with an antiques market (pricey).

Accommodation and food in Asolo

Albergo Al Sole €€–€€€ *V. Collegio 33; tel: 0423 528 111, fax: 0423 528 399.* A Venetian red building set just above the main *piazza*, with fine castle views from its spreading porch.

Melo in Fiore €–€€ *V. Caldretta 41, Maser, 1km from Villa Barbaro; tel: 0423 565 205, lodging open all year, restaurant Fri–Sun or by advance booking.* A wine estate with comfortable rooms and a restaurant serving grilled meats, seasonal vegetables and fruit from the farm.

Due Mori €€ *Pza Gabriel d'Annunzio, next to TIC; tel: 0423 952 256. Open 1800, closed Wed.* Begin with pasta and *porcini* before moving on to game birds with *polenta*. Tables on the terrace have nice views.

Bar al Castello €–€€ *Castelo della Regina.* A pleasant café inside the castle walls.

Right
Antiques shop, Asolo

The villas of the Veneto

In the 16th century, it was fashionable to quit the city of Venice in the summer and retire to a cooler country estate on the mainland. To house them there, wealthy Venetians built villas, sprawling palaces far larger than the cramped confines of Venice allowed. The favoured architect for these was, of course, Palladio, and of all those he conceived, no two are alike. His creativity seemed boundless, but always within the classical and Roman villa traditions. The architect often worked with one of the master painters of the day – Veronese, Tiepolo, Zelotti – who created frescoes to adorn the interiors.

BASSANO DEL GRAPPA***

APT *Largo Corona d'Italia 35; tel: 0424 524 351. Open Mon–Fri 0900–1230, 1400–1700, Sat 0900–1230.* One of the most accommodating and helpful in all Italy.

Parking € is just east of the old city, off Viale delle Parolini.

Museo Civico € *Pza Garibaldi. Open Tue–Sat 0900–1230, 1530–1830, Sun 1530–1830.*

Museo degli Alpini *Ponte degli Alpini. Open Tue–Sun 0800–2000.*

Museo della Ceramica, Palazzo Sturm € *V. Schiavonetti. Open Apr–Oct Tue–Sat 0900–1200, 1530–1830, Sun 1530–1830 & morning Jun–Sept, Nov–Mar Fri 0900–1200, Sat–Sun 1530–1830.*

Museo della Grappa *V. Gamba 6. Open Tue–Fri 0900–1230, Sat–Sun 0900–1300, 1430–1930, Mon 1430–1930.*

Asparagus Festival *Late Apr, early May.*

Bassano del Grappa was not named after the drink, nor vice versa, although you can learn about its making at the Poli distillery in the **Museo della Grappa**. Steps away is Bassano's best-loved landmark, the covered bridge, **Ponte degli Alpini***, designed by Palladio. Destroyed in the Second World War by Italian partisans (two of whom were executed by the Germans for doing so), it was faithfully reproduced by Alpini soldiers. The **Museo degli Alpini***, downstairs from the cheerful Taverna Al Ponte, at the bridge, has weapons, uniforms and photographs from both World Wars and material relating to the reconstruction of the bridge. The bridge is Bassano's favoured place for the evening *passiagato*, especially in summer, when it catches the slightest breeze. The 13th-century **Torre Civica**** overlooks Piazza Garibaldi, opposite the Church of **San Francesco**** (*open daily 0800–1200, 1500–1900*), built in the 1200s and with a fine portico and 15th-century frescoes. On its exterior wall is a town map showing where bombs fell, a poignant memorial. **Museo Civico****, set in the cloister and convent of a 14th-century Franciscan church, shows works by artist Jacobo Bassano and sculptor Canova, archaeology of Bassano's Roman era, and the evolution of the local ceramics. At **Palazzo Sturm**** are more local decorated ceramics, housed in a rococo setting of frescoes and stucco work.

Accommodation and food in Bassano del Grappa

Hotel al Castello € *Pza Terraglio 19; tel/fax: 0424 228 665.* A bowl of glistening fresh fruit is offered at breakfast (included), a thoughtful touch at this friendly and well-located hotel.

Hotel Positano € *Vle Asiago 88; tel: 0424 502 060; fax: 0424 502 615; www.gattei.it/positano.* Minutes from central Bassano, the Positano is newly refurbished, with spacious rooms and a restaurant with a terrace.

Taverna Al Alpini € *Ponte degli Alpini.* The best view in town, from tables on its tiny balcony over the river.

Look for dried *porcini* and other mushrooms, honey and jars of delicious condiments in **El Melario** at the foot of Ponte degli Alpini. *Grappa* (brandy) and pottery are found in several shops at the upper end of the bridge. Buy elegant picnic items, salads, pâtés and pastries at **Lino Santi** *V. Da Ponte 14.*

Market days: Thur, Sat.

Trattoria Alla Veneziana € *V. Menarola 22; tel: 0424 522 525.* This is food you hope to find and seldom do: vegetables and fish grilled to perfection, *gnocchi* with courgettes and shrimp, tender pasta with salmon.

Trattoria El Piron €€ *V. Z Bricito 12; tel: 0424 525 306. Closed Thur.* Bigoli (a locally popular fat spaghetti) is served with duck; tender *gnocchi* is prepared with *porcini* mushrooms.

CASTELFRANCO**

ARPT *V. Francesco M Preti 39; tel: 0423 495 000. Open daily; morning only Sun.*

P Parking is between the wall and moat near the west gate, often on the east side as well.

Casa di Giorgione *€ Pza Duomo. Open Tue–Sun 0900–1200, 1500–1800.*

Duomo *Pza Duomo. Open 0900–1200, 1500–1900.*

Villa Emo €€ *Fanzolo di Vedelago; tel: 0423 487 040. Open Apr–Oct Mon–Sat 1500–1900, Sun 1000–1230, 1500–1900, winter Sat–Sun 1400–1800.*

Market days: Thur, Fri morning.

Opposite
Eastern gate tower, Castelfranco

Defensive walls rising intact above portions of a moat are Castelfranco's hallmark and most interesting feature, built in 1199 to defend against Paduans. **Casa di Giorgione** was the home of Titian's teacher, whose masterpiece **Madonna and Child** hangs in the **duomo**, opposite. Coins in the adjacent box will illuminate the painting. At **Villa Emo** in nearby **Fanzolo**, Palladio created a spacious, spreading design that perfectly incorporates the farm and residence. Mid-1500s-interior frescoes by Zelotti show scenes from mythology. A farm museum of implements and local crafts is on the grounds.

Accommodation and food in Castelfranco

Alla Torre € *Piazzetta Trento e Trieste 7; tel: 0423 498 707; fax: 0423 798 737.* At the eastern tower of the city's impressive walls, this is the most centrally located hotel.

Ristorante Alle Mura €€–€€€ *V. F M Preti 69; tel: 0423 498 098. Closed Thur.* In the shadow of the walls at the west gate, this classy restaurant specialises in pricey fish, although you can order other dishes – from a menu in English.

Al Pozzo €–€€ *V. Cal di Monte 7, San Floriano di Castelfranco; tel: 0423 476 492. Open Fri & Sat evenings, Sun & holidays.* A farm restaurant, 4km from Castelfranco centre. Dine on *risotto* with quail, mixed grill and other local specialities.

Ferraro €–€€ *V. Larghe 4, San Floriano di Castelfranco; tel: 0423 487 099. Open Fri & Sat evenings, Sun & holidays, other days by advance booking.* A rural restaurant serving spit-roasted meats and seasonal dishes.

CITTADELLA*

ⓘ ARPT *Pza Scalco; tel: 0495 970 627. Open daily.*

◖ Market day: Mon morning.

The 13th-century **walls** and moat at Cittadella were the Paduans' response to the similar fortifications built by Trevisans at Castelfranco. Its four gates and thirty-two towers provided a good view of approaching danger. Today, they and the parapets provide lots of leg exercise, and good aerial views. Viewers will notice that the gates don't match the walls. In the 1800s demolition of the walls was begun. Fortunately, preservationists won the day, and the gates were rebuilt, but in the Romantic style of the time. The tower of the **Padua Gate** has the bicycle-like symbol of the Carraresi family on it. The **duomo***, which faces a large *piazza* near the centre of the enclosed town, has several paintings by 19th-century Veneto artists.

Accommodation and food in Cittadella

Hotel Filanda €€ *V. Palladio 34; tel: 0499 400 000; fax: 0499 402 111; restaurant closed Sun evening & Mon.* Reliable hotel, but best known for its excellent restaurant, **San Bassiano**, whose chef is an active promoter of the use of fresh, locally-grown products. Look for white asparagus Apr–May, woodland mushrooms in autumn.

2 Mori € *Borgo Bassano 141; tel: 0499 401 422; restaurant closed Sun evening & Mon.* Two dozen guest rooms and a good restaurant serving traditional local dishes.

MAROSTICA**

ⓘ ARPT *Pza Castello; tel: 042 472 127. Open daily 1000–1200, 1500–1800. Helpful staff and plentiful information.*

ⓟ Parking is usually available around the square at the lower castle.

ⓗ Castello Inferiore € *Pza Castello; tel: 042 472 127. Open daily 0900–1200, 1500–1800.*

Museo della Ceramica € *Nove; tel: 0424 829 807. Open Tue–Sat 0900–1300, Sun 1000–1230.*

◖ Nearby Nove is a ceramics centre, with a number of workshops. Many of these small

One of the finest remaining castellated towns, Marostica's **Castello Superiore*** crowns a hilltop, with **Castello Inferiore** directly below it on the town's famous chessboard square. For fine views, walk the medieval walls connecting the two. Finding the road to drive up to Castello Superiore is trickier. Follow Via Mazzini to the left (as you face the upper castle), exiting through Porta Breganze. Turn right, ascending Via Can Grande della Scala and keeping to the right until you reach the gate in the castle walls. Inside the lower castle are the costumes worn by the 'chessmen' and other participants in the biennial re-enactment of a 1454 chess game. Surrounding the chessboard pavement is a fine ensemble of buildings: the castle, faced by its former armoury, now a covered market, and along one side a row of arcaded buildings. Near the eastern gate, along Via Mazzini, is a row of medieval arcade buildings with decorative brickwork. Nearby **Nove*** is a ceramics centre, an industry and craft made possible by mills built in the 1700s on the Brenta River, which crushed rock quarried nearby into the fine powder needed for pottery. Today Nove is a major source of the colourful ceramic table and decorative ware found in shops all over northern Italy. You can tour the workshops to buy blems (factory

factories do not have signs advertising their showrooms, but you can find someone in the office who will show you in.

Maer V. Padre Roberto 26. Has especially good prices.

Market day: Tue.

⊗ **Partita a Scacchi** The famous human chess game is played on the town square; tel: 042 472 127; fax: 042 472 800. Second weekend Sept, even-numbered years.

Above
Castello Inferiore, Marostica

seconds) and surplus stock. **Museo della Ceramica*** shows examples of the art and crafts over its three-century history.

Accommodation and food in Marostica

Hotel Europa €–€€ V. Pizzamano 19; tel: 042 477 842; fax: 042 472 480. A full service hotel with secure parking, a restaurant and convenient location just outside the walls, near the lower castle.

La Rosina €–€€ V. Maretti, Valle San Floriano; tel: 0424 470 360; fax: 0424 470 290. Twelve rooms and a fine restaurant, featuring fresh local ingredients and views of the hills between Marostica and Bassano.

Ristorante Due Mori €–€€ V. Mazzini 73; tel: 0424 471 777; www.duemori.it

Trattoria Alla Fortuna € V. Campo Marzio 22; tel: 042 475 446. Closed Wed.

Thiene market day:
Mon morning.

Sample the local
sweet, *treccia d'oro*, at
Signorini, a café near
Castello Porto-Colleoni,
Thiene.

Suggested tour

Total distance: 116km, with detours 253km.

Time: 4 hours' driving. Allow 3 days for the main route, 5 days with detours. Those with limited time should concentrate on Bassano del Grappa and Asolo (with Villa Barbaro), and a quick stop in Marostica.

Links: From the Valpolicella and Pasubio Valley route (*see page 134*), connect via Schio to Thiene. Treviso, the starting point for the Eastern Alpine foothills route (*see page 196*), is almost directly west of Castelfranco via S53.

Route: Leave Vicenza ❶ (*see page 215*), heading east on S53 and following signs to **CITTADELLA** ❷. Several access roads lead from S53 into Cittadella as it skirts the town. Continue on S53, following signs to **CASTELFRANCO** ❸, which is just south of S53 on S667. Backtrack to S53, crossing it and continuing to **Valla** (40km). (*See Detour 1 below.*) In Valla turn left following signs to Asolo and **Riese Pio X**, named for native son Giuseppe Sarto, elected Pope Pius X in 1903 and canonised in 1954. **Museo S. Pio X** memorialises his birthplace (*free, open daily 0800–1200, 1500–1900 summer, shorter winter hours*). Continue through San Vito, turning right on S248 and immediately left, signposted **ASOLO** ❹. Leaving Asolo, return toward S248, turning left just short of its intersection and following signs to **Maser** and **Villa Barbaro**.

Travel south from Maser, signposted Monte Belluna, only until you reach S248, turning west (right) and following signs into **BASSANO DEL GRAPPA** ❺ (42km). (*See Detour 2 below.*) Leave Bassano heading south on S47, turning right onto S248. Shortly after crossing the Brenta River follow signs left into **Nove**, the region's ceramic centre (some signs read 'Nove de Bassano'). Leave Nove heading west from its centre, following signs to **MAROSTICA** ❻ (you will cross S248). Leave Marostica heading west on the unnumbered route signposted Mason Vicentino, continuing on through **Breganze** to **Thiene** ❼. (*See Detour 3 below.*) In the historic centre of Thiene is the 15th-century battlemented **Castello Porto Colleoni**, in the Venetian Gothic style, with good frescoes in the great hall and excellent 18th-century stables by Muttoni (*Corso Garibaldi 21, guided tours Sun €€*). Return to Vicenza following S349 south from Thiene to Motta where you meet S46 into the city (34km).

Malga Cason Vecio
€–€€ Val Poise, Borso
del Grappa; tel: 0423 542
051. Open daily Jun–Sept,
May & Oct Sun only. The
speciality of this mountain
restaurant (apart from the
panoramic view) is *polenta*
served with the local hard
sausage, *sopressa*, but the
onion soup and apple tart
are equally good.

APT V. Stazione 5,
Asiago; tel: 0424 462
661; www.ascom.vi.it/asiago

Parking is near the
duomo, off Via
Mattiotti at Via A Costa,
Asiago.

Detour 1: In **Valla** turn right, following signs to **Fanzolo**, to visit Villa Emo. Backtrack to **Valla** (8km).

Detour 2: Leave **Bassano** heading north on S47, turning right on the outskirts of town and following signs for **Monte Grappa** via S141. This winding and often steep mountain road ascends the 1775m

Caldonazzo Terme
Becco di Filadonna
2150
Levico Terme
Cima Dodici 2341
Primolano
Arsiè
Enego
Vezzena
Lastebasse
Folgaria
349
350
ezza del Cimone
349
Gallio
Asiago
Monte Grappa 1775
Valstagna
Cima Fonti
50
41
63
27
Cima Palòn 2235
Monte Priaforà 1659
Arsiero
1519
Piovene Rocchette
Possagno
Romano d'Ezzelino
Bassano del Grappa
Pederobba
Cornuda
Maser
Asolo
248
Marostica
Thiene
Rosà
Cassola
Rossano Veneto
Valla
Fanzolo
Montebelluna
16
Schio
Breganze
Castelfranco
Vedelago
San Martino di Lupari
Resana
o Terme
Valdagno
Malo
Dueville
Cittadella
246
46
Caldogno
A31
Piombino Dese
Trebaseleghe
245
Camposampiero
Noale
Cornedo Vicentino
la Calavena
Chiampo
Tregnago
Vicenza
Montecchio Maggiore
Piazzola sul Brenta
Campodarsego
Santa Maria di Sala
Arzignano
50bis
348
Valmar
Quero
Valdobbiadene
Il Mor
Volpa
Mò
348
53
53
47
248

0   10   20km
10 miles

Lago Cort

Piave

Sile

Tre Fonti €–€€
V. Rodighieri, Asiago;
tel: 0424 462 601. North
of town, serves local
specialities on a pleasant
terrace.

Monte Grappa, from which are panoramic views. Built in 1935, the huge circular memorial commemorates the 12,000 soldiers who died in battle here during the First World War, both Italians and members of the Austro-Hungarian Army. Via Eroica leads to a war museum. Return to **Bassano** via S141 (62km).

Detour 3: From **Thiene** travel north on S349 signposted to **Asiago**. This hilly mountain road leads to the **Altopiano di Asiago**, a region at the centre of a First World War engagement, and the site of five British cemeteries. The hill towns are rich in local culture, with a full calendar of festivals. Many good walking trails through the Dolomite foothills begin here, as do cross-country and Alpine ski trails and lifts. Backtrack to **Thiene** (67km).

Also worth exploring

Northwest of Asiago, bordering the **Val Sugana**, S349 winds scenically (and often precipitously) through the foothills and over Passo di Vezzena.

Vicenza and the Euganean Hills

Ratings

Architecture	●●●●●
Villas	●●●●●
Art	●●●●○
Gardens	●●●●○
Historical sights	●●●○○
Scenery	●●●○○
Villages	●●●○○
Vineyards	●●●○○

The gracious, lively and architecturally superb city of Vicenza is, unaccountably, not on most travellers' 'must see' list of Italy. That's a shame, because the city and the hillsides above it have so much to offer. Much of its appeal derives from the work of native son Andrea Palladio, who gave his name to the style of architecture that has inspired buildings all over the world. Southeast of the city lie the Euganean Hills, a scenic cluster of near-perfect cones formed by long extinct volcanoes. Remains of this thermal activity make this one of the largest hydro-geological basins in Italy. Thermal springs here have been used for bathing and therapy since the Romans languished in the warmth of their waters. Vineyards and farms are also common along the surprisingly steep roads that meander through these hills.

ABANO TERME AND MONTEGROTTO TERME❖

ℹ️ **IAT** *V. P d'Abano, Abano Terme; tel: 0498 669 055. Open Mon–Sat 0830–1300, Sun 0900–1200, 1500–1800. Brochures are mostly in French and German.*

🅿️ *Parking in Abano is limited to 30 minutes. That's long enough. In Montegrotto, metered parking is along Viale Stazione, but your car may be ticketed while you search for change.*

The name of Abano – the largest and best-known spa centre – is thought to derive from the Greek, meaning removal of pain. Mineral-laden, 87°C (188.6°F) waters are slightly radioactive and muds from the thermal lakes have been used for a wide variety of complaints. For those not booked into a treatment programme, a glance at the pricey spa hotels is the only reason to stop. In Montegrotto are **Scavi Romani**❖, extensive ruins of Roman baths and theatre. A live butterfly collection is shown at **Casa delle Farfalle**❖. Just west of Abano is the 15th-century Benedictine monastery **Abbazia di Praglia**❖❖, whose brothers offer tours of the Renaissance church and its cloisters. The monastery grows herbs for market and is a botanical garden. East, in Due Carrare, **Castello di San Pelagio**❖❖ is a surprising venue for a museum of air and space. The connection between this villa and flight is not so tenuous as one might imagine – it was from here that the

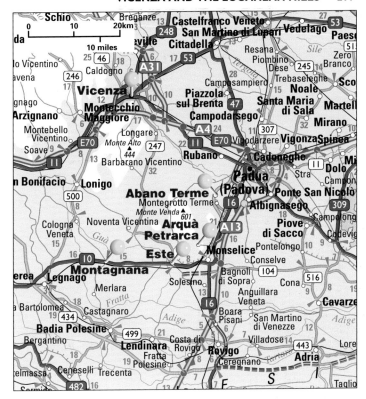

Abbazia di Praglia
Bresseo de Teolo,
6km west of Abano; tel:
0499 900 010. Open Apr–
Oct Tue–Sun 1530–1730,
Nov–Mar daily 1430–1630,
tours every 30 minutes.

Casa delle Farfalle €€
Montegrotto; tel: 0498 910
189. Open Apr–Aug daily
0900–1230, 1430–1730,
until 1630 Mar & Sept.

Castello di San Pelagio
€€ Due Carrare; tel: 0499
125 008. Open Tue–Sun
summer 0900–1230,
1430–1900, winter
0900–1230, 1400–1800.

Scavi Romani *V. Scavi; tel:*
049 793 700. Tours at
0900, 1000, 1100 and
occasionally Sat afternoon.

poet Gabriele d'Annunzio and his First World War squadron began
their 1918 flight over Vienna.

Accommodation and food in Abano Terme and Montegrotto Terme

Throughout the hills are *agriturismo* restaurants, some open weekends
only. Nearly every village has its *trattoria* serving local wine.

Terme Mamma Margherita € *V. Monteortone 63, Teolo village of
Monteortone; tel: 0498 669 350; fax: 049 667 286.* With its own thermal
baths, this amiable hotel and restaurant is a pleasant distance from
Abano.

Caffè Bar Lucia € *V. Stazione 97, Montegrotto; tel: 0380 351 8060.* Good
sandwiches and a wide street-side terrace.

Above
Chessboard, Abano Terme

ARQUA PETRARCA AND EUGANEAN HILLS❖❖❖

🅿 Parking in Arqua
Petrarca is uphill
from the main square.

🄷 Casa di Petrarca €
V. Valleselle 4; tel: 0429
718 294. Open Mar–Oct
Tue–Sun 0900–1230,
1500–1900, Nov–Feb
0900–1230, 1430–1730.

Cava Bomba € Cinto
Euganeo. Open Jun–Sept
Sat–Sun 1000–1900,
Mon–Thur 0900–1300,
Wed–Thur also 1500–1900,
shorter hours Apr–May, Oct;
Nov–Feb closed.

**Museo Naturale di Villa
Beatrice** € Baone; tel:

The centre of this hill town looks much as it did in the Middle Ages, when the poet Petrarch spent his last years at **Casa Pertarca**❖❖, amid the landscapes he had described in his poetry. The frescoed, bucolic scenes from his works date from the 1500s. Note especially the fine painted and panelled ceilings. From the balcony you can look down at the well-kept gardens. The church of the **Assumption**❖ has frescoes from as early as the 11th century. Wealthy Paduans and Venetians chose these hills for their summer villas, one of which, **Villa Barbarigo**, is surrounded by some of the finest baroque gardens in Italy. The 17th-century **Valsanzibio**❖❖❖, as the beautifully kept gardens are now called, are filled with statuary, trick fountains, a labyrinth and a monumental baroque gate, the Arch of Diana. At the crest of Monte Gemola, west of Arqua, is the old convent of Beatrice d'Este, in a lovely setting with views of surrounding Euganean Hills. **Villa Beatrice**❖❖ contains a nature museum showing the botany and zoology of this micro-climate ecosystem. The adjacent nature reserve protects a population of rare hedgehogs. In Cinto Euganeo, the old furnace of

0429 601 177. Open Jun–Sept Sat–Sun 1000–1900 Mon–Thur 0900–1300, Tue & Fri also 1500–1900, shorter hours Apr–May, Oct; Nov–Feb Sat–Sun only.

Valsanzibio € *Valsanzibio; tel: 0499 130 042. Open Mar–Nov daily 0900–1200, 1330–sunset.*

🍽 *Jujubes preserved in local liqueurs, other fruit preserves and wines are at **Enoteca Da Loris** V. Valleselle, open 0930–1200, 1430–1930.*

🍽 *Jujube Festival First two Suns in Oct. Celebrates local fruit, wine and chestnuts, with food vendors and floral decoration.*

Cava Bomba* has been restored as a museum of fossils and the unique geology of the hills.

Accommodation and food in Arqua Petrarca and Euganean Hills

Hotel Picolo Marte €–€€ *V. Casteletto 51, Torreglia; tel: 0495 211 177; www.piccolomarte.it. Restaurant closed Wed.* In a beautiful green setting, overlooking the hills and farms, the hotel is a good base for exploring the area, with a restaurant €–€€ specialising in veal *scallopini* and mixed grills.

Serena € *V. Bignano 90, Arqua Petrarca; tel: 0429 718 044; fax: 0429 718 045.* A small hotel with restaurant, in a quiet setting.

Alla Loggia € *Pza San Marco; tel: 0249 718 281. Closed Wed.* Sandwiches and *gelati* are served overlooking the quiet square or on a flower-draped terrace.

Osteria Tramontan € *Galzignano, near Villa Barbarigo.* Situated in the ruins of an old Franciscan monastery.

ESTE**

ℹ️ **ARPT** *Pza Maggiore 5; tel: 0429 3635. Open in theory Mon–Fri 0900–1230, Sat 1000–1230.*

🏛 **Museo Nazionale Atestino** € *Castello; tel: 0429 2085. Open daily 0900–1900. Children will like the playground in the castle grounds, reserved for the under-12s.*

Torre Civica € *Castello; tel: 0429 931 5711. Guided tours mid-May–Nov, Sat 1600–1900, Sun 1000–1200, 1600–1900. Gardens open until 2300 Apr–Sept, 0900–1800 Oct–Mar.*

🍽 *Market day: Thur.*

One of the two oldest settlements in the Veneto (Adria is the other), Este was home to the Ateste people for five centuries, before the Romans conquered them in the 4th century BC. Artefacts unearthed in Este – bronze vessels, jewellery, tools, architectural details – are shown in the **Museo Nazionale Atestino****, built into the walls of **Castello d'Este****. Also in the museum are examples of arts from Roman to medieval times. The castle overlooks Este's main square and inside its circling walls are gardens that rise to the keep, the **Torre Civica****. The main interest in the **duomo*** is a Tiepolo altar painting of St Tecla. The *campanile* of the 11th-century church of **San Martino** lists disconcertingly.

Accommodation and food in Este

Albergo Centrale € *Pza Beata Beatrice 14; tel: 0429 3930; fax: 0429 603 209.* Facing the main square, this convenient hotel has a most accommodating staff and parking close by.

Sapio € *V. Madonnetta; tel: 0429 602 565. Closed Mon.* The enclosed (and air-conditioned) terrace surrounds a giant tree. Expect to savour the likes of *ravioli* filled with pears and sauced in *Gorgonzola*. There's no written menu, but the genial staff will make sure you understand the evening's choices.

Below
Castle and gardens, Este

Caffè Borsa € *Pza Beata Beatrice 14; tel: 0429 3930.* Smart, modern décor and a spot overlooking the main square.

Below
Castle and gardens, Este

MONTAGNANA❖❖❖

ⓘ ARPT *Castel S. Zeno;*
tel: 042 981 320.
Open Wed–Sat 0930–1230,
1600–1900, Sun
1000–1300, 1600–1900.

ⓟ Parking is plentiful
around the Piazza
Duomo.

ⓘ Duomo *Pza Duomo.*
Open daily
0800–1230, 1600–1730.

Castel San Zeno,
Mastio di Ezzelino €
Padua Gate; tel: 042 981
220. Open Mon
0930–1230, Wed–Fri
0930–1230, 1600–1900,
Sat–Sun 1000–1300,
1600–1900.

Musico Civico *tours at*
various hours.

ⓒ Market day: Thur.

ⓐ Il Palio *First Sun Sept.*
A horserace around
the town walls, preceded
by a week of medieval
costumes and market.

The entire town is enclosed by a solid medieval brick wall with four gates and twenty-four towers, all still in good repair, making this one of the finest walled towns in northern Italy. The whole ensemble is surrounded by a grassy moat, begging photographs from every angle. The **duomo**❖❖ is not only architecturally significant, but is almost an art museum as well. Its highly successful transition between Gothic and Renaissance shows some of the best of both. The art begins at the Sansovino portal and includes a Veronese altarpiece painting of the Transfiguration. Nearly every artist of note from the period has been credited with the panels that flank the entrance. Much of the vaulting is covered in early 16th-century frescoes. Choir stalls have delicately painted wood panels above them and the main altar is flanked by a pair of fine semi-circular transept chapels with good frescoes, lighted by a coin box beside the right transept. The Rosary chapel has unusual frescoes on an astrology theme. The arcaded **loggia**❖ on the east side of **Piazza Duomo** has an excellent ceiling, with frescoes under the arches; and to remind you that this was once part of the Venetian empire, a lion of St Mark looks down from the wall above it. From the main square you can see the fine Gothic brick bell tower of **San Francesco Grande**. At the Padua Gate, inside **Castel San Zeno**❖, are museums with a variety of finds that include those from a Roman necropolis discovered in the 1980s. Clearly visible just outside the same gate is Palladio's **Villa Pisani**❖, which is not open to view.

Accommodation and food in Montagnana

Hotel Aldo Moro €€ *V. Marconi just off Pza Duomo; tel: 042 981 351; fax: 042 982 842. Restaurant closed Mon.* The only hotel inside the walled town also has a good restaurant.

Trattoria da Stona €–€€ *V. Carrarese 51; tel: 042 981 523. Closed Mon.* Local favourites include peppered rabbit with *polenta*.

VICENZA❖❖❖

ⓘ APT *Pza Duomo 5; tel:*
0444 544 122,
www.ascom.vi.iv/aptvicenza.
Open daily.

ⓟ Parking € is available
off Piazza Matteotti,
but you must move to
another spot after 2 hours.

About halfway between Verona and Padua, Vicenza seems to suffer from 'middle child syndrome' as tourists whizz past it on the *autostrada*. Without the mythical Juliet or the mystical St Anthony, Vicenza must rely on its native son, Andrea Palladio. Not a weak reed on which to lean, Palladio's revolutionary approach to architecture transformed the way the world looked at buildings. Some of his most outstanding works are in his home town. The city's gracious historic centre spreads around the 15th-century **Palazzo della Ragione**, better

A Vicenza Card includes admission to most of the major sights, including Teatro Olimpico and the museums.

Museo Civico €€
Pza Matteotti; tel: 0444 321 348. Open Tue–Sun 0900–1700. Ticket includes admission to Teatro Olimpico and other attractions.

Palazzo della Ragione
(Basilica) *Pza dei Signori. Hours vary, but usually Tue–Sun 0900–1700, 1000–1900 Jul–Aug, charge for some exhibitions.*

San Lorenzo
V. Montagna. Open 1030–1200, 1530–1800.

Santa Corona
Corso Palladio. Church open daily 0830–1200, 1430–1830, museum open Tue–Sat 0930–1200, 1415–1700, Jul–Aug 1000–1900, Sun 0900–1200.

Teatro Olimpico €€
Pza Matteotti; tel: 0444 323 781. Open Tue–Sun 0900–1700. Ticket includes admission to museums and other attractions.

Villa Rotunda € *V. della Rotunda off S247; tel: 0444 321 793. Grounds open mid-Mar–mid-Oct daily 1000–1200, 1500–1800, interior Wed 1000–1200, 1500–1800.*

Opposite
Teatro Olimpico

known as the **basilica♦♦♦**, whose soaring *loggia* was built by Palladio in 1549, when he was assigned the job of supporting Vicenza's sinking town hall. His larger-than-life statue contemplates his accomplishment, often looking over market stalls that spill from adjacent **Piazza dell'Erbe♦♦**, a busy marketplace behind the basilica. In this *piazza* stands a crenellated medieval tower, **Torre del Tormento**, looking a bit uncomfortable among all the Palladiana.

On the opposite side of the basilica is **Piazza dei Signori♦♦♦**, one of the most architecturally pleasing squares in all Italy. Above rises the slender **Torre di Piazza♦**, whose height increased over the course of three centuries, to its present 82m. Opposite stands the **Loggia del Capitaniato♦♦**, an arcade designed by Palladio. Behind this, especially along Contra Porti, are elegant *palazzi* built by Vicenza's leading families, showing both the 14th-century Venetian style and a number of Palladio's designs. Between Piazza dell'Erbe and the River Retrone are more of these older Venetian-style palaces; more of Palladio's works are along Corso Palladio. Vicenza's **duomo♦** was largely reconstructed after severe damage in the Second World War. Also worth seeing is **Santa Corona♦♦**, a 13th-century Gothic church built as a home for a thorn from Christ's Crown of Thorns. It contains paintings by Bellini and Veronese; coin boxes adjacent to side altars illuminate these. Go behind the high altar to see the intricate marble work and the inlaid wood choir stalls. The former convent houses a museum of natural history and archaeology. **San Lorenzo♦♦** has some excellent tombs and an outstanding carved stone doorway. Its cloister is one of the loveliest in the city.

Facing Piazza Matteotti is the last of Palladio's works, unfinished at his death. **Teatro Olimpico♦♦♦** would be enough reason for visiting Vicenza, if Palladio had done nothing else there. Opened in 1589, it is the oldest indoor theatre surviving in Europe. The theatre is designed to feel like a Greek open-air amphitheatre, with the ceiling painted to look like sky and seats replicating the stone steps. The **stage♦♦♦**, designed by Palladio's student, Vincenzo Scamozzi, suggests the city of Thebes, its 'streets' so cleverly proportioned and raised that they appear to be many times longer than they are. Looking into the arches of the grand, statue-studded 'façade' is like looking down the streets of a town. The theatre is entered through the **Odeon♦♦**, a concert chamber richly decorated in frescoes. Opposite Teatro Olimpico is a grand Palladian palazzo, now home to the **Museo Civico♦♦**. At least step inside to see Carpione's magnificent frescoed entrance hall ceiling. The museum contains art from local churches and works by Montagna, Tiepolo, Veronese, Bellini and others.

Three of Vicenza's sights are on **Monte Berico**, a hillside overlooking the city, two of them connected by a pleasant stone path. The whole ensemble can be reached on foot from central Vicenza, via a shaded colonnade, punctuated by chapels. Follow Viale X Giugno from Piazza X Giugno, south of the old city centre. The colonnade

Villa Valmarana
€€ *V. dei Nani* 12; *tel:*
*0444 543 976. Open
Mar–Apr daily 1000–1200,
1430–1730, May–Sept
1000–1200, 1500–1800,
Oct–Nov 1000–1200,
1400–1700.*

Market days in Piazza
dell'Erbe: Tue and
Thur.

The Feast of the
Epiphany (6 Jan) is
celebrated in colourful
processions. The annual
Gold Fair, the first week in
June, is a good time to
miss, since the area is filled
to overflowing.

leads to **Basilica di Monte Berico**✶✶, a pilgrimage church begun in the 15th century commemorating Vicenza's being spared from the plague. The ornately embellished interior is lighted by votive candles, which hang around the high altar, giving it a distinctly Byzantine feel. Montagna's fine Pieta fresco is to the right, beside a mosaic of framed votives. In the refectory are Veronese's *The Supper of Gregory the Great* and an incongruous – but fascinating – fossil collection. An anteroom displays unusual needlework votives. Opposite the basilica is a park with two notable monuments, one to the local Alpini battalion and the other an appealing bronze statue of a woman playing with child.

Villa Valmarana✶✶✶ is surrounded by a wall guarded by stubby statues, giving rise to the nickname Villa dei Nani, or 'villa of the dwarfs'. Inside, each room is decorated with frescoes by Tiepolo, based on mythology, including the *Iliad* and Virgil's *Aeneid*. Plentiful light from large windows underscores Tiepolo's light and airy style, and the frescoes and grisaille work are in fine condition. In the Forestierre, a smaller building across the garden, are pastoral frescoes by the younger Tiepolo in a very different, more representational style. A short stone path leads from the front gate of Villa Valmarana down to **Villa Rotunda**✶✶✶, perhaps Palladio's most famous single work. Its perfect symmetry, clean lines and graceful proportions have inspired buildings on nearly every continent. The two best views for photographing the building are from the front approach, framed in roses, or from the bosky corner to the left at the top of the walk, both best in the afternoon. The interior is lavishly decorated.

Right
Villa Rotunda

Thomas Jefferson and La Rotunda

American travellers may wish to sit on the conveniently placed bench under the trees and contemplate why Jefferson was so impressed with Palladio's masterpiece that he adapted it for his own home, Monticello, in Virginia, and promoted the use of the style in America's new public buildings. Palladio's design was the very essence of Jefferson's philosophical vision for his new United States: dignity without pomp, everything in balanced proportion, and enough of the classical to satisfy the Federalist mind.

Accommodation and food in Vicenza

Giardini €€ *V. Giuriolo 10; tel/fax: 0444 326 458.* A small hotel with parking and a very convenient location near the Teatro Olimpico and TIC.

Antica Trattoria Tre Visi €€ *Corso Palladio 25; tel: 0444 324 868. Closed Sun evening.* Set inside a grand *palazzo* in the centre of the old city, this warm *trattoria's* speciality is goose cooked with mushrooms. Reservations suggested.

Gran Caffè Garibaldi €–€€ *Pza dei Signori, next to Loggia del Capitaniato.* The most elegant and stylish place to watch Vicenza go by.

Nogarazza €–€€ *V. S Agostino; tel: 0444 288 900.* Friendly little place tourists rarely find, but a favourite of pilots stationed nearby. The sweet 'Bunga Cake' is named for one of them.

Pizzeria Vesuvio € *Corso Palladio 204; tel: 0444 324 546.* Close to Teatro Olimpico, with a lovely little courtyard, the restaurant is almost hidden, down a small passageway. Pizza and many other options.

Suggested tour

Total distance: 162km, with detours 173km.

Time: 4 hours' driving. Allow 3 days for the main route, 3–4 days with detours. Those with limited time should concentrate on Vicenza.

Links: Vicenza is connected to Verona (*see page 118*) and Venice (Venezia) (*see page 172*) via S11 or A4. The Euganean Hills are just south of Padua (Padova) (*see page 222*), reached via S10.

Route: Leave Padua (Padova) ❶ via its inner ring road, following signs south to Rovigo and **ABANO TERME** ❷. Continue to **MONTEGROTTO TERME**. Leave on the unnumbered road signposted **Torreglia**, turning left at its centre, to **Galzignano Terme**. The gardens at **Valsanzibio** are a short distance to the south (*see page 212*). Continue through Galzignano, to **Faedo** and **Fontanafredda**, turning left, following signs to **Cinto Euganeo**. In about 1km, turn left,

ℹ ARPT *V. Roma 2, Monselice; tel: 042 972 380. Open daily.*

🍴 Ristorante Torre *€–€€ Pza Mazzini, Monselice; tel: 0429 737 529. No surprises on the menu, but a reliable stop.*

◉ La Giostra della Rocca *Monselice. First three Suns, Sept, brings medieval merriment.*

following signs to **Villa Beatrice** (49km). Return and continue south through Cinto Euganeo, turning left and following signs to **ARQUA PETRARCA ❸**. Leave Arqua, turning right at the T-junction and following signs to **ESTE ❹**. (*See Detour 1 below*.) Leave Este, heading west on S10 to **MONTAGNANA ❺**. Leave Montagnana via the Padua (Padova) (east) Gate, turning left immediately and heading north to **Pojana Maggiore**. On the southern end of the town, the road passes between the 16th-century **Villa Pojana** (*open Tue–Sun, 1000–1800*) and the older, castellated villa/farm opposite. Follow signs from Pojana to Noventa Vicentina, turning north (left) on S247, signposted **VICENZA ❻**. (*See Detour 2 below*.) Follow S247 into the city, passing the left turns for Villa Rotunda and Villa Valmarana, both well signposted (84km). From Villa Valmarana, follow Via Tiepolo to Borgo Berga, turn right and follow signs right to **Villa La Rotunda**. Return to Borgo Berga, turning left and following it into Vicenza (26km). To return to Padua (Padova), use the A4 to avoid the heavy traffic on S11 (29km).

Detour 1: Instead of turning right to **Este**, turn left, signposted **Monselice**. The town clusters around its 13th-century **duomo**◆, with a fine, high altar painting depicting St Justine. Climb the **Via del Santuario**◆◆ to visit the **Santuario San Giorgio**◆◆, whose interior is decorated in delicate designs of inlaid marble. The six chapels along the way were also designed by Vincento Scamozzi, Palladio's student. Inside the sanctuary church are tombs of early Christian martyrs. **Ca'Marcello**◆◆◆ (*€€, hourly tours morning & afternoon except Mon*), a cluster that includes a castle, a chapel and two palaces, with good frescoes, armour, tapestries and Renaissance furnishings. Continue to Este on S10 (17km).

Detour 2: North of **Noventa Vicentina**, in **Ponte di Barbarano**, turn left on a road signposted **Barbarano Vicentino**. The road climbs from the town into the Berici Hills, signposted for Vicenza. After passing through **Perarolo** and **San Gottardo**, the road drops to **Monte Berico** and its sanctuary, overlooking Vicenza. Follow Via d'Azeglio downhill, turning right onto Via San Bastiano to its end at **Villa Valmarana**.

Also worth exploring

🍴 Ostello Amolara *€–€€ V. Capitello 11, Adria; tel: 0426 943 035. Simple foods in an old mill with a small museum.*

Southeast of the Euganean Hills lies the low, canal-webbed farmland between the Po and Adige deltas, called the Polesine. **Rovigo** has the fine octagonal **La Rotunda** church, with paintings and statues in niches. **Adria**, 22km east, joins Este as the oldest settlements in the Veneto. When the Po delta wandered at will over thousands of acres, the town of Adria was a thriving port, but alluvial deposits have left it more than 25km from the Adriatic Sea. Its **Museo Archeologico** (*€, V. Badini 59; tel: 042 521 612, open daily*) has a complete iron chariot from the 4th century BC.

Opposite
Bar, Arqua Petraca

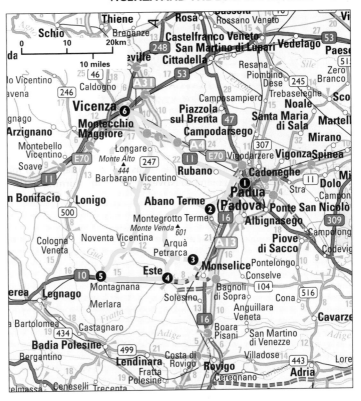

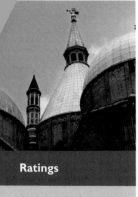

Padua and the Brenta Canal

Ratings

Architecture ●●●●●

Art ●●●●○

Boat trips ●●●●○

Historical sights ●●●●○

History ●●●●○

Religious interest ●●●●○

Gardens ●●●○○

Food and drink ●●○○○

St Anthony was born in Lisbon, Portugal, but that has not stopped Padua from making him very much their own. The basilica built to honour his relics is one of Europe's major pilgrimage sites. St Anthony is not Padua's only claim to fame, however. Its university is among the oldest in the world, and their pioneering medical school created Europe's first botanical garden in 1545 to study medicinal plants. The university also conferred the world's first degree awarded to a woman. The *Risorgimento* that finally freed Italy from Austrian control was planned in the Caffè Pedrocchi, still thriving, still stylish and still a place for a lively exchange of ideas. It sits in the centre of Padua's old city, surrounded by distinguished palaces and public buildings. Above all, Padua is pleasant and hospitable, well accustomed to its role as host after greeting centuries of pilgrims.

❶ APT *Stazione Ferrovie Stato; tel: 0498 752 077; fax: 0498 755 0008. Open Mon–Sat 0900–1900, Sun 0900–1200, and at Pza del Santo; tel: 0438 753 087; Mar–Oct Mon–Sat 0830–1330, 1500–1900.*

Informazione *Galleria Pedrocchi; tel: 0498 766 860. Open Mon–Sat 0830–1330, 1500–1900.*

❷ Park at the **Prato della Valle** on the south end of town, within walking distance of the

Getting there

Most motorists arrive in Padua via the A4, which connects it to Venice, Milan, Verona and Vicenza. *Autostradas* encircle the city, and avenues describe an inner ring around the city's remaining walls.

Getting around

From the basilica, public transportation runs to the historic centre. Alternatively, walk up the Via dei Santo (which becomes Via Zabarella) to the Scrovegni Chapel and Chiesa degli Eremitani, just under 1km.

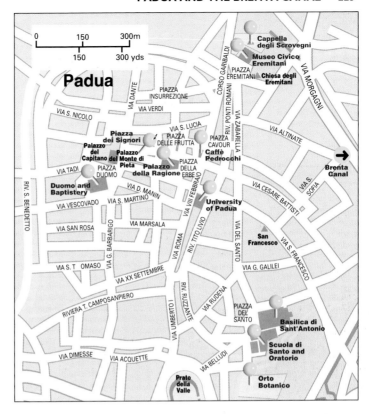

Sights

Basilica di Sant'Antonio✦✦✦

basilica. From the city's ring road, take Via Paoli which becomes Via Alberto Cavalleto and leads you directly into the Prato. More parking is around Piazza Erimitani.

Construction began in 1232, only a year after St Anthony's death, and it immediately became a major pilgrimage site. The entombed relics in the Capella dell'Arca are the object of worshippers' devotion, set in a chapel of exquisite marble inlay and *bas-relief* by Sansovino, Tullio Lombardo and Giovanni Minello. Just beyond is the Cappella Beato Lucca Belludi, dedicated to the saint's companion, with frescoes by Giusto de'Menabuoi. In the ambulatory is a large Jesse Tree and several beautifully frescoed chapels. The Donatello bronze panels on the main altar are hard to see, but his stone *bas-relief* is visible. The Contarini and Bembo tombs, facing one another across the aisle, are by Sanmicheli. Cappella del Tesoro, in the apse, contains the saint's tunic and reliquaries containing teeth and other remains. From the lovely cloister are fine views of the Pisan-style Romanesque church, which shows Gothic and heavy Byzantine influences. In the *piazza*, Donatello's *Gattamelata* was the first monumental equestrian statue since Roman times.

Ⓐ **Antiques market** Prato della Valle, 3rd Sun monthly.

Ⓑ **Basilica di Sant'Antonio** Pza del Santo. Open daily Mar–Oct 0630–2200; Nov–Feb daily 0630–1900.

Caffè Pedrocchi €
V. VIII Febbraio 15.
Museum open Tue–Sun
0930–1230, 1530–1800.

Cappella degli
Scrovegni €€€
Pza Eremitani 8; tel: 0498
204 550. Open Mar–Jan
0900–2200 by advance
reservation (72 hours);
tel: 049 201 0020.

Duomo and baptistery
Pza del Duomo. Open
Mon–Sat 0730–1200,
1545–1930; Sun
0745–1300, 1545–2030.
Baptistery *Apr–Oct daily*
0930–1330, 1500–1900;
Nov–Mar daily 0930–1300,
1500–1800.

Musei Civici €€ *Pza*
Eremitani 8. Open Tue–Sun
0900–1900. **Eremitani**
Church *Mon–Sat*
0815–1215, 1600–1800;
Sun 0930–1215,
1600–1800.

Orto Botanico €
Off Prato della Valle, near
the basilica. Open daily
May–mid-Sept 0900–1300,
1500–1800, shorter hours
off-season.

Palazzo della Ragione
€€ *Pza del Erbe. Open*
Feb–Oct Tue–Sun
0900–1900, Nov–Jan
0900–1800.

Caffè Pedrocchi*

The neo-classical building has housed this historic café since 1831. Manin and other *Risorgimento* leaders plotted the ousting of the Austrians, and students and intellectuals have gathered here ever since. Up a Greek stairway are theme-decorated rooms and a small Risorgimento Museum.

Cappella degli Scrovegni***

When Dante consigned Reginaldo Scrovegni to hell in the *L'Inferno* for usury, he may well have caused the building of this superb chapel. Finished in 1305 by the son to atone for his father's sins, the interior is covered with Giotto's most complete and outstanding fresco cycle. Beneath the luminescent blue ceiling, three rows of wall frescoes tell the story of Christ and of the Madonna with vivid Giotto colour on a cool blue background. Beneath, in monochrome, are the vices and virtues, while on the entry wall is the Last Judgement, a sobering reminder as worshippers left the chapel.

Duomo and baptistery**

The church itself is not the draw, although in the sacristy are paintings by Tiepolo, Bassano and others. The treasure is the baptistery, from an earlier 4th-century church, containing an astonishingly vivid cycle of frescoes by Menabuoi depicting the Creation, and Christ's miracles, Passion, Crucifixion and Resurrection. Facing Piazza del Duomo is the splendid façade of the 16th-century **Palazzo del Monte di Pieta***.

Musei Civici**

Along with art and one of Italy's most outstanding archaeological collections, the complex includes the Eremitani Church and Scrovegni Chapel (*see above*). Archaeology covers Egyptian, Etruscan, Greek, Roman and later periods, including a 1st-century tomb of the Volumni family. Painting and sculpture is 13th- to 17th-century, with works by Giotto, Bellini, Veronese, Riccio and Jacopo Sansovino. The 13th-century Eremitani (hermitage) church was heavily damaged in 1944, destroying much of Mantegna's fresco work. Two outstanding panels and the altarpiece remain.

Orto Botanico (Botanical Garden)**

Europe's oldest botanical garden dates from 1545, with trees from its first plantings. The garden is a pleasant place to stroll, fascinating for those interested in herbs and medicinal plants.

Palazzo della Ragione*

Europe's largest medieval hall was created in 1218 as law courts. Reconstructed after a 1420 fire, the walls have frescoes by Nicola Miretto. Months of the year, mythology and the zodiac are depicted in 333 panels. Inside, too, is a huge wooden horse made for a parade in

Above
Cloisters, Basilica of
St Anthony, Padua

1466. The arcaded *loggia*, designed by Palladio in the 14th century, needs upkeep after use as a market.

Piazza dei Signori*
Paduans savour city life in this gracious square surrounded by small shops, cafés and bars. At one end, **Palazzo Capitano** has a clock tower (1599) and an astronomical clock (1344). Concerts are held in the adjacent 14th-century **Corte Capitano**, whose frescoes include a portrait of Petrarch.

Scuolo di Santo
€ *Pza del Santo 11.*
Open Apr–Sept 0900–1200,
1430–1900; Oct–Mar
0900–1230, 1430–1700.

Scuola di Santo and Oratorio**
Adjacent to the basilica, the Oratorio is a small chapel, its walls covered with elegant frescoes, two scenes of the life of St Anthony, by Titian (1511), and the lives of other saints and Christ, by Altichiero da Zevio and Jacopo Avenzo (1378–84).

University of Padua € *V.*
Marzolo 8. Open for guided
tours on the hour Mon, Wed,
Fri 1500–1700, Tue, Thur,
Sat on the hour 0900–1100.

University of Padua*
Italy's second oldest university (1222), it was the first in the world to award a degree to a woman, Elena Piscopia, in 1678. Visit Palazzo del'Bo and the oval Anatomy Theatre built in 1594, the first in the world. The Auola Magna (Great Hall) is a baroque room with walls completely covered in crests. Galileo worked here for 18 years, developing his law of accelerated motion and designing the first astronomical telescope lens.

Accommodation and food in Padua and Brenta Canal

Hotel Donatello €€ *V. del Santo 102–104, 35123; tel: 0498 750 634; fax: 0498 750 829; e-mail: infor@hoteldonatello.net* A full-service hotel opposite Basilica di Sant'Antonio. The restaurant serves local specialities, parking available and public transport nearby.

Hotel Maritan €–€€ *V. Gattamelata 34, 35128; tel: 049 850 177; fax: 049 812 076.* In the centre of town, it is near the station and public transport, with parking available.

Riviera dei Dogi Hotel €€ *V. Don Minzoni 33, Fraz Mira Porte; tel: 041 424 466.* Comfortable hotel facing the canal, with good **Trattoria Nalin** € next door.

Trattoria al Pero €–€€ *V. Santa Lucia 72; tel: 0498 758 794.* Well-prepared local cuisine in a friendly atmosphere.

Trattoria Porto Menai dall'Antonia €€ *V. Argine Destro, Mira; tel: 0415 675 618.* Very popular with locals for the extraordinary seafood; genial owners will bring you small samples of local specialities to try.

La Vecchia Enoteca €–€€ *V. San Martino e Solferino 32; tel: 0498 752 856.* A block south of the Piazza della Erbe, popular so reservations are suggested.

The Brenta Canal

Villa Foscari (La Malcontenta) €€ *V. dei Turisti, Gambarare di Mira; tel: 0415 470 012. Open Apr–Oct Tue, Sat 0900–1200.*

Villa Pisani (Villa Nazionale) €€ *Stra; tel: 049 502 074. Open daily 0900–1800. Labyrinth open Apr–Oct.*

From Stra, just east of Padua, the Brenta Canal shortened the route to Venice and the Adriatic. Wealthy Venetians used it as their summer escape, creating the Brenta Riviera. Their sumptuous villas still line the canal, which is paralleled by S11. *Il Burchiello* cruises depart from Padua and Venice on alternate days, stopping at two or all three of the villas open to the public. Return is by public transport. Motorists can visit the villas at more leisure, stopping at canal-side cafés. **Villa Pisani** (Villa Nazionale)♦♦♦ is not by Palladio, which is remarkable for a major villa in this area. Built more than a century after Palladio's death, Pisani was designed by Girolamo Frigimelica, a 114-room mansion to rival any in the Veneto in size and splendour. Tiepolo (with his assistants) decorated the interior. Its garden contains one of the world's most difficult hedge mazes – so difficult that some visitors don't have time to see the other two villas. **Villa Foscari** (La Malcontenta)♦♦♦ is one of Palladio's best known, most admired and most copied villas, for its perfect proportions, temple portico and elegant double staircase. Elaborate Zelotti frescoes decorate the interior, only a small part of which is shown. The large salon that forms the core of the building is cross-shaped, with light entering from all four of the building's sides. Its setting is splendid, with its best side looking onto the Brenta canal, framed in willows. Beside the villa are *parterre* gardens.

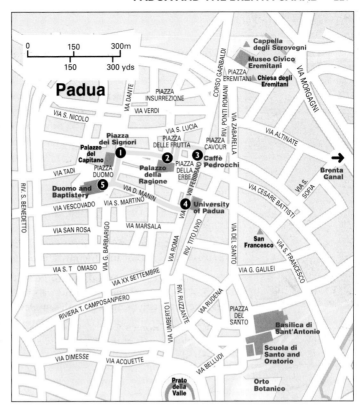

Walking tour – Padua (Padova)

Time: 45 minutes.

Route: Start at the **Palazzo del Capitano** on the **PIAZZA DEI SIGNORI** ❶, crossing the street and travelling along the left side of the square on **Via San Clemente** into **Piazza delle Frutta** (the old fruit market). Diagonally across the square is the **Palazzo Communali** with its 13th-century tower, and directly across the square is the back of the **PALAZZO DELLA RAGIONE** ❷. Continue ahead, bearing left onto **Via Gorizia**. At the end of the street, on the right, is **CAFFÈ PEDROCCHI** ❸. Turn right onto Via VIII Febbraio, following it to the **UNIVERSITY OF PADUA** ❹ on the left. On your right you will pass **Piazza della Erbe**; the front of Palazzo della Ragione encloses the *piazza* on the right. Turn right onto **Via Manin**, past arcaded storefronts to **Via Monte de Pieta**, then turn left into **Piazza Duomo**. The **DUOMO** and **BAPTISTERY** ❺ are ahead on the right. Recross the *piazza* past the front of **Palazzo del Monte di Pieta** and turn left onto **Via Monte de Pieta**, which leads back into **Piazza dei Signori** ❶.

Bologna to Florence via the Adriatic Coast

Ratings

Art	●●●●●
Beaches	●●●●○
Castles	●●●●○
Food and drink	●●●●○
Historical sights	●●●●○
Scenery	●●●●○
Children	●●●○○
Mountains	●●●○○

While you can rush from the many attractions of Bologna to Florence in a few hours along the spine of the Apennine mountains on the A-1 Autostrada, you would miss a beautiful and historic region of the Emilia-Romagna. East of Bologna, near the Adriatic coast, one of Christendom's richest treasure troves of Byzantine mosaics illuminates the churches of Ravenna. South along the coast, connected by silver-sand beaches, are colourful fishing villages, holiday resorts and the ancient Roman city of Rimini. Beyond and above stands the independent Republic of San Marino.

Within sight of the deep blue Adriatic waters, increasingly steep hills rise quickly to the beautiful Apennines, over which this route climbs to reach Florence. Hidden among these mountains' folds and crags are hillside farms, nature reserves and charming castle-topped villages rarely visited by travellers.

BOLOGNA✦✦✦

ⓘ TIC CST *Pza Maggiore; tel: 051 234 735. Open Mon–Sat 1000–1400, 1500–1900, Sun, hols 1000–1400.*

ⓟ Parking: € Cars are allowed in the city centre only with central lodging reservations.

ⓦ Internet: The Sala Borsa, opposite the Neptune Fountain, has free access for visitors.

Few cities offer such a concentration of art, history, gastronomy and culture, and yet remain so little visited by tourists as Bologna. Reminders of its rich history are everywhere. Begin at the **Basilica S Petronia✦✦✦**, designed to be larger than St. Peter's in Rome and never finished, but still impressive. Each of its side chapels is like a small church. Ask in the small **museum✦** to see the drawings for completing the half-finished façade – especially numbers 10, 11 and 12 by Andrea Palladio. Along the floor of the nave is a meridian line.

S Dominic died in Bologna, in the convent of the order he founded, and his tomb is among the city's most important treasures, carved in marble by a remarkable ensemble that includes Pisano and Michelangelo. Also in **Basilica S Dominico✦✦✦**, the choir is highlighted by outstanding wood inlay. **S Stefano✦✦✦** contains five Romanesque churches in all, dating from the 11th to 13th centuries.

The tiny and newly re-opened 1604 **Oratorio S Maria della Vita✦✦✦**,

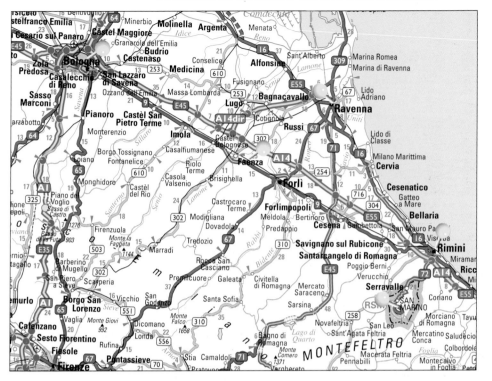

Museo de Basilica
Open Mon–Fri
0930–1230, 1430–1730,
Sun, hols 1430–1730.

**Museo Civico
Archeologico** € V.
dell'Archiginnasio 2; tel: 051
233 849. Open Tue–Sat
0900–1830, Sun, hols
1000–1830.

**Museo Civico
Medioevale** € V. Manzoni
4; tel: 051 203 930. Open
daily 0900–1830, Sun, hols
1000–1830.

Pinoteca Nazionale €
V. Belle Arte 56; tel: 051
420 9411. Open Tue–Sun
0900–1900.

**Palazzo
dell'Archiginnasio** Pza
Galvani. Open Mon–Sat
0900–1300.

almost hidden upstairs off Via Clavature, has a fresco ceiling so incredible that two benches are provided so you can admire it prone. At one end is a gold altar, on the other terracotta relief, among the most admired artworks in Bologna. Another 'lost' treasure recently reopened on Via Zamboni, is the **Oratorio S Cecelia**✦✦ its interior covered in a medieval fresco cycle.

Bologna's museum list is endless, boosted by the various university collections. Primary among them are the **Archaeology**✦✦ **and Medieval**✦✦ **museums** and the **Pinoteca Nazionale**✦✦, an outstanding art museum. In the Palazzo dell'Archiginnasio, the **Teatro Anatomico**✦✦, where medical students once learned anatomy, is panelled in cedar wood.

Among the beauties of Bologna are its ornamented buildings and colonnaded streets, which can be enjoyed during after-hours strolls. Few remain of the many towers that once crowned the palaces, but two stand side by side at alarming angles. The energetic can ascend the taller, **Torre Asinelli**✦✦.

Accommodation and food in Bologna

Al Cappello Rosso €€€ V. De'Fusari; tel: 051 261 891; fax: 051 227 179; www.alcapellorosso.it. A few steps from Piazza Maggiore, this posh, modern hotel is among the few central lodgings that offers parking.

ⓣ Torre degli Asinelli
€ *Pza di Porta. Open Apr–Sept 0900–1800, rest of year 0900–1700.*

Best Western City Hotel €€€ *V Magenta 10; tel: 051 372 676; fax: 051 312 161; www.bestwestern.it/city-bo.* Comfortable rooms, a garden and free parking.

Hotel Roma €€€ *V. D'Azeglio 9; tel: 051 226 322, 800 219 868; fax: 051 239 909.* One of the closest hotels to the sights, right in the historic centre.

Trattoria Gianni €€–€€€ *V. Clavature 18; tel: 051 229 434.* Torteloni with marrow flowers and the definitive Veal Bolognese.

Le Navate Cafe €€ *V. Val D'Aposa 7; tel: 051 262 793.* Cosy restaurant with a piano bar.

Trattoria Leonida €€ *Vicolo Alemagna; tel: 051 239 742.* Upholding the city's gastronomic reputation with dishes such as veal scallops with artichokes and pancetta in a delicate white wine sauce. Wines from under €10.

Below
Fountain of Neptune,
Piazza Maggiore

Trattoria Romagnola €€ *V. Rialto 13; tel: 051 239 310.* Some distance past S Stefano, but worth the trip for creative seasonal dishes.

FAENZA✧✧

ⓘ TIC IAT *Pza del Popolo; tel/fax: 054 625 231.*

ⓟ Parking € *Pza S Francisco.*

Shopping: Ceramics are the chief attraction; stop at Antonio Liverani, *Corso Garibaldi 19; tel: 0546 21900.*

Markets *are Tue, Thur and Sat mornings.*

ⓜ Museo delle Ceramiche € *V. Campidori 2; tel: 0546 697 311. Open Tue–Sun 0900–1230, 1500–1700.*

Known for the ceramics to which it gave its name, Faenza spreads gracefully around its long Piazza Republica, framed in arcaded buildings. The **Duomo**✧✧, built 1474–1515, but with an unfinished façade, is filled with paintings and sculpture of the 15th to 19th centuries. **Museo delle Ceramiche**✧✧ explores the history of ceramics, with worldwide as well as local examples and works by Matisse and Picasso.

Accommodation and food in Faenza

Albergo Vittoria €€–€€€ *Corso Garibaldi; tel: 054 621 508; fax: 054 629 136.* The Liberty style (Art Nouveau) interior has been restored; the dining room is a respected restaurant.

Osteria de Bergnaza €–€€ *V. Porta S Francisco;* local wines and a small menu.

RAVENNA✧✧✧

ⓘ TIC IAT *V. S Vitale; tel: 054 435 404; www.turismo.ravenna.it. Open Mon–Sat 0830–1900, Sun and holidays 1000–1600.*

ⓟ Parking € *is available at S. Vitale and several other locations.*

Festivals: *Jun–Jul,* **Ravenna Festival** uses the churches and squares as venues for opera, symphony, dance and ethnic music.

ⓦ World Heritage mosaic sites €€ *Tel: 0544 541 688. Open daily 0900–1900.*

Museo Nazionale €, *S Vitale; tel: 054 435 512. Open Tue–Sun 0830–1930.*

The churches of Ravenna combine to form perhaps the world's richest collection of Byzantine mosaics, important enough to be named a World Heritage Site.

The interior of the 5th-century **Neonian Baptistery**✧✧✧ is a riot of design, in tesserae so small that the pupils of the apostles' eyes are visible in the dome. Fine carved marble pieces, including a 6th-century pulpit, in the **Cathedral**✧✧ next door are easily overlooked among the city's mosaics.

Clustered at **S Vitale** are the mosaic-lined **basilica**✧✧✧, **Mausoleum Galla Placida**✧✧✧, and **Museo Nazionale**✧✧. The basilica's large circular interior is covered in mosaics of astonishing finesse and brilliant colour. Equally vivid are the ceiling panels in the small mausoleum, illuminated in intricate designs of cobalt and gold.

For a break from Byzantine, stop at **Basilica di S Giovanni**✧✧, where the mosaics, many with animal themes, are older and more primitive. At **S Aploinare**✧✧✧, the entire upper walls above the arches are devoted to larger-than-life images of saints and the nativity. In the cloister a fascinating display shows materials and techniques of mosaic art, including samples of 19 different shades of gold.

Dante's tomb✧ is outside **Basilica di S Francisco**✧✧, where it's worthwhile to see the flooded 5th-century crypt, the stone-carved columns by Tullio Lombardo and *freschi* by Pietro da Rimini in the left aisle.

Accommodation and food in Ravenna

Albergo Capello €€ *V. IV Nov. 41; tel: 0544 219 813; fax: 0544 219 814.* Well-located opposite the market, the hotel has a restaurant €–€€ serving grilled lamb chops, carpaccio and pasta dishes.

Ca de Ven €–€€ *V. Corrado Ricci 24; tel: 054 430 163.* Traditional foods of the Romagna and a vegetable buffet are the specialities.

Cupido € *V. Cavour 43; tel: 054 437 529.* Fast and inexpensive piedini (sandwiches), pizza and their own daily pastas (skip the gnocchi).

RIMINI✢✢

ⓘ TIC IAT *FS Rail station, Pza Caesar Battisti 1; tel: 054 151 331; www.commune.rimini.it. Open Mon, Wed, Fri, Sat 0900–1300.*

ⓟ Parking € *along city walls and outlying streets.*

ⓦ Internet *Point at Via Ponte 12.*

ⓝ Tempio Malatestiana *Open Mon–Sat 0750–1230, 1530–1850, Sun, hols 0900–1300, 1530–1900.*

An ancient Roman city, Rimini retains a surprising amount of its past, considering that its busy harbour was a major target for World War II bombs. The Roman Corso Augusto runs straight through its centre, from the striking **Porta Augusto**✢✢ to the five-arched **Ponte Tiberini**✢✢, a Roman bridge. Halfway, it passes through the **Forum**, later the Medieval marketplace and now Piazza Tre Martiri. Excavated segments of street, like other landmarks in the city, have historical signs in English.

Tempio Malatestiana✢✢ reconstructed by the Malatesta family in the 1400s, has carved marble works and a transcept painting by Piero della Francesca. The elegant fountain in Pza Cavour was admired by Leonardo da Vinci in 1502.

Stretching endlessly along the coast are fine beaches solidly lined with hotels, restaurants, cafes and shops.

Accommodation and food in Rimini

Hotel de Londres €€€ *V. Vespucci 24; tel/fax: 054 150 168; www.hoteldelondres.it.* An historic classic at the beach, completely refurbished to add all the mod cons.

Hotel Rondinella €€ *V. Neri 3; tel/fax: 0541 380 567.* At the beach, the hotel has a restaurant for its guests only.

Café Teatro €–€€ *Pza Cavour.* The place for a light meal, coffee or glass of wine and people-watching.

San Domingo € *Vale Dessié 7, Bellaria Igea Marina; tel: 0541 331 528.* Balconies overlook the Adriatic and the restaurant offers Romagnola specialities.

SAN MARINO**

ℹ TIC Ufficio Turismo *Contrada Omagnano 20; tel: 378 0549 882 998. Open Mon–Fri 0830–1830, Sat–Sun 0900–1330, 1400–1830.*

🅿 Parking: *Car parks € are located at various levels below the historic centre.*

⚓ Festivals: *Late Jul–early Aug, Medieval Days, filled with costumed pageantry.*

◑ Market day *is Thursday morning.*

Shopping: *Stamps and coins are popular with collectors.*

🏛 Palazzo Pubblico and Museo Nazionale *€ Tel: 378 0549 885 370. Open mid-Jun–Oct daily 0800–2000, shorter hours off-season.*

Rocca Malatestiana € *Verucchio, open mid-Apr–Sept daily 0930–1230, 1430–1930, weekends Oct–Dec.*

◐ Relais Torre Pratesi *V. Cavina 11, Brisighella; tel: 054 684 545; fax: 054 684 558. The Medieval watchtower, converted to spacious lodgings, crowns a garden-painted hilltop with views to the sea. Multi-course dinners use only seasonal local ingredients, many grown in the chef's garden, accompanied by their own fine wines.*

The views from this hilltop domain are splendid, especially from the castles that crown the long mountaintop. The guard, in colourful uniforms, changes hourly at the half hour in front of the **Palazzo Pubblico***, which can be toured on a combined ticket with the **National Museum****. Collections there include local Neolithic and later archaeological finds, paintings, sculpture, Egyptian antiquities and Byzantine icons. A paved walking route lined with eateries and kiosks connects the castles, beginning at the earliest, **Rocca Guaita*** (1253). **Rocca Cesta****, at the highest point, contains an arms museum.

A short side trip to hilltop **Verucchio**** is worthwhile, to see the 12th-century **Malatesta castle****, with views of a string of other hilltop castles and the Adriatic.

Accommodation and food in San Marino

L'Angelo Divino € *Pza Malatesta 15, Verucchio; tel: 378 0541 679 407.* Very inexpensive sandwiches and wine.

Righi La Taverna €€ *Pza Liberta 10; tel: 378 0549 991 196.* Café and meals at pavement tables or inside.

La Rocca €€ *Salita alla Rocca 34; tel: 378 0549 991 166, fax: 378 0549 992 430.* Attractive rooms with sweeping views and a restaurant serving local dishes.

Suggested tour

Total distance: 313km, with detours: 458km

Time: 12 hours' driving. Allow 4–5 days for the main route, 6 days with detours. Those with limited time should concentrate on Bologna and Ravenna.

Links: Florence (*see page 236*), the end point for this route, is the start of the Florence to Pisa route (*see page 254*).

Route: Leave **BOLOGNA ❶** on Via Massarenti to route S9, following signs to **FAENZA ❷** (50km). Leave Faenza by Via Garibaldi, following S302 east to **RAVENNA ❸** (31km).

Leave **RAVENNA** on S16 heading south along the shore to **Cesenatico ❹**, whose charming old canal/fishing harbour is filled with a colourful collection of historic boats, described in English. Restaurants, shops and cafes line the banks and a tiny walk-on ferry crosses it. Continue south on S16 to **RIMINI. ❺**

Albergo-Ristorante La Capanna €–€€ V. Corbari 40, Rocca S Casciano; tel: 0543 960 215. Rooms overlook a park and swimming pool (guests have access). The restaurant, specialising in porcini and other mushroom dishes, has good lasagna.

Ca'de Be Museo Enoteca €–€€ Belvedere, Bertinoro; tel: 0543 444 1426 shop open 1030–1230, shop and wine bar 1600–0030. Serves local wine and light foods.

Below
Faenza pottery

Leave **RIMINI** on Via Flaminia, turning right to S72, signposted to **San Marino ➏** (24km). Follow signs ever upward to **Borgo Maggiore ➐**, then to **Centro Storico ➑**.

From San Marino, backtrack toward **Rimini**; exiting northwest on route S9 to **Cesena ➒** (30km).

After crossing E45, follow signs south to the hilltop wine town of **Bertinoro ➓** for views from the belvedere and to see the curious hospitality pillar, where strangers once tied their horses. Descending, follow signs to Forlimpopoli to rejoin S9.

Forli is worth a stop to see the **Abazzia del S Maria✦✦**, facing its central piazza. The interior stone carving, in Istrian rock, resembles terracotta. The town is encircled by impressive bastioned walls.

Detour (52km): From Forli, continue on S9 to the **Faenza** access, but turn south onto S302 to **Brisighella✦✦**. This hillside town is distinguished by a curious 14th-century covered gallery, **Via degli Asini✦✦** that overlooks Pza Marconi. An even more compelling reason

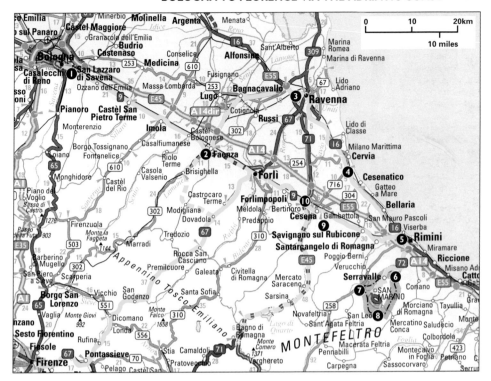

TIC IAT *V. D Manin*
Open Mon–Fri
0900–1200, 1600–1800,
Sat 0900–1330.

**Hotel Tosco
Romagnolo**
€€–€€€ *Bagno di
Romagna; fax: 0543 911
014.* Family-owned spa
resort with a wide variety
of rooms and an excellent
dining room and
sumptuous breakfasts.
Spa programmes are in
Italian, but English is
spoken at the hotel.

Locanda Giovanna
€–€€ *V. D Manin 5;
tel: 0543 911 057.* The
delicious mixed grill serves
two amply and house-made
pastas are excellent. Simple
rooms include meals in
budget-friendly rates.

to visit this region is to stay and dine in the mountaintop eyrie of **Relais Torre Pratesi****, a perfect mid-trip respite.

To rejoin the main route, follow the vinyard-lined unnumbered road from Brisighella following signs to Modigliana and Davidola to S67, just south of Davidola.

End Detour

Leave **Forli** travelling southwest on S67, signposted to **Firenze (Florence)** (105km). This route traversing the Apennines is relatively easy, passing the mountain resorts of **Rocca S Casciano** and **Benedetto in Alpi** before entering **Florence** along the Arno River.

Also worth exploring

Shortly past **Cesena**, E45, signposted 'Roma', almost immediately enters the scenic and rugged Apennine foothills. The roadway remains relatively level via tunnels and bridges to **Bagno di Romagna** (51km). This appealing old spa town with Roman origins hides in a deep, shady valley, and lacks the pretensions of the better-known watering holes. Children love the free **Gnome Trail** in the wooded **Parco dell'Armina** across the river.

Florence

The showplace of the Italian Renaissance, Florence finds itself in a difficult position today. The largesse of important buildings and art makes it a magnet for tourists – many travellers place it ahead of Rome on their 'must see' list. They come in hordes, so many that they often literally fill the streets in a solid mass. And Florence is caught between welcoming these cultural pilgrims and trying to maintain the treasures and their environment.

The traveller must overlook these obstacles and appreciate those masterpieces they came to see – the simply stunning Duomo-Baptistery complex, the art-filled churches and galleries and icons such as Ponte Vecchio and the Boboli Gardens. There is so much to see in Florence that one trip cannot possibly do more than skim the surface, so don't try to do everything. Concentrate on really absorbing a few sights – and come back often.

Arriving and departing

❶ APT Firenze
V. Cavour 1; tel: 0552 908 323; fax: 0552 760 383.

Commune de Firenze
Piazza Stazione 4 (opposite the rail station); tel: 055 212 245. Open Mon–Sat 0830–1900, Sun, hols 0830–1400.

Borgo S Croce *29; tel: 0552 344 044. Open Mon–Sat 0900–1700, Sun, hols 0900–1400.*

Arriving in Florence by plane is surprisingly difficult, as the city lacks a major airport. Its small airport, if used, connects to the centre via a regular bus. The nearest large airport with flights from abroad is in Pisa, from where one can ride directly to Florence on local trains – the travel time is approximately one hour. Longer-distance travellers may need to fly into Milan, then catch a train for Florence. Rail passengers arrive at Florence's handy rail station (also known as FMN), just a half-mile's walk from the *duomo*, the Arno and most of the major sites. There's luggage storage in the station, though fees are per-piece and quickly add up.

Getting around

Florence is a very compact place, yet there's tremendous congestion for such a small city centre; driving is not advised, and there is no

Florence

Palazzo degli Affari
Cenacolo di Foligno
VIA GUELFA
S. Barnaba
PIAZZA SAN MARCO
Palazzo Fenzi
PIAZZA ADUA
Air Terminal
Biblioteca Merucelliana
Galleria dell'Accademia
Santissima Annunziata
Museo Arch
Stazione Centrale Santa Maria Novela
Accademia di Belle Art
PIAZZA D. SANTISSIMA ANNUNZIATA
Mercato Centrale
PIAZZA MERCATO CENTRALE
Opificio delle Pietre Dure
Palazzo della Regione
Spedali degli Innocenti
San Jacopino in Campo Carbolino
Palazzo da Montauto
Palazzo Gerini
AZZA DELLA STAZIONE
Palazzo d. Cartelloni
Palazzo Bandinelli
Palazzo Medici-Riccardi
Palazzo Panciatichi
Cappellone egli Spagnoli
PIAZZA DELL' UNITA ITALIANA
Cappelle Medici
Palazzo Niccolini
Santa Maria Novela
San Lorenzo
San Giovanni
Palazzo Pucci
San Michele Visdomini
Ospedale S. Maria Nuova
PIAZZA SANTA MARIA NOVELLA
Biblioteca Laurenziana
Palazzo Niccollini
Rotonda del Brunelleschi
VIA DEL PANZANI
VIA DEI CERRETANI
Santa Maria Maggiore
Duomo Santa Maria del Fiore
Museo del Duomo
Teatro della Pergola
VIA DEL BANCHI
Palazzo Orlandini
Baptistery (Battistero)
PIAZZA S. GIOVANNI
Campanile
PIAZZA DEL DUOMO
Palazzo Guadagni
Museo Firenze Corn'era
S. Tommaso d'Aquino
Palazzo Antinori
San Gaetano
Laggia d. Bigallo
S. Maria in Campo
Palazzo d. Canonci
Museo Marino Marini
Palazzo Larderelli
Palazzo Corsi
Madonna da Ricci
Palazzo Salviati
Palazzo Nonfinito
Palazzo Altoviti
Palazzo Albizi
Palazzo Rucella
Palazzo Vechietti
PIAZZA DELLA REPUBLICA
Casa di Dante
BORGO DEGLI ALBIZI
VIA DELLA VIGNI NUOVA
VIA DEGLI STROZZI
Palazzo Strozzi
Palazzo Strozzino
Orsanmichele
S. Carlo d. Lomb
Palazzo Pazzi
Palazzo Alessandri
San Nicole
Palazzo Corsini
Palazzo Giaconi
Poste e Telegrafi
Palazzo Altovita
Badia Fiorentina
Casino Borghese
Palazzo Salviati
Palazzo Quaretari
Santa Trinita
GHIBELLINA
Bargello
Palazzo Ferroni
Palazzo Canacci
Palazzo di Parte Guelfa
Palazzo Fenzi
PIAZZA DELLA SIGNORIA
Palazzo Ugccioni
Palazzo Gondi
San Firenze
Teatro Verdi
Santa Simone
Palazzo Serristori
S.S. Apostoli
Palazzo Vecchio
PIAZZA DE SANTA CROCE
Palazzo Frescobaldi
S. Stefano
Uffizi
Loggia d. Grano
S. Remiglio
Casa d. Peruzzi
Casa dell' Antella
San Jacopo Soprarno
Palazzo Vita
Palazzo R.Firidolfi
Ponte Vecchio
Museo di Storia della Scienza
Borsa
Palazzo Corsini
Palazzo Rasponi
Biblioteca Nazionale
Casa di Blanca
Palazzo Bardi Serzelli
Museo Horne
Palazzo Ridolfo
Palazzo Alberti
Palazzo Corsini
Palazzo Guicciardini
Palazzo Mannelli
LUNGARNO DELLE GRAZIE
PIAZZA DEI PITTI
Santa Felicità
Palazzo Capponi
San Girolamo
Santa Lucia di Magnoli
Spirito Santo
Palazzo Torriagiani
Museo Bardini
LUGARNO SERRISTORI
Palazzo Serristori
Palazzo Pitti
Palazzo Alamanni
San Niccolò
Palazzo dei Mozzi
Giardino di Boboli
Forte di Belvedere o di San Giorgio
Fiume Arno
Porta San Minit

0   400m
400 yds

P Large car parks are near the main train station (Fortezza da Basso) and the cheaper Piazza della Libertà (Parterre). Most of the city centre is Zona Blu ('blue zone'), meaning only residents are allowed to park on the streets; cars parked illegally in this zone are towed away and held for ransom at V. dell'Arcovata 6; tel: 055 355 231. Making sure signs don't say 'ecetto residenti autorizatti' ('no parking except for residents'). Don't park in or near the notorious (for break-ins) Piazzale Michelangelo.

◖ Florence profits from its past but remains a working city engaged in an astonishing range of crafts and trades, particularly shoes, leather, handbags, textiles, nightgowns, bookbinding and art restoration. Most of the work is done in the Oltrarno (the left bank of the Arno) in small shops, some of them the size of a cupboard.

🛈 Baptistery € Pza del Duomo/San Giovanni. Open Mon–Sat 1200–1830, Sun 0830–1330.

Museo Nazionale del Bargello €€ V. del Proconsolo 4. Open Tue–Sun 0815–1350.

Campanile €€ Open daily 0830–1630.

Opposite
Piazza del Duomo

underground. That makes walking by far the best option in the heart of the city. Bridges cross the Arno at convenient points, making a visit to Oltrarno easy. The local buses are cheap; taxis are nearly impossible to find or call and cost more than they're worth in such a walkable place.

Driving: If Dante were alive today, he would surely add driving in Florence to the punishments of hell – a maelstrom of Vespa scooters, cabs, pedestrians and overly aggressive Italian drivers awaits. Avoid it at all costs, as you won't need a car anyway to see any of the important sights.

Buses: Florence's city buses can take you to the suburbs rather cheaply, though drivers drive like hellions and then make frequent stops. Among the options are single-ride tickets valid for 75 minutes (about €1), 24-hr tickets (about €2.50), and 48-hr tickets (about €5).

Sights

Baptistery✦✦✦

The origins of the Baptistery (Battistero) are mysterious, but the foundations are probably from the 4th–8th centuries, while the current building dates from 1059–1128. Medieval Florentines, including Dante (baptised here in 1265) thought it was built by the Romans and it does, in fact, stand at the former intersection of the town's two main Roman roads. See all three sets of its bronze doors, especially Ghiberti's east door. His crowning achievement, it is one of the finest artworks created during the Renaissance (the original ten gilded panels are in the Museo del Duomo); even Michelangelo, normally a merciless critic, called them the 'Doors of Paradise'. Inside, 13th-century mosaics in the apse inspired Dante while writing L'Inferno.

Bargello✦✦✦

The Bargello is strangely neglected, though its collection of sculpture rivals that of any museum in the world. The ground floor displays the only bust Michelangelo ever carved, of Brutus, and the same room contains his Tondo Pitti and David-Apollo. Upstairs is Donatello's homoerotic, under-age David – the first nude statue of the Renaissance, and one of the most remarkable works of art in Florence. Other high points include Ammanati's Leda and the Swan and Ghiberti's powerful The Sacrifice of Isaac. They're easy to overlook, but on the wall of the first floor are two panels submitted by Brunelleschi and Ghiberti in fierce competition for the commission to do the baptistery doors.

Campanile✦✦

Giotto was appointed architect of Florence's cathedral in 1334, but never got beyond building this tower. He decorated it with octagonal

Duomo *Pza del Duomo. Open Mon–Sat 1000–1700, Sun 1300–1700.*

Dome €€ *Open Mon–Fri 0830–1820, Sat 0830–1700 (closes 1520 first Sat each month).*

Giardino di Boboli € *Palazzo Pitti. Open Apr, May & Sept daily 0900–1830, Jun–Aug 0900–1930; shorter hours in winter. Closed first/last Mon of month. Last admission is one hour before closing.*

Museo del Duomo €€ *Open Apr–Oct Mon–Sat 0900–1930; in summer also Sun 0900–1340; Nov–Mar Mon–Sat 0900–1730. If you want to see the workshop that is now used to repair the duomo, walk around the corner to Via dello Studio 23r.*

Galleria Palatina €€ *Open May–Oct, Tue–Sat 0815–1850, Nov–Apr, Tue–Sat 0830–1900, Sun 0830–1400. Other museums in Palazzo Pitti open Tue–Sat 0900–1400, Sun 0900–1300.*

pilasters and a colour scheme that would later be applied to the cathedral – white marble (quarried in Carrara), green marble (from Prato) and red marble (from Maremma). The reliefs were added over the next century by Andrea Pisano, Luca della Robbia and Donatello and portray the history of humanity.

Duomo Santa Maria del Fiore***
When it was built, Florence's magnificently patterned *duomo* was the largest church in the world: 53m long and 38m wide. Today, it is still the fourth largest cathedral in Europe and tremendously impressive. Arnolfo di Cambio, began the *duomo* in 1296, but it was Brunelleschi who put his stamp on it, winning a heated competition to design the ingenious double-shelled dome (1420–34). Climbing to the top of it is one of the most unforgettable experiences of a trip to Florence, for its simultaneous views of the city's red-tiled rooftops and a plunging look into the marble canyon of the church's interior.

Giardino di Boboli**
The 16th-century Medici rulers used this vast fantasy-filled garden overlooking the city as a retreat; the public didn't get its first peek until 200 years later, and has been ambling happily through it ever since. Avenues lined with cypresses intersect ensembles of Roman and Renaissance statues, and stately cedars of Lebanon shade strange grottoes. Fountains are ubiquitous, and deeper inside beneath stalactites is Giambologna's well-endowed *Venus*. The steep climb to the top of the gardens is rewarded with a cinematic view of Florence and the surrounding Tuscan countryside.

Museo del Duomo***
Many of the most impressive pieces of the baptistery, *duomo* and *campanile* are kept here to preserve them from pollution and vandalism. Sculptures from the unfinished cathedral façade torn down in 1587 line the walls of the ground floor, as do the original panels of Ghiberti's 'Doors of Paradise'. The 80-year-old Michelangelo sculpted the moving *Pietà* (1548–55) for his own tomb in Rome, portraying himself in the figure of St Nicodemus. Donatello is represented by the early, powerful sculptures of prophets Jeremiah and Habakuk (1420) and a late Maria Magdalena in wood (1455). It's interesting to note that the 13th-century building behind the *duomo* served as its workshop for centuries. Michelangelo sculpted *David* there in 1501–4.

Palazzo Pitti**
The vast Pitti Palace was built at the edge of Florence by Luca Pitti and greatly expanded by Medici tyrant Cosimo. Today the palace contains no less than eight museums devoted to fashion, silver, coaches and other items. The **Galleria Palatina**** is one of Europe's great art museums, containing a brace of Caravaggios, more than a few

Above
View of the *duomo*

🛈 **Palazzo Vecchio**
€€ *Pza della Signoria.*
Open Mon–Wed & Fri
0900–1900, Sun
0800–1300.

paintings by Raphael (such as *Portrait of a Lady*) and Titian, and other works by Rubens (including *The Consequences of War*), Tintoretto and Giorgione.

Palazzo Vecchio✦✦

The palace is still the City Hall of Florence. It was the work of di Cambio (1299–1314), although Michelozzo added the early Renaissance courtyard in 1453. Two centuries after its completion, Vasari decorated the walls with frescoes, now badly faded, of Austrian cities to celebrate a wedding between the house of Medici and an Austrian princess. The clock, added in 1667, still ticks.

Ponte Vecchio✦✦

One of Europe's most photographed structures, the 'old bridge' occupies a place used in Roman times as a crossing over the Arno for

Uffizi €€ *Pzle degli Uffizi. Open Tue–Sun 0815–1850; reservations Mon–Fri 0830–1830; tel: 055 294 883; fax: 055 264 406. Booking a ticket means you don't have to wait in line but it costs a little more. Opening hours are subject to change.*

Capelle Medici €€ *Open Tue–Sun 0815–1645.*

the Via Cassia. Today's bridge was built in 1345. Originally, there were butcher shops and tanners lining it, but Ferdinand I replaced them with upmarket jewellers and goldsmiths.

San Lorenzo◆◆◆

As parish churches go, S Lorenzo goes a long way. It was, after all the parish of the Medicis, who dropped generous amounts into the collection plate. In the church are bronze pulpits by Donatello, and the old sacristy is crowned by another of Brunelleschi's domes, painted by Donatello, who also did the bronze doors. Michelangelo designed the stairs to the Medici's library and sculpted the tombs in the **Capelle Medici**, entered at the side of the church, and richly inlaid in coloured stone.

Uffizi◆◆◆

Giorgio Vasari designed the Uffizi ('offices') for Medici ruler Cosimo I in the 16th century. Today, it is Italy's most popular museum (around 1.5 million visitors a year and growing) with 1000 works of art from the 13th to the 17th centuries displayed in 45 rooms. Its most famous icon, Botticelli's *Birth of Venus*, challenges the *Mona Lisa* for the status of the world's most recognised painting. If your focus is the Renaissance, plan to spend the day in the first 15 rooms alone; save another day for the tremendous international collections, which hold major works by such northern Europeans as Dürer, Cranach, Brueghel and Rembrandt.

Accommodation and food

There is no off-season in Florence, merely busy and busier seasons; Apr–June, Sept and Oct are worst of all. Some hotels do drop rates 25–50 per cent in winter. Make advance reservations or day-trip into the city.

Culture shock

Something strange happened to French novelist Stendhal one day in 1817 during a visit to the Uffizi. His heart raced and he began to sweat and tremble; shortly afterwards, he broke down in tears. Florentine doctors and psychologists still treat dozens of cases of *sindrome di Stendhal* each year, a recognised medical condition that is basically a kind of nervous breakdown brought on by an overdose of culture.

Helvetia & Bristol €€€ *V. dei Pescioni 2; tel: 055 287 814; fax: 055 288 353; www.thecharminghotels.it.* Just as welcoming today as it was to the leading intellectuals of a century ago, whose favourite hotel it was. The décor is positively sumptuous.

Grand Hotel Minerva €€€ *Pza S Maria Novella 16; tel: 055 272 30; fax: 055 268 281; www.grandhotelminerva.com.* City centre location makes this historic hotel a short walk to all the sights; close to several moderately-priced restaurants.

Hotel Villa La Vedetta €€€ *V. Michelangelo 78; tel: 055 681 631; fax: 0556 583 544; www.villavedettahotel.com.* On a breezy hillside overlooking the city, this Liberty-style villa hotel has it all – free parking, free shuttle to the centre of town, beautifully decorated rooms, a terrace swimming pool, gardens, hospitable staff and an excellent restaurant €€€.

Right
Statuary in the Piazza della
Signoria

**Cucina alla
Fiorentina**

Florentine cuisine is simplicity itself. *Crostini* – toasted Tuscan bread with chicken-liver pâté, tomatoes or mushrooms, or simply dipped in indescribably good olive oil. Soup often takes preference over pasta, *Ribollita* in winter and *pappa di pomodori* in summer. Florentines also like to eat hare, wild boar and pheasant. The *Bistecca alla fiorentina* is simply a steak – of local Tuscan beef, from the Valdichiana, marinated in herbs, garlic and the finest olive oil, and cooked to perfection over wood coals. *Tortino di carciofi*, an artichoke omelette and *funghi alla griglia* ('grilled mushrooms') are among the few things for a vegetarian. Expensive restaurants sometimes have bargain lunch menus, and many eateries charge for *pane e coperto* (a 'cover' charge for sometimes stale bread) and sometimes for *servizio* (10 per cent); check the menu.

Hotel J and J €€€ *V. di Mezzo 20; tel: 0552 345 005; fax: 055 240 282; www.jandjhotel.com*. Few hotels in Florence have such a beautiful setting: 19 rooms are located off the courtyard of a 16th-century convent and decorated with frescoes, wrought-iron beds and fine hardwood furniture. The *duomo* is just 500m away. Parking at a nearby garage.

Royal €€ *V. delle Ruote 52; tel: 055 483 287; fax: 055 490 976.* One of the more accessible hotels by car, yet central. You can drive here directly from the peripheral road between Fortezza da Basso and Piazza della Libertà. Parking is in the courtyard.

Hotel Crocini € *Corso Italia 28; tel: 055 212 905; fax: 055 210 171.* The long established, Crocini is one of Florence's last 'authentic', English-style *pensiones*. Located in a quiet residential area, its rooms are spacious for Florence, and there is a back garden and parking lot. A 10-minute walk from the centre of town.

La Torricella € *V. Vecchia di Pozzolatico 25; tel: 0552 321 808; fax: 0552 047 402; e-mail: mbox940@mbox.infomark.it.* Two-night minimum stay. A B&B in a villa on the outskirts of Florence, run by the attentive and friendly Giannozzi family. It is an easy drive from the Certosa exit of the A1 *autostrada*. There is public transportation to the city centre.

Relais Certosa Hotel €€€ *V. di Colle Ramole 2 (Certosa); tel: 0552 047 171; e-mail: hbrelais@bettojahotels.it.* Also just off the Certosa exit of the A1, this rambling villa has spacious, attractive suites, a good restaurant and courtesy bus to the city centre.

Trattoria Antichi Cancelli € *V. Faenza 73; tel: 055 218 927.* Tourists rarely find this pleasant little place near the market, where generous portions are well prepared and cheap.

Caffe Bigallo €€ *V. del Proconsolo 73; tel: 055 291 403; www.caffebigallo.com.* Close to the Duomo, this restaurant claims 'the world's best bar', but we go for the carpaccio, offered in six varieties.

Il Cibreo €€ *Pza Ghiberti 35; tel: 0552 341 100. No reservations. Closed Sun, Mon, last week of July & Aug. Trattoria* attached to a more expensive restaurant next door; the food is outstanding at modest prices, but it doesn't accept reservations and is always packed. Arrive early, before 8 p.m. *Anatra ripiena al forno* ('stuffed roast duck') is a speciality; they don't do pasta.

Trattoria Marione €–€€ *V. della Spada 27; tel: 055 214 756; www.marione.firenze.net.* The queue waiting for tables doesn't come for the surly service, but for the prodigious plates of homey Florentine food.

La Pentola dell'Oro € *V. di Mezzo 24r; tel: 055 241 808.* Chef Giuseppe Alessi goes one better than traditional by serving Renaissance-style dishes – *Piatti Rinascimentale* – and vegetarian meals.

Osteria Pepo € *V. Rosina 4; tel: 055 283 259.* Although à la carte dishes are inexpensive, the fixed daily menu is a real bargain and includes wine. It's a good idea to reserve.

La Spada € *V. della Spada 62; tel: 055 218 757.* Begin with the tris (trio) of pastas to get the chef's daily favourites and order the excellent side-dish of grilled vegetables – main courses are so inexpensive that you can splurge on extras here.

Pitti Gola e Cantina €€ *Pza Pitti 16; tel: 055 212 704.* A little pricier than some wine bars, but you're paying for the view of Pitti Palace and for the delicious snacks that accompany the wine.

Shopping

Florence is not a bargain-hunter's dream. If money is no object, walk Via Tornabuoni or Via della Vigna Nuova for high fashion, and price tags to match. Leather lovers shop Florence for high-quality coats and shoes – you can find an open-air market atmosphere at **San Lorenzo Market**, or trawl through the shops at **Piazza Santa Croce** for moderately priced leather goods. For a complete Italian shopping experience, explore **San Lorenzo Market's** fresh produce and well-priced clothing. Finally, **Ponte Vecchio** is the place to find Italy's best gold, silver and other jewellery items.

Mario Buccellati €€–€€€ *V. dei Tornabuoni 71r; tel: 0552 396 579.* Jeweller rendering exquisite gold and silver pieces at a modest price.

Coin €–€€€ *V. dei Calzaiuoli 56r; tel: 0552 398 963.* Four-storey department store featuring affordable, made-in-Italy goods.

Leather School €–€€€ *Pza Santa Croce; tel: 055 244 533.* Reasonably priced leather goods such as wallets and handbags.

Alice's Masks €€–€€€ *V. Faenza 72; tel: 055 287 370; www.alicemasks.com; open Mon–Sat 0900–1300, 1530–1930.* As much a museum as a shop, this studio also has workshops in *papier mache* mask making.

Entertainment

There's surprisingly little nightlife in Florence, although the classical music scene is far more lively. Churches are often venues for chamber music, and the **Teatro Communale** divides its year between opera, ballet and orchestral performances *(tel: 055 211 158; www.maggiofiorentino.com).* Florence has quite a few Irish pubs catering to an American, British and Aussie audience. Among the most popular are **Fiddler's Elbow** *(Pza Santa Maria Novella 7r; tel: 055 215 056)* and **The Lion's Fountain** *(Borgo Albizi 34r; tel: 0552 344 412).* For wine, try one of the city's *enoteche* (wine bars), which offer light meals and often have no seating.

Walking tour

Total distance: 2km.

Time: To see everything on this route would require at least three days. If you only have a day, visit the *duomo* sights, walk the route below and, along the way, choose between the Uffizi or Bargello.

Links: Florence falls at the end of the Bologna to Florence route across the Apennines *(see page 235)* and at the beginning of the Florence to Pisa route *(see page 254).*

Note that this tour skips the Accademia, which holds the famous *David* statue, but little else of interest; queues here are invariably very long, not worth experiencing for the time-short traveller.

Route 1: Piazza del Duomo is the ancient heart of Florence where two Roman roads once met. Begin here with a look at the **BAPTISTERY** ❶, then visit the **DUOMO SANTA MARIA DEL FIORE** ❷ – to appreciate it fully, climb the steps to the dome. A second, even more dizzying view is possible over the edge of the **CAMPANILE** ❸. *(See Detour on page 246.)*

On the north side of the *duomo*, take Via de Martelli. After one short block, have a look at the **Palazzo Medici-Riccardi** ❺ and walk into its arcaded courtyard, one of the finest in Florence. This was the family home of the Medici until they moved to the Palazzo Vecchio in 1659. SAN LORENZO ❻ is just a stone's throw away on Canto dei Nelli. The unfinished façade hides one of the most perfectly proportioned buildings of the Renaissance. The entrance to the **Cappelle Medici** ❼ is behind the church. Just a few paces further on is Florence's gastronomic paradise, the elegant 19th-century iron and glass **Mercato Centrale** ❽ (*V. dell'Ariento. Mon–Sat 0730–1300; Sat also 1600–2000*). This is the city's main market and one of the best places in Italy to buy food. Around it are market stalls, selling foods, silk, leather, paper goods and everything else.

Route 2: The narrow street of Borgo dei Greci leads into Piazza de Santa Croce, a neighbourhood where residents actually outnumber tourists. The largest Franciscan church in Italy, **Santa Croce** ❿, was the work of Arnolfo di Cambio (but the façade is 19th-century). It has been called the Westminster Abbey of Florence; inside are masterpieces by artists from Giotto to Donatello, and tomb-spotters will quickly find Michelangelo, Machiavelli, Galileo and Rossini. Few pay the price of admission to see the **Cappella dei Pazzi** (1430–46) next door, now part of a museum – the **Museo dell'Opera di Santa Croce**. Yet it is arguably the most perfect of all the designs created by Brunelleschi, built according to the golden mean.

Walk right into the imposing open *piazza* and along Borgo dei Greci to **PALAZZO VECCHIO** ❸. This was the scene of the Bonfire of the Vanities, when Savonarola convinced Florentines to burn their carnival costumes and licentious paintings only a few short months before they subjected him to the same treatment. The huge square fronting it, **Piazza della Signoria** ❹, is Florence's open-air drawing room – a gathering place for locals and tour groups alike. The U-shaped **UFFIZI** ❺ gallery stands at the southerly end of the square; allow several hours at the very least to explore what may be Italy's finest museum, or, if you're pressed for time, follow its length (and the waiting line of tourists) to the river and the **PONTE VECCHIO** ❻. This bridge is lined with goldsmiths and people taking pictures. Across the bridge, it is just one block further to the **PALAZZO PITTI** ❼. The **GIARDINO DI BOBOLI** ❽ is behind the palace. From here, buses return to the central train station.

Detour: Walk around the cathedral past the newly restored **MUSEO DEL DUOMO** ❹ where you can see Ghiberti's original 'Doors of Paradise'. Now enter **Via del Proconsolo**, a pedestrian zone, though you will have to dodge taxis and mopeds. The **Palazzo Nonfinito** ❾ contains the Museo Nazionale di Antropologia e Etnologia, the first anthropological museum in Italy (founded in 1869, free admission). The Romanesque cloister of **Badia Fiorentina** ❿ is a small oasis of peace where Dante once wistfully spied on Beatrice at Mass; the lanes around it are known as the 'Dante quarter'. Opposite the Badia is the grim façade and tower of the **BARGELLO** ⓫.

Florence

Florence to Pisa

Ratings

Architecture	●●●●●
Art	●●●●●
Gardens	●●●●○
Historical sights	●●●●○
Museums	●●●●○
Children	●●●○○
Crafts	●●●○○
Food and drink	●●●○○

From the almost too-well-known leaning campanile in Pisa to the secret treasures of lovely Lucca and the even less-visited towns of Prato and Pistoia, the short distance between Florence and the Mediterranean shore shouldn't be skipped past in the two hours it takes via autostrada A11.

While Pisa's closely grouped sights can be seen in a day, Lucca is a city to settle into for a few days. Follow the locals' example and rent a bike to explore it, or just wander to savour its architecture and friendly atmosphere.

Perhaps because they are so close to Florence, Prato and Pistoia go largely unnoticed by tourists. But each has a central core of attractions; Pistoia's collection of art-filled churches alone would have made it a tourist mecca in any other location.

LUCCA✦✦✦

ℹ️ **TIC APT** Pza S Maria 35; tel: 0583 919 931; www.luccaturismo.it. Open daily.

🅿️ Parking is restricted within the city walls, but several car parks € lie just outside.

🏪 **Market**: An antiques market fills Pza S Martino the third weekend of each month.

🏛️ **S Giovanni Reparata** € Open

Lucca is a thoroughly pleasant city, relaxed and not jaded by tourists. Manageable in size, it is filled with sights and enjoyable strolls, especially atop the **city walls✦✦✦**, shaded by large trees planted in the early 1800s by Napoleon's widow, Marie Louise.

Perhaps the most fascinating is the petrified shell of its **Roman Amphitheatre✦✦✦**, visible inside as an oval piazza and outside as a ring of streets with odd stone arches imbedded into their facades. View the whole city from tree-crowned **Torre Guinigi✦✦✦** a surprisingly easy climb, thanks to historic cartoons that give an excuse to stop at each landing. In the separate Guinigi Villa is the **Museo Nazionale✦✦**, with Roman and Etruscan antiquities, medieval altarpieces and sculpture.

The **Duomo✦✦✦** façade deserves more than passing notice for its arched porch, colonnade and ornately carved figures. Inside, the exquisitely-carved marble **Tempieto✦✦** holds the **Volto Santo✦✦**, a simple wood crucifix. Lucca's most precious holy relic, it is believed to

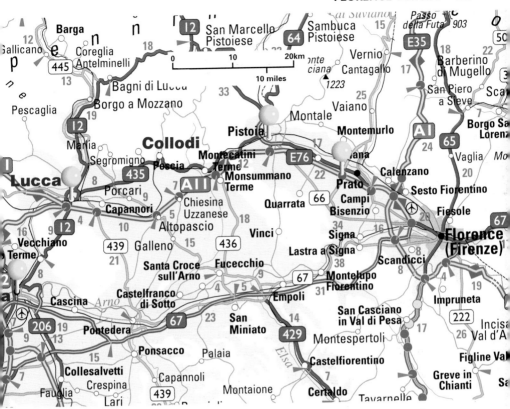

Apr–Oct Mon–Fri
1000–1800, Sat–Sun, hols
1000–1700.

Duomo Sacristy *Open
Mon–Fri 0930–1745, Sat
0930–1845, Sun, hols
0930–1100, 1300–1800.*

Torre Guinigi € *V. S
Andrea 42. Open daily
May–Sept 0900–2400,
shorter winter hours.*

Palazzo Pfanner € *V.
degli Asili 33, open Apr–Nov
daily 1000–1800.*

S Michele *Open daily
0900–1200, 1500–1800.*

Museo Nazionale € *V.
della Quarquonia; tel: 058
346 033. Open Tue–Sat
0900–1900, Sun, hols
0900–1400.*

be the only true portrait of Christ, sculpted by Nicodemus. In the Sacristy is the marble tomb of **Ilaria del Carretto**** by Jacobo della Quercia. In a side chapel, Tintoretto's *Last Supper* takes an unusual perspective. The **Cathedral Museum**** shows illuminated hymnals and intricate medieval gold work, including a Pisani crucifix.

S Giovanni Reparata** covers extensive excavations of a Roman bath, a first-century BC Roman home and stone sarcophagi. Enter through fragments of a baptistery floor (12th century) and Paleochristian mosaics – it is like descending through levels of time.

The **S Frediano**** façade is crowned by a large mosaic, and inside is a baptismal font carved with fanciful creatures, a della Robbia panel and a chapel with incorrupt relics of St. Zita. The carved and inlayed marble façade of **S Michele in Foro**** seldom repeats a design on its pillars. Inside are works by della Robbia and Lippi; Puccini sang here as a choirboy. In Pza Citadella, a statue of Puccini stands below **Casa Puccini***, his birthplace and childhood home, with original music manuscripts and letters and the piano at which he composed *Turandot*.

Palazzo Pfanner* combines ornately frescoed rooms with a beautiful garden that appears larger because of statue-lined walkways. At least look into it from the city wall.

Museo della Cattedrale € V. Arcivescovado; tel: 0583 490 530. Open Apr–Oct 1000–1800, Nov–Mar 1000–1400, Sun, hols 1000–1700.

Casa Natale di Giacamo Puccini € Corte S Lorenzo; tel: 0583 584 028. Open Jun–Sept daily 1000–1800, Mar–May, Oct–Dec Tue–Sun 1000–1300, 1500–1800.

Accommodation and food in Lucca

Lodging is scarce in Lucca, especially in the summer and on weekends. Reservations are a must.

Grand Hotel Guinigi €€ V. Romana 1247; tel: 0583 4991; fax: 0583 499 800. Outside the walls, with free parking and easy to reach by car, the modern art deco-style hotel has large rooms and Internet access.

La Luna €–€€ Corte Compagni 12; tel: 0583 493 634; fax: 0583 490 021. Set inside the walls in two historic palazzi.

Universo €€€ Pza del Giglio 1; tel: 0583 493 634; fax: 0583 954 854. Near the Duomo in the city centre, this venerable hotel has parking and a reliable restaurant.

Cafe l'Emiliana € Pza dell'Anfiteatro 134; tel: 0583 496 767. Inside the oval piazza, this is one of the few places serving breakfast.

Canuleia €€ V. Canuleia 14; tel: 0583 467 470. A more upscale menu than most of its neighbours, with a pleasant garden.

Locanda Buatino €€ Borgo Giannotti 505; tel: 0583 343 207. Outside the walls, this rustic restaurant offers rabbit cacciatore with olives, duck with mushrooms, risotto with trout. Modest rooms upstairs.

Trattoria Leo €–€€ V. Tegrimi 1; tel: 0583 492 236. Friendly, family-run restaurant serving carpaccio with arugula or veal with pignoli nuts and red wine. No credit cards.

Locanda Prociutto e Melone €€ V. Anfiteatro 29; tel: 0583 496 124. Huge cold plates, calzone, focaccie and pastas at pavement tables or the air-conditioned dining room.

I Santi Vineria €–€€ V. Anfiteatro 13; tel: 058 348 845. Salad plates, vegetable terrine and lighter dishes are on the wine bar's highly creative menu.

PISA✦✦✦

TIC APT Campo de Miracole; tel: 050 422 91. Open Mon–Sat 0900–1800, Sun, hols 1030–1630, guarded baggage check.

Parking: Near Campo €, free Sundays.

The irony of the tilting campanile, **Torre Pendente**✦✦✦, is that even if it stood straight, its delicate arcaded form would make it one of Italy's most important monuments. But tilt it does, as it has from its construction. Recently stabilised, it is again open for visitors to climb (at a very high price).

The **Duomo**✦✦✦, begun in the mid-eleventh century, is the definition of the Pisan-Romanesque architectural style that influenced churches throughout Tuscany. The mosaic in the apse is by Cimabui; Pisano created the pulpit.

Combined tickets
€–€€ are sold for monuments and museums.

Baptistery € *Open Apr–Sept daily 0800–1930, rest of the year 0900–1630.*

Camposanto € *Tel: 050 560 547. Open daily Apr–Sept 0800–1930, rest of the year 0900–1630.*

Duomo € *(free in winter); tel: 050 560 921. Open Apr–Sept, Mon–Fri 1000–1930, Sat, Sun, hols 1300–1950, rest of the year open Mon–Fri, 1000–1230 and 1500–1630, Sat, Sun, hols 1500–1630.*

Museo dell'Opera del Duomo € *V. Arcivescovado; tel: 050 560 547. Open daily Mar–Oct 0800–1930, rest of the year open 0900–1620.*

Leaning Tower €€€ *Open daily Apr–Sept 0800–2000, rest of the year 0900–1700 (later Mar, Oct).*

The Baptistery***, begun a century later, is largely the work of the Pisano family, with a magnificent pulpit by Nicolo Pisano. Shiploads of earth from the Holy Land were brought back by crusaders to fill the Camposanto** so that influential Pisans could rest eternally in holy soil. Along with tombs and second-century sarcophagi are frescoed walls under restoration. In adjoining chambers more *freschi* include vivid 14th-century depictions of the inferno.

The excellent **Museo dell'Opera del Duomo**** displays an ivory Madonna by Giovanni Pisano, gold and silver work and reliquaries, including a thorn from the *spina corona*. The view of the Leaning Tower from the courtyard balcony is among the best.

Not far from the Campo dei Miracoli, busy **Piazza dei Cavalieri**** is surrounded by palaces.

Accommodation and food in Pisa

Many of Pisa's restaurants close for the month of August.

Royal Victoria Hotel €€€ *Lungarno Pacinotti 12; tel: 050 940 111; fax: 050 940 180; www.royalvictoria.it.* Beautifully maintained historic building (parts are many centuries old) overlooking the Arno.

Villa di Corliano €€€ *San Giuliano Terme, Rigoli district; tel: 050 818 193; fax: 050 818 897. Open Mar–Nov.* The stately villa is set in gardens near the spa of San Giuliano, with a noted restaurant.

Villa Kinzica €€ *Pza Arcivescovada; tel: 050 560 419; fax: 050 551 204.* Some rooms have views of the Leaning Tower and their **Restaurant Maiori** €–€€ is better than expected in a busy tourist location.

Osteria dei Cavalieri €€ *V. San Frediano 16; tel: 050 580 858. Closed Sat lunch, Sun and Aug.* Typical dishes, but with the chef's own creative flair. Excellent wine list, many by the glass.

Trattoria La Mescita € *V. Cavalca 2 (Pza delle Vettovoglie); tel: 050 544 294. Closed Mon.* Fresh vegetables rule at this crowded spot near the

Above
Leaning Tower, Pisa

market, although fish and meats appear as well. Not your usual Tuscan menu.

Al Ristoro dei Vecchi Macelli €€€ *V. Volturno 49; tel: 050 204 24.* Fresh, local seafood and wild game are treated respectfully.

PISTOIA❖❖

ⓘ TIC AIT *Pza Del Duomo; tel: 057 321 622. Open Mon–Sat 0900–1300, 1500–1800.*

ⓟ Parking € is plentiful just outside the southeast corner of the city walls, near the Fortezza di S Barbara.

ⓜ Museo Civico € *Pza del Duomo; tel: 0573 371 296. Open Tue–Sat 1000–1900, Sun 0900–1230, winter 1000–1230.*

Principal churches *open 0830–1900, Baptistery closes 1200–1500.*

Giardio Zoologico € *V. di Pieve a Celle 160; tel: 0573 911 219; www.zoopistoia.it. Open Apr–Sept 0900–1900, Oct–Mar 0900–1700.*

The **Duomo**❖❖ is from the 11th century; apply at the Sacristy or look through the gate to see its masterpiece, the Medieval silver altar with intricate depictions of saints. The **Baptistery**❖❖, faced in carved and inlaid marble panels, has a coffered green and white marble interior with a 13th-century font. The **Museo Civico**❖❖ is well worth the long climb to upper floors to see extraordinary medieval art.

Near Piazza della Duomo on Via Cavour, the church of **S Giovanni**❖ has a pulpit supported on lion-held columns with intricate free-standing marble figures. A five-minute walk in the opposite direction is the **Ospedale del Ceppo**❖❖, its façade surmounted by a wide ceramic frieze by della Robbia. The church of **S Andrea**❖ has a magnificent pulpit by Giovanni Pisano.

West of town is one of Italy's best zoos, **Giardio Zoologico di Pistoia**❖❖. In addition to jaguars (bred there), polar bears and elephants, a special section encourages children to approach animals safely and teaches about protecting rare domestic breeds.

Accommodation and food in Pistoia

Hotel Firenze €–€€ *V. Curtatone e Montanara 42; tel/fax: 057 323 141; www.hotel-firenze.it.* Close to the Duomo, with parking and in-room Internet connections.

Albergo Le Rose €€ *Viale Auda 87; tel: 057 320 785; fax: 0573 976 161.* Just out of the town centre, with air conditioning and a good restaurant featuring local dishes.

Tenuta di Pieve a Celle €€ *V. Pieve a Cella 158; tel: 0573 913 087; fax: 0573 910 280.* Agroturismo on a country estate with stylishly furnished rooms and swimming pool. Guests' meals by reservation.

San Jacobi €–€€ *V. F Crispi 15; tel: 057 327 786.* Homey local dishes, including Tuscan tripe.

Liberty Cafe €–€€ *V. degli Orafi 54; tel: 0573 975 535.* In one of Tuscany's finest Art Nouveau buildings, serving light meals, cold dishes, waffles and pizza.

Opposite
Duomo, Pistoia

La Torretta € *V. Prov Lucchese 488; tel: 0573 572 434.* West of town, in a 17th-century palazzo with a terrace. Serves updated Tuscan cuisine – old favourites with a flair.

Caffè San Giovanni €–€€ *V. Cavour 18; tel: 057 321 623.* A relaxing stop for coffee and the local *cantuccini* (biscuits).

PRATO✧✧

ⓘ TIC APT *Pza S M della Carceri 15; tel/fax: 057 424 112; www.prato.turismo.toscano.it. Open daily 0900–1830.*

Monday, when attractions are closed elsewhere, is a good day to visit Prato, which has Tuesday closings.

Ⓟ Parking € is in Pza S Francisco and Pza Mercanti.

ⓓ Duomo € Stefano *Open Mon–Sat 0700–1200, 1530–1900, Sun, hols until 2000.*

Museo dell'Opera del Duomo € *Open Mon, Wed–Sat 0930–1230, 1500–1800, Sun, hols 0930–1230.*

Museo del Tessuto (Textiles) € *V. S Chiara 24. Open Wed–Mon 1000–1800.*

L Pecci Centro €€ *V. della Republica 277. Open Mon, Thur, Fri 1200–1900, Sat–Sun 1000–1900, Wed 1000–2100.*

Castello Imperatore € *Pza SM del Carceri. Open Apr–Sept Wed–Mon 0900–1300, 1600–1900, Oct–Mar Wed–Mon 0900–1300.*

A centre for the woollen industry since the early Middle Ages, Prato grew rich and the results are seen in its churches and public buildings today. The green-and-white-striped **Duomo✧✧** has an unusual broad pulpit on its façade, an exact replica of the original by Donatello (now in the **Museo dell'Opera del Duomo✧** in the adjoining Palazzo Vescovile). The church's sacred relic is a belt worn by the Virgin Mary, displayed in a chapel off the left nave, along with an outstanding marble and silver altar and a lovely Pisano Madonna. The high altar chapels are decorated by huge fresco cycles including Filippo Lippi's *Banquet of Herod*, with the dancing Salome (currently under restoration).

⛟ Terme Tettuccio, Montecatini Terme, is under renovation, but you can drink the water 0730–1200, 1700–1900. *Nightly concerts are in the elegant Art Nouveau atrium Jun–Jul 2115.*

🍴 Quaglino Rist-Pizzaria €€–€€€ *V. della Toretta, Montecatini Terme; tel: 057 278 652. Grilled veal, frito misto del mare.*

⛟ Parco di Pinocchio €€ *Collodi; tel: 0572 429 342, www.pinocchio.it. Open daily 0830–sunset.*

🅾 Shopping: This is the place to buy puppets, sold from shops and kiosks everywhere.

⛟ Villa Torrigianni € *Tel: 0583 928 008. Open Mar–Oct Wed–Mon 1000–1200, 1500–1800.*

Villa Mansi € *Tel: 0583 920 096. Open Tue–Sun 1000–1230, 1500–1900, winter until 1700.*

Villa Reale € *Tel: 058 330 108, gardens open by guided tour only, Mar–Nov 1000, 1500, 1700.*

Museo Archeologico *Artimino Tel: 0558 718 124. Open Feb–Oct Mon, Tue, Thur–Sat 0930–1230, Sun by tour at 1000 or 1100. Nov–Jan Sun tours only.*

The nearby **Piazza del Commune** is enclosed by the Medieval **Palazzo Pretorio** and the **Palazzo del Commune**. The Gothic **S Dominic**✶ houses a fresco museum off its cloister € (*open Wed–Mon 0900–1300, Fri–Sat also 1500–1800*). The well-preserved 13th-century **Imperial Castle**✶ was built by Holy Roman Emperor Frederick II to impress his Italian subjects.

The new **Textile Museum**✶✶ shows more than 6000 examples from all periods, and the **Luigi Pecci Contemporary Art Centre**✶ proves Prato's continued dedication to art.

Accommodation and food in Prato

Hotel Flora €€–€€€ *V. Carioli 31; tel: 057 433 521; fax: 0574 400 289.* In the historic centre, with parking and all the mod cons.

Giglio € *Pza S Marco 14; tel: 057 437 049; fax: 057 604 351.* Close to the castle, modest but hospitable.

Caffe Buonamici € *V. Ricasoli 3; tel: 057 430 170.* Generous sandwiches and a view of the Duomo from pavement tables.

I'Rifrullo €–€€ *Pza Mercatale 18; tel: 057 425 062, (closed Mon).* Seafood and typical Tuscan dishes.

Suggested tour

Total distance: 105km With detours: 124km

Time: 4 hours driving. Allow 3 days for the main route, 4 days with detours. Those with limited time should concentrate on Lucca and Pisa.

Links: Florence (*see page 236*), where this route begins, connects with the Bologna to Pisa route (*see page 233*). Pisa, this route's end, is the starting point for the Southern Riviera di Levante route (*see page 262*).

Route: Leave **FLORENCE ❶** on the *autostrada* A11, exiting at **PRATO ❷** (24km). Leave **PRATO** heading west on route S435 to **PISTOIA ❸** (15 km). Continue on route S435 to **Montecatini Terme** (15km).

Continue on route S435 through the plant and tree nurseries of **Pescia**, turning north on the unnumbered road signposted to **Collodi**, 'birthplace' of Pinocchio (14km).

Return to S435, continuing west through **Zone** (*see Detour*) and into **LUCCA ❹**. Leave **LUCCA** heading south on route S12 (beware of poor signage here), climbing the ridge of Monte Pisano and dropping into **S Giuliano Terme** before arriving in **PISA ❺**, where signs lead to **Campo dei Miracoli** (37km).

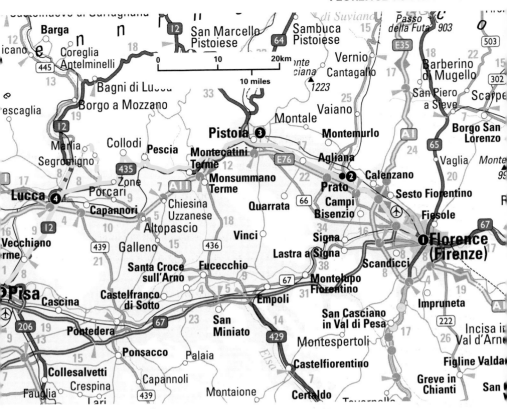

Detour: At **Zone**, turn north on the unnumbered road signposted **Segromigno**, following signs to **Villa Torrigianni** in **Camigliano**, **Villa Mansi** in **Segromigno** and **Villa Reale** in **Marlia**. Just past **Marlia**, turn south on route S12 into LUCCA (19km).

Also worth exploring

Those with a passion for archaeology and early history will find the area south of Prato fascinating. A 7th-century BC Etruscan site has been excavated at Artimino, and artifacts from this and a number of necropoli and tumuli are shown in the **Museo Archeologico** at Artimino. You can visit the Etruscan **Montefortini Tumuli** (*tel: 055 871 9741, open Mon–Sat 0900–1400*). From Prato, follow SS325 and SS66 to Poggio a Caiano, then follow signs to Comeana and Artimino.

The southern Riviera di Levante

Ratings

Scenery	●●●●●
Villages	●●●●●
Walking	●●●●●
Children	●●●●○
Geology	●●●●○
Outdoor activities	●●●●○
Vineyards	●●●○○
Beaches	●●●○○

From the Art Nouveau pleasure palaces of the Ligurian beach towns to the rugged vertical cliffs of the Cinque Terre, this section of Mediterranean coast certainly doesn't lack variety. Nor does it lack history: Romans first coaxed marble out of the mountains of Carrara, from the same quarries that later supplied Michelangelo with his palette of stone.

Because of its golden beaches and scenery, and the attention that UNESCO recognition has brought the newly-established Parco Nazionale delle Cinque Terre, the region can be very crowded in the summer. But the mild year-round climate makes the Ligurian coast ideal for off-season travel, and the months of October, November, March and April bring good weather and uncrowded roads.

CARRARA ❖❖

ⓘ V. Le XX Settembre; tel: 0585 632 519; www.massacarrara.it

ⓘ TIC Marina de Carrara V. A Vespucci at Pza La Rotunda Paradiso; tel: 0335 834 3272; www.massacarrara.it. Open Apr–Sept daily 0930–1300, 1500–1930 (Jul–Aug until 2300), on the beach side of road, 3 traffic lights north of the statue.

⭕ Market day is Monday.

Its very name synonymous with marble – and not just any marble, but the world's finest – Carrara is also inextricably linked with the name of Michelangelo. The artist believed that the search for the right piece of stone was just as important as its sculpting, and he often explored the mountainsides above town. His efforts were rewarded, for his finest works are of the almost translucent Carrara marble. The **Duomo** ❖❖ shows off the stone's architectural uses, with a delicate rose window whose tracery and frame seems like stone lace. At the **Museo del Marmo** ❖❖, near the TIC between the city and the port, exhibits explore the quarries' history from Roman origins and show slabs of every imaginable variety of the stone. Above, the mountainsides look snow-covered, so white are they with marble quarries. To visit these, ask at the TIC for a quarry map.

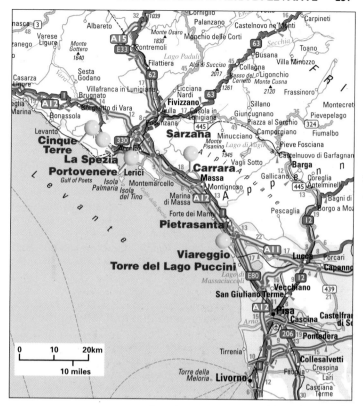

Museo del Marmo
€ Vle XX Sept; tel:
0585 845 746. Open
Jul–Aug daily 1000-2000,
May, Jun, Sept Mon–Sat
1000–1800, Oct–Apr
Mon–Sat 0830–1330.

CINQUE TERRE✦✦✦

The region's only
true TIC is at the rail
station in Monterosso; tel:
0187 817 059. Open
Easter–Oct.

**Cinque Terre
National Park** V.
Telemaco Signorini 118,
Riomaggiore; tel: 0187 760
000.

Cinque Terre Card
€€–€€€ Allows free
train and discounted boat
travel, access to paths and
use of shuttle busses in the
park for 1, 3 or 7 days.

The Cinque Terre (Five Lands) includes five villages that cling to vertiginous slopes and cliffs that centuries of hard work have made arable and habitable. Many of the old vineyards are overgrown now, and the whole area is a national park and UNESCO World Heritage Site. Although the towns are packed with tourists and hikers, their charm endures, especially when you leave **Riomaggiore**✦✦ and **Manarola**✦✦, the two connected by the shortest and easiest path, the **Via dell'Amore**✦✦ €. This largely-paved portion is relatively level and usually very crowded. The entire trail, the **Sentiero Azzurro**✦✦✦ € is more demanding – and interesting, but the views are stupendous from any part.

Most visit the towns by train, since the hair-raising road through the area runs along a corniche high above the towns, and it's a long, steep walk to the villages (and back up). Best to leave your car in La Spezia (*see page 260*) or Sestri Levante (*see page 269*) and ride the almost-hourly trains.

Riomaggiore✦✦ is small – almost too small for the number of people that throng it. At the train station are murals by Silvio Benodetto,

Ⓟ **Parking €** The only
town you can reach
by car is Corniglia, where
a hefty fee **€€€**
discourages entering.

Hiking times:
Riomaggiore–Manarola
20 min
Manarola–Corniglia
1 hr
Corniglia–Vernazza
1 hr 30 min
Vernazza–Monterosso
2 hrs

depicting early life in the Cinque Terre. **Manarola**** rises in steep terraces above a rocky pool where kids swim. **Corniglia*** sits high above the water, with few overlooks to admire the view. The climb from the train station below is scenic, but brutal; a bus is an alternative way to the top.

Beyond **Corniglia** the trail becomes its wildest, least crowded and loveliest. It is steep and very rough in places and several of the cornices are toe-curlingly narrow and without rails to separate hikers from the cliffs and ocean below. But it is bordered with wildflowers and passes through olive groves and vineyards.

Steep steps drop into **Vernazza*****, the prettiest of the five towns, to a harbour lined with brightly painted boats and equally bright café umbrellas, under pink, yellow, red and ochre walls. Above is a castle tower, and a natural arch under the cliff has houses built across its top. The northernmost town, **Monterosso***, is the largest, flattest and least scenic.

Accommodation and food in the Cinque Terre

While formal hotels are few in the Cinque Terre, rooms are abundant in private homes and small informal B&Bs. They are not inexpensive, but staying in one brings you close to the life of the locals. Look for 'Affittacamere' or 'Zimmer' signs or ask at the TIC for a list.

Mike & France €€ *Vernazza; tel: 0187 812 374.* Rooms with a garden terrace atop a cliff.

La Posada € *V. Feischi 212, Corniglia; tel/fax: 0187 812 384; www.cinqueterre-laposada.com.* Airy rooms on a wooded ridge above the town and adjacent to the trail. The terrace restaurant **€** offers views and excellent mussels, fried anchovies and grilled swordfish. The bus from the station stops at the door.

Villa l'Eremo sul Mare €€ *V. Gerai, Vernazza; tel: 3392 685 617; www.eremosulmare.com.* A bit of a hike up hill (about 0.5km), but right on the path, so you have a head start in the morning. The 3 guest rooms share facilities, but have kitchen privileges.

Albergo Ca'd'Andrean €€ *V. Discovolo, Manarola; tel: 0187 920 040; fax: 0187 920 452; www.cadandrean.it.* Family-run hotel with a lovely garden of lemon trees.

Cafe Ananasso €–€€ *Pza Marconi 17, Vernazza.* A good stop for cool refreshment between hiking segments or for sandwiches; perfect for people-watching.

La Lanterna € *V. San Giacomo 46, Riomaggiore; tel: 0187 920 589. Open daily to 2300.* Creative Ligurian dishes using local seafood.

Above
Vernazza, Cinque Terre

Locanda Cà dei Duxi €€ *V. Pecunia 19, Riomaggiore; tel: 0187 920 036; fax: 0187 920 036; www.duxi.it.* In the centre of the old town, the building dates from the 1600s and includes a restaurant.

Miki €€€ *V. Fegina 104, Monterosso al Mare; tel: 0187 817 608. Open Mar–Nov; closed Tue.* Well prepared seafood and pizza with sea views.

Porto Roca €€€ *V. Corone 1, Monterosso al Mare; tel: 0187 817 502; fax: 0187 817 692.* Large villa furnished with antiques; 42 rooms and a suite, serenely with a restaurant.

GULF OF POETS**

ⓘ TIC Lerice, *Loc Venere Azuria, open Mon–Sat 0900–1300, 1530–1830, Sun, hols 0930–1230.* Located in the northern settlement around the bay from Lerici's marina.

Portovenere *Pza Bastreri 7; tel: 018 779 091; fax: 0187 790 215.*

The Gulf of Spezia earned its more common name, the Gulf of Poets, nearly two centuries ago, when Shelley, Byron and their literary kin took villas here. La Spezia occupies the northern end of the bay and the attractive holiday towns of **Lerici**** and **Portovenere**** face each other across its entrance.

The buildings around Lerici's marina could fool you into thinking the architecture of their ornate facades was real. But it's all skilful *trompe l'oeil* – the stonework quoins, window surrounds, corbels and cornices are all painted fakes. The 12th-century **castle**** above is real, however, and contains a small museum of archaeology.

The road from **La Spezia** to **Portovenere** is so twisting and precipitous that most drivers prefer to arrive by boat, an easy trip from

Museo Geopaleontologico
€ *Castello, Lerici; tel: 0187 969 042. Open Tue–Sun, summer 1000–1300, 1700–2400, rest of the year 0900–1300, 1500–1800.*

Lerici (€€, *tel: 0187 967 676, five return trips daily*). The town clings to a steep cliff, at the end of a peninsula, with islands set just off its shore. Tall, narrow houses in candy colours line the waterfront and cafés sprawl along the quay below them. Two churches, **San Pietro+++**, with fourth-century origins, and **San Lorenzo++** (*both open daily 0700–1800*) are worth visiting, as is the **castle+**. The rocky point at the end of town is one of the best places in Italy to watch the sun set.

Boats from Portovenere connect to all the villages of the Cinque Terre, as well, a good alternative for visiting these and viewing them from the sea (€€, *tel: 0187 967 676, six return trips daily*).

Accommodation and food in the Gulf of Poets

Albergo Byron €€–€€€ *V. Biaggini 13, Lerici; tel: 0187 967 104; fax: 0187 967 409.* On the water, an easy walk to the marina and town centre.

Ristorante Albergo il Nido €€ *V. Fiascherino 75, Lerici; tel: 0187 967 286.* Well-kept rooms and a reliable dining room.

Barcollo Pub € *Pza Caesar Battisti 14, Lerici; tel: 0187 967 539.* Serves good sandwiches.

Il Brigantino €€ *Pza Caesar Battisti 12, Lerici; tel/fax: 0187 969 012; closed Wed.* Good *frito misto del mare*.

Punto Pizza € *Largo Marconi 6, Lerici; tel: 0187 967 269.* Good selection of bruscetta, seafood salads and wood oven pizzas.

LA SPEZIA

i *Vle Mazzini 45; tel: 0187 770 900; fax: 0187 770 908; www.aptcinqueterre.sp.it*

Museo Amedeo Lia €€ *V. Prione 234, www.castagna.it/mal. Open mid-Jun–Aug Tue–Sun 1000–1300, 1700–2000, rest of year 1000–1800.*

Museo Tecnico Navale € *Open Mon, Fri 1400–1800, Tue–Thur, Sat 0900–1200, 1400–1800, Sun 0830–1315.*

When it seems as though everyone on the Ligurian coast is either on holiday or catering to those that are, stop in work-a-day La Spezia for a reality check. It's also a good place to shop for practical items that beach-side boutiques don't have, or to provision for a day's walking in the nearby Cinque Terre. The daily market is large and colourful, with cheeses, cured meats, breads and fruit for picnics. This is the jumping-off point for the Cinque Terre, with almost-hourly trains and lodgings when the five towns are overflowing in the summer.

La Spezia's importance and prosperity is based on the vast naval complex there, and maritime enthusiasts should visit the **Museo Tecnico Navale++** to see ship models and exhibits on World War I.

Museo Amedeo Lia++, in a converted convent, is a remarkable private collection recently donated to the city. Among its treasures are portraits by Titian and Bellini, bronzes by Giambologna and Ammannati and the star of the show, Benedetto da Maiano's 15th-century polychrome terracotta, *Addolorata*.

Accommodation and food in La Spezia

Firenze e Continentale €€ *V. Paleocapa 7; tel: 0187 713 210; fax: 0187 714 930; www.hotelfirenzcontinental.it.* Spacious air-conditioned rooms with Carrara marble floors; parking available.

Parodi €€€ *Vle Amendola 212; tel: 0187 715 777.* Booking is essential at this cutting-edge restaurant, where food is artfully presented. Look for star-shaped ravioli, for example.

PORTOVENERE❖❖❖

Paradiso €€ *V. Garibaldi, Portovenere 34/40; tel: 0187 790 612; fax: 0187 766 056.* Family-owned *pensione* with restaurant.

Taverna del Corsaro €€–€€€ *Calata Doria 102, Portovenere; tel: 0187 790 622; fax: 0187 766 056. Closed Nov–Jan, all Mon & mid-June–early-Aug.* Housed in a converted 12th-century fort, the restaurant specialises in seafood.

VIAREGGIO AND THE BEACH TOWNS❖

ℹ *Pza Mazzini 22; tel: 0584 962 233.*

TIC Forti dei Marmi
Tel: 0584 786 322. Open Mon–Sat 0900–1230.

Warning: Red flags on the beach mean stay out of the water – even to wade – because of dangerous surf or undertow, which erodes sand from under your feet as you stand.

For admirers of Art Nouveau architecture and décor, **Viareggio**❖❖ is a must-see. When fire destroyed the entire town in 1917, it was rebuilt in the latest mode, its buildings designed by none other than the father of Liberty Style (as Italians call Art Nouveau), Galileo Chini, one of the founders of the style. Today these buildings still line the promenade: **Gran Caffe Margherita** and **Bagna Balina** are the icons, but in all 48 villas, hotels and public buildings are listed in that style, including the **Hotel Plaza & de la Russe** (*see Accommodation*) the best in this part of Italy, but book early for a room.

As you continue north along the coast to **Forti dei Marmi**❖, through the string of beach towns, you will see other examples. Each of these towns has a somewhat different character, but each revolves around the wide golden beaches that stretch for many miles. Umbrellas and canopies are so thick on these that passersby cannot see the ocean. A spot of sand is expensive and the hotels have reserved the spots near the water for their guests. In July and Aug, it is difficult to get a space at all, and almost impossible to get one within sight of the sea. North of Forti dei Marmi, however, is one of the few good stretches of free beach. Forti dei Marmi is best known for shopping; designer shops and boutiques line the streets.

Pza Mazzini 22; tel: 05 844 881; fax: 058 447 406.

Villa Puccini € *Tel: 584 341 445. Open for tours Tues–Sun 1000–1100, 1500–1730 every half hour, limit 15 per tour. Expect long waits and much standing around to spend about 10 minutes inside.*

Lake tour boats € *leave the landing in front of Villa Puccini in Torre de Lago; tel: 0584 350 252.*

Accommodation and food in Viareggio and the Beach Towns

In Forti dei Marmi, restaurant prices reflect the designer-shopping clientele. Few have posted menus, so ask to see one before taking a table. Check your bill carefully for 'mistakes'.

Hotel Il Negresco €€€ *Lungomare Italico 82, Forte dei Marmi; tel: 058 478 820; www.hotelilnegresco.com.* A beautifully-maintained beachfront hotel with a garden-enclosed swimming pool and excellent restaurant. Well-appointed rooms have balconies overlooking the promenade and sea.

Plaza e de Russie €€€ *Pza d'Azeglio 1, Viareggio; tel: 058 444 449; fax: 058 444 031; www.plazaederussie.com.* Elegant and historic hotel on the promenade, with fine dining at its La Terrazza **€€€** restaurant.

Ristorante Freddy €€ *Pza Garibaldi 2, Forti dei Marmi; tel: 058 480 862.* One of the few restaurants in town that posts a menu; excellent seafood.

Suggested tour

Below
Boat on a street at the waterfront, Portovenere

Total distance: 90km with or without detours to La Spezia.

Time: 2 hours' driving. Allow 2 days in order to spend a day exploring the Cinque Terre. Those with limited time could use the A12 *autostrada* from Pisa to Carrara to save time.

Links: Pisa, the starting point for this route, is the western terminus of the Florence (Firenze) to Pisa route (*see page 254*). La Spezia, the end of this route and a convenient spot in which to drop your car, is the beginning of the northern Riviera di Levante route (*see page 270*).

Route: Leave Pisa ❶, heading north on the coastal S1 highway (also known as the Via Aurelia), perhaps stopping at **Torre del Lago Puccini** and then continuing north via **VIAREGGIO** ❷ to **Pietrasanta** (*see Detour 1 on page 263*), CARRARA ❸, **Sarzana** and **LA SPEZIA** ❹ (*see Detour 2 on page 263*). It's best to leave your car at La Spezia and catch a boat for the Gulf of Poets towns or a train for the five **CINQUE TERRE** towns ❺; once in Portovenere, you can also take a boat for any of the five towns. There's a winding road to Portovenere; and a worse one into Cinque Terre, rough, frequently closed and inconvenient to the towns below.

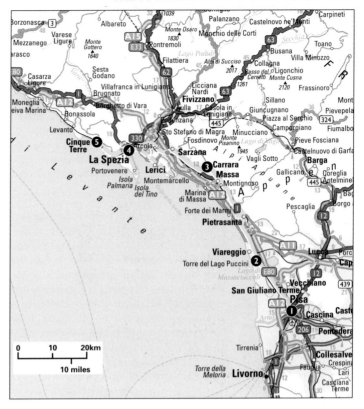

Detour 1: Instead of leaving **Viareggio** on S1, follow the coastal promenade to see the elegant villas and hotels that line the beach front as far as **Forti dei Marmi**, where a right turn signposted 'Serravezza' will take you back to S1.

Detour 2: From **Carrara**, follow Viale XX Sept to **Marina di Carrara**. Turn right at the junction, in front of the statue of a man carrying a slab of marble. Follow the coastal road to **Ameglia**, turning left at the signpost for **Montemarcello**. Follow the scenic wooded road through pretty **Montemarcello** and other cliff-top towns to **Lerici**, continuing on along the Gulf of Poets to **La Spezia**.

Also worth exploring

The mountains east of **Pietrasanta** and **Massa**, known as the **Alpi Apuane**, are part of a high natural region. A very scenic, although winding and often precipitous, route winds through these, heading west from S1 at **Querceta**. The unnumbered road passes through **Seravezza**, to **Ami**, where it intersects with another unnumbered road heading west again into **Massa**. Here it rejoins the main route at S1.

The northern Riviera di Levante

Ratings

Villages	●●●●●
Architecture	●●●●○
Beaches	●●●●○
Scenery	●●●●○
Castles	●●●○○
Geology	●●●○○
Historical sights	●●●○○
Walking	●●●○○

After the rugged perpendicular landscapes of the Cinque Terre, the Gulf of Tigullio and Gulf of Paradise seem almost benign. Candy-coloured villages circle coves of bright blue water, small boats bob in tiny harbours, and the whole area has an air of prosperous seaside retreat. Behind these towns and villages rise green-clad hills, making them especially attractive viewed from the sea. Regular boat service connects the entire coast, from Genoa to the Gulf of Poets, but to explore the winding roads that connect them is part of the attraction, as are the views from the headlands that rise between and behind them.

At the Northern end of the route is the sprawling port city of Genoa, historic, filled with art and culture and largely ignored in the modern version of the Grand Tour. The city deserves far more attention than it gets from most travellers.

CAMOGLI♦♦

❶ *V. XX Settembre 33; tel: 0185 771 066; fax: 0185 771 066.*

❶ Museo Marinaro *V. Gio Bono Ferrari 41; tel: 0185 729 049. Open Apr–Sept Mon, Thur, Fri 0900–1200, Wed, Sat, Sun 0900–1200, 1500–1800; rest of the year, shorter hours.*

M/V Laura €€ *Tel: 085 773 417; www.minicrociere.it.* Cruises to San Fruttuoso.

Unlike some of its dandified neighbours, Camoglie remains what it always was, a fishing town. Its beach and fishing port are backed with unusually tall buildings, some only one window wide and all in a full palette of colours. An archway leads to the small working fishing port. Boats leave from here to tour S Frutuoso. The town's fishing and marine heritage is explored in the good maritime museum, **Museo Marinaro♦♦**, that also has a reconstruction of an Iron Age settlement excavated nearby. Be sure to see the giant skillets used at the spring sardine festival, when huge pans of sardines are cooked and served free. The **basilica♦♦** is awash with gold inside, in votive offering from safely-returned local seafarers.

Accommodation and food in Camogli

Cenobio dei Dogi €€€ *V. Cuneo 34; tel: 01 857 241; fax: 0185 772 796;*

e-mail: reception@cenobio.it A *palazzo* originally built for Genoa's doges, this large hotel has rooms with balconies for outstanding water views.

Albergo La Camogliese €€€ *V. Garibaldi 55; tel: 0185 771 086.* Attractive rooms overlook the beach in the town centre; seafood is happily paired with pasta in the restaurant.

Bar Porticciolo € *V. al Porto 11; tel: 0185 771 629.* Under the arch, its terrace tables overlook the colourful little fishing harbour. Good sandwiches and seafood salads.

GENOA❖❖

ⓘ On the waterfront beside the *Aquarium* at *V. al Porto Antico; tel: 010 248 711; www.genoatouristboard.net; www.apt.genoa.it*

Also at Stazione Principe, the city's main train station, west of the port area; *tel: 0102 462 633.*

Once a great naval power equal to Venice, Genoa remains a major port. And alongside a proud history that includes native son Christopher Columbus comes the somewhat unsavoury reputation of 'sailor towns'. Don't be put off by that; Genoa is a smart city of striking architecture and great culture. The San Felice Opera House is among Italy's finest, a new state-of-the art venue with flawless acoustics and approachable prices.

Stroll down Via XX Settembre and adjacent streets to see the outstanding Art Nouveau façades or along Via Balbi or Via Garibaldi to

P Parking is tight in this city of narrow lanes. Try Piazza Matteotti or Piazza Piccapietra (both just off the Piazza Ferrarri), or Via Turati just south of the Aquarium.

Q Frequent boat excursions tel: 010 265 712 leave from Genoa's docks to Portofino, Portovenere, the Cinque Terre and other towns described in this and the previous chapter. Especially in high tourist seasons, it's worth considering this over driving.

🏨 **Acquariuo €€€** Ponte Spinola; tel: 0102 481 205. Open Mon–Fri 0930–1930, Thur until 2200, Sun, hols until 2030.

Cathedrale di San Lorenzo € V. san Lorenzo; tel: 010 311 269. Open daily 0900–1200, 1500–1800, Sun afternoon only.

Galleria Nazionale di Palazzo Spinola € Pza Pelliceria 1; tel: 0102 705 300. Open Tue–Sat 0830–1930, Sun 1300–2000.

Museo di Palazzo Reale € Open Tue–Wed 0900–1330, Thur–Sun 0900–1900.

admire some of the palazzi of noble families. Two of these, **Galleria Nazionale di Palazzo Spinola**∗∗ and **Palazzo Reale**∗∗ are open to tour the eye-boggling interiors of marble work, *trompe l'oeil* decoration, crystal, mosaic floors and paintings. The Spinola Palace is in a maze of narrow streets known as the Sailors' Quarter, interesting to wander (but by daylight only, please – not all the city's reputation is unwarranted).

The top attraction in the port area must be the city's **Aquarium**∗∗, with widely admired collections of both native and unusual sea mammals and fish.

Of the city's many richly-endowed churches, the most important is the Duomo di S Lorenzo, not far from the port. The striped marble of the arches in the nave reflect the striped façade; from the centre of the nave you can see the rose window and the excellent stone carvings over the largest of the side chapels. Dedicated to S John the Baptist, it was built to hold his remains, in the 13th-century carved arc at its centre. The saint's ashes, along with a bowl reputed to be the Holy Grail and the platter on which the saint's head was served up to Salome are now in the **Museo del Tesoro della Cattedrale** (€€, *guided tours only, Mon–Sat 0900–1130, 1500–1730*), and more works of art from the church are in the **Museo Diocesano** (€€, *open Tue–Fri, Sun 1500–1830, Sat 1000–1300, 1500–1830*). Just up the hill, in the Jesuit church of S Ambrose, is a theatrical painting by Rubins, just right for the exuberant high-baroque interior of the church.

Accommodation and food in Genoa

Agnello d'Oro € *Vico delle Monchette 6; tel: 0102 462 084; fax: 0102 462 327; e-mail: hotelagnellodoro@libero.it.* Simple, friendly *pensione*, some rooms retaining touches of the building's 16th century origins. Covered parking garage.

City €€€ *V. San Sebastiano 6; tel: 010 5545; fax: 010 586 301; e-mail: city.ge@bestwestern.it.* Perfectly located only a few steps from the Duomo, opera house and shopping streets, but quiet and with parking.

Da Genio € *Salita San Leonardo 61r in the Carruggi area; tel: 010 588 463. Closed Aug and Sun.* Try *trenette al pesto* for a taste of the city's famous basil and pine nut sauce.

For late night food, head for Pza della Erbe, near the Duomo, where students gather at open-air bars and eateries until all hours.

THE NORTHERN RIVIERA DI LEVANTE 267

PORTOFINO✦✦✦

ℹ *V. Roma 35; tel: 0185 269 024.*

You can also use Santa Margherita's larger tourist office (see page 268) for Portofino when its own office is closed.

Castello € *Open Apr–Sept, Wed–Mon, 1000–1800, rest of the year to 1700.*

Entered via a highly scenic road from nearby Santa Margherita, Portofino lies below in such a studiedly perfect arrangement that it seems almost like a stage set. It fairly screams 'money' with its little round harbour full of classy pleasure yachts, pricey boutiques and well-tanned starlets. You'll have to park your four-wheeled yacht out of town (no room, and besides, it would spoil the view) and walk in. An alternative to this – and to the hourly parking fee – is to arrive by one of the boats that ply the area regularly.

While such a smashing setting doesn't really need attractions, Portofino provides them. First, head up to the patterned-stone terrace above for the best **view**✦✦✦ of the harbour and surrounding painted houses – just like the postcards. Beyond the little church of S Giorgio is **Castello di San Giorgio**✦, originating from the 1500s. Parco di Portofino protects the wooded hillsides, the well-marked walking trails and the marine life of the peninsula. It's about a two-hour walk through the park to San Fruttuoso (*see page 270*).

Accommodation and food in Portofino

There are far better places in the area to stay and to dine than crowded, pricey Portofino. But if you're hoping to spot a celeb or two when the sailing day is over, the cafés and restaurants here are the place.

Eden Hotel €€–€€€ *V. Vico Dritto 18; tel: 0185 269 091; fax: 0185 269 047; www. hoteledenportofino.it.* Bland, functional small hotel that's the least exorbitant option in town, and very central to the town's chic central square. There is a restaurant, too.

Ristorante Puny €€€ *Pza Martiri dell'Olivetta; tel: 0185 269 037. Closed Thur.* Expect to wait awhile for a table at this eatery, which serves the usual *pesto* and seafood dishes.

Right
Villas near Portofino

Rapallo**

🛈 Lungomare, V. Veneto 7; tel: 0185 230 346; fax: 018 563 051. Open Mon–Sat 0930–1230, 1500–1930, Sun, hols 0930–1230, 1630–1930.

Museum of Lace Villa Tigullio; tel: 018 563 305. Open Oct–Aug, Tue–Wed & Fri–Sat 1500–1800, Thur 1000–1130.

Museo Gaffoglio € Convento delle Clarisse, Pza Libia; tel: 0185 234 497. Open Tue–Wed, Fri–Sat 1500–1830, Thur 1000–1200.

Funivia € Pza Solari; tel: 0815 239 008, free parking.

At first glance, you could mistake Rapallo's long, curving seafront **promenade**, backed by the gleaming white façades of balconied Belle Epoch hotels, for one of its compatriots on the French Riviera. The little **castle** sitting on its rock, waves lapping at three sides, completes a very pretty picture, and there are plenty of terrace cafés near the castle to admire it from.

The excellent **Museo Gaffoglio** exhibits a collection of rare jewellery, porcelain, enamels (including Faberge eggs) and ivory carvings that range from a 15th-century Venetian box to sailors' scrimshaw. Rapallo was a major lace-making town, and the **Museo del Merletto** shows both local and foreign examples of this art. More than 1400 examples of handmade lace dating back to the 1500s are shown, along with lace patterns and drawings. Fine laces of silver and gold, christening dresses and a collection of high fashion clothing are displayed in the historic Villa Tigullio, set in **Parco Casale**, which is itself filled with rare plants and trees.

Views out over the Gulf of Paradise are the reward for an 8-minute ride on the **funivia**. At the top is the **Santuario Basilica di Montallegro**. From there walkers have access to a good network of scenic trails, including one back down to the town centre.

Accommodation and food in Rapallo

Albergo Italia E Lido €€ Lungomare Castello 1; tel: 018 550 494; www.italiaelido.com. Unbeatable location facing the castle and the sea. Its restaurant **Grand Italia** € serves crispy frito misto and veal with asparagus.

Riviera €€–€€€ Pza IV Novembre 2; tel: 018 550 248; fax: 018 565 668; www.hotel-riviera.biz. Many rooms have balconies, and there is parking and a restaurant.

Ristorante Monique €€ Lungomare Via Veneto 5; tel: 081 550 541. Offers a view of the castle and specialises in local seafood.

Santa Margherita Ligure*

🛈 V. XXV Apre 2b; tel: 0185 287 485; www.portofinobayarea.com

Santa Margherita is an absolute gem of a town, more down-to-earth than chic next-door neighbour Portofino and yet possessing a rather beautiful beach and a rather genuine Italian character. This isn't the most historic village in Italy, but the beach is fine, a stroll uphill into the historic district is rewarding and the village square is – as usual – the place for a coffee. **Parco di Villa Durazzo** (open 0900–1900 Apr–Sept, 0900–1700 Oct–Mar) is a typically fine Ligurian green space with English-style gardens and views of the sea; the villa itself (*open Tue–Sun, 0900–1800 in summer, shorter hours in winter*) is worth a look inside for its stucco work, murano glass and tapestries.

Accommodation and food in Santa Margherita Ligure

Fasce €–€€ *V. Luigi Bozzo 3; tel: 0185 286 435; fax: 0185 283 580; e-mail: hotelfasce@hotelfasce.it.* Friendly, family-run hotel with lush courtyard. Spacious rooms, a car park and free bikes. Its restaurant € is good, too.

Il Faro €€ *V. Maragliano; tel: 0185 286 867.* Family-run restaurant with excellent seafood (try grilled fish with pesto).

SESTRI LEVANTE❖❖

Pza Sant'Antonio 10; tel: 0185 457 011; fax: 0185 459 575. Open 0930–1230, 1500–1930 (1630 Sun).

Galleria Rizzi € *V. Cappuccini 8; tel: 018 541 300. Open Apr–Oct Sun 1000–1300, May–Sept also Wed 1600–1900.*

Coming from La Spezia, the S1 coastal highway plunges inland through rugged mountains bypassing the Cinque Terre, before rejoining the coast at Sestri Levante. Sestri is a decent-sized resort town, occupying a lovely position with a jutting point of land to one side and a long, sweeping bay to the other. Once upon a time it was, as so many other villages on this stretch of coast were, a strategic post. Later it became a fishing town.

Today it's a garden-filled resort town, but large enough to have a life of its own. It's a place to savour some of the finest hotels and restaurants on the entire coast, and an excellent option for lodging while visiting the Cinque Terre (*see page 257*). Access to the towns by train is as good as from La Spezia.

Sestri Levante's waterfront Piazza Matteotti and promenade are lined with colourful buildings whose elegant architectural detail is painted in *trompe l'oeil*, and two of its outstanding buildings, now the hotels Nettuno and Villa Balbi, are recently restored and face each other across Viale Rimembranza. At the piazza is the baroque S Maria di Nazareth, whose primary treasure is a 12th-century crucifix. Those interested in art should visit the waterfront **Rizzi Gallery**❖❖ containing works by Tiepolo, Rubens and Raphael.

The town ends in a steep wooded, rock-bound promontory crowned by a castle-palazzo that is another hotel. Below is the little **Baiai del Silenzio**❖❖ almost completely encircled by a free beach backed by pink and yellow houses, a former convent and church punctuating its point.

Right
Il Malo, Portofino

Accommodation and food in Sestri Levante

Vis à Vis €€€ *V. della Chiusa; tel: 018 542 661; fax: 0185 480 853; www.hotelvisavis.com.* One of Italy's finest hotels, crowning the hilltop with views into the postcard-perfect Bay of Silence, the Vis à Vis descends in stunning layers from its swimming pool set in an olive orchard, past terraced cafés to balconied guestrooms. Its **Restaurant Olympia €€€** is superb, with service to match the creative menu. If you can afford only one magnificent meal on your trip, savour it here.

Il Brigantino €–€€ *V. Rimembranza 38; tel: 0185 458 265.* Local fish *en brochette*, succulent grilled lamb steaks or creamy salmon with *trofie*, the local pasta speciality, are served by a particularly genial staff.

Marina € *V. Fascie 100; tel: 0185 487 332; fax: 018 541 527; e-mail: marinahotel@marinahotel.it. Closed Jan and Feb.* Medium-sized *pensione* of 17 rooms; the least expensive choice in town. Serves meals for guests only.

Suggested tour

Total distance: 125km.

Time: 2–3 hours' driving. Allow 1–2 days with or without detours. Those with limited time can save a little by using the A12 toll road for the first 45km of this route, from just outside La Spezia to Sestri Levante. Few towns of note are skirted by this short cut, though the slower S1 road cuts through coastal foothills and is more scenic if you've the time.

Links: La Spezia, the starting point for this route, is part of the southern Riviera di Levante route (*see page 262*). Genoa, the end point, is the beginning of the Genoa to the French border route (*see page 280*). Both are easily reached by toll roads and trains.

Route: Leave La Spezia ❶, heading north on the S1 (signs and maps will also indicate it as the Via Aurelia), which slices through coastal mountains before rejoining and then hugging the coast through **SESTRI LEVANTE ❷** on its eventual way to **RAPALLO ❸**, 75km away. Swing south 9km on the S227 (also known as the Strada Panoramica) to visit **SANTA MARGHERITA LIGURE ❹** and **PORTOFINO ❺** before backtracking to the coastal S1 via the winding road to San Lorenzo della Costa and then continuing the remaining slow 30km to **GENOA** (Genova) ❻.

Detour: At Portofino, either catch a summertime ferry boat (*tel: 0185 284 670*) or don your walking shoes and hike the 5km through beautiful groves of protected forest to **San Fruttuoso Abbey**, a splendid grey stone structure on the sea with a pleasant beach at its

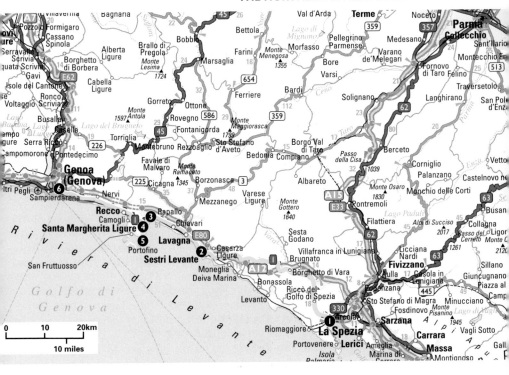

foot. The abbey, founded by Benedictine monks, knew hard times but has been restored by locals and opens to the public daily (except Mon) year-round, closing only in Nov. You can also catch a ferry (*tel: 0185 772 091*) to the abbey's tiny village of San Fruttuoso from **CAMOGLI** as well.

Also worth exploring

The inland drive or train ride from La Spezia to Parma is hardly ever done by anyone but locals, which makes it all the more appealing to the back-road adventurer – be aware that there are few architectural or historical sights along this way, only remote towns perched at angles on the hills and streams. Both the A15 toll road and the slower S62 make this 100km trip a snap; regular trains take a slightly different, mostly parallel route as well. The beginning miles are steep as one climbs from sea level into mountains; almost halfway to Parma is **Pontremoli**, useful as a coffee break. More towns follow and then one winds back downhill, emerging at little **Fornova di Taro** and its attractive **church**++. From here, the land is starkly flat and dull past industrial concerns and gigantic fields before reaching the old Etruscan city of **Parma**++, one of Italy's greatest eating cities but also an amazing **baptistery**+++, **duomo**++ and plenty of Correggio artwork.

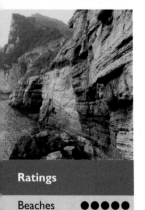

Genoa to the French border: the Riviera di Ponente

Ratings

Beaches	●●●●●
Castles	●●●●●
Geology	●●●●○
Scenery	●●●●○
Architecture	●●●○○
Outdoor activities	●●●○○
Walking	●●●○○
Historical sights	●●○○○

The final long stretch of coast in extreme western Italy, bending from Genoa to the French border, offers very fine scenery, hilltop castles and numerous small fishing towns – mixed in with occasional ugly industrial zones and modern, overbuilt resort areas. As a result, there's really only one choice of route, snug along the coast: worth driving mostly for villages like Noli and Finale Ligure. Once you've pivoted round the shipbuilding business in Savona, you'll be rewarded with yet another long sequence of undiscovered villages. San Remo's a name you might recognise, but continue west and you'll find Italy stubbornly clinging to its character right up to the French border. Ventimiglia finishes off this tour with an unexpected collection of terraced vegetable and flower gardens, Italy's last wave goodbye to travellers headed for Nice and beyond.

ALBENGA✧✧

ⓘ Vle Martiri della Libertà 1; tel: 0182 558 444.

ⓑ Baptistery €
V. Episcopio. Open Tue–Sun, 0930–1230, 1530–1930 mid-Jun–mid Sept, shorter hours in winter.

Museo Navale Romeo
Pza San Michele 12; tel: 018 251 215. Open Tue–Sun, 1000–1200, 1600–1900 summer, shorter hours in winter.

Grotte di Toirano €
Open daily 0930–1230, 1400–1500.

⬤ Market day: Wed.

Quite an old Roman town and no longer on the ocean at all, its harbour silted up long ago, board-flat Albenga offers a surprising medieval complex for such a small, nearly forgotten place. From the sea, turn right along the eastern bank of the Centa River to park and find a mini-Pisa of off-kilter towers in the town's central square, Piazza San Michele; an unusual, ten-sided **baptistery✧✧✧** with an octagonal interior; a **cathedral✧**, bell tower; and an amazing number of tall, tilting towers, seven of which are completely intact. Particularly good for history buffs is the **marine museum✧✧**, exploring the town's shipbuilding back to Roman times. Alassio, its twin just a few kilometres beyond on the S1, has a better beach and hops with nightlife, well worth the nocturnal jaunt to dance or drink.

Near Albenga, at Toirano, are **caves✧✧** which are not only beautiful, but filled with evidence of prehistoric man –′ and animals. Huge numbers of bear bones, along with mixed human and bear footprints have been found here.

ALBISSOLA MARINA***

ℹ Pza Sisto IV; tel: 0194 002 008, fax: 0194 003 084.

🏛 **Casa Museo Giuseppe Mazzotti**
€ Vle. Matteotti 29; tel: 019 489 872. Open daily 1000–1200, 1600–1800.

Villa Farragianna € V. Salomoni 177; tel: 019 480 622. Open May–Sept Wed–Sun 1500–1900, last entry 1815.

Half of one of those 'two-part towns' so common here, Albissola Marina forms the seaside half of its equation. There's the usual collection of boats, beaches and waterside cafés, but also an artistic twist: this town is one of *the* places in northern Italy to buy pottery, owing to a long-established tradition of working the ruddy local clays into pieces of higher-than-functional art. Along with galleries and workshops to visit is the **Casa Museo Giuseppe Mazzotti***. The house is by futurist architect Nicolai Diulgheroff, and it contains a collection of 20th-century ceramic works, from Liberty-style to contemporary. Pretty **Villa Farragianna***, just northeast of the centre in a park, is also worth a look, as are the decorated walkways along the shore.

Accommodation and food in Albissola Marina

Hotel Garden €€ Vle Faraggiana 6; tel: 019 485 253; fax: 019 485 255; www.hotelgardenalbissola.com. Permanent contemporary art exhibits decorate this hotel, which offers exercise facilities, sauna, outdoor pool, Internet access and car park.

Da Mario €€ *Corso Bigliati 70; tel: 019 481 640. Closed all Sept and Wed the rest of the year.* Try dishes featuring local fish at this sunny eatery with outdoor seating.

BORDIGHERA❖❖

ℹ *V. Roberto 1; tel: 0184 262 322; fax: 0184 264 455.*

🏛 **Museo Bicknell** €
*Tel: 0184 263 601.
Open Mon–Fri 0930–1700.*

🛒 Market day: Thur.

Hemmed in by cliffs and bedecked with flowers and palm trees, Bordighera makes a fine, unhurried stopping point. The place was nothing more than a sailors' town for centuries and centuries, until the English discovered its quiet charms and began building a winter resort by word of mouth. The upper town of fortifications and warrens drops to a flat beachside portion with an entirely different character. The **Museo Bicknell**❖, a museum of natural history and archaeological exhibits, is the chief sight of interest. It's worth noting that Bordighera supplies the Vatican with its palm fronds each Palm Sunday, a plum commission it won more than four centuries ago, when a quick-thinking local sailor averted a disaster in St Peters square.

Accommodation and food in Bordighera

Grand Hotel Capo Ampelio €€ *V. Virgilio; tel: 0184 264 333; fax: 0184 264 244.* Rooms with balconies overlook seascapes from a renovated hilltop villa. Extras include exercise facilities and a swimming pool.

Villa Elisa €€ *V. Romana 70; tel: 0184 261 313; fax: 0184 261 313; e-mail: villaelisa@masterweb.it.* Another well-appointed villa hotel, this one with a lush garden, pool and sauna.

Piemontese €€ *V. Roseto 8; tel: 0184 261 651.* An unexpected surprise in a seaside town: dishes typical of Italy's Piedmont region such as *risotto* with Barolo wine or fondue, plus local fish dishes.

CERVO❖❖

ℹ *Pza Santa Caterina 21; tel: 0183 408 197; fax: 0183 409 822.*

🛒 Market day: Thur.

🍴 **San Giorgio** €€€
V. Alessandro Volta 19; tel: 0183 400 175. Closed Jan and Nov; no dinner Mon and Tue Oct–Easter.

After rounding tough Cape Mele, the coastal S1 road calms down again, passing a number of shallow bays. The Golfo di Diano, one of them, is the beginning of yet another short section of beach resort towns, at whose easternmost end lies exceptionally pretty little Cervo, with a good annual summer classical music festival, and a relatively undisturbed atmosphere. A surprising baroque church, **San Giovanni**❖❖ (*tel: 0183 408 095*), tops the small rise which spills houses down to the water. Built by local fishermen, its decoration reflects their gratitude for safe return.

DIANO MARINA*

Pza Martiri della Libertà 1; tel: 0183 408 197; fax: 0183 494 365.

Market day: Tue.

Diano caps the other end of the gulf named for it and is a more self-consciously touristy town than Cervo at the opposite end. It also has a far better beach. Its appearance, different from other towns here, results from rebuilding after an 1887 earthquake levelled it. You can see all the art and altars rescued from the ruined churches now assembled in **Sant'Antonio Abate***. Vineyards dotting the nearby hills deserve exploration and the whites they pour are superb.

Accommodation and food in Diano Marina

Gabriella €€–€€€ *V. dei Gerani 9; tel: 0183 403 131; fax: 0183 405 055; www.hotelgabriella.com.* Swim in the heated pool, lounge on the beach, or rest in the garden at this posh *pensione* (*closed Nov–Dec*). Parking is available and there's a restaurant.

Il Caminetto €€ *V. Olanda 1; tel: 0183 494 700.* A *trattoria* serving typical local specialities.

FINALE LIGURE**

V. San Pietro 14; tel: 019 681 019; fax: 019 681 804. Open Mon–Sat 0900–1200, 1500–1830, Sun, hols 0900–1200.

Market day: Thur.

Pleasant Finale Ligure marks the beginning of yet another scenic little cape, this one known as Caprazoppa. Finale's seaside has one of the better beaches along this stretch of coast, set below rocky cliffs studded with villas and gardens and more, close to the town centre. Behind its tree-lined promenade, narrow streets are filled with cafés, restaurants and shops. The wildly pealing bells of **S Giovanni Battista*** summon the faithful through its yellow baroque exterior into an interior where only a row of plain round columns provide serenity amid the stucco swirls and frills. Accommodation is easy to find here, as is nightlife and good food. A kilometre uphill from the water is an even older, fortified settlement complete with its own crumbling **castle****. This is a good place to stay the night, sampling Ligurian charm and food with just a dash of history.

Accommodation and food in Finale Ligure

Punta Est €€€ *V. Aurelia 1; tel: 019 600 611; fax: 019 600 611.* Terraced along a garden-draped hillside that drops almost straight to the beach, this villa-turned-hotel sets standards other villas should follow. In summer, the excellent restaurant €€–€€€ moves to the pebbly terrace, under a canopy of trees.

Rosita € *V. Mànie 67; tel: 019 602 437; fax: 019 601 762*. Small, inexpensive *pensione* with meals on a terrace with splendid views of the water; parking is available.

Ai Torchi €€–€€€ *V. dell'Annunziata, Finalborgo; tel: 019 690 531. Closed Jan and Tue except in Aug*. It's advisable to reserve a spot here to sample some of Italy's best *pesto* a few kilometres outside Finale Ligure.

NOLI**

ℹ *Corso Italia 8; tel: 0197 499 003; fax: 0197 499 300. Open Mon–Sat 0900–1230, 1500–1830.*

🏛 **San Paragorio** *Open mid-Jun–mid-Oct, Tue–Sat, Sun 1000–1200, 1700–1900.*

🛒 Market Day: Thur.

Drive slowly around beautiful **Cape Noli***, as this round of land protruding into the Mediterranean is more attractive and wilder than most of Liguria – which is saying something. Noli, a little mountain-backed beauty of a town lined with tiny streets, is at its beginning. Take time for a stroll down its amazingly well-preserved main street, **Corso Italia****, imagining, if you can, a grandeur that once rivalled that of port republics like Venice and Genoa. Towers, part of the original loggia, gates and walls remain from those heady medieval days. From the steps of the cathedral, S Pietro, you can see four of these towers. **San Paragorio Church**** rivals many of its better-known cousins for Romanesque splendour and is one of Liguria's best. If you've got the time, hiking the trail to the ruined mountaintop **castle*** is an energetic way to spend a few hours. Beyond Noli, the cape road opens up tantalising views of the ocean, then ducks back behind thick trees again.

Accommodation and food in Noli

Miramare €€ *Corso Italia 2; tel: 019 708 926; fax: 019 748 927*. This 16th-century fortified *palazzo* with outdoor garden contains 28 rooms, all with sea views.

Lilliput €€€ *Regione Zuglieno; tel: 019 748 009. Closed Mon; also closed Jan–Feb and Nov*. Award-winning traditional Ligurian cuisine, which serves lunch only at weekends.

Romeo Albergo Ristorante € *V. Colombo 81; tel: 019 748 973*. Veal Milanese, fillet of sole and other unadorned typical and tasty dishes. Guest rooms, as well.

Trattoria/Locanda de Massimo € *Pza Militi Ignoto 2; tel: 0197 485 230*. Inexpensive upstairs dining room with simple guest rooms.

Bar Torino € *Corso d'Italia 17*, serves gigantic bruscetta (try prosciutta cotto and gorgonzola) at amazingly low prices.

SANTO STEFANO AL MARE*

V. Boselli Arma di Taggia; tel: 018 443 733.

After Imperia, olive groves begin to replace the vineyards and gardens, as things become less frantic and towns farther apart. Santo Stefano only jumps to life in summer, when the good local beaches attract holiday-seekers. Restaurants here are excellent, perhaps even a cut above the usual high Ligurian standard.

Accommodation and food in Santo Stefano al Mare

Lucciola €€€ *Lungomare di Alvertis 69; tel: 0184 484 2236.* Small, family-run hotel of 34 well-appointed rooms and Italian-speaking staff; breakfast is included.

La Reserva €€ *V. Roma 51; tel: 0184 484 134. Closed Mon, no dinner Sun except in Aug.* Rustic, lovely seaside restaurant.

SAN REMO**

Below
Beach at San Remo

By far the largest true resort on this section of coast, bayside San Remo is the Italian version of Monte Carlo, at a somewhat more affordable price. The chief attractions are the lush foliage, villa gardens and beach life; a quick walk down the Corso dell'Imperatrice gives a sense

ⓟ There's convenient
parking at a large
garage in the centre of
town at Via Asquasciati;
this central square is a right
turnoff the coast road as
you enter from the east.

Above
San Remo casino

of having arrived somewhere important. The famous local **casino*** (about half a mile west of the centre via Corso Matteotti), is divided into upscale and downscale areas. The downscale area, limited mostly to coin-gobbling machines, can be played for free in any dress, but the attractive upscale rooms host games of chance and skill – for well-dressed clientele, at a small admission charge. If you don't fancy a gamble, head uphill for the maze-like **La Pigna*** district, which winds in roughly concentric circles through a slightly ragged old quarter of arches and alleys. The most important church in town is **San Siro*** on Via Palazzo, with its separate baptistery and oratory, while the nearby **Museo Civico*** housed within the **Palazzo Borea**

Museo Civico €
Corso Matteotti 143;
tel: 0184 531 942. Open
Tue–Sat 0900–1200,
1500–1800.

Early each morning
during summer a huge
and fragrant flower market
dominates the town
centre.

Casino Corso Inglese; tel:
0184 5951. Open daily
1430–0300. It's free to
play the casino's slot
machines, but there's a
cover charge €€ to play
the tables.

Market days: Tue, Sat.

d'Olmo* should satisfy history buffs. Equally interesting is the handsomely domed Russian Orthodox church, **Cristo Salvatore****, just beyond the casino at the waterfront Piazza Battisti.

Accommodation and food in San Remo

Royal €€€ Corso Imperatrice 80; tel: 0184 5391; fax: 0184 661 445. Lavish hotel in the heart of the action with direct access to both the famed casino and downtown. There's a posh restaurant on the terrace, plus parking, mini-golf, saltwater pool and tennis court.

Paradiso €€ V. Roccasterone 12; tel: 0184 571 211; fax: 0184 578 176; e-mail: paradisohotel@sistel.it Refined, relaxed hotel where flowers tumble out of boxes and guests enjoy drinks in the garden. Parking in a covered garage, Internet access in rooms and half-pension in a convivial restaurant.

Antica Trattoria Piccolo Mondo € V. Piave 7; tel: 018 450 912. Closed Sun, Mon and all July. Friendly staff and outstanding local dishes such as octopus stew.

VARAZZE*

V. Nazioni Unite 1; tel:
019 935 043; fax: 019
935 916.

Celle Ligure Open
Mon–Sat 0900–1300,
1530–1800, Sun, hols
1000–1230, 1530–1730.

Market day: Sat.

The first town of real note west of Genoa, Varazze was important long ago as a shipbuilding centre in the pre-Columbian era and was the birthplace of the famously wandering monk Jacopo. Today it's a combination of working docks and beach villas, not bad for a short stop and a bite to eat in one of the good local seafood restaurants. Several interesting churches include a 10th-century ruin and the 12th-century baptistery of San Vittore and Sant'Ambrogio with a bell tower. The Villa Mirabello houses a set of **museums*** (open Tue–Sat 0930–1230, 1400–1730) containing local history items and art.

Accommodation and food in Varazze

Hotel Eden €–€€ V. Villagrande 1; tel: 019 932 888; fax: 0199 6315; e-mail: eden-hotel@interbusiness.it Although one of the priciest hotels in town, this is still a bargain, with modern conveniences such as air conditioning, TVs, Internet access points and parking.

Antico Genovese €€€ Corso Colombo 70; tel: 0199 6482, the Hotel Eden's restaurant, serves local style foods.

VENTIMIGLIA✤

🛈 *V. Cavour 61; tel: 0184 351 183; fax: 0184 351 183.*

🅿 Friday is market day for flower wholesalers in Ventimiglia, but this also mucks up traffic and parking for everyone else; plan carefully to avoid the congestion. There's public parking on either side of the mouth of the Roia River.

Terraced gardens surrounding the town at least hint of Ventimiglia's former glory. The border town is useful mostly as a place to change trains (French and Italian trains mostly operate with different engines). The older portion of town, located just inland from the sea, is definitely the better part of Ventimiglia with fading palaces lining a main street and a very old **library**✤ of rare books (*V. Garibaldi 10; tel: 0184 351 209, open Oct–late-May, Mon & Sat 0930–1330*); summer opening hours vary.

Suggested tour

Total distance: 155km, with detours 195km.

Time: 3–4 hours' driving. Allow 2 days with or without detours. Those with limited time can take the A10 toll road, shaving substantial time from the stop-and-go of the coastal road. In summer, especially, this is an attractive option although one must often drive several kilometres inland to connect to the A10. Definitely consider at least a short hop onto the toll road to avoid built-up Savona; turn right and head due north from **ALBISSOLA MARINA** to find it, getting off about 10km south at Zinola.

Links: Genoa (Genova), the starting point for this route, is the end point of the northern Riviera di Levante route (*see page 270*).

Route: From Genoa (Genova) ❶, drive approximately 10km west on the A10 *autostrada*, getting off at Voltri. Follow the coastal S1, first 17km west to **VARAZZE** ❷ and then through Celle Ligure another 8km to **ALBISSOLA MARINA** ❸. Now the road begins to arc southward. Use the *autostrada* for 10km or so if you wish to skip over bigger **Savona** ❹, then return to the S1 and drive 7km south round lovely Cape Noli to the village of **NOLI** ❺; it's 12km further to **FINALE LIGURE** ❻, another attractive village. From here, continue southwest 20km to **ALBENGA** ❼, then 22km to and round little Capo Mele, which ends at **CERVO** ❽. Continue 8km to **DIANO MARINA** ❾, skirt Imperia, which is hardly worth a look, emerging in a slightly different, rougher landscape on the western side of town. Proceed straight through to **SANTO STEFANO** ❿ (20km beyond), always keeping to the S1, and finish with a delightful 30-km stretch of towns including **SAN REMO** ⓫, **BORDIGHERA** ⓬ and **VENTIMIGLIA** ⓭ before reaching the French border.

Detour: At Ventimiglia, turn right (north) on the SS548 and climb the Nervia Valley toward Camporosso, continuing 8km to **Dolceacqua**, a

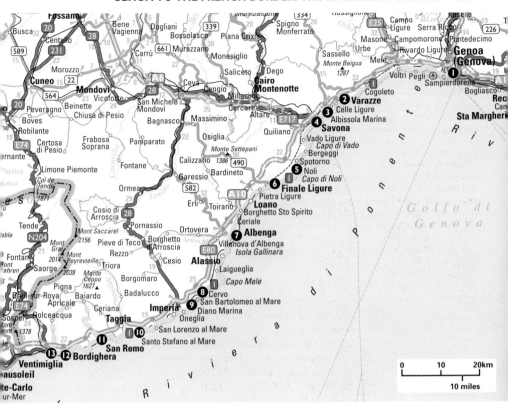

Tip: Note that on signposts, Ventimiglia is abbreviated to 'XXmiglia'.

lovely little medieval place of vineyards, olive groves, a bulky ruined castle and sprawling views. The town's single-arched stone bridge, which gracefully connects the newer town with medieval lanes, is one of the most distinctive in northern Italy. **Gastone** (€, *tel: 0184 206 577*) on Piazza Garibaldi is a good choice for local cuisine. The town might be worth a stay if you enjoy quiet country towns, though the only accommodation hereabouts is in such places as farmhouses and olive oil mills. Continue north 4km, branching right at Isolabona and then branching again on twisting roads through Apricale to more olive trees and views at **Baiardo**. From Baiardo, **Mount Brignone** can be seen, but not reached directly; descend toward Ceriana and branch right after the bridge to find the mountain. Descend via twisting, unnumbered roads to San Remo to complete the circuit.

Language

Italian shares a common Latin basis with Spanish, Portuguese and French, so a knowledge of any of those will help you recognise words once you become accustomed to the differences in pronunciation. When words fail you, first try the English word, giving it an Italian pronunciation. For example, English words ending in 'ion' will almost always be the same, ending in 'ion-e'. You will be surprised at how often English, spoken slowly and with a smile, can be understood by Italians who speak no English. Be attentive to the lilt and cadence of people talking around you, and it will help you turn everyday English words into functional Italian.

Basics

yes/no	si/no
thank you	grazie
please	per favore
you are welcome	prego
excuse me	scusi
I'm sorry	mi dispiace
I would like	vorrei
I don't understand	non capisco
I don't like that	non mi piace
I would prefer	preferisco
OK	va bene
big/little	grande/piccolo
hot/cold	caldo/freddo
open/closed	aperto/chiuso
right/left	destra/sinistra
good/bad	buono/cattivo
fast/slow	presto/lento
much/little	molto/poco
expensive/cheap	caro/economico
go away!	va via!
at what time?	a che ora?
do you speak English?	parla Inglese?
where is...?	dove...? (pronounced 'doh-veh')

Driving

car	la macchina
petrol station	il distributore
full	pieno
petrol/diesel	la benzina/il gasolio
unleaded	senza piombo
air pressure	la pressione
oil	l'olio
water	l'acqua
breakdown	il guasto
accident	l'incidente
does not work	non funziona
motor	il motore
ignition	l'accensione

Signs and directions

attenzione	watch out
deviazione	detour
divieto di accesso/senso vietato	no entry
divieto di sosta/sosta vietata	no parking
gira a destra/sinistra	turn right/left
incrocio	crossroads
limite di velocità	speed limit
parcheggio	parking
pericolo	danger
pronto soccorso	first aid
rallentare	slow down
sempre diritto	straight ahead
senso unico	one-way street
strada chiusa	road closed
strada senza uscita	dead-end, cul-de-sac
tenere la destra	keep right
traffico limitato	restricted access
uscita veicoli	exit
vietato fumare	no smoking
vietato il sorpasso	no overtaking (passing)
vietato il transito	no through traffic
zona rimorchio	tow-away zone

Strong language

sparisci	disappear
smettila	stop it
lasciami in pace	leave me alone
scemo, stupido	idiot
buffone	joker
testa di cazzo	s***head
porco	pig

Numbers and measures

1	uno	50	cinquanta
2	due	60	sessanta
3	tre	70	settanta
4	quattro	80	ottanta
5	cinque	90	novanta
6	sei	100	cento
7	sette	101	centuno
8	otto	110	centodieci
9	nove	200	duecento
10	dieci	500	cinquecento
11	undici	1000	mille
12	dodici	5000	cinquemila
13	tredici	10,000	diecimila
14	quattordici	50,000	cinquanta mila
15	quindici	1,000,000	un milione
16	sedici	2,000,000	due milione
17	diciassette		
18	diciotto	$1/2$	un mezzo
19	diciannove	$1/4$	un quarto
20	venti	$1/3$	un terzo
21	ventuno	100gm	un etto
22	ventidue	1kg	un chilo
30	trenta	1 pound	mezzo chilo
40	quaranta	1 litre	un litro

Index

Acknowledgements

Project management: Cambridge Publishing Management
Project editor: Karen Beaulah
Series design: Fox Design
Cover design: Liz Lyons Design
Layout: PDQ Digital Media Solutions Limited/Cambridge Publishing Management
Map work: Lovell Johns
Repro and image setting: PDQ Digital Media Solutions Limited/Cambridge Publishing Management
Printed and bound in India by: Replika Press Pvt Ltd

We would like to thank Barbara Radcliffe Rogers and Stillman Rogers for the photographs used in this book, to whom the copyright belongs, with the exception of the following:

John Heseltine (pages 42, 46, 48, 51, 228, 239, 272, 277, 278)

Neil Setchfield (pages 47, 236, 241, 248, 259)

Edith Summerhayes (page 243)

Front cover: Lake Como, Robert Everts/Getty Images
Back cover: Canal scene, Venice, The Travel Library

Feedback form

If you enjoyed using this book, or even if you didn't, please help us improve future editions by taking part in our reader survey. Every returned form will be acknowledged, and to show our appreciation we will give you £1 off your next purchase of a Thomas Cook guidebook. Just take a few minutes to complete and return this form to us.

When did you buy this book? ....
....

Where did you buy it? (Please give town/city and, if possible, name of retailer)
....
....

When did you/do you intend to travel to the Italian Lakes and Mountains?.........................
....

For how long (approx.)? ....

How many people in your party? ....

Which cities, towns and resorts did you/do you intend mainly to visit?
....
....
....
....

Did you/will you:
❏ Make all your travel arrangements independently?
❏ Travel on a fly-drive package?
Please give brief details: ....
....

Did you/do you intend to use this book:
❏ For planning your trip?   ❏ Both?
❏ During the trip itself?

Did you/do you intend also to purchase any of the following travel publications for your trip?
A road map/atlas (please specify) ....
Other guidebooks (please specify) ....
....

Have you used any other Thomas Cook guidebooks in the past? If so, which?
....
....

Please rate the following features of *Drive Around Italian Lakes and Mountains* for their value to you (Circle VU for 'very useful', U for 'useful', NU for 'little or no use'):

The Travel facts section on pages 14–23   VU   U   NU
The Driver's guide section on pages 24–9   VU   U   NU
The touring itineraries on pages 40–1   VU   U   NU
The recommended driving routes throughout the book   VU   U   NU
Information on towns and cities, etc   VU   U   NU
The maps of towns and cities, etc   VU   U   NU

Please use this space to tell us about any features that in your opinion could be changed, improved or added in future editions of the book, or any other comments you would like to make concerning the book:

....
....
....
....
....
....
....
....

Your age category: ❏ 21–30   ❏ 31–40   ❏ 41–50   ❏ over 50

Your name: Mr/Mrs/Miss/Ms ....
(First name or initials) ....
(Last name) ....

Your full address: (please include postal or zip code)

....
....
....
....
....

Your daytime telephone number: ....

Please detach this page and send it to: The Series Editor, Drive Around Guides, Thomas Cook Publishing, PO Box 227, The Thomas Cook Business Park, 15–16 Coningsby Road, Peterborough PE3 8SB.

Alternatively, you can e-mail us at: *books@thomascook.com*

We will be pleased to send you details of how to claim your discount upon receipt of this questionnaire.